The Ottoman Road to War in 1914

Why did the Ottoman Empire enter the First World War in late October 1914, months after the war's devastations had become clear? Were its leaders "simple-minded," "below-average" individuals, as the doyen of Turkish diplomatic history has argued? Or, as others have claimed, did the Ottomans enter the war because War Minister Enver Pasha, dictating Ottoman decisions, was in thrall to the Germans and to his own expansionist dreams? Based on previously untapped Ottoman and European sources, Mustafa Aksakal's dramatic study challenges this consensus. It demonstrates that responsibility went far beyond Enver, that the road to war was paved by the demands of a politically interested public, and that the Ottoman leadership sought the German alliance as the only way out of a web of international threats and domestic insecurities, opting for an escape whose catastrophic consequences for the empire and seismic impact on the Middle East are felt even today.

MUSTAFA AKSAKAL is Assistant Professor in the Department of History, American University, Washington, DC. His dissertation won the Bayard and Cleveland E. Dodge Memorial Prize for Best Dissertation in Near Eastern Studies at Princeton.

Cambridge Military Histories

Edited by

HEW STRACHAN, Chichele Professor of the History of War, University of Oxford and Fellow of All Souls College, Oxford

GEOFFREY WAWRO, Major General Olinto Mark Barsanti Professor of Military History, and Director, Center for the Study of Military History, University of North Texas

The aim of this new series is to publish outstanding works of research on warfare throughout the ages and throughout the world. Books in the series will take a broad approach to military history, examining war in all its military, strategic, political, and economic aspects. The series is intended to complement *Studies in the Social and Cultural History of Modern Warfare* by focusing on the "hard" military history of armies, tactics, strategy, and warfare. Books in the series will consist mainly of single-author works – academically vigorous and groundbreaking – which will be accessible to both academics and the interested general reader.

Titles in the series include:

E. Bruce Reynolds *Thailand's Secret War: OSS, SOE and the Free Thai Underground during World War II*

Robert T. Foley *German Strategy and the Path to Verdun: Erich von Falkenhayn and the Development of Attrition, 1870–1916*

Elizabeth Greenhalgh *Victory through Coalition: Britain and France during the First World War*

G. C. Peden *Arms, Economics and British Strategy: From Dreadnoughts to Hydrogen Bombs*

John Gooch *Mussolini and his Generals: The Armed Forces and Fascist Foreign Policy, 1922–1940*

Alexander Watson *Enduring the Great War: Combat, Morale and Collapse in the German and British Armies, 1914–1918*

The Ottoman Road to War in 1914

The Ottoman Empire and the First World War

Mustafa Aksakal

CAMBRIDGE
UNIVERSITY PRESS

CAMBRIDGE UNIVERSITY PRESS
Cambridge, New York, Melbourne, Madrid, Cape Town, Singapore,
São Paulo, Delhi

Cambridge University Press
The Edinburgh Building, Cambridge CB2 8RU, UK

Published in the United States of America by Cambridge University Press,
New York

www.cambridge.org
Information on this title: www.cambridge.org/9780521880602

First published 2008

Printed in the United Kingdom at the University Press, Cambridge

A catalogue record for this publication is available from the British Library

Library of Congress Cataloguing in Publication data
Aksakal, Mustafa, 1973–
The Ottoman road to war in 1914: the Ottoman Empire and the First World War /
Mustafa Aksakal.
    p.   cm. – (Cambridge military histories)
Includes bibliographical references and index.
ISBN 978-0-521-88060-2
1. Turkey – History – Mehmed V, 1909–1918.   2. World War, 1914–1918 –
Turkey.   3. Turkey – History, Military – 20th century.   I. Title.
DR588.A39   2008
940.3′56–dc22

                                                                2008037112

ISBN 978-0-521-88060-2 hardback

For my parents

Contents

Acknowledgments   *page* viii
Author's note   x
Abbreviations   xii
Glossary   xiii
Maps   xv

Introduction: pursuing sovereignty in the age
of imperialism   1

1   The intellectual and emotional climate after the
    Balkan Wars   19

2   1914: war with Greece?   42

3   The Ottomans within the international order   57

4   The Great War as great opportunity: the Ottoman July
    Crisis   93

5   Tug of war: Penelope's game   119

6   Salvation through war?   153

    Conclusion: the decision for war remembered   188

Bibliography   195
Index   208

Acknowledgments

I am delighted to acknowledge the support of a large number of individuals. They have offered a great deal of their time, expert knowledge, and words of encouragement. Margaret Lavinia Anderson and M. Şükrü Hanioğlu generously provided all. Professor Anderson read several versions of the manuscript at various stages, and I could not possibly thank her adequately for her many observations and constant prodding; I owe her a debt of gratitude. Professor Hanioğlu taught me much of what I know about the late Ottoman period, first as my teacher at Princeton, then as a colleague, and always as a friend. Hew Strachan's support of this project improved it in key respects. Cemil Aydın, Ussama Makdisi, and Yücel Yanıkdağ read individual chapters; their insights have greatly enriched the end result. I am grateful to Justin McCarthy for allowing me to adapt his maps from *The Map Project, The Middle East Studies Association of North America, CD-ROM* (Tuscon: University of Arizona, 2003). The stimulating environment provided by my colleagues in the Department of History at American University made writing the book's final stages both intellectually engaging and pleasant. Professor Robert Griffith has been a most considerate department chair. My former colleagues in the Department of History and Anthropology at Monmouth University could not have offered a more supportive surrounding. There is a long list of friends and colleagues who humored me by listening to winding stories about the late Ottomans not once but on many occasions. Their comments have contributed in ways immeasurable: Bassam Abed, Marc Abramson, Fikret Adanır, Holger Afflerbach, Feroz Ahmad, Cemil Aydın, William Blair, Harry Bone, Michael Cook, Robert Crews, Christopher DeRosa, Michael Doran, Howard Eissenstat, Edward Erickson, Yasser Freij, Stephen Fritz, Mustafa Gencer, Fatma Müge Göçek, Hasan Kayalı, Janet Klein, Sinan Kuneralp, Peter Laipson, Frederick McKitrick, Annika Mombauer, Wolfgang Mueller, Dean Owens, Katherine Parkin, Michael Provence, Michael Reynolds, Dominic Sachsenmaier, Joshua Sanborn, Saliba Sarsar, James Sheehan, Peter Sieger, Kenneth Stunkel, Ronald Suny,

Haydar Taş, Baki Tezcan, Mesut Uyar, Eric Weitz, Friedrich Wesche, and İpek Yosmaoğlu.

Since arriving at the Ottoman archives in 1999 with only a faint idea of what direction my research would take, I have benefited from the financial support of numerous institutions. I extend my deep gratitude to these institutions and to the individuals who undertook the unenviable task of selecting this project among others for support. These institutions are Princeton University – where I thank in particular the Department of Near Eastern Studies, the Graduate School, and the Center for International Studies – the Ford Foundation, the Mellon Foundation, the American Council of Learned Societies, the German Academic Exchange Service (DAAD), the Institute of Turkish Studies, the Monmouth University Grant-in-Aid program, and the College of Arts and Sciences, American University, and its dean, Dr. Kay Mussell. Without their support I could not have traveled and benefited from a number of archives and libraries and their superb staffs: the Ottoman Archives of the Turkish Prime Ministry, Istanbul; the Archives of the Turkish General Staff, Ankara (ATASE), and, in particular, its director, Colonel Dr. Ahmet Tetik; the Bundesarchiv-Militärarchiv, Freiburg i.Br.; the Political Archive of the German Foreign Office, Berlin; the Bundesarchiv Berlin-Lichterfelde; the African and Middle Eastern Reading Room at the Library of Congress, Washington, DC, and, in particular, Dr. Christopher Murphy and Dr. Levon Avdoyan; the Library of the Grand National Assembly of Turkey, Ankara, and, in particular, Mr. Ömer İmamoğlu of the periodicals reading room; the Atatürk Library, Istanbul; Firestone Library at Princeton University; Widener Library at Harvard University; the Monmouth University Library; and the American University Library. My editor at Cambridge University Press, Michael Watson, has been as efficient as he has been patient.

Any author is painfully aware of the burden that writing a book brings on one's family, so much so that not only gratitude for their understanding but apologies seem called for in equal measure. I thank my parents, Servet and Mevlüde, my siblings, Özgür and Yeşim, and my other parents, Ziad and Naila, for their constant faith in my endeavors. My son Gabriel and now his sister Clara have mastered the art of welcome interruption. Above all I am grateful to my wife, Layla, who has not only read the manuscript line by line and pointed in new directions, but whose loving companionship has provided me with nourishment and happy cheer throughout all stages of this book.

Author's note

Is it Istanbul or Constantinople? This is a question that may prove vexing to the uninitiated reader, who would be well within her right not to stop there but to ask further. Is it Turkey or Ottoman Empire, Porte or Sublime Porte, Turks or Ottomans, Middle East or Near East, or even the politically neutral eastern Mediterranean? There seems to be no convention without its own set of pitfalls. Historians working in European history have remained true to the parlance of the period, and they have stuck to "Constantinople," "Turkey," "the Porte," "Turks," and "the Near East." For historians working in Ottoman history and with Ottoman Turkish language sources, however, this usage, by definition, represents European and, worse, imperialist perspectives. Historians working with Ottoman sources point out that the usage inside the "Well-Protected Domains" (*Memalik-i Mahruse*) was quite different. It was the Family of Osman (*Al-i Osman*), and later the Sublime Ottoman State (*Devlet-i Aliye-i Osmaniye*), not Turkey, and not an "empire," that governed the multi-ethnic, multi-religious, and multi-lingual society of Ottomans, not Turks.[1] Its highest offices were accessed through the famous Exalted Gate or Sublime Porte (*Bab-ı Âli*).

And yet, even in this usage the Ottomanist must concede deficiencies. In its own international correspondence, written mostly in French, the state itself used "Constantinople" and "Turquie." In the nineteenth century it insisted on being referred to as an empire with an emperor, as in "Sa Majesté Impériale le Sultan" and "Sa Majesté le Sultan Empereur des Ottomans," on par with European powers. Its own paper money designated the issuer as "Banque Impériale Ottomane."[2] Much more important, it seems anachronistic to speak of an "Ottoman government"

---

[1] See the thoughtful discussion on the occasion of the Ottoman Empire's seven hundredth anniversary celebration in Christoph K. Neumann, "Devletin Adı Yok – Bir Amblemin Okunması [The State Has No Name – The Reading of an Emblem]," *Cogito* 19 (Summer 1999): 269–83.

[2] Ibid.

x

and an "Ottoman cabinet" in 1914 when the major players had explicitly repudiated "Ottomanism" and were set on constructing a government by and for the Turks, and when major dailies and books freely used "Turks" (*Türkler*) and "Turkey" (*Türkiye*). And if Turkish-speakers referred to the capital as Istanbul among a variety of names, about half of the population spoke other languages and used different names. The Turkish Republic under Mustafa Kemal undertook an official name change from Constantinople to Istanbul in 1930.

Since labeling and categories are no trivial matter in reconstructing decision-making, perceptions, fears, and hopes, I have tried to offer the necessary nuance without also adding muddle; otherwise, I have used the following, inadequate conventions: Ottomans and Ottoman Empire, Istanbul and the Porte, and the Near East. Where I have cited Ottoman published (primary) works I have sought to provide translations of titles in the notes and bibliography. For Ottoman dates, whether expressed in the lunar *hicri* or the solar *rumi* calendars, I have included Gregorian equivalents.

Abbreviations

A.VRK: Sadaret Evrakı, papers of the Grand Vezirate
ATASE: Archives of the Turkish General Staff, Ankara
BA-MA: Bundesarchiv-Militärarchiv, German Federal Military
                Archives, Freiburg i.Br.
BA-B: Bundesarchiv Berlin-Lichterfelde, German Federal
                Archives, Berlin-Lichterfelde
BDH: Birinci Dünya Harbi, First World War
BDOW: *British Documents on the Origins of the War, 1898–1914*
BEO.NGG: Bab-ı Âli Evrak Odası, Nezaretler Gelen-Giden,
                Document Office of the Sublime Porte, Incoming and
                Outgoing Correspondence
BOA: Başbakanlık Osmanlı Arşivi, Ottoman Archives of the
                Turkish Prime Ministry, Istanbul
GP: *Die Grosse Politik der Europäischen Kabinette, 1871–1914*
MMZC: *Meclis-i Mebusan Zabıt Ceridesi*, Proceedings of the
                Ottoman Chamber of Deputies
MV: Meclis-i Vükelâ Mazbataları, Decisions of the Ottoman
                Cabinet
IBZI: *Die Internationalen Beziehungen im Zeitalter des
                Imperialismus*
PA/AA: Politisches Archiv des Auswärtigen Amts, Political
                Archives of the Foreign Office, Berlin
RM: Reichsmarine, German Imperial Navy
TTK: Türk Tarih Kurumu Arşivi, Archives of the Turkish
                Historical Society, Ankara

Glossary

Names in parentheses indicate the individual's full name, even though it was not commonly used. Surnames were introduced in Turkey in 1934.

Auswärtiges Amt, the German Foreign Office, located in Berlin

Bey, title designating high civil or military rank, notable status, or "gentleman"

(Ahmed) Cemal, pasha, 1872–1922, born on Midilli (Mytilene), Navy Minister 1914–18, II Army Commander 1914, IV Army Commander 1914–17

CUP, the Ottoman Committee of Union and Progress (*Osmanlı İttihad ve Terakki Cemiyeti*), originally formed in 1889 as the Ottoman Union Society at the Royal Medical Academy by four medical students, two ethnic Kurds, one Albanian, one Circassian; the CUP emerged as the leading Young Turk organization and its leaders controlled the government during 1913–18

Enver (İsmail), pasha, 1882–1922, born in Istanbul, War Minister 1914–18

Giers, Mikhail N., Russian ambassador in Istanbul 1912–14

Grand Vezir, *sadr-ı azam,* the first minister in the Ottoman cabinet

Grey, Sir Edward, British Secretary of State for Foreign Affairs 1905–16

Halil, bey, 1874–1948, born in Milas on the Aegean, Speaker of the Chamber of Deputies 1914–15, Foreign Minister 1915–17; later took the surname Menteşe

Jagow, Gottlieb von, German Secretary of State for Foreign Affairs 1913–16

Pasha, highest title awarded by the sultan to civil and military officials

(Mehmed) Said Halim, pasha and prince, 1863–1921, born in Cairo, Grand Vezir 1913–17 and Foreign Minister 1913–15

Sazonov, Sergei D., Russian Foreign Minister 1910–16

Sublime Porte (Bab-ı Âli), central offices of the Ottoman government in Istanbul including those of the grand vezirate, the foreign ministry, and the cabinet; diplomats and journalists writing in European languages often used "Porte" as shorthand for the entire empire and its government

(Mehmed) Talat, pasha, 1874–1921, born in Edirne/Adrianople, Interior Minister 1909–11 and 1913–18, also Finance Minister 1914–17 and Grand Vezir 1917–18

Maps

Ottoman Territorial Losses, 1878–1912   *page* 6
The First and Second Balkan Wars, 1912–1913   7
The Ottoman Empire, 1914   8

Introduction: pursuing sovereignty in the age of imperialism

The Ottoman Empire's expulsion from Europe, where it had been a major power for more than four centuries, marks one of the major turning-points in modern history, one whose consequences for Europe and the Middle East we have still to absorb. Among the stages of this expulsion – the Balkan wars of the nineteenth and early twentieth centuries, the occupation of the Ottoman capital by the Entente Powers in 1918, the empire's subsequent and comprehensive dissolution in 1922 – the government's decision to intervene in an intra-European war in 1914 played a crucial role. Yet the decision is a puzzling one, since the conflict between Europe's two alliance systems was one in which the Ottomans had no immediate stake.

Given the war's disastrous consequences and its human cost for the entire Middle East, it is not surprising that the decision taken by the leadership in 1914 has been roundly blasted by historians and memoir-writers alike. In these accounts Enver Pasha, the war minister, a hawk in thrall to Germany, more or less single-handedly pushed the empire into a war it did not want. Alternatively, intervention has been ascribed to the hare-brained ideas of a tiny inner circle of the Young Turk leadership who had hijacked Ottoman policy – either because they were corrupted by German gold, blinded by German promises, pressured by German diplomats, or moved by voracious personal ambition, megalomaniac expansionism, or *naïveté*, attributable to their "below-average" intelligence.[1] In short, instead of welcoming the war as a reprieve from international pressures and remaining aloof from the bloodshed enveloping Europe, Enver and the men around him had sped up the "Sick Man"'s demise by entering the fight on the side of Germany and Austria-Hungary on October 29, 1914.

And yet, from a global perspective, the Ottomans' entry into the First World War can be seen as a reaction against the principal historical forces

---

[1] For the quotation see the discussion of Yusuf Hikmet Bayur below in this Introduction.

1

of the time: the steady expansion of European economic, political, and military control. This book argues that Ottoman leaders in 1914 made the only decision they believed could save the empire from partition and foreign rule. Envisioning outright foreign control in the Near East required no great stretch of the imagination. By 1900, Europe's territorial control, not least thanks to tools produced by the Industrial Revolution, extended to some 85 percent of the globe's surface, rendering the Ottoman Empire one of the globe's last holdouts. For the Ottomans, the path to international security ran through an alliance with one of the Great Powers. By 1914 a general consensus had emerged around this vision, even if its implementation became subject to personal disagreements and rivalries among the top officials. For reasons that will become clear, the choice of ally fell on Germany.

While its military and political leadership became convinced that the world had entered an era in which states and peoples could survive only through the demonstration of military power, the Ottoman Empire did not leap into war at the first opportunity. In fact, much of this book, and perhaps that is its main surprise, examines the great lengths to which the Ottomans went to stay out of the war. Once it became clear, however, that their alliance with Germany would not survive further delay, they embarked upon war confident that only the battlefield could bring the empire the unifying and liberating experience it so desperately needed.

Though the Ottoman Empire was an agrarian empire in the traditional mold, in the last decades it had been faced with the growth of the same kinds of nationalisms that beset the Habsburgs and would eventually overtake the empires of the "New Imperialism." But the Ottomans had to confront the ground-shaking forces of anti-colonial nationalism during the high noon of European imperialism, mixing geopolitical danger with domestic vulnerability. The Ottoman state thus had to come to terms with subject populations who increasingly felt themselves to be different precisely in an age when other empires, those backed by powerful industry, were spreading. Unlike the New Imperialists to the west, however, for the Ottoman leaders the survival of the state and the survival of the empire were one and the same.

To be sure, by 1914 the Ottoman Empire had become a perforated society, with perforations running along ethnic and religious lines. Throughout the long nineteenth century, the empire had endured dramatic shifts in its external boundaries, a vast remapping that truncated its territory and generated waves of migration, leading to the major blurring of its internal social boundaries as well. In fact, it is impossible to categorize the questions surrounding the empire's nationalities as belonging exclusively to *either* the domestic *or* the foreign realm of politics. By

1914, the empire's military security, or rather its vulnerability, had also become a function of the empire's demographic situation.

The question of whether the Ottomans could have saved the empire by employing, before nationalism became too virulent, "correct" domestic policies, thereby preserving its multi-ethnic and multi-religious, even cosmopolitan, character is now unanswerable. To us, the possibility that it could have done so carries tremendous appeal, since it would have spared the region the ugly, often bloody and murderous, process of disintegration and the subsequent, often equally horrific, process of nation-building. In 1914, however, Ottoman observers needed only to look at recent history, whether across the globe or at home, to conclude that military power alone could prevent dismemberment and colonial status. Even so, the empire's military, political, and intellectual leaders were not engaged solely in a campaign of self-defense; they firmly believed that the militarization of society and its institutions, which they based on European models, were the only road to an Ottoman modernity.

In 1914, the Sublime Porte faced four main foreign policy challenges, each in turn carrying a set of crucial domestic implications: the Armenian reform project in eastern Anatolia, the Aegean islands question, a loan agreement with one or more of the European governments, and the Liman von Sanders Affair. From the Ottoman perspective, these challenges posed life-or-death questions, and they tended to come from the Entente: Britain, France, and Russia. The archival evidence shows that for the tsarist government in St. Petersburg the Balkan Wars of 1912 and 1913, the Liman von Sanders Affair of December 1913, the possibility of a Greek–Ottoman War in 1914, and the July Crisis were all seen in the context of Russian intentions to seize control over Istanbul and the Ottoman Straits.

Once the war raged in Europe, the Entente governments, as we shall see, issued in writing a promise that they would protect the empire's territorial integrity in exchange for its neutrality, an offer the Ottoman leadership turned down. Rejecting the promise was not simply a matter of misplaced suspicion, however. Writing from Paris on August 11, 1914, the Russian ambassador, A. P. Izvolskii, reported the prevailing views in the French foreign ministry. Foreign Minister Gaston Doumergue and his colleagues had discussed Ottoman fears that the European war might precipitate the Russian seizure of Istanbul and the Straits. In the discussion, Doumergue suggested issuing the Entente guarantee of territorial integrity in order to "calm" Ottoman nerves. "According to the views of Doumergue," Izvolskii wrote, making such a guarantee now "would not prevent us from solving the Straits question in line with our thinking at war's end." Others in the French foreign ministry took yet a more aggressive line and argued that it would "be more advantageous for us to include Turkey on the side of our enemies and in that way to finish her off" for good.[2]

Were the Ottomans privy to exchanges such as this one, exchanges that spelled out explicitly the empire's partition? We know that this was so on at least some occasions, though the archives have remained silent as to whether the Sublime Porte's intelligence services succeeded in obtaining the exchange above. One occasion on which they did acquire such information was a note of August 6, 1914, penned by the Russian ambassador at Istanbul, M. N. Giers. In that note, Giers was proposing to his government that the empire be kept neutral until "that point in time when circumstances permit our own firm entrance into the Straits."[3] From the Ottoman perspective it was of little consolation that S. D. Sazonov, the Russian foreign minister, steered a policy aimed at later rather than immediate annexation of the Straits.[4]

Hence, when the Entente in August and September 1914, after much diplomatic wrangling, issued its guarantee of territorial integrity for the duration of the war, it should come as no surprise that the decision-makers in Istanbul treated the Entente promise as an empty one, a diplomatic hoodwink intended to buy time and to prevent the conflict from spreading.[5]

On the eve of the Great War, it was modernizing ideology that dominated the Ottomans' political and military leadership. Becoming modern meant the establishment of a sovereign, economically and politically independent state that enjoyed full membership in the international state system and access to international law. In theory, the Ottoman Empire had been a member of the Concert of Europe since 1856, when the Ottomans were signatory to the Treaty of Paris ending the Crimean War. In reality, this Great Power status and membership in a system whose mandate it was to preserve peace by defending the international status quo had not prevented the empire from suffering a series of

[2] *IBZI*, Series II, vol. 6/1, no. 65, Izvolskii to Sazonov, August 11, 1914, 44, and Note 2. Izvolskii reported these French attitudes a day after the two legendary German battle-cruisers, the *Goeben* and the *Breslau*, made their famous escape into the Ottoman Straits, discussed in chapter 4. The French talks took place before news of the ships had reached Paris, however, and hence had not been prompted by the crisis that ensued over them.

[3] BA-MA, RM 40–457, sheet 254, Giers to St. Petersburg, August 6, 1914, no. 631. Also in *IBZI*, Series I, vol. 2, no. 9, Giers to Sazonov, August 5, 1914, 6–7.

[4] From the Ottoman perspective it mattered little that S. D. Sazonov was genuine in his desire to keep the Ottomans out of the war and to preserve neutrality, see Ronald P. Bobroff, *Roads to Glory: Late Imperial Russia and the Turkish Straits* (London: I. B. Tauris, 2006), 96–115.

[5] Discussed in chapter 5.

territorial and diplomatic losses that left the country utterly demoralized and in financial ruin.[6] Since 1878 alone, these territorial losses included: Cyprus (British administration under Ottoman sovereignty, 1878); Ardahan, Batum, and Kars (to Russia, 1878); Montenegro, Romania, and Serbia (all gaining independence, 1878); Bosnia-Herzegovina (Austro-Hungarian occupation, 1878; Austro-Hungarian annexation, 1908); Tunisia (French protectorate, 1881); Egypt (British occupation, 1882); Crete (Great Powers impose autonomy, 1898); Kuwait (British protectorate, 1899); Bulgaria (independence, 1908); Tripoli (Italian annexation, 1912); Dodecanese Islands (Italian occupation, 1912); western Thrace (to Bulgaria and Greece, 1912); Aegean islands, including Chios and Mitylene (to Greece, 1912); Albania (independence, 1912); Macedonia (partitioned among Bulgaria, Greece, and Serbia 1912–13). And although the Great Powers did intervene on behalf of the Ottoman Empire at the Berlin Congress of 1878, following the war between the empire and Russia, they did so because they feared Russian expansion, which suggested to the cynical that when Western and Russian interests coincided, European concern for Ottoman integrity would cease.

Until the beginning of this period of staggering losses, perhaps as many as half of the empire's subjects resided in its European provinces, collectively known as *Rumeli* (i.e. land of the Romans). The Balkans thus formed an integral, if not crucial, part of the empire's economic, political, and cultural life. By the twentieth century, *Rumeli* had shrunk significantly; it now represented but one-fifth of the empire's total population.[7]

The state's massive reform programs of the nineteenth century proved unable to reverse the slippage in the empire's international footing. Beginning with its military and bureaucratic reforms in the late eighteenth and early nineteenth centuries, the Ottoman state implemented policies designed to regain its rank as one of the most prosperous and orderly states in the world, a proud position it had occupied in the sixteenth century. With Western European powers now in the driver's seat, however, by the mid-nineteenth century the empire's statesmen had embraced both the principle and the work of reform, not because reforms were forced on them but because they believed in these measures as the best way of regaining strength and stability. This reform movement grew from inside the empire in response to the pressures and challenges posed by the

---

[6] See, for example, the three-hour-long report by Finance Minister Cavid Bey on the budget for 1330 (March 1913–March 1914) in the Ottoman chamber of deputies in *MMZC*, 18 Haziran 1330 (July 1, 1914).

[7] Donald Quataert, *The Ottoman Empire, 1700–1922*, 2nd edn. (Cambridge: Cambridge University Press, 2005), 54.

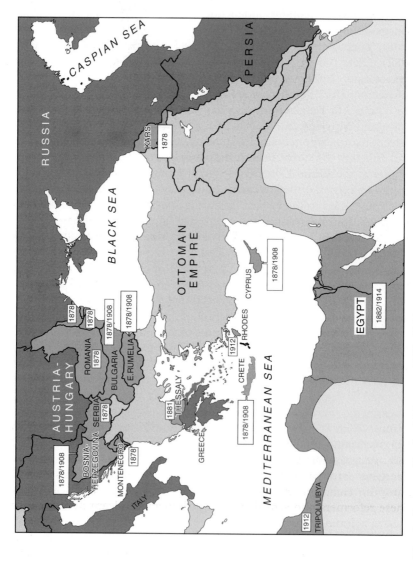

Map 1: Ottoman Territorial Losses, 1878–1912

Map 2: The First and Second Balkan Wars, 1912–1913

European Great Power system. Thus these reformers initially adopted European methods and techniques not with resentment or hostility but with a great deal of respect and even admiration. In this effort to fit into the emerging international society of states, the Sublime Porte hired European technical experts to reform its army, bureaucracy, and law. These reformers also sent their own technocrats to learn new methods in Berlin, London, and Paris. Nor did these reformers adopt European methods out of a sense of humiliation or "Eastern inferiority"; while other Asian and African states engaged in the same drive for modernization, so did various European governments. The Spanish and Swedish governments, to choose western European examples, also sent officers for training to Berlin, London, and Paris. Further to the east, Bulgaria, Greece,

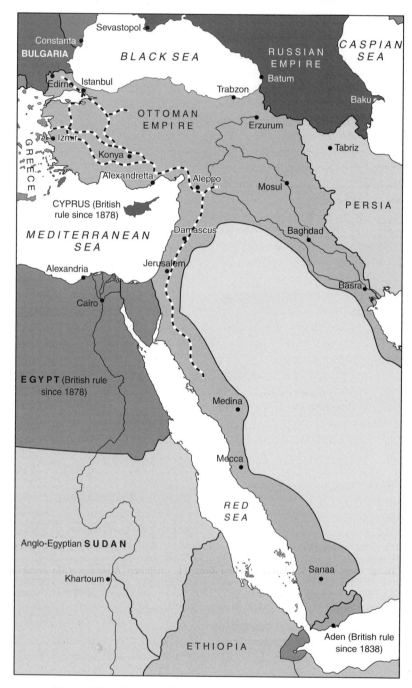

Map 3: The Ottoman Empire, 1914

and even Russia all participated in this process of acquiring new skills and technologies.[8]

This embrace of European-based reforms gradually gave way to the conviction that Western arguments for reform were simply tools of European imperialism. The new Ottoman leadership of the twentieth century viewed Great Power diplomacy as a fixed game: the Great Powers were the House, and you could not beat it by playing by the rules. In the face of these territorial losses, diplomatic defeats, and severe economic difficulties, the generations of pro-European reformers were eventually replaced by increasingly radical, younger leaders who believed that diplomatic history had taught a single lesson: only military power could preserve the empire.

This new generation of leaders organized itself as the Ottoman Committee of Union and Progress and succeeded in 1908 in toppling the regime of Sultan Abdulhamid II (r.1876–1908/9). In what became known as the Young Turk Revolution of 1908, the Ottoman Committee of Union and Progress (CUP) compelled the regime to reinstate the Constitution of 1876 and to call for general elections for a new chamber of deputies. With a bloodless revolution, empire-wide elections, and the opening of the chamber in 1908, the Ottoman Empire, it seemed, had transformed itself into a liberal, constitutional monarchy. While the revolution's aftermath saw the birth of a lively press and the expressions of high hopes for "union and progress" and "liberty, justice, and brotherhood," as so many postcards and placards proclaimed, the years that followed were also marked by deep crises of internal violence, including the massacre of 20,000 Armenians in the Adana region in 1909, wars in North Africa and the Balkans in 1911–13, and continued financial insecurity. Finally, in the context of the Balkan Wars, the CUP seized near-authoritarian control over the state apparatus in 1913 and continued to tighten its grip through the war years.[9]

---

[8] Brian Silverstein, "Islam and Modernity in Turkey: Power, Tradition and Historicity in the European Provinces of the Muslim World," *Anthropological Quarterly* 76 (Summer 2003): 497–517; David Ralston, *Importing the European Armies: The Introduction of European Military Techniques and Institutions into the Extra-European World, 1600–1914* (Chicago: University of Chicago Press, 1990); William R. Polk and Richard L. Chambers, *Beginnings of Modernization in the Middle East: The Nineteenth Century* (Chicago: University of Chicago Press, 1968).

[9] There are a number of excellent studies of CUP history: M. Şükrü Hanioğlu, *Preparation for a Revolution: The Young Turks, 1902–1908* (New York: Oxford University Press, 2001), and *The Young Turks in Opposition* (New York: Oxford University Press, 1995); Zafer Toprak, *İttihad-Terakki ve Cihan Harbi: Savaş Ekonomisi ve Türkiye'de Devletçilik* (Istanbul: Homer, 2003); M. Naim Turfan, *The Rise of the Young Turks: Politics, the Military and Ottoman Collapse* (New York: I. B. Tauris, 2000); Hasan Kayalı, *Arabs and Young Turks: Ottomanism, Arabism, and Islamism in the Ottoman Empire, 1908–1918* (Berkeley: University of California Press, 1997); Feroz Ahmad, *The Young Turks: The Committee of*

In selecting the sources for this study, I have mostly avoided reliance on the main secondary publications appearing in the war's highly charged aftermath. These studies too often misportray Ottoman intervention as the work of a single individual, War Minister Enver Pasha, who has gone down in history as dazzled by Prussian military prowess and dreaming of a pan-Islamist/pan-Turkist empire stretching from the Bosporus to Central Asia. I have equally avoided reliance on political memoirs. While these sources undoubtedly offer a wealth of information on the late Ottoman period more generally, they aim at deflecting responsibility and shifting blame elsewhere when considering the question of the Ottoman entry into the war. To illustrate the point we may turn to the memoirs of Halil Menteşe, the speaker of the Ottoman chamber of deputies in 1914, who participated in the alliance negotiations with Germany and the subsequent decision-making that paved the way for intervention. Halil looks back approvingly on the decision for war, surmising that there existed no other option. This perhaps was no surprise, since he had supported the war very publicly in 1914. And yet his memoirs, published in 1986 with an excellent introduction by İsmail Arar, also claim that the Ottomans entered the war "accidentally" and that no orders for attacking Russian forces in the Black Sea were ever issued.[10] As we shall see in the later chapters of this book, the archival evidence fully contradicts this point.

In the middle of the July Crisis, on July 13, 1914, and about two weeks after the assassination of the Habsburg heir apparent Franz Ferdinand in Sarajevo, the grand vezir and foreign minister, Said Halim Pasha, dispatched a confidential note, written in his own hand, to War Minister Enver Pasha, conveying the strong possibility of the outbreak of war between Austria-Hungary and Serbia. Said Halim beat the alarm bells based on information from an "*authoritative*" and "high ranking" source in the German foreign office itself. The contact had revealed remarkable news: "I can tell you confidentially that next week war will break out between Austria and Serbia ... We hope that the war is no longer avoidable, because it is perhaps the final chance for Austria to deal with Serbia. But one does not have full confidence that Vienna will demonstrate the energy necessary for this decision."[11] While the note exposes the attitudes of at least some in Berlin during the July Crisis, it also demonstrates that

Union and Progress in Turkish Politics, 1908–1914 (Oxford: Oxford University Press, 1969). See also more generally Palmira Brummett, *Image and Imperialism in the Ottoman Revolutionary Press, 1908–1911* (Albany: State University of New York Press, 2000).

[10] Halil Menteşe, *Osmanlı Mebusan Reisi Halil Menteşe'nin Anıları* [Memoirs of the Speaker of the Ottoman Chamber of Deputies, Halil Menteşe], ed. İsmail Arar (Istanbul: Hürriyet Vakfi, 1986), 188, 206, 208 and Arar's discussion, 49–54.

[11] ATASE, BDH, Klasör 243, Yeni Dosya 1009, Fihrist 1 and 1–1. Said Halim received Berlin's letter via the Ottoman consul at Bremen. (Emphasis in original.)

those plying the Ottoman rudder were by no means benighted as to the real possibility of a major European war in late July 1914.

In hindsight, these gathering war clouds on the European horizon offered the empire a precious opportunity for domestic reform. In Turkey, Yusuf Hikmet Bayur made this point forcefully in his monumental *History of the Turkish Revolution*, published between 1940 and 1967 in more than five thousand pages. Bayur drew not only on the vast document collections made public by the European governments after 1919 but also on the unpublished Ottoman archival material, newspapers, and political memoirs.[12] On the basis of this rich documentation, he concluded that the Ottoman government led by the "triumvirate Talat-Enver-Cemal" had entered the war "without any compelling reason."[13]

Bayur was the grandson of the former grand vezir and CUP arch-rival, Kâmil Pasha, and he criticized harshly the attempts of successive CUP governments at reorganizing the state's administrative, financial, and military apparatus after the two Balkan Wars. In mid-1913, the then grand vezir and war minister, Mahmud Şevket Pasha, had enlisted British, French, and German officers and technical specialists into the state's service. Mahmud Şevket had hoped both to improve and modernize the state's institutions and to establish more cordial foreign relations with the European powers in the process. Writing from the perspective of the new Turkish Republic established in 1923, Bayur found such policies terribly imprudent, because, in his view, they had only fueled the imperial rivalries in the region. Leaders such as Enver, Said Halim, and Talat (the interior minister), Bayur surmised, failed to understand the effects of their policies because they were men who lacked the skills and abilities of true statesmanship. In Bayur's words, they were "below-average" and "simpleminded" individuals.[14]

Finally, Bayur accused the CUP leadership of chasing "ideals like Turanism [i.e. pan-Turkism] and pan-Islamism"[15] and entering a world war unnecessarily and with calamitous consequences. Their course stood in stark contrast to Turkey's splendid isolation during the Second World War. Once the navy had mined the Straits – the southern one, the Dardanelles, connecting the Mediterranean and the Sea of Marmara, and the northern one, the Bosporus, connecting the Sea of Marmara to

---

[12] Yusuf Hikmet Bayur, *Türk İnkılâbı Tarihi*, 3 vols. (Ankara: Türk Tarih Kurumu Basımevi, 1940–1967).

[13] Bayur, *Türk İnkılâbı Tarihi*, vol. III/i, *1914–1918 Genel Savaşı*, 267 and 269.

[14] Bayur, *Türk İnkılâbı Tarihi*, vol. II/iii, *Paylaşmalar*, 2 and 5.

[15] Bayur, *Türk İnkılâbı Tarihi*, vol. III/i, *1914–1918 Genel Savaşı*, 268 for the quotation, and see 267–74, where he addresses the question "Was the Ottoman government correct in entering the war?"

the Black Sea – and closed them first to warships in August 1914 and then to all traffic in late September, the German government would have "treated [the Ottomans] with kindness and would have provided each and every type of support" to the Istanbul government in exchange for this invaluable service of cutting off British and French supply lines to Russia.[16] Thus even Bayur implicitly endorsed a policy that sided with Germany, although not an alliance and intervention. Whatever the majority of historians and memoir-writers may have claimed after the war, as we shall see, the sources examined in this study strongly suggest that it was not only Enver Pasha who supported the option for war in 1914.[17]

Nonetheless, Bayur's work has remained unique both inside Turkey and beyond for its comprehensiveness and its use of all the published European archival material. His access to the then-restricted and uncatalogued archives of the foreign ministry permitted him to shed light on Ottoman decision-making as well. It is not surprising that Bayur's study quickly became the standard historical account of the period in general and on the question of the Ottoman entry into the First World War in particular. Its influence can also be seen in the extensive military history publications of the Turkish General Staff, which followed Bayur very closely, focusing on both Western imperialism and the Ottoman leaders' alleged secrecy and incompetence.[18] As a result, historiography has judged strongly the leaders whose actions led to the empire's entry into the war.[19] The war minister and deputy commander in chief, Enver

[16] Bayur, *Türk İnkılâbı Tarihi*, vol. II/iii, *Paylaşmalar*, 271.
[17] For a single example, see the speech by Ubeydullah Efendi, representative from Izmir, in the Ottoman chamber of deputies, in *MMZC*, 6 Temmuz 1330 (July 19, 1914).
[18] Republic of Turkey, Chief of the General Staff, *Birinci Dünya Harbi'nde Türk Harbi*, vol. I, *Osmanlı İmparatorluğu'nun Siyasî ve Askerî Hazırlıkları ve Harbe Girişi*, Genelkurmay Askeri Tarih ve Stratejik Etüt Başkanlığı Yayınları, rev. Cemal Akbay (Ankara: Genelkurmay Basım Evi, 1970; rev. 1991), 1–154, 201–20; Kâzım Yetiş, "İkinci Meşrutiyet Devrindeki Belli Başlı Fikir Akımlarının Askeri Hareketlere ve Cepheye Tesiri," in *Bildiriler: Dördüncü Askeri Tarih Semineri* (Ankara: Genelkurmay Basımevi, 1989), 59–69; Y. T. Kurat, "How Turkey Drifted into World War I," in *Studies in International History*, ed. K. Bourne and D. C. Watt (London: Longmans, 1967), 293; Veli Yılmaz, *1nci Dünya Harbi'nde Türk-Alman İttifakı ve Askeri Yardımlar* (Istanbul: Cem, 1993), 1–16, 73–94; Doğan Hacipoğlu, *29 Ekim 1914: Osmanlı İmparatorluğu'nun 1. Dünya Harbine Girişi* (Istanbul: Deniz İkmal Grup Komutanlığı, 2000), 5–25, 103; Durdu Mehmed Burak, *Birinci Dünya Savaşı'nda Türk–İngiliz İlişkileri* (Ankara: Babil, 2004), 59–72. See also Geoffrey Miller, *Superior Force: The Conspiracy behind the Escape of Goeben and Breslau* (Hull: University of Hull Press, 1996), 252–5.
[19] Şevket Süreyya Aydemir, *Makedonya'dan Ortaasya'ya Enver Paşa*, 3 vols. (Istanbul: Remzi Kitabevi, 1971), vol. II, 505–6.

Pasha, in particular, has frequently been presented as "selling out" the country to Germany and forcing the Ottomans into war.[20]

The history of the late Ottoman period has been shaped by what we now know about the war and its outcome. The war's relatively long duration, for instance, led historians like Bayur to depict the Ottoman decision for war as a death wish. This understanding fails to recognize that despite the intense militarism and armaments race in Europe, many contemporaries believed that a general war, if it broke out at all, could last no more than "a matter of months," and that it would be concluded by a negotiated peace rather than decisive military victory of one side over the other.[21] If the Ottoman leaders could plausibly have expected a shorter confrontation, room must be allowed for the possibility that they were seeking not the grandiose creation of a Muslim empire in Central Asia and elsewhere, as has been charged, but rather a long-term alliance with a Great Power, and, in particular, with Germany. From that alliance, Ottomans could hope for a period of stability, a period marked by international security and economic advances.

But perhaps what accounts most for the deep entrenchment of the reigning view on the Ottoman decision for war is what has been referred to as "imposed historical amnesia"[22] or a "post-war amnesia"[23] in the Turkish historiography of the early republican era. Following the Turkish War of Independence (1919–22) and the establishment of the Republic of Turkey (1923), Turkish historiography embraced vigorously the precepts of the nation-state and sought a complete break with the Ottoman Empire even as the republic continued to rely on the political, social, and institutional structures of the late Ottoman period.

In 1914 the July Crisis and the possibility of war between Austria-Hungary and Serbia seemed to offer an escape from what many Ottomans perceived to be a dead end. With the support and guidance of the German Empire, Ottoman leaders hoped to carry through the kind of radical transformation they deemed necessary for the creation of a modern, sustainable state. Wartime, some of these leaders believed, presented

---

[20] See, for example, the lead story headline on the front page of a prominent Turkish daily, "Savaşın bedeli 5 milyon altın [The War's Price: Five Million in Gold]," *Cumhuriyet*, August 11, 1996, reporting a "find" in the archives of the German Foreign Office documenting that Cemal-Enver-Talat received 5 million Ottoman pounds from Germany in exchange for entering the war.

[21] David G. Herrmann, *The Arming of Europe and the Making of the First World War* (Princeton: Princeton University Press, 1996), 1.

[22] Kemal H. Karpat, *The Politicization of Islam: Reconstructing Identity, State, Faith, and Community in the Late Ottoman State* (New York: Oxford University Press, 2001), 354.

[23] Stéphane Audoin-Rouzeau and Annette Becker, *14–18: Understanding the Great War*, trans. Catherine Temerson (New York: Hill and Wang, 2002), 46.

a suitable, even ideal, environment for the realization of such drastic changes. The Young Turks intended to transform the empire into a politically and economically independent, modern country by removing foreign control and cultivating a citizenry that would be loyal to the state. These individuals imagined that conditions of war could offer an appropriate pretext for the expulsion of foreign businesses and the nullification of fiscal and legal exemptions for foreign nationals, the so-called "capitulations" (their actual cancellation on October 1, 1914, announced on September 9, produced massive public celebrations). Wartime, moreover, presented the state with additional tools for the mobilization of the citizenry behind the Istanbul government.[24]

Resituating the decision for war in the psychological climate of prewar society makes it possible to see Ottoman intervention as the product of wider political trends rather than of the immediate pressures of the July Crisis. Feroz Ahmad has remarked that the CUP leaders, civilian and military alike, were united in their strong desire to achieve full independence and were prepared to go to war for this cause: "Thus Turkey's intervention in 1914 was not the result of collusion between the Germans and the war party. It was mainly determined by the nationalist aspirations of the [CUP] which Enver Paşa came to personify."[25] If we follow Ahmad's lead that Enver's actions reflected the wider circles of Ottoman leadership and society, then the empire's entry into the First World War must be re-examined in light of the prevailing political arguments circulating on the eve of the war.

Scholars who have maintained that Enver single-handedly shoved the empire into war have inadvertently provided evidence to the contrary. The Turkish historian Tuncer Baykara, for example, has pointed out how the ignominious defeats in the Balkan Wars of 1912 and 1913, which forced hundreds of thousands of displaced Ottoman Muslims to seek refuge in Asia Minor, created a deep sense of violation and a call for revenge. From a geography textbook published in 1913, Baykara quoted this revealing passage: "In 1912 the Balkan states formed an alliance against Turkey [*Türkiye*]. After fierce battles, Turkey lost all of Rumelia [the Ottoman provinces in Europe] except for Istanbul, the Straits, and Edirne Province ... Much innocent Muslim and Turkish blood was shed

---

[24] Hanioğlu, *Preparation for a Revolution*, 302–5; Zafer Toprak, *Milli İktisat-Milli Burjuvazi: Türkiye'de Ekonomi ve Toplum (1908–1950)*, Türkiye Araştırmaları, no. 14 (Ankara: Tarih Vakfı Yurt Yayınları, 1995), 4–6, 51–4, 66–74; Fikret Adanır, "Der jungtürkische Modernismus und die nationale Frage im Osmanischen Reich," *Zeitschrift für Türkeistudien* 2 (1989): 79–91.

[25] Feroz Ahmad, "Ottoman Armed Neutrality and Intervention, August–November 1914," *Studies on Ottoman Diplomatic History* 4 (1990): 60 and 69.

during this period. Women and children, indiscriminately, were cut up and butchered [*kesildi, biçildi*]. Villages were burnt and razed. Now, in Rumeli, under every rock and beneath the soil lie thousands of dismembered bodies, with eyes gouged out and stomachs slit ... It is our children's and grandchildren's national duty to right this wrong, and to prepare for taking revenge for the pure and innocent blood that has flowed like waterfalls."[26] This passage conveys just how deep-seated was the need for revenge and how accepted was the idea of an Ottoman forward, offensive action. The fact that in attempting to regain some of the lost territory the Ottoman armies had fought alongside some of the same Balkan states during the Second Balkan War in early 1913 they had fought against in the first did not change the situation. By July 1914, bellicose notions of revenge, retribution, and recovery had become embedded in Ottoman identity.

During the late nineteenth and early twentieth centuries, as the political, military, and intellectual elites in the capital embraced and promoted the ideologies of anti-imperialism and social Darwinism, the belief in struggle and war as the only avenues to Ottoman liberation increasingly acquired currency. A number of historians have acknowledged this aspect of the Ottoman decision for war in 1914 by appropriately referring to the entire period from 1914 as a "war of independence."[27] Enver Pasha shared these values, but he differed from his many like-minded contemporaries in important respects: he held the office of war minister and he considered himself to be the ultimate leader and hero of the movement opposing European imperialism. Enver's grandiosity, however, in no way lessens the fact that his contemporaries shared in his *Weltanschauung* and his strategy.

The story of Enver's death in 1922 while fighting alongside the Muslims of Central Asia against the Red Army has contributed to the close association of Enver Pasha, and indeed the decision to enter the First World War, with pan-Turkism and pan-Islamism. It should be remembered, however, that by 1922 Enver had been discredited, even ostracized, by the new Turkish leadership forming in Anatolia under Mustafa Kemal. In a letter from Moscow, dated April 21, 1921, Enver's strong opposition to Western imperialism persisted unabated: "I am pursuing today the same purpose that I pursued before and during the Revolution of 1908, during

---

[26] Tuncer Baykara, "Birinci Dünya Savaşı'na Girişin Psikolojik Sebepleri," in *Bildiriler: Dördüncü Askeri Tarih Semineri* (Ankara: Genelkurmay Basımevi, 1989), 362–3, citing Faik Sabri Duran, *Avrupa* (Istanbul: n.p., 1913). For Baykara's insistence on Enver's role as culprit, see Baykara, 363–5.

[27] Yetiş, "İkinci Meşrutiyet Devrindeki Belli Başlı Fikir Akımlarının Askeri Hareketlere ve Cepheye Tesiri," 64; Toprak, *Milli İktisat-Milli Burjuvazi*, 6.

the Tripolitanian War, the Balkan Wars, and the First World War. And this purpose is very simple: to organize and bring to action the Islamic world of four hundred million people ... and to save it from the European and American oppression which enslaves it."[28] After his escape on board a German submarine during the war's final days, Enver found a new, Islamic constituency in Central Asia and adjusted his language and politics accordingly, but this shift was a result of his changed circumstances rather than long-held convictions.

Enver's foreign policy ambitions have frequently been depicted not only as pan-Islamic but, at different times, as pan-Turkic dreams as well. It has been claimed, for example, that "Greed rather than necessity drove the Ottoman Empire into the First World War. Its war aim was to realize the imperialist vision of the powerful minister of war Enver Pasha: a tangled web of grievances and revanchist hopes geared toward reassertion of Ottoman imperial glory and unification of the Turkic peoples within an expanded empire."[29] Such conclusions overlook the fact that the German emperor, Kaiser Wilhelm II, backed by a wide circle of German scholars and politicians, promoted pan-Islamist ideology to a much greater extent than Enver ever did. To these Germans, pan-Islamism meant the fomentation of revolution in the imperial territories of the Entente, while Germany played the role of liberator.[30] It is important to take note, therefore, that Enver considered inexpedient the declaration of a "holy war" by the Ottoman sultan as urged by Berlin in 1914. Enver, perhaps more accurately attuned to the illusory nature of a global, pan-Islamic revolution, reminded Berlin that the declaration of *jihad* would necessarily

---

[28] Selçuk Gürsoy, "*Liva el-Islam*'da Enver Paşa'nın Yazıları," *Toplumsal Tarih* 50 (February 1998): 24; America received much attention in the Ottoman press, for example, see "Amerika-Meksika Muharebesi [The US-Mexican War]," *Tanin*, April 23, 1914.

[29] Efraim Karsh and Inari Karsh, *Empires of the Sand: The Struggle for Mastery in the Middle East, 1789–1923* (Cambridge, MA: Harvard University Press, 1999), 138. See also: Baykara, "Birinci Dünya Savaşı'na Girişin Psikolojik Sebepleri," 363–5; Aydemir, *Makedonya'dan Ortaasya'ya Enver* Paşa, vol. II, 11–21, 505–6; Jacob M. Landau, *Pan-Turkism: From Irredentism to Cooperation*, 2nd edn. (Bloomington: Indiana University Press, 1995), 51–6, and, for a more balanced presentation, Jacob M. Landau, *The Politics of Pan-Islam: Ideology and Organization* (New York: Oxford University Press, 1994), 94–103; cf. discussion above of Bayur.

[30] Wilhelm van Kampen, "Studien zur deutschen Türkeipolitik in der Zeit Wilhelms II," Ph. D. diss., University of Kiel, Germany (1968), 57–68; Herbert Landolin Müller, *Islam, ğihād ("Heiliger Krieg") und Deutsches Reich: Ein Nachspiel zur wilhelminischen Weltpolitik im Maghreb, 1912–1918* (New York: Peter Lang, 1991), 173–85. Donald M. McKale, *War by Revolution: Germany and Great Britain in the Middle East in the Era of World War I* (Kent, OH: Kent State University Press, 1998), 17–96. For an example of German pan-Islamism, see Max Freiherr von Oppenheim, "Die Revolutionierung der islamischen Gebiete unserer Feinde" [Fostering revolution in the Islamic territories of our enemies], undated manuscript in Jäckh Papers, Yale University Library, Box 2, Folder 47.

have to be directed against all "infidel" powers, including Germany, and hence could not be an option. He therefore suggested that rather than declaring *jihad*, Sultan Mehmed V (Reşad) would "call upon all Muslims to take up arms against the powers of the Triple Entente."[31] Nonetheless, some two weeks after the Ottoman entry into the war, on November 14, 1914, the highest-ranking religious official, the sheiyhülislam, proclaimed *jihad* to a crowd gathered outside the mosque of Mehmed the Conqueror.

Rather than the pursuit of pan-Islamist or pan-Turkist objectives, examination of the official documentation and the political literature of the time suggests that the Ottoman leadership viewed the war as a "historic opportunity" of a different kind. Shortly after the attack on Russia across the Black Sea that finally brought the Ottomans into war on October 29, 1914, the German general and reformer of the Ottoman army, Colmar von der Goltz, sent a congratulatory telegram to Enver Pasha. "Bravo," Goltz exclaimed, "Old Turkey now has the opportunity … in one fell swoop, to lift itself up to the heights of its former glory. May she not miss this opportunity!"[32] To the Ottomans, the alliance with Germany and the war held out the promise of regaining, if not "former glory," as Goltz had put it, then at least the empire's security and independence.[33]

Throughout their wartime partnership with Germany, the Ottomans made it clear that they were acting in the deliberate pursuit of their national interests. When the Ottoman navy minister, Cemal Pasha, and Enver rejected a sum of money Berlin had offered to finance an expedition against the Suez Canal in early 1915, Enver declared the amount sadly wanting, and he aired some of his general views about the German–Ottoman alliance: "If Germany supports Turkey materially and financially, it does so for its own advantage. If Turkey accepts [German aid] and thereby ties its fate to that of Germany, then it, too, does so exclusively to its own advantage. There can be no illusion about that."[34] Similarly, Enver complained about the fact that General Otto Liman von Sanders, the head of the German military mission in the Ottoman Empire, took decisions without consulting the German ambassador, Baron Hans von Wangenheim, with whom Enver enjoyed much better rapport. Having reminded the German side that both Germany and the Ottoman Empire were acting out of self-interest, Enver continued: "everything has

---

[31] BA-MA, RM 40 – 4, sheets 34–5, Humann to Wangenheim, October 22, 1914.
[32] BA-MA, N 80–1, sheet 201, Goltz to Mudra, November 9, 1914.
[33] BA-MA, RM 40 – 456, sheet 371, Humann to Souchon, April 22, 1915.
[34] Ibid.

to remain orderly in this 'deal.' The German Empire's representative here is the German Embassy and not Liman."[35]

Addressing the "unspoken assumptions" of the European leaders on the eve of the First World War, James Joll in a now classic essay pointed to the importance of the intellectual climate affecting policy-making elites and their decision-making, and the historian's methodological difficulties in reconstructing that intellectual climate.[36] In the Ottoman case, publications appearing during the period preceding the First World War shed light on key aspects of the intellectual baggage that influenced political decision-making in 1914. These publications reflect the patriotic-militarist attitude that belies the generally accepted explanation of the Ottoman entry into the First World War, namely that it resulted from Enver Pasha's underhand collaboration with the Germans while the majority of the Ottoman leaders preferred neutrality. Given the ideas promoted by the Ottoman elite in their publications and the forceful language in which they were advanced, the entry into the war emerges as a continuation rather than a new chapter in Ottoman political thinking.

To emphasize this climate of opinion is not to downplay the vulnerable position the Ottoman Empire certainly occupied in the international order of the early twentieth century. Had it not been for the heated domestic climate that is reflected in the contemporary literature, however, the Ottoman leaders might have behaved differently during the July Crisis. An alternative course of action could have aimed at collaboration with the Triple Entente, but it would have required willingness to engage with these powers and confidence that their interests were reconcilable. That willingness, however, could not be found in the climate of the late Ottoman period.

---

[35] Ibid.
[36] James Joll, "1914: The Unspoken Assumptions," inaugural lecture delivered April 25, 1968, The London School of Economics, 7–8 and 17–18; see also Paul Kennedy, *The Realities behind Diplomacy: Background Influences on British External Policy, 1865–1980* (London: Fontana Press, 1981), 36–65.

1 The intellectual and emotional climate after the Balkan Wars

> When I contemplate all that Russia has done for centuries to bring about
> our destruction, and all that Britain has done during these last few years,
> then I consider this new crisis that has emerged to be a blessing. I believe
> that it is the Turks' [*Türklerin*] ultimate duty either to live like an hono-
> rable nation or to exit the stage of history gloriously.[1]
>
> Cemal Pasha, navy minister, November 2, 1914

The Committee of Union and Progress resolved to enter the First World
War on the side of Germany in the long shadow of Great Power intervention in the internal affairs of the Ottoman Empire. Publications
addressing international questions reflected the deep conviction that the
country's survival could be secured only on the battlefield. These arguments, to be sure, reflected elite thinking, and it is doubtful that they had
made much headway among rural, let alone illiterate, populations by
1914. Nonetheless, Ottoman political writing after the two Balkan Wars
of 1912 and 1913 focused on the mobilization of all segments of society in
the defense of the empire. This mobilization required a comprehensive, or
total, process, a process that could equip the people with patriotic passion
and industry to fend off the dangers the empire faced. In books, journals,
and newspapers appearing in Istanbul and elsewhere, writers and politicians referred to this process as *hareket-i intibahiye*, "the movement of
awakening."[2] Military and political leaders depicted the empire as
engaged in a final, life-or-death struggle. By August 1914, the political
public was thoroughly familiar with the values and changes its leaders
regarded as essential for the empire's recovery: if Ottomans were to
survive, and to survive honorably, they had to embrace an unfaltering

---

[1] ATASE, BDH, Klasör 87, Yeni Dosya 449, Fihrist 1–2 and 1–3, Cemal to Sofia Embassy,
20 Teşrin-i Evvel 1330 (November 2, 1914).
[2] "Meclis-i Mebusan Reisinin Nutku [The Speech by the President of the Chamber of
Deputies]," *Tanin*, May 20, 1914.

patriotism of toil and self-sacrifice in the empire's service. This mentality prevailed among the decision-makers as well, and it is reflected in the words of Cemal Pasha above.

This chapter is not an attempt to offer a genuine cross-section of the press appearing on the eve of the Great War or to present the variety of perspectives present. Nor is the press examined in order to gauge popular support or "war enthusiasm." The goal instead is to draw on a number of prominent publications expressing, first, Ottoman views of the international order and, second, visions of the future place the empire might take safely within that international order. It is unlikely that all of the publications discussed here were "independent" or formed part of what might be called "public opinion" in the modern sense. However, since this chapter is meant to shed light on the ideological world of the decision-makers, the proximity of the daily *Tanin* (Echo), for example, to the CUP, poses few methodological or theoretical challenges. In fact, it permits a more comprehensive, if not deeper, understanding of Ottoman thinking in 1914.[3]

Kâzım Karabekir (1882–1948), the prominent general and army commander whose career stretched from the suppression of the 1909 counter-revolution to the Balkan Wars, the First World War, the Turkish War of Independence, and eventually to speaker of the Turkish parliament, wrote extensively on the period, although some of his works have appeared only recently.[4] As early as 1937, he pointed to the importance of the publications appearing on the eve of the First World War: "Like all social events, our entering the war was not the work of a single individual, but the result of various complex factors [*Her içtimaî hadise gibi harbe girişimiz dahi bir tek insan iradesinin eseri değil, bir takım girift amillerin muhassalasıdır*]." Of these factors, he accorded a significant portion of his study to "our press, our publications [*matbuatımız,*

---

[3] For recent studies drawing on this material, see Handan Nezir Akmeşe, *The Birth of Modern Turkey: The Ottoman Military and the March to World War I* (New York: I. B. Tauris, 2005); Eyal Ginio, "Presenting the Desert to the Ottomans during WWI: The Perspective of *Harb Mecmuası,*" *New Perspectives on Turkey* 33 (2005): 43–62, and "Mobilizing the Ottoman Nation during the Balkan Wars (1912–1913): Awakening from the Ottoman Dream," *War in History* 12 (April 2005): 156–77; Zeki Arıkan, "Balkan Savaşı ve Kamuoyu," in *Bildiriler: Dördüncü Askeri Tarih Semineri* (Ankara: Genelkurmay Basımevi, 1989), 168–88. For a contemporary study examining the press, see Ahmed Emin [Yalman], "The Development of Modern Turkey as Measured by Its Press," *Studies in History, Economics, and Public Law* 59 (1914): 1–142.

[4] Kâzım Karabekir, *Tarih Boyunca Türk–Alman İlişkileri* [Turkish–German Relations in History], ed. Orhan Hülagü and Ömer Hakan Özalp (Istanbul: Emre, 2001), and *Türkiye'de ve Türk Ordusunda Almanlar* [Germans in Turkey and in the Turkish Military], ed. Orhan Hülagü and Ömer Hakan Özalp (Istanbul: Emre, 2001).

neşriyatımız]" and a third section to "public opinion [*efkâr-ı umumiye*]."[5]
And indeed, as was the case in so many societies worldwide before the
First World War, in the Ottoman Empire the "intelligentsia as vanguard
of nationalism" attempted to mobilize all of society in order to stem the
tides of what were, in the eyes of many, radical transformations caused by
foreign intrusion.[6]

In European states, the militarization of society had become institution-
alized with the inception of the *levée en masse* following the French
Revolution and intensified in the cauldron of nineteenth-century industrialization.[7] States began reaching into the previously untapped resources
of civilian society, often in the form of educational and cultural movements, a development we can clearly see emerging in the Ottoman Empire
as well.[8]

The Ottoman Empire and the international order

During the Balkan Wars, political associations organized fever-pitched
mass demonstrations. Intended to mobilize the general public, these
demonstrations employed such emotional slogans such as "Honor or
Death! [*Ya Namus Ya Ölüm*]." The editorials in the Izmir daily *Ahenk*
(Harmony), for example, expressed an opinion that was becoming rapidly a
permanent fixture in the press: the paper argued that international law
offered no viable platform for countering the external threats to the empire.
The only alternative, *Ahenk* proclaimed, was war: "We must now fully
realize that our honor and our people's integrity cannot be preserved by
those old books of international law, but only by war."[9]

---

[5] Kâzım Karabekir, *Cihan Harbine Neden Girdik, Nasıl Girdik, Nasıl İdare Ettik* [Why We Entered the War, How We Entered It, and How We Administered It], vol. II, *Cihan Harbine Nasıl Girdik?* [How We Entered the World War] (Istanbul: Tecelli Basımevi, 1937), 32–86.

[6] The phrase comes from Aviel Roshwald, *Ethnic Nationalism and the Fall of Empires: Central Europe, Russia and the Middle East, 1914–1923* (New York: Routledge, 2001), 34, who offers not only a comparison of several nationalist movements but also demonstrates direct links between them. See especially 34–69.

[7] Daniel Moran and Arthur Waldron, eds., *The People in Arms: Military Myth and National Mobilization since the French Revolution* (Cambridge: Cambridge University Press, 2003), passim.

[8] Martha Hanna, *The Mobilization of the Intellect: French Scholars and Writers during the Great War* (Cambridge, MA: Harvard University Press, 1996); Wolfgang J. Mommsen, ed., with Elisabeth Müller-Luckner, *Kultur und Krieg: Die Rolle der Intellektuellen, Künstler und Schriftsteller im Ersten Weltkrieg* (Munich: R. Oldenbourg, 1996).

[9] Arıkan, "Balkan Savaşı ve Kamuoyu," 172–3 and 176, quoting *Ahenk*, 30 Eylül 1328 (October 13, 1912); see also the excellent works by the diplomatic historian Ahmed Salâhaddin, *Berlin Kongresi'nin Diplomasi Tarihine Bir Nazar* [The Diplomatic History of

Politicians and prominent public figures rejected the notion that international law could offer the empire any kind of security, and argued time and again that international relations should be seen as determined entirely by military power. By according primacy to military matters, opinion-makers increasingly equated the functions of the military with those of society as a whole. In the Ottoman chamber of deputies a delegate argued that:

it does not matter however many books we write on international law or however many human rights laws we implement. In order to get states to respect these [laws] we must still possess additional means, means of coercion. Every state has adopted this position and for that reason builds up its [military] strength. [A state] will use all of its defensive or offensive strength in order to defend and protect its rights. We are a state, too, and we therefore cannot escape this truth.[10]

While such a statement could be understood as an ordinary assertion of sovereignty, in the Ottoman Empire of 1913–14 it constituted a powerful rallying cry for social mobilization and a call to action. In such a heated climate, it was no surprise that the war ministry's budget, presented personally by Enver Pasha to the chamber on July 16, 1914, was speedily approved, without the usual long-drawn-out debate.[11]

The experience of the Balkan Wars had sent shockwaves reaching far beyond the confines of the political elite. The wars meant the loss of 80 percent of the empire's European territory, home to a population of over 4 million, or 16 percent of the empire's total population.[12] The fact that the First Balkan War of 1912 had ended in terrible defeat, that the adversary was not a Great Power but a coalition of the small Balkan states, that the loss of territory came within a hundred miles of the capital and included such prominent metropolises as Salonica, and that perhaps as many as

---

the Berlin Congress], Külliyat-ı Hukuk ve Siyasiyatdan Birinci Kitab (n.p., 1327 [March 1911–March 1912]), and *Makedonya Meselesi ve Balkan Harb-i Ahiri* [The Macedonian Question and the Aftermath of the Balkan Wars] (Dersaadet: Kanaat Matbaası, 1331 [March 1915–March 1916]); Yusuf Ziya, afterword to *Anadolu'nun İstikbali ve Akdeniz Meselesi* [*Problème méditerranéen*, 1913], by Charles Vellay, trans. Yusuf Ziya, Kütübhane-i İntibah, Tüccarzade İbrahim Hilmi, no. 10 (Dersaadet: Kütübhane-i İslam ve Askerî, 1329 [March 1913–March 1914), 115–27; Süleyman Nazif, *İki İttifakın Tarihçesi: İttifak-ı Müselles-İttifak-ı Müsenna* [The History of the Two Alliances: Triple Alliance-Dual Alliance] (n.p.: Muhtar Halid Kütübhanesi, 1330 [March 1914–March 1915]); for the defeats' impact on Muslims in India, see Azmi Özcan, *Pan-Islamism: Indian Muslims, the Ottomans and Britain (1877–1924)* (New York: Brill, 1997), 146–50.

[10] Ferhad Bey in *MMZC*, 30 Haziran 1330 (July 13, 1914).

[11] War Minister Major General Enver Pasha in *MMZC*, 3 Temmuz 1330 (July 16, 1914).

[12] Erik Jan Zürcher, "Greek and Turkish Refugees and Deportees, 1912–1924," 1, *Turkology Update Leiden Project (TULP)* (January 2003), http://tulp.leidenuniv.nl/content_docs/wap/ejz18.pdf.

half of the CUP's leaders themselves hailed from the Balkans, all accentuated the gravity of the situation.[13]

Nor had this crush of defeat let up during the final months before the First World War. On the contrary, as some 400,000 Muslim refugees arrived from the former Ottoman territories, the experience of the Balkan Wars profoundly impacted the empire.[14] In typical fashion, a newspaper article appearing in May 1914 indignantly reported the "violations committed against the honor and dignity of the Muslim population that lived in Macedonia and, especially, the Muslim population that lived in the areas now under Greek administration; and the violations committed against their religion, property, communal and educational institutions ... and even against their dead and their graves."[15] Thus the Balkan Wars intensified Ottoman and Muslim feelings of vulnerability, sense of violation, and revenge.[16]

These psychological effects were not the only results of the Balkan Wars. If the painful defeats suffered by the Ottoman armies in late 1912 spread panic across the empire, the successful recovery of Edirne (Adrianople) in July 1913 under the leadership of the charismatic young army officer Enver set off a spark of optimism and pointed in a new direction. The fact that the city had been reclaimed by military means and that this military recapture *de facto* reversed the diplomatic directives of the Great Powers endorsed the belief that through steadfast commitment and fierce action the empire could perhaps be saved after all.

This attitude was not only heavily represented in contemporary publications but also informed the debates in the chamber of deputies. The chamber assembled for its third legislative period on May 14, 1914, and continued meeting for what turned out to be an abbreviated two-and-a-half-month session before it was prorogued on August 2. While in session, the members of the chamber were energetic and optimistic about the tasks that lay ahead. The deputy from Izmir, Ubeydullah Efendi, for example,

---

[13] Erik Jan Zürcher, "The Young Turks – Children of the Borderlands?" 5–6, *Turkology Update Leiden Project (TULP)* (October 2002), http://tulp.leidenuniv.nl/content_docs/wap/ejz16.pdf.

[14] Zürcher, "Greek and Turkish Refugees and Deportees, 1912–1924," 1.

[15] "Makedonya Müslümanları [The Macedonian Muslims]," *Tanin*, May 1, 1914. See also Justin McCarthy, *Death and Exile: The Ethnic Cleansing of Ottoman Muslims, 1821–1922* (Princeton: Darwin Press, 1995), 1, who estimates that some 5 million Ottoman Muslims were uprooted between 1821 and 1922, and 5.5 million Ottoman Muslims died as the result of wars, starvation, and disease. This is certainly a problematic statistic, not only because it covers an entire century, but also because it covers a wide range of causes.

[16] Elçin Kürsat-Ahlers, "Die Brutalisierung von Gesellschaft und Kriegsführung im Osmanischen Reich während der Balkankriege (1903–1914)," in *Gewalt im Krieg: Ausübung, Erfahrung und Verweigerung von Gewalt in Kriegen des 20. Jahrhunderts*, ed. Andreas Gestrich (Münster: Lit-Verlag, 1995): 51–74.

delivered an emotional speech describing how he had felt upon hearing the news of the defeats in the Balkans and, in particular, the loss of Edirne. He had left Izmir and "wanted to get even farther away [from Istanbul]. Going farther and farther, I was determined never to return here [Istanbul]." When he did return, he did so "filled with great hope upon hearing that Edirne" had been recaptured and returned to the Ottoman domains.[17] Edirne imparted the crucial lesson that only military victory held the key to saving the empire.

The causes of the empire's chronic fragility were no secret and they were discussed at great length both in the chamber and in the press. There was a similar consensus as to the prescription for this enfeebled condition. The empire would have to make great strides in each area of the modern state and modern society: military, financial, and industrial strength; administrative efficiency; and an educated and diligent citizenry united in its desire to serve and to defend the state. Until the Young Turk Revolution of 1908 (July 23), which compelled Sultan Adülhamid II to reinstate the suspended constitution of 1876 and to call for elections, political discourse had focused on overcoming the sultan's autocratic regime. In subsequent years, however, as the new constitutional government suffered a series of territorial and diplomatic losses, the public's focus shifted away from ousting Abdühamid II (r.1876–1908/9) and replacing him with the constitution and parliamentary politics. The new vision crystallized around the imperatives of national unity, progress – and war.

Writing in 1910, Ahmed Saib, for example, still held Sultan Abdülhamid II's misrule responsible for the acts of international hostility the Ottomans had faced since the Berlin Congress of 1878. Abdülhamid II's policies, such as those towards Armenia and Macedonia, and his granting of commercial concessions, Ahmed Saib argued, had transformed the Ottoman Empire into a target of Western imperialism.[18] Following the Young Turk Revolution of 1908 and Abdülhamid II's removal, Ahmed Saib continued, the lack of unity among political groups had precluded a fruitful foreign policy. Party politics came at the cost of domestic polarization, and it cost the Sublime Porte's diplomats the opportunity to negotiate a better alternative to the double-punch of 1908: the Austro-Hungarian annexation of Bosnia-Herzegovina and the Bulgarian

[17] Ubeydullah Efendi, *MMZC*, 6 Temmuz 1330 (July 19, 1914).
[18] Ahmed Saib, *Tarih-i Meşrutiyet Ve Şark Mesele-i Hazırası* [The History of the Constitutional Period and the Current Eastern Crisis] (Istanbul: Necm-i İstikbal Matbaası, 1328 h. [1910]), 45–9, 130, and passim.

declaration of independence.[19] Ahmed Saib was a seasoned political writer who had played a leading role in the opposition movement against the Hamidian regime before 1908, and that history perhaps explains his emphasis on the former sultan.[20]

Unlike many of the younger authors who concerned themselves with the inevitability of warfare, he was not a militarist writer. Rather, Ahmed Saib decried both the continued lack of political unity and the absence of the rule of law. How, he asked, could the project of recovery (*tecdid-i kuvvet*) be sustained without the presence of either?[21]

By 1913 the language of politics had turned decidedly nationalist.[22] Writing at some point in 1913 under the pseudonym "Habil Adem," the political writer Naci İsmail published what was meant to look like a European view of Ottoman society. Naci İsmail's choice of title was indicative of the near despair among the Ottoman elite. In *Will Turkey Survive in Anatolia?* he argued that the Turkish intellectual and political elite must quickly bring about the formation of a Turkish nation, of "Turkey in Anatolia [*Anadolu'da Türkiye*]."[23] To ground his argument historically, Naci İsmail presented a quintessentially nationalist argument, typical in its insistence that the Turkish nation was "rooted in the remotest past."[24] While the expressions "*millet*," "*ırk*," and even "*Türk*" cannot simply be understood as the equivalents of "nation," "race," or "Turk/Turkish" in their modern sense,[25] Naci İsmail was unequivocal

---

[19] Ibid., 102.

[20] M. Şükrü Hanioğlu, "Jön Türk Basını," in *Tanzimat'tan Cumhuriyet'e Türkiye Ansiklopedisi*, ed. Murat Belge (Istanbul: İletişim Yayınları, 1985), vol. III, 848–9, and *Young Turks in Opposition*, 156–8.

[21] Ahmed Saib, *Tarih-i Meşrutiyet Ve Şark Mesele-i Hazırası*, 104–5.

[22] For the origins of Turkism in its cultural rather than political form, see David Kushner, *The Rise of Turkish Nationalism, 1876–1908* (Totowa: Frank Cass, 1977), 7–19, 27–49, 81–9.

[23] Naci İsmail, writing under the pseudonym Habil Adem, attributed the work to Jones Moll, *Londra Konferansı'ndaki Meselelerden: Anadolu'da Türkiye Yaşayacak Mı? Yaşamayacak Mı?* [One of the Matters at the London Conference: Will Turkey Survive in Anatolia?], trans. Habil Adem [pseud.] (Istanbul: İkbal Kütübhanesi, n.d.), 79. On Naci İsmail, see Mustafa Şahin and Yaşar Akyol, "Habil Adem ya da nam-ı diğer Naci İsmail (Pelister) hakkında …," *Toplumsal Tarih* 11 (November 1994): 6–14.

[24] Naci İsmail, *Anadolu'da Türkiye*, 130–1, and Mehmed Emin, *Ey Türk Uyan* [O Turk, Awake!] ([Istanbul]: Babikyan Matbaası, 1330 (March 1914–March 1915), 6, where Turkish history is said to extend back 5,000 years. For the primordial nature of nations as claimed by nationalist ideologies, see Eric Hobsbawm and Terence Ranger, eds., *The Invention of Tradition* (Cambridge: Cambridge University Press, 1983; Canto edn., 1996), 14; Edward Shils, "Primordial, Personal, Sacred and Civil Ties," *British Journal of Sociology* 8 (June 1957): 130–45; and Clifford Geertz, "The Integrative Revolution," in *Old Societies and New States: The Quest for Modernity in Asia and Africa*, ed. C. Geertz (New York: The Free Press: 1963).

[25] Kushner, *Rise of Turkish Nationalism*, 23–6.

regarding his own definition of these terms. Among the causes of the Turks' political plight, he declared, was the fact that non-Turks such as Arabs, Greeks, Indians, and Persians had entered Turkish government and brought about its deterioration.[26] His "Turks" in 1913, therefore, were the Turkish-speaking Muslims of Anatolia.

Will Turkey Survive in Anatolia? explicitly demanded a "return" to the Turkish nation and a clear break with the empire's imperial past, advocating separation from territories that were not predominantly Turkish. The author dismissed "Ottomanist politics [*Osmanlı siyaseti*]," which had operated on the principles of decentralization and the inclusion of non-Muslim and non-Turkish citizens, as mere "Armenian politics [*Ermeni siyaseti*]." In his view, Turks had to form their own, Turkish government: "One government means one nation [*bir hükûmet, bir milletdir*]." The corollary was clear: the Ottoman government, like Ottoman literature and culture, even the Ottoman people, were all aspects of an artificial edifice, a house of cards, doomed to collapse.[27]

Naci İsmail devoted a lengthy segment of his book to the dominant and allegedly suffocating role of Greek Orthodox and Armenian Ottomans in trade and commerce, a common point of discussion in the press at the time.[28] These ethnic groups, he continued, controlled the economy with a crippling effect on the Turkish population.[29] The creation of a national economy (*millî iktisad*), as Zafer Toprak has shown, became a crucial aspect of Turkish nationalism during this period.[30] "Once the national movement has started," Naci İsmail went on, "all patriots will patronize the shops of their fellow [Turks] and this support will lead to the establishment of large companies ... The Turk who is not a businessman today can be one tomorrow."[31] In several statistical tables, he purported to document the minority presence in the various Ottoman provinces. And because they were in a minority, he concluded, none of these ethnic groups enjoyed the right to an independent government. In eastern Anatolia, he argued, Armenians and Kurds did not comprise a majority in any province – though neither did Turks, he neglected to add. Thus, no basis existed, according to the author, for an independent Armenian state (*Ermenistan*), or a Kurdish one (*Kürdistan*).[32]

---

[26] Naci İsmail, *Anadolu'da Türkiye*, 9–11.   [27] Ibid., 15–17, 78–9.

[28] See Hilmar Kaiser on the German dissemination of this perception, *Imperialism, Racism, and Development Theories: The Construction of a Dominant Paradigm on Ottoman Armenians* (Ann Arbor: Gomidas Institute, 1998).

[29] Naci İsmail, *Anadolu'da Türkiye*, 34–9, 43, 45–9, 52.

[30] Toprak, *Millî İktisat-Millî Burjuvazi*, 101–24.

[31] Naci İsmail, *Anadolu'da Türkiye*, 99 and 100.   [32] Ibid., 54–60, 62, 69–71, 73–4.

Turning to the hostile policies of the Great Powers, Naci İsmail sketched each power's aims in the Ottoman Empire and the Near East in detail. The Russians hungered for the Istanbul Straits, while the British pursued interests in Egypt and the Gulf, and, as a result, tried to keep Russia at bay by supporting an independent Armenia to serve as a buffer zone. The Germans, he continued, were using the Anatolian and Baghdad railway lines as means to colonize Anatolia. Because of these and other European schemes, he claimed, the history of Anatolia had been a history of upheaval. The Turkish reformer could never succeed by simply devoting his energies to domestic reforms and putting his own house in order: "The reformer in Turkey must keep in mind Europe. He cannot just think about his homeland [vatan]."[33]

To avert the Europeans' destructive plans, Naci İsmail argued, the Turks must unite in a nationalist movement, channel its unified strength and successfully defeat these enemies. The Turks were capable of such action because they were a true nation; they required only awakening: "When the foreigners attack Anatolia, the Turks and the Turkish government will prove [their] patriotism [eser-i asabiyet]. Because Turkey exists."[34] While Naci İsmail was not an outright militarist, advocating war with irredentist objectives, in his writings war is considered inescapable, and therefore he exhorted all Turks to ready themselves in full anticipation.

This attitude was widely echoed in the outlets of public opinion. In a speech that was as celebrated as it was characteristic of its time, the speaker of the chamber of deputies, Halil Bey, admonished the assembled delegates never to accept the empire's territorial losses. The recent military defeats had been terrible "accidents" made possible by the failure to keep alive memories of past battles and struggles; or, in other words, to keep alive the right kind of history:

I now have one plea to my people: Not to Forget! Don't forget the cradle of our freedom and our constitution: our beloved Salonica, verdant Manastır, Kosovo, İşkodra, Yanya, the entire beautiful Rumeli [i.e. all the European provinces of the Ottoman Empire]. I ask of our teachers, of our writers and poets, of all our leaders of thought to use their lessons, their writings, their poems, and their spiritual influence to keep alive in this generation and in future generations, the memories of our brothers and sisters who have remained on the other side of our borders and who must be saved; and to keep alive the memories of the limbs of our homeland on the other side of our borders that must be liberated.[35]

---

[33] Ibid., 80–95, 101–2.   [34] Ibid., 96.
[35] "Muazzez Refiklerim [Dear Friends]," MMZC, 6 Mayıs 1330 (May 19, 1914).

Halil Bey was calling for the formation of a nationalist movement led by intellectuals. He need not have feared; the intellectual movement he was calling for was already well underway.

Naci İsmail's "Habil Adem" heavily underscored the need for unity and common action among the Turkish elite and the Anatolian Turks at large. Employing the rhetoric of nationalist history, he called on his readers to unite and to prepare for violent conflict, because "when the Anatolian Turk put down his weapon, he saw that he was lost."[36] Naci İsmail even went as far as to divide the Ottoman Empire into "the real Turkey" and "colonial Turkey" (*hakikî Türkiye* and *müstemleke Türkiyesi*), and he returned to his argument that Turkey must free itself of its burdensome colonies. He explained that colonies, such as those constituted by the territories in the Balkans, had only forced the government to divert its energies to foreign affairs and had distracted it from more significant internal interests.[37]

The acquisition of colonies had served to muddle national identity and to squander national resources. Touching on the rival ideology of Turanism, which upheld the solidarity and unification of Turkic peoples from Anatolia to western China, he added that to pursue Turanist ideas would be to commit the same fallacy as the old Ottoman Turks, who eventually paid a heavy price for territorial expansion.[38] Naci İsmail's Anatolia-based nationalism, therefore, represented a revolution in patriotic-nationalist thinking and differed substantially from Halil Bey's irredentism.

"Habil Adem" concluded by underscoring that all true nations strive towards an "ultimate purpose: the nation has a multitude of feelings, thoughts, and ideas ... these must be united," and he argued that "all members must contribute to this effort." Nor would the new Turkish state, based in Anatolia alone and without any costly colonial possessions, mean that the Turks had demonstrated failure in successfully governing themselves. Comparing the Turks of the Ottoman Empire to the Italians of the Roman Empire, he argued that such a decolonization process simply represented a natural evolution. Turkey was just like Italy, even if it occupied a different historic stage for the moment: "Turkey is at the beginning of its journey, while Italy has already reached its destination."[39]

The ideas put forth in *Will Turkey Survive in Anatolia?* were shared, as we shall see, by other publications of the time. These ideas deepen our understanding of the values embraced by the elite in the capital, if not by the broader sections of the population, and they help recover the contemporary

[36] Naci İsmail, *Anadolu'da Türkiye*, 109–14.   [37] Ibid., 118.
[38] Ibid., 123–4.   [39] Ibid., 123–5.

intellectual climate in which the decision for war was taken. Naci İsmail's vision of the political future was in fact extremely close to the ideology of the Kemalist Republic that followed after 1923, underscoring the deep ideological connections between modern Turkey and the late Ottoman period. Naci İsmail's work opens a window into the contemporary intellectual and emotional world of the Turkish–Ottoman elite. Even though his work did not call for the reconquest of the Balkans, it becomes apparent that, in regard to 1914, the intellectual and emotional climate was consistent with, and, in fact, fostered, the embrace of war in 1914. That decision was the outcome less of irredentist ideas than the firm conviction that war inevitably would have to be faced once again in the near future.

"National struggle" and the mobilization of society

Thus a strong linkage between the questions of war, liberation, and modernity characterized political writing on the eve of the First World War. Discussions focusing on the creation of a "new society" and a "new life [*yeni hayat*]" which were to be molded by a new language and a new literature converged with the ideas of waging war and gaining independence from the imperialist powers. Liberation would have to be total. A significant portion of these publications aimed at broad segments of society and was intended to mobilize the people against the state's external enemies. The authors of these publications, intellectuals, politicians, and military leaders alike, viewed as their role the mobilization and education of the masses, and they viewed themselves as the enlightened guides of their people's "awakening [*intibah*]."[40] In their efforts this intelligentsia had to confront the difficulty of spreading their message to a population of fellow countrymen who were largely illiterate. As a result the ubiquity of public readings became an important characteristic of the national awakening movement. Popular authors like the sharp-minded CUP critic Şehbenderzade Ahmed Hilmi included straplines to their book titles such as "May every patriot read and relate this booklet to the Turks."[41]

[40] Tüccarzade İbrahim Hilmi, *Türkiye Uyan* [Turkey Awake], Kütübhane-i İntibah, no. 13 (Dersaadet: Kütübhane-i İslam ve Askerî, 1329 [March 1913–March 1914]), 1–2 and passim; Mehmed Emin, *Ey Türk Uyan* [O Turk, Awake!]; see also the addresses to the Ottoman chamber of deputies by the sultan and by the grand vezir, e.g. Mehmed Reşad V, "Muhterem Âyân ve Mebusan [Honored Senators and Deputies]," *MMZC*, address delivered 1 Mayıs 1330 (May 14, 1914), and the government program of the Said Halim Pasha cabinet, *MMZC*, address delivered by Talat Bey, 6 Temmuz 1330 (July 19, 1914); "İğne Darbeleri [Thorns in Our Flesh]," *Tanin*, April 21, 1914.
[41] Özdemir [Şehbenderzade Filibeli Ahmed Hilmi], *Türk Ruhu Nasıl Yapılıyor? Her Vatanperverden, Bu Eserciği Türklere Okumasını Ve Anlatmasını Niyaz Ederiz* [How the

It is instructive to stay with him for a while. Ahmed Hilmi, whose book appeared between March 1913 and March 1914, demanded of his readers utmost loyalty to the Turkish nation. A new age, he insisted, had opened, one that demanded that the people unite and rally behind their state. Addressing the reader as "Turk," he explained that the national groups in the Balkans had ended Ottoman rule there because the peoples of the Balkans had "awoken after centuries of slumber" and were regaining their national consciousness.[42] Now, Ahmed Hilmi claimed, "while we have remained the people of a past age," the Balkan nations have "become peoples of this age," which he labeled "the age of knowledge and struggle [*bilgi ve çabalama zamanı*]." Although the Balkan Wars had ended, Ahmed Hilmi continued, the national struggle had just begun. Such a struggle was inevitable and required the selfless effort and sacrifice of each and every Turk: "The struggle [in the Balkans] is over, but struggle will start again. Living means struggling. Absence of struggle can only be found in cemeteries. Only the dead are without struggle."[43]

By 1914, the defining characteristics of the age were part of Ottoman common knowledge. The ideas of social Darwinism had been elaborated upon and transferred, in pseudo-scientific jargon, to the realms of government and international relations. The importance of this theme, that society must organize itself and prepare its every aspect for war, cannot be overemphasized; it dominated Ottoman political discourse on the eve of the First World War.[44]

To external enemies, Ahmed Hilmi added social problems such as "hunger, poverty, and ignorance" as the most pressing issues.[45] Today's reader may rightly wonder what exactly authors had in mind when referring to "society" or "national." On this point, Ahmed Hilmi was explicit.[46] His intended audience was the Turkish-speaking Muslim population of Anatolia:

The Crimea, Rumania, Algeria, Tunisia, Egypt, Serbia, Bulgaria, the Caucasus all went one by one … Finally Tripoli [Libya] and three-fourths of the Balkans also were lost. These areas were all rich and valuable places; we gained them at the

---

Turkish Spirit is Formed: We Ask of Each Patriot to Read and Relate this Booklet to the Turks], İkaz-ı Millet Kütübhanesi, no. 1 (Darülhilâfe: Hikmet Matbaa-i İslamiyesi, 1329 [March 1913–March 1914]); see also İsmail, *Anadolu'da Türkiye*, 15–21, 78–9.

[42] Ibid., 16.   [43] Ibid., 4.

[44] Besides the works discussed here, see also A., *Balkan Harbi'nde Neden Münhezim Olduk* [Why We Were Routed in the Balkan War], pt. 1, Kütübhane-i İntibah, Tüccarzade İbrahim Hilmi, no. 9 (Istanbul: Kütübhane-i İslam ve Askeri, 1329 [March 1913–March 1914]), 4, as well as İbrahim Hilmi's afterword in ibid., 92.

[45] Özdemir, *Türk Ruhu Nasıl Yapılıyor?*, 4.

[46] Erik Jan Zürcher, however, argues that little Turkish nationalism to speak of existed prior to the First World War; see his "The Vocabulary of Muslim Nationalism," *International Journal of the Sociology of Language* 137 (1999): 81–91.

cost of our blood. But those territories, however rich they may be, were not the heart and soul of our homeland [*yurdumuzun yüreği*] ... O Turk! Anatolia is the heart and soul of our homeland. O Turk! If we continue in our old ways, if we face the enemy again in slumber, unprotected, then this time the enemy's sword will come to our [homeland's] heart and soul and kill each one of us.[47]

Ahmed Hilmi, who was not a member of the CUP, thus also adopted the vision of a Turkish homeland in Anatolia, rejecting at the same time the premises of the multi-national Ottoman Empire and the Turanist ideology of uniting all Turkic populations from Anatolia to Central Asia. The author considered it essential for the young and educated to go beyond the capital and spread the nationalist message in the towns and villages of Anatolia. Only in this way could the "Turkish spirit" be recovered after its centuries of slumber: "O Turkish youths, sons of the homeland, hope of the nation! Run out to the four corners of Anatolia and be fountains of vigor and guidance. Wake up the common classes from their slumber and rescue the middle classes from intrigue and politics, lead them all down the right path."[48] The author not only intended his work to be read aloud in public readings, but evidently also expected wide circulation; the book's front matter indicated that orders of over 200 and those of over a thousand copies each qualified for special discounts.

In the foreword to the translation of a French work, the author Recai also made an argument for national mobilization; this time, however, speaking of an "Ottoman" rather than a "Turkish" nation. Under the title *How Germany Revived and How It Is Preparing for War*, Recai criticized writers and intellectuals for not educating the people sufficiently about topics that would contribute to the formation of an "Ottoman nation." Novels and plays must never be purely literary or artistic, but needed to fulfill a social purpose, illustrating didactically the importance of being a true patriot and how this could be accomplished.[49] Novelists, playwrights, and intellectuals who put their talents at the service of the nation's interest should join together and form a National Literature Association (*Müellefât-ı Milliye Heyeti*), he suggested.[50]

Like so many nationalists responding to a sense of weakness, Recai, in fact, elevated the task of writing and thinking in the nation's interest to a matter of life and death. Prussian history provided a most instructive lesson in this regard. Following Prussia's defeat at the hands of Napoleon, its

---

[47] Özdemir, *Türk Ruhu Nasıl Yapılıyor?*, 6–7.   [48] Ibid., 18, 30–2, 36.

[49] Recai, foreword to *Almanya Nasıl Dirildi? Harbe Nasıl Hazırlanıyor* [How Germany Revived and How it is Preparing for War], translation of *La préparation de la lutte économique par l'Allemagne*, by Antoine de Tarlé (Dersaadet: Nefaset Matbaası, 1329 [March 1913–March 1914]), 7.

[50] Ibid., 10.

writers and poets had given shape to a German spirit capable of uniting the
German people and of defeating France in 1870–1. The Ottoman nation,
too, Recai continued, had to be shown the meaning of "state" and "nation,"
as well as needing to learn about foreign countries and their people.[51]
Recai's "Ottoman nation" was not ethnically but religiously defined, differ-
ing in this important regard from thinkers like Ahmed Hilmi and Naci
İsmail. Thus, the Muslim population of the empire had to be instructed in
Islamic history, made conscious of their community, and united behind the
state to overcome the empire's external foes.[52] Here again, the vision for
the future turned clearly on the building of a Turkish-Muslim nation, while
the role of the non-Muslim population remained unspecified.

In the writings of the day, a consensus existed that an army's level of
effectiveness could only be as high as the level of education in the society
that produced it. Writing just before the outbreak of the Second Balkan
War, Major Hafız Hakkı (1878–1915), who served as Enver's assistant in
the general staff in 1914 and as commander of the Third Army in 1915,
argued that "the army may try as hard as it wishes to improve a society's
military strength. The army's officers may be the most skilled in the world,
but if the society's material and moral standards are low, the army will
certainly enter the battlefield in a deficient and disorderly manner and
quickly meet with defeat."[53] Hafız Hakkı decried the crops of impover-
ished, unhealthy, and uneducated recruits that entered the army's ranks
for regular military service year after year and returned later as reserves
during periods of mobilization. The army's problems, he believed,
stemmed from those within society itself: the need for education, for
economic development, and for improving the situation of women.[54]
Hafız Hakkı argued that the people needed a shared, supreme ideal that
defined Ottoman life and towards whose purpose its members could strive
collectively,[55] a purpose that writers frequently referred to simply as the
"national ideal [mefkûre-i milliye]."[56] Hafız Hakkı fixed on the creation of a
"people in arms," as the German general Colmar von der Goltz had before
him, and whose book by that title, translated into Ottoman Turkish as

---

[51] Ibid., 8. Recai writes the following about the Prussian victory over the French: "Bu kıyamı
hazırlayan işte bütün Prusya mütefekkirleri, ve onların içinde de en ziyade edibleri,
şairleridir. [Those who prepared the rise of Prussia were Prussian thinkers, and amongst
these most importantly their writers and poets.]"
[52] Ibid., 12–13.
[53] Hafız Hakkı, Bozgun [Morale and Defeat], Tüccarzade İbrahim Hilmi Series (Dersaadet:
Matbaa-i Hayriye, 1330 [March 1914–March 1915]), 37.
[54] Ibid., 39–42, 66–7.   [55] Ibid., 51–3.
[56] "Şevketmeab [Your Majesty]," MMZC, 10 Mayıs 1330 (May 23, 1914).

early as 1886, Hafız Hakkı now quoted.[57] Like Recai, Hafız Hakkı also invoked the Prussian example of recovery and victory. While France and the case of Alsace-Lorraine provided a model of loss, Prussia provided a model of recovery. Such recovery was available to the Ottoman Empire as well, but only if its society, as a totality, prepared unconditionally for war during times of peace.[58]

Cami [Baykut], a former delegate to the Ottoman chamber who had co-founded in 1912 the National Constitution Party, the first party to be openly Turkish nationalist, argued along similar lines. In *The Ottoman Future: Its Enemies and Its Friends*, published in 1913, Cami claimed that the empire was primarily an Asian country, and that the Balkans, now lost, had been colonies, never part of the true homeland (*vatan*). Like Hafız Hakkı, Cami, a former officer, was also intimately acquainted with the ideas of Goltz. Cami praised the German general's recommendation that the empire's center of gravity should formally be shifted southward by moving the capital to Konya, or perhaps even farther south.[59]

Thus, whether Ottomanist and irredentist or Anatolian and ethnic nationalist, the idea that the Ottomans sooner or later would have to fight a war of survival and that for this purpose the population had to be equipped appropriately – mentally and physically – formed the central theme in the period's political literature. This import is also found in Cami's work: "There can be no doubt that our homeland's survival and well-being depends on the raising of our defensive strength, and this [strengthening] can only be accomplished if the people's power to resist and their power to fight in the general struggle is increased." This goal could only be accomplished, Cami posited, by improving the country's economic and social conditions and by instilling a strong sense of discipline and duty in the people.[60]

Remaining silent on the question of the Christian and Kurdish populations, Cami envisioned the new state to consist of both Turks and Arabs, and he was therefore less radical than Naci İsmail or Ahmed Hilmi. The empire's industrial base had to be developed and the population educated

---

[57] Hafız Hakkı, *Bozgun* [Morale and Defeat], 80–1. Goltz's book, *Das Volk in Waffen: ein Buch über Heerwesen und Kriegsführung unserer Zeit*, 3rd edn. (Berlin: Decker, 1884), appeared in Ottoman as *Millet-i Müselleha* (Kostantiniye: Matbaa-i Ebüzziya, 1301 [March 1885–March 1886]).

[58] Ibid., 105–6.

[59] Cami [Abdurrahman Cami Baykut], *Osmanlılığın Âtisi: Düşmanları Ve Dostları* [The Ottoman Future: Its Enemies and Its Friends] (Istanbul: İfham Matbaası, 1331 [5 Kanunisani 1328/January 18, 1913]), 6–8, 12; on Cami's National Constitution Party, see Ali Birinci, *Hürriyet Ve İtilâf Fırkası: II. Meşrutiyet Devrinde İttihat Ve Terakki'ye Karşı Çıkanlar* (Istanbul: Dergâh Yayınları, 1990), 181–3.

[60] Ibid., 9.

and instilled with common goals and ideals. School curricula, Cami
continued, had to be revised so that students could begin to embrace
shared ideals and unite in their citizenship. Up to now, he argued, schools
had produced "useless Ottomans." He thus dismissed categorically the
possibility of an Ottoman identity, adding, "We have witnessed ourselves
that the time has passed when armies were formed by societies that are
uneducated and lack ideals."[61]

Cami found a great deal of irony in the empire's dilemma, namely that
only Europe stood in the way of the "Turk's Europeanization [*Türkün
Avrupalılaşması*]." Through constant interference in the empire's internal affairs, politically and financially, the Great Powers of Europe had tied
the Sublime Porte's hands and prevented it from implementing effective
reforms, despite the numerous attempts dating as far back as the beginning of the nineteenth century. The Triple Entente, and Britain in particular, Cami argued, was waging an all-out attack on the Ottoman
Empire.[62] Cami described this dynamic sarcastically:

Yes, in order to be friends with Britain we must recognize that the Red Sea is a
British sea. And we must also cede [to the British the region stretching from] Egypt
to Syria, [and from] Iraq to India, and permit the British sphere of influence in Iran
to extend westward, that is, to extend to the port of Alexandretta. And we must be
satisfied with an Anatolian princedom based in Konya. [Once we do all that] we
can begin to speak of a friendly British policy towards us.[63]

In this view, nothing but harm could be expected from Britain and its
partners in the Triple Entente.

As to Germany, the author expressed a perspective that was typical:
"Germany is not simply pursuing its economic interests by maintaining
the status quo in the Near East, but Germany also intends to take advantage of the Ottoman state's [strategic] position in its [own] hostile relationship with Slavdom. In fact, the Slavic world is growing more rapidly than
its neighbors and poses a threat in Europe to the Germans, Hungarians,
and Romanians; and it presents the same threat, or perhaps even a greater
calamity, to the Ottomans. A strong Ottoman state must form an alliance
with Germany and take a defensive position against the Russian and
Balkan Slavs; this is the foundation of any sound policy."[64] After the
Ottoman defeat in the Balkans, Cami calculated, the German government
would have to reaffirm its commitment to the Ottoman Empire, politically
and economically, if it did not wish to witness a "Slav invasion" of eastern
Europe and Anatolia.[65] In his conclusion he reiterated the argument

[61] Ibid., 10 and 11.   [62] Ibid., 21–9.   [63] Ibid., 30.
[64] Ibid., 34; "Asabiyet Alâmetleri [Signs of Nervousness]," *Tanin*, April 30, 1914.
[65] Cami [Abdurrahman Cami Baykut], *Osmanlılığın Âtisi*, 37–8.

regarding Germany: in the aftermath of the First Balkan War, the Ottomans must put aside their former differences with Italy (over Cyrenaika and Tripoli in North Africa) and Austria-Hungary (over Bosnia-Herzegovina and Salonica), and join the Triple Alliance of Germany, Austria-Hungary, and Italy.[66]

There is stunning evidence for the extent to which an alliance with Germany was discussed publicly. When the German battlecruiser SMS *Goeben* visited Istanbul in May 1914, already at that point it was rumored that the powerful ship might be sold to the Ottoman navy, or that in the event of war between the Triple Alliance and the Triple Entente the *Goeben* would assume duties on behalf of the empire.[67] Hence, astonishingly, about six weeks prior to Franz Ferdinand's assassination in Sarajevo, participation in a general war alongside Germany was presented in a major Istanbul daily as a reasonable and acceptable course of action.

Pan-Islamism, the idea that the Muslim populations of Eurasia and North Africa should join forces and cooperate politically and perhaps even militarily, played only a small role in Cami's perception of the international order and the Ottoman place in it. He described pan-Islamism (*ittihad-ı İslam*) as a fabrication of the Triple Entente, a specter the European imperialists invoked in order to manipulate their own public opinion and to continue their aggressive schemes of expansion into Muslim territories. Cami opined that, in the end, a kind of Muslim union might appear after all, a self-fulfilled prophecy, but not the one imagined in the West: "This union ... will not be the result of the caliph's politics, but of the Europeans' oppression in the colonies: pan-Islamism is not a positive result of Islamic politics, but it will be the negative result of Christian oppression."[68] This pan-Islamism, in other words, would manifest itself in a kind of anti-colonial, defensive league of Islamic states that would form a united front against the provocations and assaults of the Triple Entente powers.

The tendency for wars to become "holy wars" or "crusades" fought in the name of God and civilization against perceived evil and barbarism would be demonstrated to perfection in the Great War, as each of the belligerent societies created and clung tightly to such myths.[69] In their

---

[66] Ibid., 39–40.
[67] "Bu Günlerde Tekrar Limanımıza Gelecek Olan *Goeben* Drednotu [The Dreadnought *Goeben*, Which is to Call on Our Port Once Again]," *Tanin*, May 7, 1914; "Amiral Suşon [Admiral Souchon]," *Tanin*, May 17, 1914; the rumor of the *Goeben*'s sale to the Ottoman Empire had also been discussed in diplomatic circles, see *IBZI*, Series I, vol. 1, no. 72, Gulkevich to Sazonov, January 24, 1914, 62–3, and ibid., Series I, vol. 1, no. 140, Sazonov to Sverbeyev, January 30, 1914, 123, and ibid., Series I, vol. 1, no. 175, Sverbeyev to Sazonov, February 4, 1914, 164.
[68] Cami [Abdurrahman Cami Baykut], *Osmanlılığın Âtisi*, 41–6, quotation on 44–5.
[69] Audoin-Rouzeau and Becker, *14–18: Understanding the Great War*, 91–171.

mobilization of the general population, the Ottoman elite employed such thinking during and following the wars with Italy in 1911 and the Balkan states in 1912–13. In a communiqué of early August 1914 to the Fourth Army headquartered in Baghdad, Enver Pasha warned of an impending attack by British and Russian forces, and he urged Arab leaders such as Naqib Talib Bey of Basra, Amir ʿAbd al-ʾAziz ibn Saʾud of Najd and al-Hasa, and the Sheiyh Mubarak al-Sabah of Kuwait to rally for "the support and protection of the state," because "as a result of this war, Islamic peoples will rise up" and put an end to Christian colonial rule over Islamic populations.[70] To Talib Bey he wrote: "But should our enemies wish to soil our land with their filthy feet, I am convinced that Islamic and Ottoman honor and strength will destroy them."[71]

Authors like Cami were explicit about their efforts to mobilize the public. To prevent European control, Cami urged, Ottomans must prepare to fight for their survival. Writing during the final days of the First Balkan War, Cami addressed his fellow citizens in this manner: "Ottomans! ... If you do not want to become slaves, if you do not want to be destroyed forever, ready yourselves for the fight." According to Cami, the fight (*cidal*) must begin prior to the war on the battlefield; it must begin in the minds and homes of all Ottomans: "Now withdraw to your mother soil [*ana toprağınıza*], and build there a true society, and lay the foundations for the civilization of the future [*medeniyet-i istikbalin temellerini*]! You require everything that is new: a new ambition, a new understanding, a new faith."[72]

The journal *Büyük Duygu* (The Great Yearning)

The journal *Büyük Duygu* also illustrates the emotional and intellectual environment that formed during and after the Balkan Wars. Its first issue appeared in Istanbul in March 1913 and was followed by twenty-five further issues before publication came to an end in January 1914. Subtitled "The Turk's Journal," *Büyük Duygu* employed nationalist language throughout its articles on politics, history, and literature.[73] The journal's first issue declared as its purpose the fostering of awareness of

---

[70] ATASE, BDH, Klasör 68, Yeni Dosya 337, Fihrist 1 and 1–1, Enver to Cavid, 24/25 Temmuz 1330 (August 6/7, 1914).
[71] ATASE, BDH, Klasör 68, Yeni Dosya 337, Fihrist 3–2, Enver to Talib, 28 Temmuz 1330 (August 10, 1914).
[72] Cami [Abdurrahman Cami Baykut], *Osmanlılığın Âtisi*, 47 and 48.
[73] The journal's founders were listed as Dündar Alp, Ş. Uluğ, and M. Fazıl; see the first issue of *Büyük Duygu: Onbeş Günde Bir Çıkar, Türkün Risalesidir* [The Great Yearning: The Turk's Bimonthly Journal], Cemiyet Kütüphanesi, Sayı 1, 2 Mart 1329 (March 15, 1913), 1.

Turkish history and national consciousness. The latter required develop-ment, the publication urged, because the Turks would soon be taking their place on the battlefield where they would fight for their national survival. Women, in particular, were accorded a major role in the for-mation of the new society.[74]

What did the journal's title, "The Great Yearning," refer to? Was it "revenge" (*intikam duygusu*), as the title of several lead articles seemed to suggest?[75] Or did it refer to the perceived need to "return" to a primordial Turkish identity (*Türklük duygusu*), as another piece claimed?[76] Whichever facet one chooses to emphasize, there can be no doubt that the journal sought to grip its readers with gory descriptions of the recent past and to instill a deep sense of violation and to build a collective identity. Only the unity of the nation, the editors proclaimed, could offer a prosperous foun-dation for existence. Continuous "battle [*kavga*]," moreover, formed the essential aspect of any meaningful survival. "Peace and tranquility," so the journal declared, could be found only in death.[77] It continued in social Darwinian terms: "Only the nation armed with national feelings [*milliyet duygularıyla*] can participate in the struggle and gain as a result of it the right to remain alive. But let us not spend much time on the word 'right,' for there is no one left who does not believe that 'right' [*hak*] is nothing other than 'might' [*kuvvet*]. 'The most obvious truth is that those who do not crush will be crushed.' The inevitable place of those who do not heed this proverb is the cemetery and history. Thus in order to live we must not strive for 'right' but for power."[78] Throughout the issues of *Büyük Duygu*, the authors' message was unequivocal. Existence depended on unfettered sovereignty and self-reliance: "Right can only be derived from power, civilization only from power, happiness only from power. Power is everything."[79]

Typical of the authors in this genre, *Büyük Duygu*'s editors were mobi-lizers and activists, and they were far from resigned to Ottoman demise. To illustrate their arguments, they turned to history for examples of peoples that had reemerged successfully from defeat.[80] Successful

---

[74] Ibid., "Milliyet," 1–2.
[75] "İntikam Duygusu," *Büyük Duygu*, Sayı 2, 16 Mart 1329 (March 29, 1913), 17–18, and "Acımak Yok … İntikam! [No Mercy … Revenge!]," *Büyük Duygu*, Sayı 8, 6 Haziran 1329 (June 19, 1913), 113–14.
[76] "Türklük Duygusu," *Büyük Duygu*, Sayı 5, 25 Nisan 1329 (May 8, 1913), 65–6, and "En Büyük Noksan [The Greatest Deficiency]," *Büyük Duygu*, Sayı 9, 20 Haziran 1329 (July 3, 1913), 129–31.
[77] "İntikam Duygusu," *Büyük Duygu*, Sayı 2, 16 Mart 1329 (March 29, 1913), 17–18.
[78] Ibid., 17.   [79] Ibid.
[80] See Naci İsmail, Belak [pseud.], *Mağlub Milletler Nasıl İntikam Alırlar* [How Do Defeated Nations Take Revenge?], trans. Habil Adem [pseud.] (Dersaadet: İkbal Kütübhanesi, 1332 h. [November 1913–November 1914]).

national recovery demanded an active, not a passive policy. "Crushed and defeated nations must rise up without delay and act swiftly ... crying Revenge, Revenge!" That the worldview of *Büyük Duygu* was not unique but reflected the sentiments of influential circles can be seen in a letter Enver wrote on May 8, 1913: "My heart is bleeding ... If I could tell you all the atrocities which the enemy has committed right here at the gates of Istanbul, you would understand the sufferings of the poor Muslims farther away. But our hatred is intensifying: revenge, revenge, revenge, there is nothing else."[81] Writers often referred to the German victory over France in 1870–1, a victory that followed the Germans' defeat by the Napoleonic armies several decades earlier. As a nation that had successfully reasserted itself, Germany presented an example to be followed. Turks also should stand up: "Oh Turkish nation! ... Has the blood of Oğuz, Genghis, and Fatih dried up in your veins? Will you forget the blows that have been dealt against your Turkish soul [*Türklüğüne*], will you forget the wounds that have been inflicted upon your heart?!"[82] Evidently, some parts of the Turkish elite in Istanbul believed not only that the empire faced a historic military confrontation in the near future, but that the Ottomans should seek out that confrontation rather than await it passively.

While we know little about the size and make-up of *Büyük Duygu*'s readership, it is significant that the journal supported public lectures and meetings in an effort to reach broader segments of the population. One such meeting was held in an Istanbul suburb in early April 1913, organized by the local women's branch of the Society for National Defense (*Müdafaa-i Milliye Cemiyeti*), a prominent and very popular organization that promoted the values of the publications under discussion. At the meeting, the branch chairwoman, N. Sebiha, delivered an address subsequently published in *Büyük Duygu*. By now, the reader will recognize the topic of Sebiha's address – that the people were "still asleep" and must be awakened to the dangers facing the empire – as the theme running through much of the contemporary political literature. Drawing on a historical example, this time the deeds of the ancient Carthaginian women when besieged by the Roman armies, Sebiha urged the women in her audience to make sacrifices, especially financial ones, in the name of the nation. She called on her listeners and readers to prove to the Europeans that "Turks" could "face the Europeans head on, be it militarily or economically."[83]

---

[81] M. Şükrü Hanioğlu, ed., *Kendi Mektuplarında Enver Paşa* (Istanbul: Der Yayınları, 1989), 242.
[82] "İntikam Duygusu," *Büyük Duygu*, 18.
[83] "Türk Hanımlarının Toplantısı [The Gathering of Turkish Ladies]," *Büyük Duygu*, no. 2, 16 Mart 1329 (March 29, 1913), 31–2; on the *Müdafaa-i Milliye Cemiyeti*, which was

These contemporary publications suggest that the necessity of fighting a 'war of independence' had become a widely-discussed, if not accepted, reality. In holding this view, the public's outlook did not differ from Enver's: war was the opportunity by which Ottoman aims of restoring a militarily powerful and politically independent empire could be achieved. Intellectuals and political leaders also believed that the empire had entered a crucial phase in its history during which it would be decided whether it would continue to exist or be destroyed. Nations and states were taken to exist in endless cycles of Darwinian struggle that no nation could escape.[84] By 1914, a broad consensus had formed around these issues, at least in the capital.

In the period following the war, however, the elite of the newly-established Turkish Republic strongly denied the existence of such a consensus and thereby distanced itself from former decision-makers such as Enver. The reasons for such distancing are not difficult to discern. It was evident in retrospect that by entering the First Word War the empire had run itself into the ground. And there were more immediate reasons as well. At war's end, the Entente allies proceeded to occupy significant portions of the empire, including the capital. High-ranking civilians and military officers were rounded up and imprisoned. Their guilt was not only that of waging war and losing, but they were also held responsible for the murderous treatment of their own Armenian civilian population during the war years.

The prewar discussion of the international order grew out of the experience of repeated diplomatic and military defeat. This experience not only meant a wealth of social and economic hardships for the population at large, but also engendered a deep psychological crisis. Although the resulting literature has been called "romantic" and "devoid of any connection with the people,"[85] it would be erroneous to think that it was only the product of a small group of insignificant writers. The takeover of the Sublime Porte on January 23, 1913, under the leadership of Enver Bey, brought to power a new government and marked the beginning of increased one-party rule under the CUP.[86] Given the authoritarian regime during those years, we might conclude that the political ideas

formed during the height of the Balkan Wars by the most influential intellectuals and politicians of the time, and its women's groups, see Nazım H. Polat, *Müdafaa-i Milliye Cemiyeti*, Kaynak Eserler, no. 52 (Ankara: Kültür Bakanlığı, 1991), 16–33 and 71–81.

[84] Ömer Seyfeddin, *Yarınki Turan Devleti* [Tomorrow's State of Turan], Türk Yurdu Kütübhanesi (Istanbul: Kader Matbaası, 1330 [March 1914–March 1915]), 3–11.

[85] Niyazi Berkes, *The Development of Secularism in Turkey* (Montreal: McGill University Press, 1964), 428.

[86] Sina Akşin, *Jön Türkler ve İttihat ve Terakki* (Istanbul: Remzi, 1987), 250–308.

appearing in the publications of 1913–14 were accepted, if not wholly embraced, by that regime.

The Ottoman elite was not unique in its concern to foster among broad segments of its population a strong feeling of loyalty and duty to the state. An "internal colonialism" that sought to accomplish these tasks through homogenization of their populations was a global trend and occurred in Western European states such as France and in regions of Eurasia such as the Russian Empire.[87] But given the Ottoman focus on the need to face external threats and to counteract foreign control, the movement to mobilize its citizens was closer in its motivation to the Chinese and Spanish experiences. Like the Ottoman Empire, Qing China was not formally colonized but its elite detested the sway of Western imperialism just the same. Chinese intellectuals decried commercial concessions and legal privileges granted to foreigners under the Qing dynasty. Soon after the Wuchang Revolution of 1911 led by nationalist army troops, the emperor was forced to abdicate, under circumstances not unlike those of Sultan Abdülhamid II's abdication.

The rhetoric of the Chinese "movement of self-strengthening," moreover, exhibited considerable similarities to the political literature of the late Ottomans, including an emphasis on a newly defined ethnic identity.[88] The Spanish military elite, too, promoted a movement intended to prioritize the well-being of the state in its citizens' outlook. Spanish "regenerationism" in the late nineteenth century was a reaction to the "great disaster" that had befallen the Iberian power and a response to the need to recover from the loss of Spain's imperial possessions: Cuba, the Philippines, and Morocco.[89]

---

[87] Jörg Baberowski, "Nationalismus aus dem Geist der Inferiorität: Autokratische Modernisierung und die Anfänge muslimischer Selbstvergewisserung im östlichen Transkaukasien, 1828–1914," *Geschichte und Gesellschaft* 26 (*Aspekte des Nationalismus*) (2000): 371–98. Examining nationalism in Russia, Baberowski invokes Eugen Weber's study of France, *Peasants into Frenchman: The Modernization of Rural France, 1870–1914* (Stanford: Stanford University Press, 1976). See also Ussama Makdisi, "Ottoman Orientalism," *American Historical Review* 107 (June 2002): 768–96, on the Ottoman state's policy and perception of its Arab subjects.

[88] Kauko Laitinen, *Chinese Nationalism in the Late Qing Dynasty: Zhang Binglin as an Anti Manchu Propagandist*, Scandinavian Institute of Asia Studies (London: Curzon Press, 1990), 35–51; Jonathan D. Spence, *The Search for Modern China* (New York: W. W. Norton, 1990), 197 and 216–44.

[89] Geoffrey Jensen, "Military Nationalism and the State: The Case of *fin-de-siècle* Spain," *Nations and Nationalism* 6 (2000): 257–74, and Francis Lannon, "1898 and the Politics of Catholic Identity in Spain," in *The Politics of Religion in an Age of Revival*, ed. Austen Ivereigh (London: Institute of Latin American Studies, 2000), 63.

For the Ottoman elite, a similar military challenge lay ahead. Like the drive to modernize its armies beginning in the late eighteenth century, nascent Turkish nationalism on the eve of the First World War stemmed from the external imperative to gear up the public for military conflict.[90]

[90] M. E. Yapp, "The Modernization of Middle Eastern Armies in the Nineteenth Century: A Comparative View," in *War, Technology and Society in the Middle East*, ed. V. J. Parry and M. E. Yapp (New York: Oxford University Press, 1975), 331–66; Glen W. Swanson, "War, Technology and Society in the Ottoman Empire from the Reign of Abdülhamid II to 1913: Mahmud Şevket and the German Military Mission," in ibid., 367–85; Ralston, *Importing the European Armies*.

2   1914: war with Greece?

The Treaty of Constantinople officially ended the Second Balkan War for the Ottoman Empire, but not, as we have seen, the conviction on the part of an aggrieved public that more war was necessary. And indeed in the months between September 1913 and August 1914, the empire teetered on the brink of war with Greece, which had captured several Aegean islands during the First Balkan War. Throughout these ten months, the foreign ministry worked hard to attract Great Power support for their return. At issue were the islands of Chios and Mytilene, within sight of the Ottoman coast, and the island of Limnos. All three were of critical strategic importance, with Limnos commanding the mouth of the Dardanelles. A war between Greece and the Ottoman Empire contained the potential to draw in the Powers. In the event of war, the Sublime Porte would certainly close the Straits, as it had done briefly after Italy invaded its North African province of Tripoli (Libya) in 1911. Russia could not remain on the sidelines if the war closed the Straits; 50 percent of all its exports, including 90 percent of its grains, shipped through it.[1] With her economy and thus the stability of the state endangered, could anyone doubt that St. Petersburg would have felt compelled to open its only route to the West "with force," as Tsar Nicholas II put it in April 1914?[2] And could anyone doubt that a Russian intervention, threatening Austria-Hungary's position in the Balkans and crowding Britain's in the eastern Mediterranean, would have triggered an international crisis of the first order, and perhaps German and British intervention as well?

The dispute over the future of the northern Aegean islands also fueled a high-stakes arms and naval race between Athens and Istanbul. The immediate factor intensifying the stand-off was the impending delivery of two dreadnought-class battleships which the Ottoman government had

---

[1] Norman Rich, *Great Power Diplomacy, 1814–1914* (New York: McGraw-Hill, 1992), 425.
[2] *IBZI*, Series I, vol. 2, no. 238, Paléologue to Doumergue, April 18, 1914, 243.

on order with the British shipbuilding firms Armstrong and Vickers.[3] As the delivery date approached, with the first ship due in late July 1914, Greek planners considered blockading Izmir and waging a pre-emptive war.[4] For the Greeks, such a war would not only consolidate their hold on the islands. More importantly, it would force the British to intervene, causing, they hoped, the cancellation of the Ottomans' two ships before they could be delivered.

This prospect meant that the Ottomans could not allow the saber-rattling between Athens and Istanbul to develop into war prematurely. The arrival of the two dreadnoughts would hand the Ottomans the naval advantage in the Aegean; without them they would have to contend with a superior enemy. To compensate for this temporary weakness at sea, the Sublime Porte sought to extend its land power across the Balkan peninsula. Thus in 1914 rumors of a Bulgarian–Ottoman alliance circulated in the capitals of Europe.[5] At the very moment that shots brought down Franz Ferdinand, on June 28, 1914, the Ottoman government was actively pursuing a Bulgarian promise of neutrality in the event that the empire invaded Greece.[6] Whether they actually planned to attack Greece once they had secured Bulgarian neutrality, or whether they hoped to use Bulgarian neutrality as a lever to pry the islands away from Greece's grasp remains uncertain. Most probably, the Ottomans were bargaining for both options, to exercise depending on how events unfolded.

The broader circumstances of the Greek–Ottoman confrontation during 1913/14 illustrate the explosive links between the empire's domestic problems and its foreign conflicts, as would the Armenian question (discussed in the next chapter).

By 1914 the possibility of population exchanges and ethnic cleansing had entered Ottoman strategic thinking. At least for Ottoman leaders like Talat Bey, the interior minister, the presence of large ethnic minorities, especially when backed by a foreign power, threatened the stability and

---

[3] Paul G. Halpern, *The Mediterranean Naval Situation, 1908–1914* (Cambridge, MA: Harvard University Press, 1971), 317, 324; "Osmanlı Ve Yunan Drednotları [The Ottoman and Greek Dreadnoughts]," *Tanin*, May 2, 1914; "Yunan Donanması [The Greek Navy]," *Tanin*, May 10, 1914; "Ganbotlarımız [Our Warships]," *Tanin*, May 11, 1914; "Osmanlı-Yunan Münasebatı [Ottoman–Greek Relations]," *Tanin*, May 12, 1914.
[4] *IBZI*, Series I, vol. 3, no. 70, Giers to Sazonov, May 23, 1914, 64; ibid., Series I, vol. 3, no. 142, Poklevskii to Sazonov, June 2, 1914, 131–2.
[5] *IBZI*, Series I, vol. 1, nos. 44, 66, 108, 134, 156, 160, 168, 187, 223, 224, 227, 268, 289, 302, 382; ibid., Series I, vol. 2, no. 55, Demidov to Sazonov, March 20, 1914, 42; ibid., Series I, vol. 2, no. 61, Giers to Sazonov, March 22, 1914, 49; ibid., Series I, vol. 2, no. 70, Giers to Sazonov, May 23, 1914, 64; "Yunan Kralının Beyanatı [The Statement by the Greek King]," *Tanin*, May 16, 1914.
[6] Wolfgang-Uwe Friedrich, *Bulgarien und die Mächte, 1913–1915* (Stuttgart: Franz Steiner Verlag, 1985), 129.

existence of the state. Hence they found it legitimate, even modern and Western, to deal with such minorities in ways that would preclude any future challenges to security. Some 200,000[7] Orthodox had been expelled from Izmir and Thrace through what Erik J. Zürcher has described a "campaign of threats and intimidation."[8] In June 1914 Talat proposed a formal exchange of populations to make the expulsions official. The Greek and Ottoman governments would calculate the material losses suffered by refugees on both sides, pay the balance in cash, and resettle the refugees according to their religious affiliation. No attempts should be made, in other words, to restore the refugees to their original homes. Claiming that only a few Orthodox residents remained in and around Izmir – although the region's Orthodox population numbered some half a million at the time and a sizeable Orthodox population remained there until 1922[9] – Talat suggested to the Russian foreign minister S. D. Sazonov that the Ottomans could now even countenance an alliance with Greece on the basis of a population exchange. He explained to the Russian ambassador Giers that since the coast of Izmir and Aydın Province, situated adjacent the disputed islands of Chios and Mytilene, had been "cleansed" of their Orthodox population, the imminent threat Greece posed had temporarily subsided.[10] His government therefore was now in a position to make concessions regarding these islands, such as granting them (with their largely Greek populations) a degree of autonomy.[11] On the surface, Talat was arguing that Istanbul could now conceive of Greek administration on the islands so close to the Ottoman mainland because the danger of a Greek seizure of the region around Izmir, launched from the islands, would no longer be a strategic soft spot. Yet it is doubtful that Talat and his colleagues seriously considered surrendering the islands without a war once their navy had acquired the dreadnoughts.

With the dispute over the Aegean islands raging, the Ottomans engaged in the diplomatic equivalent of a full-court press. In February 1914, Grand Vezir Said Halim Pasha, working through K. N. Gulkevich, the

---

[7] Erik J. Zürcher, "The Ottoman Empire, 1850–1912: Unavoidable Failure?" 9, *Turkology Update Leiden Project (TULP)* (n.d.), http://tulp.leidenuniv.nl/content_docs/wap/ejz31.pdf.
[8] Erik J. Zürcher, *Turkey: A Modern History*, 3rd edn. (New York: I. B. Tauris, 2004), 126.
[9] Alexis Alexandris, "The Greek Census of Anatolia and Thrace (1910–1912): A Contribution to Ottoman Historical Demography," in *Ottoman Greeks in the Age of Nationalism*, ed. Dimitri Gondicas and Charles Issawi (Princeton: Darwin Press, 1999), 58, gives 495,936 for Aydın Province based on a 1910–12 census carried out by Orthodox Church and Greek consular officials.
[10] Giers used "cleansed," see *IBZI*, Giers to Sazonov, Series I, vol. 3, no. 386, June 26, 1914, 334. The Russian original reads *ochishchenie*. I am grateful to Michael Reynolds for his assistance with the Russian.
[11] Ibid., 334–5.

chargé d'affaires at the Russian embassy in Istanbul, attempted to get the Russian government to recognize Ottoman sovereignty over the islands. Although Gulkevich supported the effort, suggesting to Sazonov that the Ottomans would probably succeed in regaining Chios, Limnos, and Mytilene sooner or later in any case, and that St. Petersburg might as well reap the credit for such an outcome, the foreign minister dismissed any such overtures.[12]

For Sazonov and the St. Petersburg government much was at stake. It was of vital importance that the Ottoman Straits remained open to Russian shipping, and that a war, for now, be averted. Gulkevich and Giers, in Istanbul, were following a slightly different line. They were not only concerned that the Straits remain open, but were also determined to prevent any additional Ottoman territories that eventually might come under Russian rule from being seized by smaller powers, such as Greece or Bulgaria. The Bulgarian representative at Istanbul, Andrei Toshev, expressed this point to an Ottoman colleague after the Second Balkan War, when he described Russian satisfaction at the Ottomans' reconquest of Edirne in June 1913: "The Russians consider Constantinople their natural inheritance. Their main concern is that when Constantinople falls into their hands it shall have the largest possible hinterland. If Adrianople is in the possession of the Turks, they shall get it too."[13]

In August 1914, when the Entente was attempting to prevent the Ottoman Empire from joining the Central Powers, one proposed agreement offered the return of Limnos as the carrot. Ambassador Giers wrote in an "urgent" telegram to Sazonov that he strongly favored trading Limnos for Ottoman neutrality. If Limnos became Ottoman once again, it would eventually come under Russian control, they hoped, in any case: "Mudros Bay [on Limnos] is the key to controlling the Straits, which we may not leave out of our sight."[14]

The Russian government thus took a keen interest in the possibility of war between Greece and the Ottoman Empire during spring 1914.[15] In its exchanges with the British, St. Petersburg's diplomats criticized the work of the British naval mission in Istanbul. The modernization of the

---

[12] *IBZI*, Series I, vol. 1, no. 318, Gulkevich to Sazonov, February 24, 1914, 317–18, and for Sazonov's response, ibid., Series I, vol. 1, no. 321, Sazonov to Giers, February 25, 1914, 322–3.
[13] Richard C. Hall, *The Balkan Wars, 1912–1913: Prelude to the First World War* (New York: Routledge, 2000), 125, citing Andrei Toshev, *Balkanskite voini* (Plovdiv and Sofia: H. G. Danov, 1931), vol. II, 453.
[14] *IBZI*, Series II, vol. 6/1, no. 138, Giers to Sazonov, Urgent, August 19, 1914, 102–3.
[15] The Romanian government also feared the closing of the Straits and the detrimental effect it would have on Romanian trade, see *IBZI*, Series I, vol. 3, no. 291, Benckendorff to Sazonov, June 17, 1914, 257–60.

Ottoman navy, and the considerable expansion of its firepower through the purchase of the two British-made dreadnoughts, the Russians argued, only encouraged Ottoman aggression towards its Balkan and Russian neighbors. Sazonov instructed his ambassador at London to impress this point on the British government. Admiral Arthur Henry Limpus, the head of the British naval mission then in the Ottoman Empire, should be enlightened as to the Entente's broader strategic objectives, and his reform efforts should be adjusted accordingly. (Later, when the German rear-admiral Wilhelm Souchon took charge of the Ottoman navy, he repeatedly complained that the British naval mission had systematically sabotaged Ottoman equipment and organization.) For Russia's states-men, this was a critical point: "It is clear what calamitous results the loss of our superior position in the Black Sea would have for us," Sazonov declared. "And therefore we certainly cannot stand idly by and watch the continued and also very rapid expansion of the Ottoman naval forces."[16] Against these and subsequent objections to the Limpus Mission, Sir Edward Grey, the British foreign secretary, argued that the mission had not been sent to Istanbul to arm the Ottomans against Russia. If London recalled the mission, Grey observed, British naval officers would only be replaced with a German naval mission, a development that would serve neither British nor Russian interests.[17]

Rejected by Russia, the Ottomans attempted to engage the Romanian government as mediator. This time Enver Pasha led the initiative, working through the Romanian representative in Istanbul. According to Enver's proposal, Greece would return Chios, Limnos, and Mytilene to Ottoman control and receive in exchange several Dodecanese Islands, grabbed by Italy in 1912 but due to be handed back to the Ottomans in a few months' time. The Greek prime minister, Eleftherios Venizelos, however, turned down Romanian mediation. His government, Venizelos believed, lacked the political strength to make concessions on the islands question. Greek public opinion loathed the recent evacuation of another prize of the Balkan Wars, southern Epirus, to be ceded to the new state of Albania, and would never permit the government to give up the islands.[18]

The governments of Austria-Hungary and Italy also proved unsuppor-tive in the Ottoman bid for international support for the return of the islands. By March 1914, all the European governments had indicated politely but firmly that the Ottomans could count on no such support. In fact, these governments favored continued Greek possession of the

---

[16] *IBZI*, Series I, vol. 2, no. 384, Sazonov to Benckendorff, Confidential, May 8, 1914, 381–2.
[17] *IBZI*, Series I, vol. 3, no. 253, Aide-mémoire, Grey to Benckendorff, June 9, 1914, 225–6.
[18] *IBZI*, Series I, vol. 1, no. 370, Giers to Sazonov, March 3, 1914, 369–70.

islands in exchange for Greece's evacuation of the Epirus region.[19] In the end, it was Prime Minister Venizelos who succeeded in securing the Great Powers' official recognition of Greek sovereignty over the islands, though he failed to obtain an additional promise from the Powers to protect the islands militarily. It would be up to Greece to militarize and defend its new possessions.[20] The Ottoman ambassador at Vienna, Hilmi Pasha, did not hesitate to decry the injustice he perceived in the Powers' decision to accord the islands to Athens: "the Great Power response to the Greek government renders any agreement in the near future between the Porte and Greece impossible. It will also cause the Ottoman Empire to seize the first opportune moment to regain the islands of Chios and Mytilene, which it requires."[21]

In spring 1914, therefore, it looked as if once Armstrong and Vickers delivered the dreadnoughts, the Ottomans would employ them, either as instruments of intimidation or as men-of-war, to reclaim the lost islands. Thus a third Balkan war between Greece and the Ottoman Empire, with the potential to engulf the Balkan states and even the Great Powers, would threatenen the international system. Facing this prospect, St. Petersburg sought to shore up its own security by proposing an alliance with Great Britain on the terms of the Anglo-French *Entente Cordiale* already in place.[22] Although the British proved unwilling at the time, the Russian ambassador in London, Count A. K. Benckendorff, assured his government three weeks later that in the event of a European war, Britain would not remain a bystander; if a European war broke out, he believed, St. Petersburg could count on British action.[23]

Back on the ground in western Anatolia, the situation of both Orthodox and Muslim refugees (from the Balkans) continued to be a flashpoint. The *Rum*, members of the Greek Orthodox Church, were compelled to leave the empire indefinitely, and without notice.[24] Officials in Thrace forced

---

[19] *IBZI*, Series I, vol.1, no. 306, Gulkevich to Sazonov, February 20, 1914, 304–5, and ibid., Series I, vol. 1, no. 309, Sazonov to Benckendorff, February 24, 1914, 306–7.
[20] *IBZI*, Series I, vol. 2, no. 80, Krupenski to Sazonov, March 24, 1914, 71; ibid., Series I, vol. 2, no. 286, Demidov to Sazonov, April 24, 1914, 279. The representatives of the six Great Powers submitted the joint note on April 24, 1914.
[21] *IBZI*, Series I, vol. 2, Note 3 to no. 246, Sazonov to Izvolskii and Benckendorff, April 21, 1914, 249–50.
[22] *IBZI*, Series I, vol. 2, no. 224, Benckendorff to Sazonov, April 15, 1914, 332–3.
[23] *IBZI*, Series I, vol. 2, no. 363, Benckendorff to Sazonov, May 6, 1914, 353–6.
[24] Mehmed Şerif, *Edirne Vilayetinden Rumlar Niçin Gitmek İstiyorlar? İzmir Mebusu Emanuelidi Efendi'ye* [Why Do Greek Ottomans Want to Leave Edirne Province? (A Letter) To Emanuelidi Efendi, Member of the Chamber of Deputies from Izmir] (Edirne: Edirne Sanai'i Mektebi Matbaası, 1330 (March 1914–March 1915).

Orthodox residents to sign documents surrendering land and property.[25] To counter the voices that deplored such practices, *Tanin* published tens of articles claiming that the suffering of the *Rum* did not compare in the least to the atrocities visited upon Muslim populations recently expelled from the Balkans.[26]

In response to public criticism of the treatment of the empire's Orthodox population, Interior Minister Talat Bey personally inspected Edirne Province in April 1914.[27] Upon his return, the government issued a communiqué to the Great Power cabinets claiming that Talat had cautioned the local authorities in eastern Thrace to safeguard the rights and property of its Orthodox residents, adding that troops had been assigned to police all necessary measures. Grand Vezir Said Halim Pasha used the opportunity to demand that the Great Powers enforce analogous measures for the protection of the safety and property of Muslims residing in former Ottoman Macedonia now under Greek control.[28]

Talat's assurances, however, flew in the face of reality. Since the previous year, Talat himself had orchestrated a policy of Turkification in western Anatolia, empowering local militias to expel Orthodox residents from their homes and businesses.[29] The Ottoman press, as we have seen, undergirded this policy of expulsion by balancing the atrocities with accounts of atrocities committed against Muslims and Turks – in the Balkans, the Caucasus, and the Crimea since the eighteenth century.[30] So many of the Turkish leaders, including Talat himself, originated in these very borderlands and former areas of the empire that the territorial losses often touched off a highly emotional and sensitive memory, one in which revenge and retribution figured prominently. For the Muslim and Turkish descendants of refugees, Anatolia became the new homeland of Muslim Turks, while its Christian population was either killed or deported. Anatolia's subsequent demographic trajectory bears out this

[25] *IBZI*, Series I, vol. 2, no. 246, Sazonov to Izvolskii and Benckendorff, April 21, 1914, 250; see also ibid., Series I, vol. 2, no. 270, Giers to Sazonov, April 22, 1914, 269, and ibid., Series I, vol.3, no. 22, Sazonov to Giers, May 18, 1914, 15.

[26] For an example, see "Bir Mukayese [A Comparison]," *Tanin*, April 29, 1914.

[27] "Çorlu Seyahatı [The Çorlu Visit]," *Tanin*, April 28, 1914, which dismissed Greek Ottoman complaints and claimed that Greek Ottomans were departing, among other reasons, in order to escape their military service; for the government's position see also BOA, A.VRK, 788–90, Justice Ministry to Greek Orthodox Patriarchate, 3 Mayıs 1330 (May 16, 1914).

[28] *IBZI*, Series I, vol. 2, no. 349, Giers to Sazonov, May 4, 1914, 344–5.

[29] Zürcher, "Greek and Turkish Refugees and Deportees, 1912–1924," 2.

[30] See chapter 1.

point: in 1912 80 percent of Anatolia's population was Muslim, a figure that had risen to 98 percent by 1923.[31]

The Greek government attempted to apply pressure on the Ottomans by playing on Russian fears regarding the closure of the Straits. The Greek press adopted an increasingly belligerent voice, demanding support for its co-religionists in the Ottoman Empire. The foreign minister sent word to St. Petersburg that war appeared imminent and that it could be averted only through a concerted international effort that would rein in the Ottomans and "halt the persecutions."[32] According to the Ottoman point of view on the matter, seconded by none other than E. P. Demidov, the chief Russian diplomat in Athens, the Greek government was playing an obvious game: it was trumping up charges of Ottoman misconduct in order to create an international uproar that would prevent the scheduled delivery of the two powerful dreadnoughts from the British shipmakers.[33] Once they received these dreadnoughts, the entire balance of power in the eastern Mediterranean would shift in the Ottomans' favor. Their navy would enjoy such strength that it would be able to retake by force the disputed islands in a confrontation with the Greek navy. From this position of strength, the Ottoman leaders had made it clear to the Great Power ambassadors that they would not accept Greek occupation of the islands forever, challenging openly the status quo now backed by the Powers.

The strong resolve on both sides meant that Athens and Istanbul were indeed on a collision course; each side was counting on the Great Powers to temper the other while at the same time threatening the international system with a local yet dangerous war.

The correspondence of the Russian ambassador at Istanbul documents this worry very clearly. The Russian correspondence shows that the tsarist government would not have remained passive had the Greek–Ottoman stand-off developed into war. The Ottomans, Giers reported back to St. Petersburg, were convinced that Athens was clamoring for international intervention on behalf of the Greek Orthodox Christians of Anatolia. The Ottoman leadership would not cave in, Giers posited; rather, they would count on the Great Powers to restrain Greek action in order to maintain passage and commerce at the Straits. At this point, in mid-June 1914, Giers warned that the outbreak of war between the two

---

[31] Zürcher, "Greek and Turkish Refugees and Deportees, 1912–1924," 6; see also on this point the same author's "The Young Turks – Children of the Borderlands?," 1–9, and the excellent article by Nesim Şeker, "Demographic Engineering in the Late Ottoman Empire and the Armenians," *Middle Eastern Studies* 43 (May 2007): 461–74.

[32] *IBZI*, Series I, vol. 3, no. 199, Urussov to Sazonov, June 10, 1914, 183.

[33] *IBZI*, Series I, vol. 2, no. 325, Demidov to Sazonov, Confidential, April 29, 1914, 318–20.

powers seemed more likely than its prevention. For that eventuality, he suggested, Russia must be ready to launch "immediate counter meas-ures,"[34] recommending that military preparations necessary for forcing open the Straits be taken.

In mid-June western Anatolia continued to be such a tinderbox that the Russian consul there requested the dispatch of a warship because of the prevailing "anarchy in Izmir Province [*sic*: Aydın Province], the misdeeds of those engaged in the boycott, and the absence of any [Ottoman] troops." The fact that the request was approved and Tsar Nicholas II ordered a warship for cruising along the Anatolian coast underscores once again the potential for escalation and a much wider international conflict.[35]

In case of war, the Athens government could count on the support of its Serbian ally, or so it thought. Yet when it presented the Sublime Porte with a list of demands on June 12 – not an "ultimatum" for it bore no deadline – the Serbian government made it known immediately that it would not march with Greece if war broke out, and for several reasons. It maintained that (1) Athens had taken an extreme stance throughout the crisis; (2) the situation of Greek Orthodox citizens in the Ottoman Empire was not yet hopeless, and that this issue, in any case, was not in itself a sufficient cause for war; (3) Serbia considered itself for financial and military reasons in no state to fight another war after two recent wars and operations in Albania, and for a cause not vital to Serbia or Greece; and (4) a war against the rejuvenated Ottoman Empire could mean the loss of Kavala, Salonica, and other areas that had changed hands only recently. The Serbian government's third point is particularly remarkable for its timing, coming as it did a mere two weeks before the assassination of Franz Ferdinand. Thus, at this point, the Serbian government and St. Petersburg were collaborating in the effort to restrain Athens, and to prevent war.[36]

The Greek note of June 12 called for the immediate end to persecu-tions, the resettlement of displaced persons, and the restoration of con-fiscated property or financial compensation.[37] In their reply, the Ottoman authorities pledged full commitment to addressing these points and claimed that public order had already been restored in eastern Thrace and that the same efforts to restore public order were in motion in Aydın Province as well. Then the Ottomans turned the tables, pinning the blame

---

[34] *IBZI*, Series I, vol. 3, no. 265, Giers to Sazonov, June 15, 1914, 236; see also ibid., Series I, vol. 3, no. 217, Giers to Sazonov, June 11, 1914, 204.

[35] *IBZI*, Series I, vol. 3, no. 228, Giers to Sazonov, June 12, 1914, 208–9, and Note 1.

[36] *IBZI*, Series I, vol. 3, no. 239, Hartwig to Sazonov, June 14, 1914, 218–19.

[37] *IBZI*, Series I, vol. 3, no. 244, Argiropulo to Giers, June 15, 1914, 221–2.

for Ottoman ill will against the Orthodox population and Greece itself on the brutal persecution and expulsion of Muslim populations in the Balkans. It was the destitute state of these refugees arriving in Anatolia, they claimed, that had so fomented the public's hostility.[38]

Russian diplomats continued to restrain Greece from unleashing a war that would lead to the closure of the Straits and perhaps spark a much wider war. The foreign ministry at St. Petersburg suggested the Ottomans be given an opportunity to reinstate order and warned the Athens government that Greece might very well lose some of the territories it had recently gained if the crisis spiraled into war.[39] Giers urged Said Halim Pasha to allocate regular troops to Talat and to charge the interior ministry with the duty of protecting the empire's Orthodox population. He also urged Said Halim to soften the aggressive tone taken by the Ottoman press,[40] which included organs of powerful foreign interests as well.[41] The Ottomans met Giers's demands, declaring martial law for Aydın Province and the Dardanelles region, and allegedly dispatching troops to resettle Orthodox populations in the towns and villages from which they had been displaced. Even the press, according to Said Halim, had been issued official instruction to moderate its rhetoric.[42]

Eager to contain the crisis, Ambassador Giers defended the Ottoman position on the question of the treatment of the *Rum*. He reported back to his superiors in St. Petersburg that the Greek accusations of persecution had been exaggerated and politically motivated. Athens's primary concerns aimed at achieving international recognition of its ownership of the disputed Aegean islands and preventing the delivery of the two British dreadnoughts, scheduled for late July 1914. "It has become clear," Giers wrote, "to what great extent the Greek Patriarchate [in Istanbul] had exaggerated the emergency which the Anatolian Greeks have suffered at the hands of the Muslim refugees from Macedonia."[43] The Ottoman leaders were concerned not to be viewed in the European capitals as the aggressors in this conflict. The Istanbul government sent a circular note to the ambassadors of the six Great Powers inviting international monitors to

---

[38] *IBZI*, Series I, vol. 3, no. 304, Giers to Sazonov, June 18, 1914, 269.
[39] *IBZI*, Series I, vol. 3, no. 245, Argiropulo to Urussov, June 15, 1914, 222.
[40] *IBZI*, Series I, vol. 3, no. 263, Giers to Sazonov, June 15, 1914, 234–5.
[41] Because many of these were financed in secret, it is unclear which newspaper or writers received "subventions" from vested interests. For German propaganda work in the Ottoman press, see Irmgard Farah, *Die Deutsche Pressepolitik und Propagandatätigkeit im Osmanischen Reich von 1908–1918: Unter Besonderer Berücksichtigung des "Osmanischen Lloyd"* (Stuttgart: Steiner, 1993).
[42] *IBZI*, Series I, vol. 3, no. 286, Giers to Sazonov, June 16, 1914, 254.
[43] *IBZI*, Series I, vol. 3, no. 267, Giers to Sazonov, June 16, 1914, 237; see also ibid., Series I, vol. 3, no. 269, Sazonov to Neratov, June 16, 1914, 238–39.

observe conditions at first hand. The Ottomans pointedly expressed the hope that such joint tours of inspection could also be undertaken in the empire's former territories now part of Greece.[44] The Athens government accepted the proposal, and suggested the creation of a mixed Greek–Ottoman commission to determine the property losses of Orthodox and Muslim refugees.[45] Thus, after the Balkan Wars had produced some 400,000 Muslim refugees and the Ottoman policy of Turkification in western Anatolia some 200,000 Orthodox refugees, the two governments agreed to take stock of the damage.[46]

With the assassination of Franz Ferdinand, the Great Powers' attention shifted away from the Greek–Ottoman confrontation, but the conflict continued to define the relations between the two Mediterranean states. In July 1914, the Greek members of the Ottoman chamber of deputies, led by the delegate from Aydın Province, Emanuelidi Efendi, succeeded in holding a formal hearing (sual-i takrir) as to the rights and safety of Greek Orthodox Ottomans. The questioning of Interior Minister Talat Bey, in particular, took place in a heated and raucous session of the chamber.[47]

How the Bulgarian government would have behaved in the case of war between Greece and the Ottoman Empire remains unclear. In the Balkans, the Ottoman Empire represented the friendliest of Bulgaria's neighbors, whereas Bulgarian relations with Greece, Romania, and Serbia had been strained since the Second Balkan War and the August 1913 Treaty of Bucharest (which had excluded Ottoman participation, however). Meeting with his Russian counterpart on June 20, 1914, the Bulgarian military attaché in Istanbul declared that Sofia would remain neutral in the case of war between Athens and Istanbul and that, in exchange for its neutrality, it would expect a favorable revision of the Bulgarian–Ottoman border. If diplomacy failed, such a revision, to be sure, could have been achieved through a swift Bulgarian military operation, returning to her the access to the Aegean Bulgaria briefly enjoyed after the First Balkan War. Although Bulgaria still retained a small strip of the Aegean coast, the Treaty of Bucharest had granted the Aegean port of Kavala to Greece.[48] Nevertheless, fearing that St. Petersburg might step up its support of Sofia's rivals Greece and Serbia, the Bulgarian prime minister, Vasil Radoslavov, deferred to St. Petersburg and pledged that

---

[44] *IBZI*, Series I, vol. 3, no. 289, Argiropulo to Demidov, June 17, 1914, 256–7.
[45] *IBZI*, Series I, vol. 3, no. 342, Sazonov to Giers, June 24, 1914, 300.
[46] For these figures, see Zürcher, "Greek and Turkish Refugees and Deportees, 1912–1924," 1–2.
[47] *MMZC*, 23 Haziran 1330 (July 6, 1914).
[48] *IBZI*, Series I, vol. 3, no. 318, Leontiev to Danilov, June 20, 1914, 279; Richard C. Hall, *Bulgaria's Road to the First World War* (Boulder: East European Monographs, 1996), 255.

his government would neither support an Ottoman attack on Greece nor grant free passage to Ottoman land forces.[49]

Thus the Balkan Wars had proven to many the impossibility of coexistence of Christians and Muslims. As co-religionists, Christian Ottomans were perceived as sympathetic to the Balkan powers, especially the Greek Orthodox population (known in Ottoman as *Rum*, meaning "Romans"). As a result, Ottoman newspapers and patriotric societies called on Muslims to boycott Christian businesses and to shop only at Muslim stores. The Greek Orthodox patriarch, Germanos V, attempted to defuse the situation by asking the Ottoman government to take steps towards ending the boycott. His requests rebuffed, the patriarch threatened publicly to turn to the international community – or international intervention, as others would see it – causing an even louder outcry. The patriarch's appeal to foreign powers seemed to demonstrate precisely the Christian population's lack of loyalty that had necessitated the boycott in the first place. Hüseyin Kâzım Bey, the former governor of Salonica Province, lost to Greece, published an open, and openly hostile, letter to the patriarch.[50] Hüseyin Kâzım justified the "Muslim boycott" by claiming that the *Rum* had acted with unabashed disloyalty during the Balkan Wars. They had not served in the Ottoman army, and, on the contrary, they had provided financial support to Greece and thus, by extension, to all of the Balkan states. Moreover, Hüseyin Kâzım pointed to the lack of financial contributions made by Orthodox citizens to patriotic efforts like the Ottoman Navy and National Aid Society (*Osmanlı Donanma ve Muavenet-i Milliye Cemiyeti*). Founded in 1909, the Society enjoyed wide popularity and had succeeded in collecting large donations for modernizing the navy.[51] Thus the Ottoman naval build-up was financed at least in part by direct donations collected by this highly popular organization. In this climate the Ottoman arms race was a great source of national pride, as the strengthening of the navy symbolized Ottoman efforts at modernization and renewal.[52]

In addition to the alleged lack of *Rum* loyalty, Hüseyin Kâzım provided further justifications for the economic boycott. The empire's Muslims had

[49] *IBZI*, Series I, vol. 3, no. 314, Savinski to Sazonov, June 20, 1914, 277; ibid., Series I, vol. 3, no. 371, Giers to Sazonov, June 25, 1914, 320–1.
[50] Hüseyin Kâzım, *Rum Patriği'ne Açık Mektub: Boykot Müslümanların Hakkı Değil Midir?* [An Open Letter to the Greek Orthodox Patriarch: Do Muslims Not Have the Right to Boycott?] (Istanbul: Yeni Turan Matbaası, 1330 [March 1914–March 1915]), 8 and 12; for the staged boycott see "Boykotaj [Boycott]," *Tanin*, April 24, 1914; Toprak, *Milli İktisat-Milli Burjuvazi*, 107–11.
[51] Hüseyin Kâzım, *Rum Patriği'ne Açık Mektub*, 12.
[52] "Bahriye'mizde Yeni Bir Nefha-i Faaliyet [A New Breath of Activity in Our Navy]," *Tanin*, May 1, 1914.

started down the path of communal awakening and consciousness, and they had now become painfully aware of the need to build a national economy for the empire. In his open letter, he addressed the patriarch directly: "There is no boycott, only an economic awakening, and a struggle to survive," and he pointed to the Ottoman state's miserable financial situation. Hüseyin Kâzım stopped short of scapegoating outright the empire's Christian citizens for the decrepit state of the economy. Rather, he blamed previous Muslim generations for mismanaging the economy and allowing the empire to slip into indebtedness and poverty.[53] The time had now arrived, he continued, for this generation to act in the state's interest, and this could only mean supporting Muslim businesses in order to avert total financial collapse.[54]

Writing after the outbreak of war in Europe but prior to Ottoman intervention, the Russian-born socialist and well-known journalist on Ottoman political and economic issues Alexander Helphand, who wrote under the name of Parvus, argued that Britain was responsible for the current hostilities. By the time Parvus came to Istanbul in 1910 he had spent over a decade in Germany, immersed in Marxist circles and a relentless critic of British imperialism. In Istanbul as a correspondent of a German paper, his views represented German interests but reflected much of the Ottoman press nonetheless.[55] He claimed that Germany had achieved industrial and technological superiority over Britain, and that Germany now posed a formidable threat to British political and commercial hegemony in many parts of the world.[56] To confront this challenge, Parvus argued, Britain had now resorted to defend its global position militarily.

Now we are facing a great European war that has been brought upon us [Germans and Ottomans] by the Triple Entente ... The British Prime Minister Asquith can repeat as many times as he likes that Britain entered the war only as the result of the violation of Belgian neutrality. There is not the slightest doubt that Britain carefully calculated its entry into the war ahead of time, and that it entered it purely for reasons of material gain. Britain's objective is to destroy German commerce entirely and, if possible, to remove Germany's merchant fleet and, especially, its

---

[53] Ibid., 7.   [54] Ibid., 10–13.

[55] For Parvus and his role in Young Turk circles, see M. Asim Karaömerlioğlu, "Helphand-Parvus and His Impact on Turkish Intellectual Life," *Middle Eastern Studies* 40 (November 2004): 145–65.

[56] Parvus, *İngiltere Galib Gelirse ... İtilaf-ı Müselles'in Zafer ve Galibiyetinde Husula Gelecek Tebedüllat-ı Araziye* [If England is Victorious ... Territorial Changes in the Event of Triple Entente Victory], Türk Yurdu Kütübhanesi, Umumî Harb Neticelerinden, no. 2 (Istanbul: Kader Matbaası, 1330 [March 1914–March 1915]), 12–19, 26–8.

navy from the seas ... Just as importantly, Britain is trying to break German political influence [around the world].[57]

According to Parvus, imperialist ambitions were driving Britain to wage war on Germany in the hope of consolidating its colonial empire. Once Germany was defeated, Britain would then have to contend with its current allies, France and Russia; the Ottoman Empire would be the first victim of such colonial consolidation. Britain, he maintained, aimed at creating a contiguous colonial empire from Cairo to Bombay: "The Gulf of Basra and Iraq are of the greatest importance to British rule in India."[58] Control over these areas would not only give Britain command over the Indian Ocean and cut off Germany's route to the Far East, but would also guarantee ready access to oil fields. Oil, Parvus pointed out, "has become one of the most valuable types of fuel for navies since the day battleships began using oil instead of coal."[59]

Parvus portrayed Britain not as Germany's but as the Ottoman Empire's greatest enemy. He accused Britain of causing the war, and he even speculated that it would be Britain, rather than Russia, that would take the first steps towards Ottoman dismemberment. Given the British wartime agreements, including the Constantinople Agreement of 1915, the Sykes–Picot Agreement of 1916, the Hussein–McMahon Correspondence of 1915–16, and the Balfour Declaration of 1917, Parvus, at least in this respect, was not off the mark. He also held Britain responsible for the losses the Ottoman Empire had suffered in the Balkan Wars. Should Britain win the war, Parvus posited, the Ottoman Empire would certainly be partitioned between the Entente powers. France, he reminded his readers, no longer even bothered to hide its territorial designs and spoke openly about its intentions to establish French rule in Syria. Sounding a theme similar to Cami's, Parvus concluded that the colonized peoples of the world would no longer endure European rule and were growing strong enough to "break the shackles" imposed on them by "British imperialism."[60]

In a speech delivered on November 19, 1914, about three weeks after the Ottoman entry into the war, one of the foremost Turkish nationalist intellectuals agreed fully with Parvus' assessment regarding the Triple Entente's culpability in bringing about the world war.[61] The scholar and ideologue Akçuraoğlu Yusuf (later Yusuf Akçura), a Russian-born émigré, praised the Ottoman alliance with Germany: "The policy pursued

---

[57] Ibid., 22.   [58] Ibid., 23.   [59] Ibid., 23–4.   [60] Ibid., 21–2 and 30–1.
[61] Akçuraoğlu Yusuf, "Türk, Cermen ve Islavlar'ın Münasebat-ı Tarihiyeleri [Historical Relations among the Turks, Germans and Slavs]," address delivered November 19, 1914 ([Istanbul]: Kader Matbaası, 1330 [March 1914–March 1915]), 24–30.

by the Ottoman state today is historically flawless ... I do not know of any war which Muslims, or Ottomans, have fought with greater justification than this one. In this war we are defending a principle that is accepted and embraced by all belligerents, namely the independence and freedom of nations, the independence and freedom of religions. In other words, we are only defending ourselves against an active policy of imprisonment and oppression ... And for that reason we are shedding our blood."[62] Akçuraoğlu Yusuf, an influential member of the Istanbul elite, thus viewed the Ottoman entry into the war as a historic opportunity for Ottoman liberation and self-assertion. Although this interpretation of the war has become closely associated with Enver Pasha, it was clearly entrenched within the Turkish Ottoman elite on the eve of the war.

---

[62] Ibid., 30–1.

3 The Ottoman Empire within the international order

From the Ottoman perspective the international order in 1913 looked bleak. At the height of European imperialism, the Powers, great and small, all sought to expand their strategic and financial control in the Ottoman Empire. This international rivalry, of course, was part of a much bigger game that stretched from Africa and the eastern Mediterranean across Central Asia and the Indian Ocean to the Pacific. The territorial losses and land seizures began in 1878, when Britain and Russia seized Ottoman territory in ways that resembled a tightening noose from Istanbul. Russia annexed large parts of the Caucasus for itself and supported openly the nationalist independence movements in the Ottoman Balkans. Britain first took direct control over Cyprus, then occupied Egypt, and later concluded several independent treaties in the Gulf with local rulers who at least nominally were subjects of the Ottoman state. The British also challenged Ottoman authority in Iraq, Palestine, and Syria and bumped up against Russian interests in Persia, the Ottomans' eastern frontier. In Syria, the London government was aided by its French ally, the leading investor in the empire and its principal creditor. German investments were concentrated along the Baghdad Railway, although the line remained incomplete in several critical sections by 1914. Italy, too, sought to carve out its slice of the Ottoman pie, both through commercial investments and through a bid for colonial empire in North Africa. In 1911 it nestled itself between the colonial possessions of its British and French allies there and occupied several islands in the Mediterranean.[1]

---

[1] See Frederick F. Anscombe, *The Ottoman Gulf: The Creation of Kuwait, Saudi Arabia, and Qatar* (New York: Columbia University Press, 1997); Rashid Ismail Khalidi, *British Policy towards Syria and Palestine, 1906–1914: A Study of the Antecedents of the Hussein–McMahon Correspondence, the Sykes–Picot Agreement, and the Balfour Declaration*, St Antony's Middle East Monographs (London: Ithaca Press, 1980), F. A. K. Yasamee, *Ottoman Diplomacy: Abdülhamid II and the Great Powers, 1878–1888*, Studies on Ottoman Diplomatic History (Istanbul: Isis Press, 1996), Gregor Schöllgen, *Imperialismus und Gleichgewicht: Deutschland, England und die orientalische Frage, 1871–1914*, 3rd edn. (Munich: Oldenbourg Verlag, 2000).

While no alliance with a great power appeared in the offing, the Ottomans pursued the formation of a Balkan league. Following the Greek–Ottoman War of 1897, a rare military victory for the Ottomans amidst many disasters, Sultan Abdülhamid II initiated, and later reopened, alliance negotiations with Greece, Romania, and Serbia, but these talks never came to fruition. The strategic reasons for the alliance were straightforward. The Sublime Porte hoped the alliance would offer protection against a second attack from Greece while preventing similar attempts at territorial expansion by the empire's other Balkan neighbors.[2]

If the empire's territorial integrity was fragile under the reign of Sultan Abdülhamid II, it shattered under the new constitutional government that came to power in July 1908. At the forefront of the Young Turk movement, which, despite its name, included groups of non-Turkish ethnicity, came the Ottoman Committee of Union and Progress (*Osmanlı İttihad ve Terraki Cemiyeti*), or CUP.[3] Rather than initiate a period of stability and development, or "union and progress," as the Young Turks had hoped, the revolution of 1908 set in motion a host of adverse events. The uncertainties that emerged along with the new constitutional regime prompted the Great Powers to consolidate their own interests in the Near East. Most significantly, from the Ottomans' perspective, the foreign ministers of Austria-Hungary and Russia exchanged favors at the empire's expense: Russian warships would gain the right of passage through the Straits while Austria-Hungary annexed Bosnia-Herzegovina, the territory occupied by the Habsburgs since 1878. Vienna fevered over the possibility of Serbian expansion, and it feared that Belgrade might make its own grasp for the Ottoman region during the tumultuous days of the coup. Although the Russians ultimately failed to push their agenda successfully past the other Powers, the Austro-Hungarian annexation stuck, thanks to the backing of its German ally.[4]

The bad news continued to pour into the capital, as the small Balkan states indeed interpreted the Young Turk Revolution as a moment of Ottoman weakness and thus opportunity. Bulgaria unilaterally declared its formal independence. Cretan delegates announced the island's unification with Greece, a declaration that was unrecognized by any power, including Greece, but which constituted a serious challenge to the Ottomans nonetheless. Appeals to the signatories of the Berlin Congress

[2] Ali Fuat Türkgeldi, *Mesâil-i Mühimme-i Siyâsiyye* [Key Political Events], ed. Bekir Sıtkı Baykal (Ankara: Türk Tarih Kurumu Basımevi, 1966), vol. III, 85–109.

[3] For the most detailed analysis of this movement, see Hanioğlu, *Preparation for a Revolution*, and *The Young Turks in Opposition*.

[4] M. S. Anderson, *The Eastern Question, 1774–1923: A Study in International Relations* (New York: St. Martins Press, 1966), 279–85.

of 1878, protesting the violation of the status quo in Bosnia-Herzegovina
and Bulgaria, fell on deaf ears. These unexpected and dramatic reverses
underscored the perilous condition of the Ottomans' international isolation. As a result, and for the moment still buoyed by the restoration of
the constitution on July 24, 1908, they embarked on a wide search for
allies among the European powers. Such alliances, it was hoped, would
deter further aggression against the empire's territories and provide a
measure of international security.[5]

In its efforts to find such allies, the new cabinet headed by Grand Vezir
Kâmil Pasha sought to enlist British support. Kâmil suggested that the
British foreign office endorse Ottoman alliance negotiations with Bulgaria,
Montenegro, and Serbia. His proposal met with only a cool reception,
however, and the attempt to form a Balkan entente never got off the
ground.[6] A few weeks later, in early November 1908, the Committee of
Union and Progress sent two of its leaders, Ahmed Rıza and Dr. Nazım Bey,
to London to meet with Foreign Secretary Grey to win him over to a
British–Ottoman alliance. That attempt, too, failed immediately. Three
years later, in the midst of the war with Italy, the Said Pasha cabinet
resurrected these efforts at a British alliance, only to be rebuffed once again.[7]

The lack of military power, which necessitated the empire's search for
allies in the first place, was paralleled by the state's precarious financial
situation. Heavily indebted, the state had defaulted on its foreign loan
payments, prompting the creditor nations and banks to form the Ottoman
Public Debt Administration in 1881. During its final decades the empire
saw large portions of its revenues controlled directly by this international
financial body.[8] Following the political instability of 1908, foreign capital
fled the empire and the budget deficit continued to grow by large margins.
The new leaders made attempts at financial reform, focusing primarily on
streamlining the collection of taxes and a greater reliance on domestic
rather than foreign debt.[9] But any success would be gradual, and for the

---

[5] The Bulgarian government declared its independence from the empire on October 5,
1908, one day prior to the Austro-Hungarian announcement of its annexation of
Bosnia-Herzegovina. See Charles and Barbara Jelavich, *The Establishment of the Balkan
National States, 1804–1920* (Seattle: University of Washington Press, 1977), 176.

[6] Joseph Heller, *British Policy towards the Ottoman Empire, 1908–1914* (London: Frank Cass,
1983), 17–19.

[7] Feroz Ahmad, "Great Britain's Relations with the Young Turks, 1908–1914," *Middle
Eastern Studies* 2 (July 1966): 308–9 and 318–19.

[8] Şevket Pamuk, *A Monetary History of the Ottoman Empire* (Cambridge: Cambridge
University Press, 2000), 213–16.

[9] Mehmet Beşirli, *Die europäische Finanzkontrolle im Osmanischen Reich in der Zeit von 1908
bis 1914: Die Rivalitäten der britischen, französischen und deutschen Hochfinanz und der
Diplomatie vor dem Ersten Weltkrieg am Beispiel der türkischen Staatsanleihen und der
Bagdadbahn* (Berlin: Buch und Mensch, 1999), 93–4.

short term the empire continued to depend on external loans. The search
for foreign loans proved as disappointing to Istanbul as its search for
political and military allies. In mid-1910, London and Paris rejected the
requests of the finance minister, Cavid Bey, who had traveled to the
European capitals personally, hat in hand. Britain and France withheld
loans in part to undermine the independent-minded Cavid, whose intentions of circumventing the French-dominated Ottoman Public Debt
Administration and thus making the Ottoman state less reliant on it
were understandably unpopular in the Western capitals.[10] In holding
back the loan, the European powers increased their leverage by linking
the loan question to political matters. London made its financial assistance
conditional on the abandonment of plans to extend the German-financed
Baghdad Railway to Basra, a "British" port in the Persian Gulf.[11] Anglo-
Ottoman differences over such issues as Ottoman tariff rates, British
navigation rights in the Persian Gulf, oil exploitation concessions, and the
extension of the Baghdad Railway were not solved until the signing of a
series of agreements negotiated by a special diplomatic mission headed by
the former Grand Vezir İbrahim Hakkı Pasha in mid-1913.[12]

As for Russia, the tsar's government erected obstacles in the way of
Ottoman reform whenever it could, and it insisted on a comprehensive
reform program in the provinces with large Armenian populations border-
ing Russia as a precondition before any other reforms could take place.
It not only opposed the reorganization of the military and the navy –
understandably, since these might be turned directly against Russia – but
also administrative reforms ranging from agriculture and public works to
the training of a professional gendarmerie. When Tevfik Pasha, the
Ottoman ambassador in London, proposed detailed reforms for the
empire, the British foreign office proved cooperative initially but had to
drop its support in the face of Russian objections.[13]

Sazonov, St. Petersburg's foreign minister, also stipulated that Russian
officers must be part of all reforms in eastern Anatolia. Explaining his
objections to the British, he "stated that some time ago representatives of
Armenians had approached the Russian government with a request for the
annexation of Turkish Armenia to Russia. He had replied that there could

[10] Ahmad, *The Young Turks*, 76–80; L. Bruce Fulton, "France and the End of the Ottoman
Empire," in *The Great Powers and the End of the Ottoman Empire*, 2nd edn., ed. Marian
Kent (London: Frank Cass, 1996), 156–7.
[11] Beşirli, *Die europäische Finanzkontrolle im Osmanischen Reich*, 182–8.
[12] Heller, *British Policy towards the Ottoman Empire*, 92–3.
[13] For Tevfik's proposal, see *BDOW*, vol. 10/1, Communication from Tewfik Pasha,
April 24, 1913, no. 479, 427–30; for the subsequent discussion and Russian objections,
see ibid., nos. 480–95, 430–42.

be no question of annexation but that Russia would see that effective reforms were carried out. Russia was therefore under peculiar obligations to the Armenians and she could not play second violin in this matter."[14] If the Sublime Porte rejected Russian officers in eastern Anatolia, Sazonov "would then intimate to Turkey that in the absence of a properly organized *gendarmerie* disorder and massacres of Armenians were certain to occur and that in that case Russia would intervene."[15]

Perhaps more importantly, St. Petersburg worried about the growing potential of the Ottoman Black Sea Fleet. By 1914, Admiral I. K. Grigorovich, the Russian navy minister, warned that "the Turks will have unconditional supremacy in the Black Sea" in a year's time.[16] Indeed, the Ottomans were working intensively to expand their naval capacity, in large part by shopping in European capitals and the Americas for warship contracts. To deny it the wherewithal to make such costly purchases, Russia fought the proposed increase in Ottoman tariff rates and lobbied its Entente partners, Britain and France, to turn down any loan requests.[17] When Cavid Bey traveled to Paris in January 1914 in pursuit of a loan from the French government, Russian interests hung over the negotiations like a dark cloud and precluded any agreement.[18] On another front, Russian diplomacy, this time working together with London, requested delaying the delivery of the Armstrong ship – successfully as it turned out.[19] At other times, St. Petersburg attempted to derail Ottoman purchases of capital ships by acquiring the vessels itself, adding them to its own Black Sea Fleet.[20]

For their part, the Central Powers lacked faith in the empire's future, and they showed no interest in an Ottoman alliance. Ottoman offers of alliance to Vienna in November 1909 were rebuffed.[21] While the Sublime Porte kept alive alliance negotiations with the Habsburgs in the following

---

[14] Ibid., O'Beirne to Sir Edward Grey, May 26, 1913, no. 492, 438.
[15] Ibid., O'Beirne to Sir Edward Grey, May 27, 1913, no. 494, 441.
[16] *IBZI*, Series I, vol. 1, no. 50, Grigorovich to Sazonov, January 19, 1914, 45–7; see also ibid., Series I, vol. 1, nos. 53 and 55, Grigorovich to Sazonov, January 20, 1914.
[17] Hiller, *Krisenregion Nahost*, 94–5.
[18] *IBZI*, Series I, vol. 1, no. 34, Sazonov to Giers, January 17, 1914, 31, ibid., Series I, vol. 1, no. 114, Izvolskii to Sazonov, January 14, 1914, 97.
[19] *IBZI*, Series I, vol. 1, no. 2, Etter to Sazonov, January 14, 1914, 2; see also ibid., Series I, vol. 1, no. 295, Journal einer Sonderkonferenz, February 21, 1914, 294–5, and ibid., Series I, vol. 1, no. 382, Sazonov to Benckendorff, March 5, 1914, 378–80.
[20] *IBZI*, Series I, vol. 1, no. 325, Sazonov to Stein, February 25, 1914, 324; ibid., Series I, vol. 2, no. 51, Bachmetyev to Sazonov, March 19, 1914, 40.
[21] *GP*, vol. 27/1, no. 9780, Marschall to Auswärtiges Amt, Bericht des Militärattachés in Konstantinopel Majors von Strempel [Report of Major von Strempel, Military Attaché at Constantinople], November 7, 1909; ibid., vol. 27/1, no. 9781, Tschirschky to Bethmann Hollweg, November 13, 1909.

years, simultaneous, and equally unsuccessful, approaches to the Romanian government followed.[22] Berlin remained equally aloof to an alliance, but it did bolster the Ottoman naval effort by agreeing to the sale of two large warships and four destroyers in mid-1910, something the British at the time were unwilling to do.[23] Moreover, later that year Berlin and Vienna issued the Ottomans a much-desired loan refused earlier by the Entente.[24]

When the Ottomans tried their luck at an alliance with Berlin in 1912, however, the German foreign office, like its British counterpart, could not bring itself to put its resources and prestige at the service of Ottoman security, despite Kaiser Wilhelm II's pronounced views to the contrary.[25] Ahmed Rıza Bey, the former CUP leader in exile and now a member of the senate (Meclis-i Âyân), met with officials at the German embassy in Paris and reopened in vain the question of a German–Ottoman alliance. A single word by his "Majesty the Kaiser," Ahmed Rıza claimed, would win over "the hearts of the entire Islamic world." And Noradonkyan Efendi, the Ottoman foreign minister, followed up Ahmed Rıza's efforts by raising the question with Ambassador Wangenheim in Istanbul. Despite the kaiser's favor, however, the Ottoman leaders would not be successful in achieving their alliance until the emergence of the July Crisis in 1914.[26]

The role of Germany

The fact that the German foreign office, the Auswärtiges Amt, initially rejected the Ottoman offer for an alliance in July 1914 has been cited as key evidence that Germany did not "push" the Ottomans into war.[27] Much of the analysis that has dealt with the German–Ottoman alliance was caught up in the postwar debate about war guilt. Each of the European governments published massive archival collections to document its innocence in the origins of the war. These publications were so

---

[22] See *GP*, vol. 27/1, nos. 9783–97; Austria-Hungary, Foreign Ministry, *Österreich-Ungarns Aussenpolitik*, no. 3103, Pallavicini to Aehrenthal, December 14, 1911, no. 69C; ibid, nos. 3111–12, 3117, 3150–1, 3172, 3317.

[23] Halpern, *Mediterranean Naval Situation*, 316.

[24] Beşirli, *Die europäische Finanzkontrolle*, 189–93.

[25] *GP*, vol. 27/1, no. 9782, Schoen to Marschall, November 18, 1909.

[26] PA/AA, R 1913, Schoen to Bethmann Hollweg, December 31, 1912.

[27] Frank G. Weber, *Eagles on the Crescent: Germany, Austria, and the Diplomacy of the Turkish Alliance, 1914–1918* (Ithaca: Cornell University Press, 1970), 62–3; Ulrich Trumpener, *Germany and the Ottoman Empire, 1914–1918* (Princeton: Princeton University Press, 1968), 14–16.

voluminous indeed that they prompted one historian to speak of "the world
war of the documents."[28] The American historian Robert J. Kerner, like the
British historian H. S. W. Corrigan, to give but two examples, relied on
these collections to argue that German expansionism had forced the
Ottomans into war.[29]

Over four decades ago, Ulrich Trumpener concluded his examination
of the German–Ottoman alliance of 1914 with the verdict that the
German admiral Wilhelm "Souchon's attack on Russia was not an independent coup, but planned in close collaboration with several members of
the Porte and executed upon explicit orders from the Ottoman war
minister."[30] These individuals, he declared, comprised "the Turkish
action party" and consisted of "Enver, Talaat, Djemal, Halil and their
supporters in the Committee of Union and Progress."[31] Trumpener's
"Assessment of Responsibilities" exculpated Germany from thrusting
the Ottoman Empire into an unwanted war. Nor, according to
Trumpener, would Germany have been able to do so; in a subsequent
study, he argued that German economic and political influence in the
Ottoman Empire was "effectively counterbalanced by that of the other
European powers."[32] While he conceded that the German military mission arriving in Istanbul in mid-December 1913 had "resulted in a substantial increase of Germany's general influence," Trumpener called
attention to the "high-ranking British [naval] officers" whose presence
equaled that of the German mission.[33] From Trumpener's point of view,
Germany enjoyed no particular position of strength in Istanbul in 1914.

Trumpener found erroneous the conclusions of earlier scholars who
depicted Germany as an imperialist bully and who claimed that "by 1914
the Ottoman empire was little more than a satellite of the [German]

---

[28] Bernhard Schwertfeger, *Weltkrieg der Dokumente: zehn Jahre Kriegsschuldforschung und ihr
Ergebnis* (Berlin: Deutsche Verlagsgesellschaft für Politik und Geschichte, 1929). Gregor
Schöllgen's handbook on imperialism lists twenty such document collections, with the first
published by Germany in 1921, see Schöllgen, *Das Zeitalter des Imperialismus*, 3rd edn.
(Munich: R. Oldenbourg, 1994), 183–8. While these published collections were intended
to demonstrate a respective state's innocence in the origins of the world war, the notable
exception was the documents published by the Bolshevik government, which intended to
expose the fallacies of tsarist imperialism; see editor's preface, M. N. Prokowski, "Vorwort
des russischen Herausgerbers," in *IBZI*, Series I, vol. 1, xi–xxiv.
[29] Robert J. Kerner, "The Mission of Liman von Sanders," *Slavonic Review* 6 (1927–8): 12–
27, 344–63, 543–60, and *Slavonic Review* 7 (1928–9): 90–112; H. W. S. Corrigan,
"German–Turkish Relations and the Outbreak of War in 1914: A Re-Assessment," *Past
and Present* (April 1967): 144–52.
[30] Ulrich Trumpener, "Turkey's Entry into World War I: An Assessment of Responsibilities,"
Journal of Modern History 34 (December 1962): 380.
[31] Ibid.   [32] Trumpener, *Germany and the Ottoman Empire*, 12–13, for quotation see 12.
[33] Ibid., 13.

Reich."[34] He attributed the conclusions of some East German historians to their authors' Marxist bent.[35] Trumpener was partially correct: the Ottoman Empire was not a "satellite" of Germany, but neither were the Ottomans "diplomatic equals."[36]

Writing in the 1960s, Trumpener, in part, was answering the highly controversial studies by the German historian Fritz Fischer. Drawing on extensive archival material, Fischer had postulated that Wilhelmine politicians were resolved on fighting a "preventive war" against France and Russia before these powers could combine to overpower Germany's economic and military strength.[37] Fischer had argued forcefully that Wilhelm II and his chief of staff, Helmuth von Moltke, viewed the war as the inevitable confrontation of "Germandom and Slavdom."[38] And while Fischer recognized continuity in German alliance policy towards the Ottoman Empire,[39] Trumpener saw the sudden emergence of the July Crisis as the basis for the German–Ottoman alliance of 1914.[40]

Trumpener was not alone in his conclusion regarding Ottoman "willing co-operation"[41] as Germany's ally in 1914. Basing his findings on published and unpublished German archival sources, Carl Mühlmann, a former German officer who had served in the Ottoman Empire, documented the Ottoman role in the formation of the alliance and the empire's entry into the war. From the German archives, Mühlmann even produced Enver Pasha's written order to Souchon, instructing the admiral to "seek out the Russian fleet and to attack it without prior declaration of war."[42] More so than Trumpener's, Mühlmann's work aimed directly at the

---

[34] Ibid., 6, noting the works of W. W. Gottlieb, Lothar Rathmann, and A. F. Miller.

[35] Ulrich Trumpener, "Germany and the End of the Ottoman Empire," in *The Great Powers and the End of the Ottoman Empire*, 131.

[36] Trumpener, *Germany and the Ottoman Empire*, 21.

[37] See Fritz Fischer, *Griff nach der Weltmacht: Die Kriegszielpolitik des kaiserlichen Deutschland, 1914/18* (Dusseldorf: Droste, 1961; special edition, 1967), 46 and passim, and *Krieg der Illusionen: Die deutsche Politik von 1911 bis 1914* (Dusseldorf: Droste, 1969), both works have been translated into English; see also the same author's "Deutsche Kriegsziele, Revolutionierung und Separatfrieden im Osten 1914–1918," *Historische Zeitschrift* 188 (1959): 249–310; for key participants in the "Fischer controversy" and their arguments, see H. W. Koch, ed., *The Origins of the First World War: Great Power Rivalry and German War Aims*, 2nd edn. (London: Macmillan, 1984).

[38] Fischer, *Griff nach der Weltmacht*, 34.

[39] Ibid., 24, 26, 110. Fischer developed this thesis further in *Kriegszielpolitik*, 424–43 and 481–515.

[40] Trumpener, *Germany and the Ottoman Empire*, 20.

[41] Trumpener, "Turkey's Entry," 380.

[42] Carl Mühlmann, *Deutschland und die Türkei, 1913–1914: Die Berufung der deutschen Militärmission nach der Türkei 1913, das deutsch-türkische Bündnis 1914 und der Eintritt der Türkei in den Weltkrieg (Unter Benutzung und Mitteilung bisher unveröffentlichter politischer Dokumente dargestellt)*, (Berlin-Grunewald: Rothschild, 1929), 102.

question of German war guilt, but it shared Trumpener's overall conclusion: the origins of the German–Ottoman alliance and the origins of Ottoman intervention must primarily be sought in the motivations of Ottoman statesmen, not in Berlin. While Ottoman statesmen doubtless played a crucial role, more must be said about German policies and interests in the Near East. Here the concern is not with the debate about German war guilt and the "disastrous quality" in German foreign policy, which has been such a frequent theme of historical studies examining pre-1914 Germany.[43] The aim is rather to resituate the German-Ottoman alliance of August 1914 in the context of the new international dynamic that emerged after Italy's grab for Tripoli in 1911 and that gained further momentum with the outbreak of the Balkan Wars in 1912–13.

Trumpener's general assessment of the German–Ottoman alliance characterized Germany as having been drawn more or less unwittingly into the alliance and into fighting a war in the Near East by Wilhelm II and the Ottoman war party. There had been, in other words, no pre-July 1914 planning of a military alliance with the Ottoman Empire.[44] This interpretation overlooks key aspects of the story, however. Given the level of heated anticipation surrounding the question of Ottoman partition since the nineteenth century, it is hardly surprising that Germany, like the other powers, took steps to prepare for annexation in the Near East. The vision of Germany as a global power had been formulated in 1897, when the chancellor proclaimed *Weltpolitik* as the state's new course. A decade later, that vision had lost some of the confidence and excitement with which it had been proclaimed. Gaining control over all or parts of the Ottoman Empire could energize those ambitions. Ottoman territory could be pivotal to Germany's place in the world, connecting the German and Habsburg realms to the Near East and thus the Persian Gulf and the Indian Ocean. It could also form an integral part of Berlin's other vision, that of a unified *Mitteleuropa*.[45] It would be inaccurate to attribute annexationist thinking across the board to German decision-makers, even if key figures such as Wilhelm II and General von der Goltz had embraced such thinking. But we also see that such ambitions were not confined to official circles. Even beyond them, in church

---

[43] Gregor Schöllgen, ed., *Escape into War? The Foreign Policy of Imperial Germany* (Providence: Berg, 1990), 16 and passim.

[44] Trumpener's work has enjoyed wide influence. See, for example, Wolfdieter Bihl, *Die Kaukasus-Politik der Mittelmächte*, vol. I, *Ihre Basis in der Orient-Politik und ihre Aktionen, 1914–1917*, Veröffentlichungen der Kommission für Neuere Geschichte Österreichs (Vienna: Böhlau, 1975), 47–8.

[45] Hew Strachan, *The First World War*, vol. I, *To Arms* (Oxford: Oxford University Press, 2001), 1–35, 46–8.

groups and the universities, for example, were those who dreamt the "Dream of a German Orient." Thus, as the international rivalry of the New Imperialism intensified, Berlin widened its economic and political presence in the Ottoman Empire, a presence that was buttressed within German society by a culture that revered the Near East as hallowed ground.[46]

For their part, the Ottomans welcomed this greater German involvement in the empire as a counterweight to British and Russian expansion. Certainly, the vested interest of yet another Great Power brought along a new set of dangerous circumstances. Kaiser Wilhelm II, for example, loved to pose as the Muslim world's liberator, and Berlin promoted the ideology of pan-Islamism in North Africa and Asia as a way of stirring into revolution the colonial Muslim subjects of Germany's enemies, Britain, France, and Russia. Britain sought to parry these efforts by supporting Arab nationalism against the sultan, who was also, at least in theory, the caliph of all Muslims worldwide.[47]

Wilhelm van Kampen has argued cogently that Berlin's long-term policy of preserving the Ottoman Empire shifted to a policy of acquisition following the Ottoman defeat in the Balkan Wars.[48] His final assessment, however, that German territorial pursuits resulted only from the unexpected military collapse of 1912 and thus should be understood as "a child of necessity" is debatable.[49] German aims after 1912 may be seen not so much as a redirection as an intensification of German policy. While Germany diplomatically supported Ottoman territorial integrity before the Balkan Wars, it did so for the explicit reason that its share in the event of partition would be very modest. German commercial and institutional presence in the Ottoman Empire, after all, was still relatively small in comparison to that of Britain, France, and Russia. What is more, defending these possessions in a war over Ottoman territory would pose a daunting geostrategic challenge to Germany, which had no firm military footing in the wider region. The later the partition, the greater the share Berlin could realistically hope to control eventually.

Prior to the Balkan Wars, Berlin had favored the gradual transformation of the Ottoman Empire into a German protectorate. In May 1913, with

[46] Malte Fuhrmann, *Der Traum vom deutschen Orient: Zwei deutsche Kolonien im Osmanischen Reich, 1851–1918* (Frankfurt: Campus Verlag, 2006).
[47] İlber Ortaylı, *Osmanlı İmparatorluğu'nda Alman Nüfuzu* (Ankara: Ankara Üniversitesi Sosyal Bilgileri Fakültesi Yayınları,1981; reprinted, Istanbul: İletişim Yayınları, 1998), 15–19; McKale, *War by Revolution*, 7–16.
[48] Kampen, "Studien zur deutschen Türkeipolitik," 39–57, citing both published and unpublished Auswärtiges Amt documents.
[49] Ibid., 47.

the Ottomans defeated, German policy-makers prepared for the antici-
pated territorial partition of the empire. As Kerner, and later Corrigan,
Fischer, and Kampen pointed out, the German foreign office demarcated
its sphere of influence in what it hoped would become German-controlled
territory at the time of partition. When partition appeared imminent
during the Balkan Wars, Berlin's ambassador in Istanbul, Hans von
Wangenheim, circulated color-coded maps designating the areas that
could fall under German control.[50] Once the likelihood of the empire's
wholesale partition had passed, the German secretary of state for foreign
affairs, Gottlieb von Jagow, summarized the German policy in a letter to
Wangenheim, dated July 28, 1913: "We have only a single interest in
Turkey: that it will survive in Asia long enough until we will have consolidated ourselves there in our areas of activity [*Arbeitszonen*] and have
become prepared for annexation. I want to postpone that moment for as
long as possible. The first condition for this, however, is that Turkey will
stay out of European dealings [i.e. further confrontation in the Balkans]."[51]
Hence Foreign Secretary Jagow, anxious lest another Balkan war trigger
partition, urged Ottoman *détente*. His statement referred specifically to the
recapture of Edirne the previous week,[52] a military operation that the
foreign secretary clearly did not endorse: "In my opinion the push to
Adrianople [Edirne] … only harbors great misfortune for the Turkish
Empire. The entanglement in European and Balkan affairs has always
been a [source of] weakness for Turkey. [Such entanglement] has distracted [Turkey] from its Asiatic duties … without [Turkey] ever gaining
a practical benefit from participating in the games of European intrigue.
[Such entanglement] has only wasted [Turkey's] best energies."[53] The
Ottoman Empire should cut its losses and focus on improving the
internal conditions of its Asian provinces, Jagow believed.

---

[50] *GP*, vol. 38, no. 15312, Wangenheim to Bethmann Hollweg, May 21, 1913; Kerner, "The Mission of Liman von Sanders," 15–16; Kampen, "Studien zur deutschen Türkeipolitik," 44; Corrigan, "German–Turkish Relations," 146; Fischer, *Krieg der Illusionen*, 429–30.

[51] PA/AA, R 2125, Jagow to Wangenheim, July 28, 1913, also in PA/AA, R 14524.

[52] Ottoman forces defending Adrianople/Edirne surrendered to Bulgarian and Serbian armies on March 26, 1913. The city was retaken by forces led by Enver on June 22, 1913. See Turfan, *Rise of the Young Turks*, 301 and 337. For a comprehensive assessment, see Ernst Christian Helmreich, *The Diplomacy of the Balkan Wars, 1912–1913* (Cambridge, MA: Harvard University Press, 1938).

[53] PA/AA, R 2125, Jagow to Wangenheim, July 28, 1913, also in PA/AA, R 14524. I have used "Turkey" here rather than "Ottoman Empire" in line with the German usage of "*Türkei*" as opposed to "*Osmanisches Reich*."

Ambassador Wangenheim's position also reflected the fear that formal partition at this point would hand the empire's most lucrative and strategically significant points to the Entente:

We are not at all prepared to settle down in Asia Minor. Russia, France, and England have defined spheres of interest. Our interests run alongside the Baghdad Railway and traverse all of Asia Minor; they are more of a financial nature than a material one. Our schools, churches, etc. cannot be compared with those of France, Russia, and England, which were established over the course of centuries ... Our [institutions], moreover, are located in areas which to a great extent must fall under the control of other powers. We have a great deal of catching up to do and for that we require an extended period of diligent work. The aim of our policy, therefore, can only be to delay Turkey's dissolution for as long as possible.[54]

While the German fear of partition was real, Jagow kept a poker face. He was not worried about secret Entente plans to partition Anatolia, he told Grey, even "if there have been from time to time faint rumors in the press."[55] To what extent Berlin was able to follow internal British discussion, we do not know. In November 1912, the consul-general in Egypt, Lord Kitchener, had written Grey from Cairo proposing to exploit the instability of the Balkan War and tighten its grip on Egypt, a move the cautious Grey rejected. Britain controlled Egypt already, and any change in its status would entitle the other powers to war spoils as well.[56]

Berlin's foreign policy-makers envisioned the gradual development of a protectorate, and these intentions remained consistent into the war years. Count Johann von Pallavicini, the Austro-Hungarian ambassador in Istanbul, who maintained close relations with Wangenheim, reported that he and his German colleague shared the conviction that the Central Powers must establish over the Ottoman Empire "a type of protectorate in order to maintain and develop it," and once the First World War began he concluded that Germany's "central war aim was to seize control over the Near East."[57] Berlin's Ottoman policy, then, aimed at gaining influence among decision-makers in the capital. The empire's immediate partition was undesirable, but Germany's vision would not have preserved Ottoman autonomy any more than the territorial acquisitions sought by the Entente powers.

Wilhelm II, kaiser of the German Empire since 1888, was an ardent proponent of deeper involvement in the Ottoman Empire. Although he

---

[54] *GP*, vol. 38, no. 15312, Wangenheim to Bethmann Hollweg, May 21, 1913.

[55] *BDOW*, vol. 9/2, Goschen to Grey, no. 1026, June 3, 1913, 829–30; ibid., Grey to Goschen, no. 1018, May 30, 1913, 824.

[56] Ibid., vol. 9/2, Kitchener to Grey, Private, no. 113, November 3, 1912, 88; ibid., vol. 9/2, Grey to Kitchener, Private, no. 204, November 14, 1912, 156.

[57] Bihl, *Die Kaukasus-Politik der Mittelmächte*, 50, citing Pallavicini's reports of October 29 and December 7, 1915.

repeatedly floated the idea of a formal Ottoman alliance with his advisors, the Auswärtiges Amt deemed such an alliance irreconcilable with the realities of the international state system.[58] The kaiser's minutes on memoranda relating to the Near East suggest that he strongly believed in the advantages of a formal alliance nonetheless. In September 1910, when rumors of an alliance between Austria-Hungary, Germany, and the Ottoman Empire appeared in European and Ottoman dailies, Wilhelm II noted: "let us hope it will come to that." And, referring to an article regarding the same rumors in the *Neue Wiener Journal*, the influential Viennese daily, he commented: "too good to be true, if only we were there already!"[59]

Why, then, was a German–Ottoman alliance not feasible in 1910, despite the German emperor's evidently strong support for it? For one thing, the Ottomans did not bring enough to the table; the empire was simply too vulnerable militarily, even when backed by Germany. In June 1909, just weeks after the failed counter-revolution that sought to over-throw the new constitutional government, and the Armenian massacres throughout Adana that followed it, Kaiser Wilhelm II asked General Colmar von der Goltz to embark on the project of reforming the Ottoman army.[60] Goltz had spent twelve years in Istanbul in the 1880s and 1890s teaching and training Ottoman officers, and he enjoyed great stature, even that of a hero, in Ottoman military circles.[61] In Germany, he was considered to be the foremost authority on the Ottoman Empire, and was even briefly viewed by some as a potential candidate for the German chancellorship.[62] Based on a two-month visit to Istanbul in late 1910, Goltz reported to the kaiser that the Ottoman army would emerge as a key strategic factor the moment the Anatolian and southern Syrian railway lines were connected. More specifically, he pointed out that if the Ottomans could threaten Egypt with quick troop movements to the border, Britain would be forced to take a more accommodating position on Ottoman demands and interests in the Gulf. Once the railway was completed, Goltz claimed, even an Ottoman military campaign against

[58] Kampen, "Studien zur deutschen Türkeipolitik," 57–80.
[59] PA/AA, R 1912, Auswärtiges Amt to Wilhelm II, September 17, 1910.
[60] BA-MA, N 80–1, sheets 180–1, Goltz to Mudra, June 10, 1909.
[61] For Goltz's ideas on Ottoman reforms, including those reflected in his private correspond-ence, see F. A. K. Yasamee, "Colmar Freiherr von der Goltz and the Rebirth of the Ottoman Empire," *Diplomacy and Statecraft* 9 (July 1998): 91–128. For Goltz's career more generally, see Friedrich von der Goltz and Wolfgang Foerster, *Generalfeldmarschall Colmar Freiherr von der Goltz: Denkwürdigkeiten* (Berlin: E. S. Mittler und Sohn, 1929); Pertev Demirhan, *Generalfeldmarschall Freiherr von der Goltz: das Lebensbild eines grossen Soldaten. Aus meinen persönlichen Erinnerungen* (Göttingen: Göttinger Verlagsanstalt, 1960).
[62] "Wer wird Kanzler?" *Das kleine Journal*, December 4, 1911, in BA-MA, N 737 – 23.

India would become a realistic option. For Wilhelm II, Goltz's highly optimistic assessment was not positive enough; he remarked dismally: "In other words, only after several years [will the Ottomans be capable of an alliance]! And only if the railways are completed by then."[63] Addressing directly the case of a European war, Goltz summarized the Ottoman potential as follows: "The question as to how Turkey should be taken into account in the event of a general European war is no longer a remote one. She can be useful to us against Russia, but we do not necessarily need her in that quarter, since we can reach the enemy [Russia] ourselves. Against England, however, which is not directly within our own reach, her alliance could prove extremely valuable. She [Turkey] can successfully strike at the British Empire in two very sensitive places [Egypt and India]. It is therefore in our own interest not only to look upon [Turkey's] military strengthening with favor, but to support it actively as much as we can."[64] Until the Ottomans could stand on their own feet militarily, however, no German–Ottoman alliance could be signed.

German circles agreed that the premature signing of such an alliance would probably meet with fervent hostility on the part of the Entente powers and quite possibly unleash a Europe-wide war. This consideration was still alive and well two years later, in mid-1912, when the Ottoman Empire was at war with Italy, still a formal ally of Germany and Austria-Hungary at that time. In a detailed report, Gerhard von Mutius, *Botschaftsrat*, or counselor, at the German embassy at Istanbul, in a crucial analysis, assessed the question of an Ottoman alliance. In the report addressed to the chancellor, Theobald von Bethmann Hollweg, Mutius emphasized that the continued existence of the Ottoman Empire depended on the interests of the Great Powers, which currently did not favor a radical change in the status quo, such as partitioning. An Ottoman alliance with either Triple Alliance or the Entente would render the empire a protectorate rather than an ally. Such a profound restructuring of the international order, Mutius continued, would almost certainly lead to the outbreak of war. Each of the two major alliance groups had vital political and economic interests in the empire and was prepared to defend these militarily. From the German perspective, territorial partition remained decidedly undesirable in the face of the Entente's stronger regional position: "In the event of Ottoman partition we would lose out

[63] BA/MA, N 737–5, Goltz to Wilhelm, Bericht des Generaloberst Freiherrn von der Goltz über seinen Aufenthalt in der Türkei im Oktober und November 1910 [Report of Colonel General Freiherr von der Goltz regarding his stay in Turkey in October/November 1910], December 18, 1910.
[64] Ibid.; partly quoted in Yasamee, "Colmar Freiherr von der Goltz and the Rebirth of the Ottoman Empire," 115, whose translation is loosely followed here.

simply because of our geographic situation." Mutius offered a reminder of what escalation could bring. Germany had suffered a diplomatic debacle in mid-1911, when France answered the arrival of a German gunboat in Morocco by landing troops and establishing a protectorate there by the next year: "A Turkey under the protectorate of another Great Power would be a second Morocco for us."[65]

To Wilhelm II and his advisors, the quick fall of the Ottoman front to the Balkan coalition armies in late November 1912 harbored the potential for a general war involving all of the European Great Powers. The Ottoman defeat of October/November 1912 must not be underestimated, Goltz warned, and he argued that the Balkan states, victorious and with Russian backing, were now free to turn their expansionist energies against Austria-Hungary, Germany's lone committed ally. Romania and Serbia, especially, would from now on have their eyes on Habsburg lands. The Central Powers' extreme response to Serbia in July 1914, therefore, owed much to the events of 1912 and 1913. Goltz submitted to Wilhelm II a long report detailing the implications created by the outcome of the First Balkan War:

As is well known, there are about two million Romanians living in Siebenbürgen [in Hungary], and approximately a similar number in the Banat [partly in southern Hungary] and the Bukovina [in western Ukraine]. Thus, all the [Romanians] lack is an opportunity for an expansion of its political power. The same is true for Serbia ... Of the ten million Serbs that exist, only two and a half million live on the soil of the current [Serbian] kingdom ... Most of the remaining Serbs live within Austrian borders. The number of the latter, including the Serbo-Croats, can be estimated at six million.[66]

Goltz concluded this report by emphasizing that Germany thus had no choice but to "choose the moment for action ourselves, instead of having it imposed on us." Germany must consider launching a "preventive war [*Präventivkrieg*]." Goltz's report received close attention from Kaiser Wilhelm II as well as Chancellor Bethmann Hollweg, who met with Goltz in December 1912 to discuss the matter in person.[67]

When the First Balkan War broke out in October 1912, Berlin had dispatched a naval squadron to the eastern Mediterranean. Following

---

[65] PA/AA, R 1913, Mutius to Bethmann Hollweg, June 24, 1912; see also Schöllgen, *Imperialismus und Gleichgewicht*, 360, and Kampen, "Studien zur deutschen Türkeipolitik," 78–9.

[66] BA-MA, N 80, Sheets 188–95 and reverse, Goltz to Wilhelm, Betrachtungen über die politische Lage Europas nach dem Zusammenbruch der türkischen Herrschaft [Observations regarding the Political Situation in Europe following the Collapse of Turkish Rule], November 17, 1912.

[67] Ibid. It is unclear against *whom* exactly the preventive war would be fought: Serbia, Russia?

the Ottoman defeats, the kaiser decided not to dissolve the squadron but to make it permanent, creating the Mediterranean Squadron (*Mittelmeerdivision*, or *MMD*). In his directive for the squadron's establishment, the kaiser added that he had consulted with German "experts on Islam and its psyche" and concluded that an Ottoman "rebirth" could no longer be hoped for realistically.[68] Under no circumstances, Wilhelm II noted, could Germany miss out on the inevitable partition, which would include "Turkish Asia Minor." Hence German ships in the region would be essential: "We will participate in [the partition] and therefore ships are absolutely necessary there ... Alexandretta [İskenderun] and Mersin [on the southeastern Anatolian coast] must under any circumstances remain in our hands and must never be left unoccupied."[69]

Hence, the German ships the Ottoman public would celebrate in August 1914 as friend and protector had originally been placed near Ottoman waters in order to position Germany for the empire's partition. During 1913–14, the German foreign office reviewed proposals with its two allies, Austria-Hungary and Italy, defining the manner in which Asia Minor might eventually be districted into their respective spheres of interest. They also discussed how their claims to Ottoman territory might best be defended in subsequent negotiations with the Entente.[70]

The Russian reform proposal for eastern Anatolia

The establishment of a Russian protectorate over the Ottoman Armenian population appeared a real possibility in 1878, when the tsar's armies decisively defeated Ottoman forces in a nine-month-long war. In the aftermath of that war, St. Petersburg demanded administrative reforms in the Armenian-inhabited areas of eastern Anatolia that would guarantee the security of Armenian Christians. It also proclaimed its intention of occupying the region until it was satisfied that such reforms had been carried out. Only strong Great Power opposition prevented the Russian occupation of eastern Anatolia. In the preliminary peace settlement, the

---

[68] PA/AA, R 14524, Wilhelm II's marginalia on Tirpitz to Wilhelm II, May 15, 1913. See also BA-MA, RM 40 – 575, sheet 4, Tirpitz to Chief of the Navy Cabinet, July 5, 1913.

[69] PA/AA, R 14524, Tirpitz to Wilhelm II, May 15, 1913.

[70] *GP*, vol. 37/2, Die Kleinasiatischen "Arbeitszonen" Österreich-Ungarns und Italiens, Mai 1913 bis Juli 1914 [Austria-Hungary's and Italy's "Areas of Activity" in Asia Minor, May 1913–July 1914]," nos. 15045–114; ibid., vol. 38, no. 15312, Wangenheim to Bethmann Hollweg, May 21, 1913; PA/AA, R 14503, Auswärtiges Amt to Bethmann Hollweg, December 3, 1913, no. 381, and ibid., Flotow to Auswärtiges Amt, December 5, 1913, no. 249.

Treaty of San Stefano signed on March 3, 1878, Article 16 had guaranteed the Ottoman Armenian population protection from its Muslim neighbors, "les Kurdes et les Circassiens." In the final peace settlement, however, signed at the Berlin Congress on July 13, 1878, Article 61 obliged the Sublime Porte only to undertake reforms in the Armenian provinces and to seek periodic approval of its measures from the Great Powers, a much weaker measure, since the Russian army would no longer be there to ensure its enforcement.[71]

The new urgency that attended the question of Ottoman territorial partition in 1913 resulted not only from the possibility of the Ottomans' total military collapse in the Balkans, but also from renewed Russian pressure for reforms in the empire's eastern provinces.[72] A Russian reform proposal, which was presented to the Great Powers on June 6, 1913, and deliberated upon during the subsequent months, provided for the creation of a special governorship centered in Erzurum. According to the proposal, the six Ottoman provinces of eastern Anatolia would be consolidated into a single, "Armenian" province. The administration of the new province would be headed by a team of two general-governors, nominated by the Great Powers and approved by Istanbul. The province would also be governed by a provincial chamber of deputies, with an equal number of Armenian and Muslim delegates.[73] This Russian proposal caused grave concerns in German government circles in general, and the members of the Auswärtiges Amt in particular. Foreign Secretary Jagow saw in such a special status for the eastern provinces the area's "separation from the whole," a form of partition and Russian annexation. Such an outcome, without any compensation to Berlin, would be a defeat of the first order.[74]

---

[71] The texts of both Article 16 and Article 61 are found in André N. Mandelstam, *Das armenische Problem im Lichte des Völker- und Menschenrechts* (Berlin: Georg Stilke, 1931), 23; for a discussion of the Treaty of San Stefano and its revision at the Berlin Congress (June 13–July 13, 1878), see Yasamee, *Ottoman Diplomacy*, 53–65.

[72] The provinces (*vilayets*) of Bitlis, Erzurum, Diyarbakır, Sivas, Van, and Mamuretülaziz (often Harput in Western parlance).

[73] For the account by the First Dragoman at the Russian embassy at Istanbul, see Mandelstam, *Das armenische Problem im Lichte des Völker- und Menschenrechts*, 28–31, where the author explicitly argued that the reforms were not a Russian ploy to seize the eastern Ottoman provinces. A revised version of the proposal was signed into treaty by the Ottoman and Russian governments on February 8, 1914. Eventually, the Dutchman Westenenk and the Norwegian Hoff were selected for this task; see *IBZI*, Series I, vol. 2, no. 227, Giers to Sazonov, April 15, 1914, 236; also ibid., Series I, vol. 1, no. 210, Gulkevich to Sazonov, February 9, 1914, 193–200, and Roderic H. Davison, "The Armenian Crisis, 1912–1914," *American Historical Review* 53 (April 1948): 481–505.

[74] PA/AA, R 2125, Jagow to Wangenheim, July 28, 1913, also in PA/AA, R 14524.

The swift fall of the Ottoman armed forces to the attack of the Balkan states the previous year, however, forced Berlin to rethink its position on the question of partition, and Jagow began to give serious consideration to the Russian reform proposal. If the proposal could be expanded into establishing similar administrations in "the other parts of Asiatic Turkey as well," then Berlin could gain from the arrangement. In other words, if the powers set up in concert regional administrations charged with implementing reforms in their respective spheres, the proposal on the table could be used as the basis for further negotiations.[75]

Initially such regional administrations under the aegis of the powers could work closely with the local Ottoman institutions and officials. "It would certainly be significant for us," Jagow noted, "to be able to draw on administrative "organs in our regions of interest" at the time of Ottoman "liquidation."[76] He pointed to the challenges that came with direct colonial rule: "It would be very difficult for us to simply annex large territories and to flood them with Prussian district officers (*Landräte*) and other administrative bodies. The French [struggled with it] in Algeria, and thus they preserved the Bey of Tunis and the local indigenous administration; that is more practical and cheaper. The model, in any case, is the Khedive in Egypt."[77] Hence the establishment of a German protectorate (*Protektorat*) should be facilitated by building on local administrations and placing them under a German "viceroy or governor general."[78]

Jagow at the Auswärtiges Amt began to see in the June 1913 Russian proposal an opportunity to set in motion a gradual and negotiated process of partition and a way of precluding a sudden dismemberment in which the German role would be secondary. After all, with the outbreak of the First Balkan War in October 1912 and the weak performance of the Ottoman forces, the possibility of an overnight Russian occupation of eastern Anatolia had to be taken very seriously in Berlin. In January 1913, Foreign Minister Sazonov had spoken openly of military intervention in eastern Anatolia: should anti-Christian violence flare up as a result of the hostile atmosphere created by the First Balkan War, Russian troops would march in.[79]

Other news arriving in Berlin soured the outlook further. Wangenheim reported in mid-April 1913 that Russian agents had succeeded in mediating outstanding differences between two major Kurdish factions of the Lake Van region in eastern Anatolia by pledging the Russian

---

[75] Ibid.   [76] Ibid.   [77] Ibid.   [78] Ibid.
[79] Pourtalès to Bethmann Hollweg, January 23, 1913, in *GP*, 38, no. 15284; see also Manoug Joseph Somakian, *Empires in Conflict: Armenia and the Great Powers, 1895–1920* (New York: I. B. Tauris, 1995), 48.

government's support for Kurdish independence.[80] Wangenheim also warned the Auswärtiges Amt that Russian provocateurs in eastern Anatolia were actively attempting to foment discord between Christian Armenians and Muslim Kurds: "the [Russian] purpose is to incite the Kurds to massacres against the Armenians in order to justify Russian [military] intervention."[81] Such alarming rumors kept German political and military leaders on the edge of their seat.

When St. Petersburg redeployed its troops along the Ottoman border in late April 1913, Kaiser Wilhelm II interpreted this move as the first step towards partition: "Preparations for the partition of Turkey, which apparently is closer than thought. In Palestine and Syria a secret war for life and death between England and France has already begun ... We must pay close attention that partition does not happen without us. I will take Mesopotamia, Alexandretta, and Mersin! The sensible Turks are already awaiting this fate patiently!"[82]

Just how near a Russian occupation of eastern Anatolia appeared in the mind of the Russian ambassador, Giers, is evident in his telegram to St. Petersburg on January 13, 1914. This telegram shows that Giers, in contrast to Jagow, hoped to avoid a drawn-out negotiation process among the powers:

[W]e have no time to lose in raising our war readiness, because the events in the Near East, at any moment, could take a turn which would force us to defend strongly our honor and our interests. One of the questions that would demand our decisive action is the Armenian question in the case Armenians are massacred. Through quick and decisive action we could then perhaps prevent a greater European involvement. But for such action we must be ready at the necessary moment, and we must not overlook that Turkey is gathering strength quickly, and that Turkey, after solving the [Aegean] islands question, will move its Anatolian divisions ... back to the eastern part of Anatolia. And, furthermore, it is of particular importance to us that the Turkish Black Sea Fleet will be stronger than ours by mid-year [1914], so that Turkey will be superior to us in terms of troop movements and coastal defense.[83]

[80] PA/AA, R 14501, Wangenheim to Bethmann Hollweg, Separatistische Umtriebe in der asiatischen Türkei [Separatist Intrigues in Asiatic Turkey], April 12, 1913. The two groups were those headed by the Bedirhanzades and those headed by Abdülkadir, the Ottoman senator. The Bedirhanzades were represented by Abdürrezak; see also *GP*, vol. 38, no. 15308, Wangenheim to Bethmann Hollweg, May 20, 1913.
[81] Ibid. The Ottoman government also received reports that Russia was supplying the Armenian population with arms, see BOA, A.VRK, 787 – 28, Ali Rıza (Erzurum) to Office of the General Staff, 21 Kanun-i Evvel 1329 (January 3, 1914).
[82] These are Wilhelm's marginalia in PA/AA, R 14524, Schulenburg to Bethmann Hollweg, April 30, 1913, also quoted in part in Fischer, *Krieg der Illusionen*, 429.
[83] *IBZI*, Series I, vol. 1, Note to no. 9, Giers to Sazonov, January 13, 1914, 7; for the views of Giers's colleagues, who shared his position, see ibid., Series I, vol. 1, no. 155, Gulkevich to Sazonov, January 31, 1914, 142–4; ibid., Series I, vol. 1, no. 84, Sukhomlinov to

Very different assumptions, therefore, were governing German and Russian strategic planning regarding the Ottomans' future. For Jagow and the kaiser, the empire had already become moribund and could not be saved, and thus Germany had to prepare for its impending demise. If it did not act, Berlin would see the Entente accrue even more power and a stronger strategic position in the eastern Mediterranean. For Giers and St. Petersburg, the Ottoman Empire was strong and getting stronger all the time, even to the point of threatening Russia's position in the Near East.

Foreign Minister Sazonov fully supported Giers's assessment and passed it on to the top brass – the war minister, the navy minister, and the chief of the general staff. He stressed once again that the military must be able to take "quick and energetic steps" in eastern Anatolia in order to avoid the possibility of "much more serious" confrontations with any of the European powers.[84] To prepare the armed forces for such swift action Sazonov developed a "Program of Action" for the "suitable solution of the historic problem of the Straits."[85]

The Russian foreign minister even accepted the greatest military risk of all: "it should not be assumed that our operations against the Straits could proceed without a European war." By no means was this conclusion a warning against such action; if it came to a general war, he added, St. Petersburg could count on the support of its Serbian ally, which would then move against Austria-Hungary.[86]

With the great power reform proposal for eastern Anatolia not yet finalized, key Russian decision-makers supported the idea of forcing the negotiations forward with the help of military measures. V. A. Sukhomlinov, the war minister, together with Sazonov proposed mobilizing troops in the Caucasus and pushing across the border into Ottoman Erzurum. Quite remarkably, as far as the Russian war minister was concerned, eastern Anatolia had already ceased to be an integral part of the Ottoman Empire. Sukhomlinov's operation plan did not consider the moving of troops into Erzurum Province an invasion and hence an act of war. Rather, he suggested the massing of Russian troops in Ottoman territory "in order to take up a suitable position there in the event war breaks out."[87]

Sazonov, January 22, 1914, 72–3; ibid., Series I, vol. 1, no. 295, Journal einer Sonderkonferenz, 283–96; and ibid., Series I, vol. 2, no. 308, Giers to Sazonov, April 27, 1914, 301–3.

[84] *IBZI*, Series I, vol. 1, no. 9, Sazonov to Kokovtsov, Sukhomlinov, Grigorovich, and Shilinski, January 15, 1914, 7–8.
[85] *IBZI*, Series I, vol. 1, no. 295, Journal einer Sonderkonferenz, February 14, 1914, 283.
[86] Ibid., 285.
[87] *IBZI*, Series I, vol. 1, no. 84, Sukhomlinov to Sazonov, January 22, 1914, 72.

On February 9, 1914, the day after the Ottoman government accepted and signed the Great Powers' Armenian reform proposal, K. N. Gulkevich, the chargé d'affaires at the Russian embassy in Istanbul, wrote a glowing summary of the negotiations over the past seven months. His report also points to the fine line between humanitarian interventionism, on the one hand, and imperialist expansionism, on the other. He wrote, in a passage that would be deleted in a 1915 publication of the telegram: "I am so bold as to believe that Russia, if its historical fate leads it to Constantinople, will be able to rely on the 200,000-strong Armenian population of Constantinople in the inevitable struggle with the Greek element."[88] The idea of using the help of Ottoman Armenians in order to establish Russian control over the Straits, therefore, was not far from the minds of Russian statesmen.

The Ottomans in the aftermath of the Balkan Wars

In June 1913 the Ottoman ambassador at London, Tevfik Pasha, launched a renewed attempt to win the foreign office over to an Anglo–Ottoman alliance, only to learn that the British position had not changed. At the foreign office, Sir Louis Mallet, soon to replace Sir Gerard Lowther as ambassador in Istanbul, strictly opposed engaging Tevfik's proposal. Mallet stayed close to the argument employed earlier by Mutius, maintaining that an alliance would incur the vengeance of the other powers and cause a "European war." Hence Mallet advocated interna-tional cooperation rather than alliance, suggesting the "participation by all the Great Powers in financial control [of the Ottoman Empire] and the application of reforms."[89]

To the Ottomans, the First Balkan War had been another bitter lesson learned in the empire's precarious international relations. The attack of the Balkan states in October 1912 had followed the Italian occupation of Tripoli in Libya (1911–12), an act of imperialism the Great Powers had tolerated quietly, as neither side of the alliance blocs wished to "fatally antagonize" Italy.[90] Strategic realities once again reminded Ottoman

---

[88] *IBZI*, Series I, vol. 1, no. 210, Gulkevich to Sazonov, February 9, 1914, 200. See the editor's note for the deletion of the passage from the Russian *Orange Book*.

[89] *BDOW*, vol 10/1, Memorandum by Sir L. Mallet, June 19, 1913, 901–2; also quoted at length in Ahmad, "Great Britain's Relations with the Young Turks," 321–3, and briefly in Elie Kedourie, *England and the Middle East: The Destruction of the Ottoman Empire, 1914–1921*, new edn. (Boulder: Westview Press, 1987), 10–11; *BDOW*, vol. 10/1, Edward Grey to Tevfik, Secret, July 2, 1913.

[90] R. J. B. Bosworth, "Italy and the End of the Ottoman Empire," in *The Great Powers and the End of the Ottoman Empire*, 63.

decision-makers and the public alike that neither the Ottoman military nor the international state system was providing the empire's security. Seizing the Italian attack as their opportunity, the Balkan states had launched a war of their own against the Ottoman Empire.[91]

From the Ottoman perspective the Great Powers had clearly applied a double standard to the conflict and ignored established conventions of international law. Just prior to the Balkan attack the powers had issued a collective note affirming the status quo of the Ottoman boundaries in Europe.[92] Once the Balkan allies emerged triumphant, however, the powers changed tack and officially recognized the Balkan states' territorial gains. There was no question as to why the Great Powers had altered their original stance. Foreign Minister Sazonov, the initiator of the Powers' declaration, openly stated that the declaration's purpose had been to preclude any kind of *Ottoman* territorial acquisition.[93] The double standard hence was hardly a veiled one, and the Ottomans were hit by yet another act of international humiliation.

Unable to draw on the means of protection presented theoretically by the international state system, the Ottomans felt deeply the bitter pain of isolation. Events, moreover, continued to confirm their fears regarding the intentions of the Great Powers. In late October 1912, a multi-national fleet gathered in Istanbul, ready to occupy the city and other parts of the empire in the name of protecting the foreign and religious minority populations and their businesses. The German records, for example, show plans for going ashore and setting up an interim administration if necessary.[94] And in London, Foreign Secretary Grey suggested making Istanbul an international city. That outcome was scuttled largely by Sazonov, who believed that the city should come under direct Russian

---

[91]　Helmreich, *Diplomacy of the Balkan Wars*, 84–5.

[92]　The Great Powers presented their note to the Sublime Porte on October 10, 1912, two days after Austria-Hungary and Russia had submitted a similar note to the governments of Bulgaria, Greece, Montenegro, and Serbia. See Edward C. Thaden, *Russia and the Balkan Alliance of 1912* (University Park: Pennsylvania State University Press, 1965), 129. For the origins and making of the Balkan Wars, see Helmreich, *Diplomacy of the Balkan Wars*, 103–24 and passim.

[93]　PA/AA, R 14503, Pourtalès to Bethmann Hollweg, February 14, 1914.

[94]　BA-MA, RM 40 – 564, sheets 16–22, Sievers to Wilhelm, November 7, 1912, and subsequent documents; ibid., sheets 55–8 and reverse, November 18, 1912, Militärpolitischer Bericht über den Aufenthalt S. M. S. *Hertha* in Malta und die Lage im Vilajet Adana [Military-political report regarding SMS *Hertha*'s call in Malta and conditions in Adana Province], November 18, 1912; ibid., sheets 82–5 and reverse, Militärpolitischer Bericht S. M. S. *Geier* für die Zeit vom 19. Oktober bis 30. November 1912 [Military-political report of SMS *Geier* for October 19–November 30, 1912. For a list of foreign warships in Istanbul on November 15, 1912, see BA-MA, RM 40 – 564, sheet 483.

control if it did not stay Ottoman, opposing any other foreign power's direct involvement in controlling the capital.[95] Then, in a collective note of January 17, 1913, the Great Powers admonished the Sublime Porte to halt all military activities immediately and to accept all terms imposed on it as a result of the war; otherwise, it risked the loss of Istanbul and perhaps even the empire's Asian provinces altogether![96]

Outraged by Grand Vezir Kâmil Pasha's willingness to engage the powers' proposal, the CUP staged a bloody coup d'état the next week. Led by Enver and Talat, and armed with pistols, a small group of ten stormed the grand vezir's chambers and forced the veteran politician to resign at gunpoint, shooting and killing War Minister Nazım Pasha in the process. The new government would be led by Mahmud Şevket Pasha, a brilliant general who had been war minister until July 1912. The *bab-ı âli baskını* (the Raid on the Sublime Porte), as the coup became known, was a clear signal that no liberal government could survive under the weight of such diplomatic and military defeats. Thus the Raid marked a major change in the political direction of the Ottoman Empire, one in which resolute military action, not diplomatic wavering, would dominate.

Mahmud Şevket assumed the offices of both grand vezir and war minister and devoted his energies to modernizing the army and police corps begun by previous governments.[97] Just prior to the "Raid on the Sublime Porte," Foreign Minister Noradonkyan Efendi had raised with Wangenheim the possibility of a German military mission headed by a senior officer. Throughout the first half of 1913, Mahmud Muhtar Pasha, the Ottoman ambassador in Berlin, secretly negotiated the terms of the mission. Once the Second Balkan War drew to a close, Kaiser Wilhelm II selected General Otto Liman von Sanders in June 1913 as the mission's head. Almost a year after Noradonkyan's initial request, General Liman von Sanders arrived in Istanbul as the freshly minted President of the Reform Commission (*Heyet-i Islahiye Reisi*) on December 14, 1913.[98]

---

[95] Harry N. Howard, *The Partition of Turkey: A Diplomatic History* (Norman: University of Oklahoma Press, 1931), 24–5.

[96] *BDOW*, vol. 9/2, Enclosure 1 in no. 583, January 17, 1913, 468.

[97] Swanson, "Mahmud Şevket and the German Military Mission," 382–5.

[98] ATASE, BDH, Klasör 1649, Yeni Dosya 41, Fihrist 1 and 1–1; Liman von Sanders, *Fünf Jahre Türkei*, 2nd edn. (Berlin: August Scherl, 1920), 9–12 and passim; *GP*, vol. 38, Die Liman Sanders-Affäre, Januar 1913 bis Juni 1914 [The Liman von Sanders Affair, January 1913 to June 1914], nos. 15435–532; BOA, BEO 318658, 1 Kanun-i Sani 1329 (January 14, 1914); for a copy of the contract between Liman and the Ottoman ambassador at Berlin, Mahmud Muhtar Pasha, dated October 28, 1913, see BA-MA, RM 40 – 106, sheets 10–15.

The German military mission

The diplomatic crisis surrounding the Liman von Sanders mission plunged the Great Powers into the "last conflict before the catastrophe." Fearing that the mission would essentially place the Ottoman capital in German hands, St. Petersburg issued stern warnings even before the general's arrival.[99] It saw the presence of a German commander in Istanbul and the Straits region as a fundamental shift in the balance of power, a change for which Russia demanded compensation. Adequate compensation, Sazonov intimated, could take the form of Russian command over Erzurum Province in eastern Anatolia, and the foreign minister sought immediately the support of his none-too-eager counterparts in London and Paris for such action.[100]

Grey warned his German colleagues that the Liman von Sanders mission, and the Russian response it would precipitate in eastern Anatolia, would undoubtedly lead to Ottoman partition. Berlin proved unwilling to back down. Karl Max Lichnowsky, the German ambassador in London, explained to Grey that the mission was similar to the British naval mission headed by Admiral Limpus. Hence, under no circumstances ought the German mission be regarded as a legitimate basis for Russian claims for compensation. Grey, who had no desire to see the Russians in Erzurum, acknowledged that Limpus did indeed occupy the position of commander (Commander-in-Chief of the Ottoman Navy). In retrospect, Grey's reply does not add up to a great deal of resistance; he argued that Limpus was occupying the role of his immediate predecessor, whereas Liman outranked his. Thus the mission and Liman's appointment meant an expansion of German power, and therefore the Russian objection, Grey suggested, was justified.[101] Grey's mild interjection did little to decelerate the course of confrontation, however.

As for St. Petersburg's other ally, the French government deferred to Grey throughout the crisis, as it did generally in matters concerning the Straits and Anatolia. St. Petersburg did succeed, however, in persuading

[99] Martin Kröger, "Letzter Konflikt vor der Katastrophe: Die Liman-von-Sanders-Krise, 1913/14," in *Vermiedene Kriege: Deeskalation von Konflikten der Großmächte zwischen Krimkrieg und Erstem Weltkrieg, 1856–1914*, ed. Jost Dülffer, Martin Kröger, and Ralf-Harald Wippich (Munich: R. Oldenbourg, 1997), 657–71.

[100] PA/AA, R 14503, Radowitz to Auswärtiges Amt, December 7, 1913, no. 434.

[101] PA/AA, R 14503, Lichnowsky to Auswärtiges Amt, December 15, 1913, no. 375. See also Geoffrey Miller, *Straits: British Policy towards the Ottoman Empire and the Origins of the Dardanelles Campaign* (Hull: University of Hull Press, 1997), 165–71; Heller, *British Policy towards the Ottoman Empire*, 111–16.

the French foreign ministry to postpone a loan agreement it had all but settled with the Ottomans.[102]

The weak British reaction to the installation of Liman and the mission resulted partly from the expectations of upcoming British–German negotiations on a series of issues relating to their interests in the Near East.[103] But it was also a product of considerations regarding the British naval mission in the empire. Limpus did, after all, exercise direct command over the Ottoman navy, and the mission under his direction consisted of no less than seventy-two British officers – the fact that the German military mission consisted of the same number of personnel was not missed by contemporary observers. The foreign office was not ready to question the legitimacy of its own mission, which not only exercised considerable influence over naval matters, but also facilitated lucrative contracts for British industrial concerns like Armstrong and Vickers.[104]

Most importantly, Grey was concerned about the potential crisis that a harsh stance might provoke. Sazonov had requested nothing less than a British endorsement of his plan for occupying Trabzon and Bayazit while Britain and France occupied Izmir and Beirut, respectively. Grey left this aspect of the proposal unanswered and pointed out that neither London nor Paris was willing to risk war with Germany over the Liman von Sanders mission. Sazonov and Tsar Nicholas II, even if only for the moment, were evidently prepared to take that risk. In the effort to restrain the Russian leaders, who saw their position in the eastern Mediterranean weakening drastically, with the possible strangling of its trade relations – half of its exports passed through the Straits – both Prime Minister Asquith and Grey made it clear that London would remain on the sidelines if war broke out. Eventually Grey agreed to the presentation in Istanbul of a joint verbal protest in the name of the Triple Entente, a considerably weaker measure than Sazonov had pressed for.[105]

Sazonov's aggressive course was also undermined by his failure to win the votes of key figures in the government, such as those of the prime minister, V. N. Kokovtsov, and the ambassador at London, Count Benckendorff, who counseled diplomatic measures. Despite Sazonov's threats, the Russian government as a whole was not prepared in early 1914

[102] Marlene P. Hiller, *Krisenregion Nahost: Russische Orientpolitik im Zeitalter des Imperialismus, 1900–1914* (New York: Peter Lang, 1985), 84 and 88.
[103] Schöllgen, *Imperialismus und Gleichgewicht*, 329–416.
[104] *IBZI*, Series I, vol. 1, no. 3, Etter to Sazonov, January 14, 1914, 2–3; ibid., Series I, vol. 1, no. 12, Izvolskii to Sazonov, January 15, 1914, 14; ibid., Series I, vol. 1, no. 122, Benckendorff to Sazonov, January 28, 1914, 107–9; Hiller, *Krisenregion Nahost*, 88–9 and 98; Kröger, "Letzter Konflikt," 664–7.
[105] Ibid.; for the trade statistics, see Rich, *Great Power Diplomacy, 1814–1914*, 425.

to take drastic, unilateral steps such as the military occupation of eastern Anatolia or the seizure of the Straits region, since such moves entailed risking war against one or more of the Great Powers. In a series of secret conferences regarding the Straits and its surrounding region, Russian military planners had designated a timeframe of two to three years as a necessary period of preparation before they could reach for the Straits and risk a general war.[106] This need for military preparation had prevented Russian decision-makers from sending troops into eastern Anatolia or against the Straits during the crises brought on by the Balkan Wars in 1912/13. By strongly opposing the installation of a German command over the Ottoman First Army, therefore, St. Petersburg sought to undermine any significant attempts at Ottoman military reform and greater German influence in Istanbul. Such was also the conclusion of the German military attaché at St. Petersburg, Bernhard von Eggeling, who reported that the leading circles in Russia believed further preparation was necessary before "*all* the consequences of a war with Turkey could be accepted."[107]

In April 1914, St. Petersburg's position was summarized in a widely circulated report penned by its delegate in Bucharest, S. A. Poklevskii: "the possession of the Dardanelles represents for Russia a question of its very existence [*eine Lebensfrage*]." The report emphasized that the Great Powers must reach an agreement on partition, but that until such an agreement could be reached the Sublime Porte had to be kept on its wobbly legs. Tsar Nicholas II hoped for such an international agreement as much as he hoped to avoid a general war. But if war did break out among the Great Powers, Poklevskii claimed, Russia would prove the least vulnerable.[108]

Such pronouncements were neither stunning nor considered secret information, as Russian intentions had been all too well known since at least the Bosnian Crisis of 1908, when in response to its outcries over Austria-Hungary's annexation of Bosnia-Herzegovina, Austria-Hungary had publicized Izvolskii's own plans to seize control of the Straits, causing

---

[106] Robert J. Kerner, "Russia, the Straits, and Constantinople, 1914–1915," *Journal of Modern History* I (September 1929): 402–3, and "The Mission of Liman von Sanders," 92–8; Hiller, *Krisenregion Nahost*, 95–6; and Alan Bodger, "Russia and the End of the Ottoman Empire," in *The Great Powers and the End of the Ottoman Empire*, 95.

[107] PA/AA, R 14503, Eggeling to War Ministry, January 3, 1914, Türkische Sorgen in Armenien, russische Kriegsbereitschaft und die deutsche Militärmission [Turkish Concerns in Armenia, Russian Readiness for War, and the German Military Mission].

[108] PA/AA, R 14503, Auswärtiges Amt to Bethmann Hollweg, March 30, 1914, no. 81. Berlin reported the Poklevskii conversation to its embassies at Istanbul, St. Petersburg, and Vienna on April 16, 1914. For additional quoted deliberations among Russian high officials, based on published Russian sources, see Fischer, *Krieg der Illusionen*, 491.

Russia an international embarrassment. The Russian ambassador at Istanbul, M. Charykov, for instance, in 1911 had made a much-discussed statement similar to Poklevskii's.[109] In such a high-stakes atmosphere, with the Russian cards squarely on the table, the Ottomans had no doubt as to which of the Great Powers represented the greatest threat: Russia.

In the end, the international crisis over the appointment of General Liman von Sanders to the helm of the First Army in Istanbul was resolved diplomatically by promoting him to the rank of marshal in the Ottoman army. As a result, Liman would act as general-inspector of the Ottoman armed forces but would not exercise actual command over any troops.[110]

Russian challenge and Ottoman response

In the spring of 1914, at a time when the European cabinets had begun to address successfully issues concerning the Near East, the Ottoman leaders stepped up their diplomatic activity. Observing an eerie calm that followed the turbulent days of the Liman von Sanders crisis, they worried that the new level of cooperation among the Great Powers could diminish Ottoman sovereignty even further and impede its programs for reform and recovery. On the surface, there appeared some reason for optimism. In particular, the Great Powers settled disagreements over the extension of the Baghdad Railway. Though anxious about greater European cooperation in the Near East, the Ottomans hoped to gain finally, after years of deliberations, the Powers' approval of a 4 percent increase of tariff rates on goods imported to the empire. But as the Baghdad Railway agreement and similar negotiations remained contingent on additional treaties, requiring the consensus of all the six powers that claimed areas of interest in the Near East, none of these agreements was ever ratified.[111]

---

[109] Hiller, *Krisenregion Nahost*, 95.

[110] *IBZI*, Series I, vol. 1, no.18, Sverbeyev to Sazonov, January 15, 1914, 20–1; ibid., Series I, vol. 1, no. 21, Sverbeyev to Sazonov, January 16, 1914, 22–3; ibid., Series I, vol. 1, nos. 23 and 24, Giers to Sazonov, January 16, 1914.

[111] Murat Özyüksel, *Osmanlı-Alman İlişkilerinin Gelişim Sürecinde Anadolu ve Bağdat Demiryolları* (Istanbul: Arba, 1988), 233–8; Schöllgen, *Imperialismus und Gleichgewicht*, 374–5; for the Russian demands, see *IBZI*, Series I, vol. 1, no. 19, Sazonov to Izvolskii and Benckendorff, January 16, 1914, 21; St. Petersburg, for example, demanded the conclusion of the Armenian reform proposal, the signing of a commerce and railway agreement, and the addition of a Russian delegate to the Ottoman Public Debt Administration before it could approve the increase in Ottoman custom duties from 11 to 15 percent, see ibid., Series I, vol. 1, nos. 26, 34, 39, 56, 143, 158, 170, 211, 214, 287, 327; and ibid., Series I, vol. 2, no. 296, although Gulkevich also feared that such pressures would lead only to greater German influence in the Ottoman Empire, ibid., Series I, vol. 2, nos. 247 and 261.

In early 1914, the Ottoman ambassador in Vienna, Hüseyin Hilmi Pasha, reopened efforts at a Habsburg–Ottoman alliance. He tried to convince the Austro-Hungarian foreign minister, Leopold Count von Berchtold, of the need for a formal entente between the two powers. Hüseyin Hilmi added a sense of urgency to the question, warning that Russia was mediating an alliance between Bulgaria and Serbia directed against both Istanbul and Vienna. Berchtold's reply was disheartening; echoing Jagow, he maintained that the Sublime Porte should steer clear of any alliance and concentrate on its domestic issues.[112]

Grand Vezir Said Halim Pasha supported these efforts from the Ottoman capital. He advised Pallavicini, Vienna's ambassador, of an alleged Russian attempt at *rapprochement* with the Sublime Porte, suggesting the possibility of greater Russian influence in Istanbul. Said Halim also mentioned the establishment of a new society designed to promote "Ottoman–Russian friendship," and he did not fail to embellish the society's inaugural celebration at the chamber of deputies on March 24, 1914.[113] For the moment, however, these tactics achieved little success.

Ottoman organizations devoted to building closer business and cultural ties like the Ottoman–Russian society were also established with British and French partners, in February and April 1914, respectively.[114] The warming of commercial and diplomatic relations between Istanbul and the powers of the Entente in the spring of 1914 rested on the desperate Ottoman need to secure a loan from one of these governments. Without Entente goodwill, no such loan could be forthcoming. Moreover, any loan would have to be achieved with a reasonable rate of interest, and with relatively few strings attached in terms of how the Sublime Porte could spend such monies.[115]

In January 1914, with the Armenian reform proposal almost signed and the Liman von Sanders crisis resolved, the Russian ambassador in Paris, A. P. Izvolskii, suggested that the Entente's prevailing "financial boycott" of the Ottoman government might now be laid aside carefully. Lest the Ottomans be driven into the arms of Germany, Izvolskii recommended, his government should signal a qualified green light to the granting of a French loan of 350 million francs. Of this amount, 250 million francs should be applied directly against outstanding debt. The balance, it should be stipulated, was to be spent on "absolute necessities" limited

---

[112] PA/AA, R 14503, Auswärtiges Amt to Bethmann Hollweg, February 15, 1914, no. 46.
[113] PA/AA, R 14503, Embassy of Austria-Hungary at Berlin to Auswärtiges Amt, March 27, 1914.
[114] *IBZI*, Series I, vol. 2, Note (a) to no. 215, Giers to Sazonov, April 13, 1914, 438.
[115] *IBZI*, Series I, vol. 1, no. 114, Izvolskii to Sazonov, January 14, 1914, 97; and ibid., Series I, vol. 1, nos. 226, 288, 300, 424.

to "peaceful and productive purposes."[116] The Russian government also
feared that Cavid Bey, the finance minister, might secure a loan, if not
with Berlin, then with Washington.[117] Thus by April 1914 Cavid eventually succeeded in negotiating the final terms of a much-needed French
loan to be paid out in two installments.[118]

Back in Istanbul, Enver, too, worked towards alliance with Austria-
Hungary and Germany in the spring of 1914. Meeting with Wangenheim
in early April, he falsely claimed that his government had received a
Romanian offer for alliance, an alliance that would include Greece and
that would be protected by the Triple Entente. The Romanian proposal,
said Enver, provided for the return of the disputed Aegean islands, Chios
and Mitylene. Although these offers had been on the table for the taking,
Enver claimed, he could not trust either British or Russian intentions.
Instead, he hoped "to supply one day a German-trained Turkish army of
500,000 men to fight alongside the Triple Alliance" and, especially,
Germany.[119]

In reality, no such offers, either from the Greek or the Romanian side,
had actually existed. The Ottomans were maneuvering to raise anxiety in
the capitals of the Central Powers about losing the empire to the Entente.
In May 1914, Talat and İzzet Pasha, the former war minister, traveled to
the Crimean spa town of Livadia, where Tsar Nicholas II vacationed for
its mud baths and mineral treatments. Ostensibly, the Ottoman delegation made the trip to convey the sultan's greetings in an act of royal
respect.[120] But while the Sublime Porte had sent such delegations as a
matter of diplomatic courtesy in previous years, the delegation of 1914
was extraordinary because it was a summit meeting – headed by some of
the leading Ottoman statesmen – between traditional enemies. Thus the
1914 visit attracted a great deal of international attention and gave cause
to speculation regarding a new direction in the relations between the two

[116] *IBZI*, Series I, vol. 1, no. 133, Izvolskii to Sazonov, January 29, 1914, 117–19; see also
ibid., Series I, vol. 1, no. 236, Izvolskii to Sazonov, February 11, 1914, 230.
[117] *IBZI*, Series I, vol. 1, no. 154, Gulkevich to Sazonov, January 31, 1914, 142.
[118] *IBZI*, Series I, vol. 2, no. 199, Izvolskii to Sazonov, April 10, 1914, 210. The first
installment of 500 million francs, earmarked in its entirety to service the Ottoman
debt, was paid out on April 24, 1914. The second installment had been scheduled for
late 1914, see ibid., Series I, vol. 2, no. 266, and Note (a), Izvolskii to Sazonov, April 22,
1914, 265–6 and 442.
[119] PA/AA, R 1913, Wangenheim to Auswärtiges Amt, April 12, 1914, no. 165.
[120] PA/AA, R 14503, Pourtalès to Auswärtiges Amt, Talaats Besuch in Livadia [Talat's visit
to Livadia], May 23, 1914; "Livadia Telâkisi: Heyet-i Mahsusa [The Livadia Meeting,
Special Delegation]," *Tanin*, May 9, 1914; "Livadia Heyet-i Mahsusası [The Special
Livadia Delegation]," *Tanin*, May 10, 1914.

powers.[121] Accompanied by Giers, the Russian ambassador, the delegation arrived in early May and remained there for about a week.[122]

At Livadia, did the Ottomans proffer a military alliance to the Russians? And did they do so with sincerity, or was it a diplomatic ploy? There can be no question that Talat raised the issue of an alliance with Sazonov, but what were Talat's intentions in doing so? According to Sazonov, "Talat uttered the word 'alliance' twice, upon which I responded that this question required, of course, further investigation, but that from this point on we would be willing to support a mutual improvement of our relations."[123] Once the delegation had departed, Sazonov informed the Russian ambassadors in London, Paris, and Vienna of his conversation with Talat. He authorized his colleagues to share the general contents of his discussions with the governments to which they were posted, but he instructed them not to mention "Talat Bey's proposal to conclude an alliance with us."[124]

Following the visit, Talat expressed his deep gratitude for the reception he had received in Livadia, saying he had been "deeply touched." Talat then raised the issue of an alliance once again, this time with Ambassador Giers, arguing that it would be of the "greatest benefit" for the Ottoman Empire. He added quickly, however, that he realized fully that the empire at the moment made a weak alliance partner, and that therefore he and his government would first endeavor to make "the Ottoman Empire a strong state, entirely independent of all foreign influence."[125] In other words, Talat attempted to assuage Russian fears that Ottoman recovery – military, economic, administrative – was pointed at Russia. Then he broached the issue of the two battleships on order with British shipmakers and due in Ottoman waters by August 1914. In three months' time, Talat went on, the Ottomans would be strong at sea, but despite this strength his government would always be reasonable in its diplomacy and conduct.[126]

At Livadia, in a trip designed to generate Russian goodwill, Talat had also sought to ease Sazonov's worries about a war with Greece and the subsequent closure of the Straits. Presenting Ottoman–Greek relations as basically repaired, he claimed that Greece had agreed to recognize the

---

[121] *IBZI*, Series I, vol. 2, no. 295, Giers to Sazonov, April 25, 1914, 292; ibid., Series I, vol. 3, no. 26, Giers to Sazonov, May 18, 1914, 18–19.

[122] *IBZI*, Series I, vol. 2, no. 352, Sazonov to Giers, May 5, 1914, 346.

[123] *IBZI*, Series I, vol. 2, not numbered, Sazonov to Izvolskii, Benckendorff, Shebeko, and Sverbeyev, Beilage, no date, 408–10; this report seems to have been sent shortly following the Ottoman delegation's departure from Livadia on May 12, 1914.

[124] Ibid.   [125] *IBZI*, Series I, vol. 3, no. 27, Giers to Sazonov, May 18, 1914, 19–20.

[126] Ibid.

Ottomans' sovereignty over Chios and Mytilene, and that in return the Sublime Porte would lease the islands back to Athens for a period of several years. Furthermore, the two powers would form a defensive alliance.[127]

Like Enver's, these claims were untrue. If the Ottomans hoped for such a resolution, it was far from a done deal. Instead, Talat, this time visiting Bucharest and meeting with King Carol I and Prime Minister Ion Bratianu, proposed an alliance to the Romanian government, a power close to – and in fact secretly allied with – the Central Powers. Presenting his case, Talat argued that a Bulgarian–Ottoman–Romanian alliance would not bring about but prevent war. If Greece faced such a formidable enemy, it would have to settle for a diplomatic solution and recognize Ottoman sovereignty over Chios and Mytilene. The Ottomans would not be bullies but grant the islands autonomy over their internal affairs and thus permit them the self-rule they demanded. Talat reassured the Romanian statesmen that the islands issue would be settled diplomatically. Diplomatic talks would be opened as soon as the English companies delivered the two ships and the Ottoman navy established itself as the superior naval power in the Aegean. Once the ships arrived, Talat posited, Athens would have to rethink its determination to maintain sovereignty over the islands by military means. The proposal was rejected out of hand. For the Romanians, the alliance as proposed would embolden the Ottomans into an aggressive stance in the Aegean. The possibility of a Greek–Ottoman war and the closure of the Straits to commercial traffic was fraught with perilous consequences not only for the Russian but also for the Romanian economy. Bucharest's intelligence services already reported Greek plans for pre-emptive war ahead of the delivery of the two ships.[128]

These attempts to put Russia and Romania at ease thus had failed miserably. The Romanian government stated brusquely that it would intervene in any land war between Greece and the Ottoman Empire. And because so much of Russian trade depended on unfettered access through the Straits, Sazonov firmly believed, the Russian government would have to take action even in the event of a "temporary" closure of the Straits.[129]

[127] *IBZI*, Series I, vol. 3, no. 131, Neratov to Giers, June 1, 1914, 113–15; ibid., Series I, vol. 3, no. 129, Poklevskii to Giers, May 31, 1914, 112.
[128] *IBZI*, Series I, vol. 3, no. 129, Poklevskii to Giers, May 31, 1914, 112; ibid., Series I, vol. 3, no. 142, Poklevskii to Sazonov, June 2, 1914, 129–32.
[129] *IBZI*, Series I, vol. 3, no. 185, Sazonov to Nicholas II, June 9, 1914, 169–71; Rich, *Great Power Diplomacy*, 425.

For European statesmen in June 1914, a Greek–Ottoman war, just as the two Balkan Wars had done before it, continued to raise the specter of a European, if not worldwide, war. Writing to Prime Minister Bratianu just two weeks prior to the assassination of Franz Ferdinand, Sazonov warned that a Balkan conflict could also pull in Austria-Hungary and Russia. In a letter to Tsar Nicholas II, Sazonov stressed once again that Russia would have to take military action against Austria-Hungary should "Austria be willing to attack Serbia – be it because of the Albanian question or some other pretense – in order to substantially weaken the [Serbian] kingdom."[130]

In addition to its diplomatic efforts to prevent Ottoman restrengthening by working through the Great Powers, the Russian government also sought to undermine the empire by interfering directly in its domestic affairs. Since many of these projects were organized covertly, only some instances of such operations have been recorded in the regular Russian diplomatic correspondence. St. Peterburg, for example, financed the political opponents of the Said Halim Pasha government and organized these into "secret bureaus."[131] In April 1914, the Russian government also worked with and financed the Kurdish leader Abdürrezak Bedirhan, under whose direction an Armenian-Kurdish organization was founded with the purpose of uniting the Armenian and Kurdish populations in an effort to challenge the Ottoman government.[132]

Following the Ottoman delegation's visit to Livadia, the Russian governor for the Caucasus region, Prince I. I. Vorontsov-Dashkov, elaborated on this policy further. He argued for the need to pay "great attention" to the Kurdish population and to provide it with "energetic support," so that "in this way it would be possible to unite the Kurds inside Turkey into a power factor, which could form a very serious counterweight against the further development of Turkey's military and political strength."[133] The contrast to the view from Berlin could not be clearer. St. Petersburg's anxiety resulted from an Ottoman Empire that was becoming stronger, whereas for Berlin the fear went in the opposite direction. Berlin worried that the empire was becoming enfeebled and thus susceptible to partition, a partition in which Germany would get little more than a few crumbs. For Russia, the moment for seizing on these

---

[130] *IBZI*, Series I, vol. 3, no. 339, Sazonov to Nicholas II, June 24, 1914, 293–9.
[131] *IBZI*, Series I, vol. 3, no. 240, Giers to Sazonov, June 1914, 219; ibid., Series I, vol. 1, no. 73, Vorontsov-Dashkov to Sazonov, January 21, 1914, 63.
[132] *IBZI*, Series I, vol. 2, no. 177, Klemm to Vorontsov-Dashkov, April 8, 1914, 187–9.
[133] *IBZI*, Series I, vol. 3, no. 203, Vorontsov-Dashkov to Giers, Vorontsov-Dashkov's Report of June 7, 1914, for Nicholas II, June 10, 1914, 188–90.

preparations would arrive in August 1914, when Russian forces in northern Persia were poised to arm Kurdish groups there.[134]

The CUP leaders certainly engaged in the same game, and they sought to pave the way for rebellions led by Russian Muslims against the tsar's government. Even if the much grander aims of rising Muslim populations in all of the colonial territories of the Entente from North Africa to India to Central Asia were never seriously undertaken, inciting the Muslims of the adjacent Caucasus proved much more feasible. These duties would be discharged by the "Caucasus Desk" of the *Teşkilat-ı Mahsusa*, the Special Organization formed in 1913 or 1914 charged with covert operations.[135]

In May 1914, however, a rosier picture still belied this atmosphere of mobilization between Istanbul and St. Petersburg, and the Ottoman government sought to take advantage of this leverage. In Vienna, Berchtold's trepidation about the reportedly friendly relations between the Sublime Porte and St. Petersburg grew considerably during this period. He also feared an Ottoman–Romanian alliance under Russian aegis, such as the one broached by Enver and Talat. Such an alliance, as Berchtold worried, would bolster Romanian claims on its nationals living inside Habsburg borders.[136] Berchtold discussed the issue Ambassador Hilmi Pasha, and reiterated that it had been Austria-Hungary, after all, that had supported the Ottomans during the recent Balkan Wars, while Russia had sided with their enemies. Hilmi responded, ever so diplomatically, that his government pursued friendly relations with all the Great Powers.[137] The apparent Ottoman–Russian rapprochement, however, caused near panic in Vienna, and in May 1914 Berchtold even considered pre-empting the possibility of an Ottoman–Russian alignment by proposing the final partitioning of the Ottoman Empire in which Istanbul and the Straits would go to St. Petersburg![138]

As the Ottoman dance for alliance gained momentum, Ambassador Wangenheim advised supporting the creation of a small triple alliance of Bulgaria, the Ottoman Empire, and Romania under the protection of the

---

[134] *IBZI*, Series II, vol. 6/1, no. 40, Klemm to Korostovetz, August 9, 1914, 26.
[135] Tarık Zafer Tunaya, *Türkiye'de Siyasal Partiler*, vol. III, *İttihat ve Terakki, Bir Çağın, Bir Kuşağın, Bir Partinin Tarihi*, rev. edn. (Istanbul: İletişim, 2000), 342 and 337–59 more generally. See also Michael A. Reynolds, "The Ottoman–Russian Struggle for Eastern Anatolia and the Caucasus, 1908–1918: Identity, Ideology, and the Geopolitics of World Order," Ph.D. diss., Princeton University (2003); Cemil Aydın, *The Politics of Anti-Westernism in Asia: Visions of World Order in Pan-Islamic and Pan-Asian Thought* (New York: Columbia University Press, 2007).
[136] PA/AA, R 14503, Auswärtiges Amt to Bethmann Hollweg, May 22, 1914, no. 145.
[137] *IBZI*, Series I, vol. 3, no. 134, Giers to Sazonov, June 1, 1914, 116–17; ibid., Series I, vol. 3, no. 135, Giers to Sazonov, June 1, 1914, 117.
[138] Weber, *Eagles on the Crescent*, 54, citing Pallavicini to Berchtold, May 13, 1914.

Triple Alliance. The Ottomans certainly would have embraced such a combination, but it never proved workable since Bucharest and Sofia could not resolve their mutual antagonism after the Second Balkan War.[139]

Throughout spring 1914, the empire cultivated friendly diplomatic relations with the Entente. The delegation visiting Livadia in May 1914 was one significant manifestation of this policy, and the trip to France by the navy minister, Cemal Pasha, in July 1914, yet another. Once the consensus took shape after the First World War that joining the Central Powers had been a terrible mistake, historians emphasized these Ottoman attempts at forming alliances with the Entente. Only when the Sublime Porte's offers to the Entente powers were rebuffed, they argued, were the Ottomans compelled to join the Central Powers.[140] But, in the case of Cemal, it remains unclear whether he ever put forth such an offer. True, he claimed to have done so in his memoirs published shortly after the war, in 1920.[141] But no evidence of the offer has been found in the French records.[142] Nor was Talat's offer, if it was an offer, made with any clarity, leaving Sazonov guessing as to the nature of the proposal.[143]

Until the Ottoman defeats in the First Balkan War, Germany strove towards the gradual establishment of a protectorate over the Ottoman Empire. It was clear to Berlin that this process could under no circumstances be rushed, as the German position in the Near East was inferior to that of the Entente. The establishment of a protectorate had to be considered in the long term. For the short term, Berlin pursued a policy of defending Ottoman territorial integrity, a policy that became increasingly untenable in 1913 after the empire's catastrophic defeats at the hands of the Balkan states. At that point, Berlin's thinking necessarily included the possibility of extending direct control, and the Auswärtiges Amt held negotiations with Germany's allies, Austria-Hungary and Italy, on the subject of Ottoman partition. While the Ottomans were certainly not blind to German ambitions, Russia's stated intention to seize the Straits region was an insurmountable obstacle to real cooperation with St. Petersburg, or with Russia's allies, Britain and France. The latter

[139] PA/AA, R 1913, Wangenheim to Jagow, May 7, 1914.
[140] Republic of Turkey, *Birinci Dünya Harbi'nde Türk Harbi*, vol. I, *Osmanlı İmparatorluğu'nun Siyasî ve Askerî Hazırlıkları ve Harbe Giriş*, rev. Akbay, 30–44; Y. T. Kurat, "How Turkey Drifted into World War I," 291–5.
[141] Metin Martı, ed., *Bahriye Nazırı Ve 4. Ordu Kumandanı Cemal Paşa: Hatırat*, 5th edn. (İstanbul: Arma, 1996), 113–16.
[142] Fulton, "France and the End of the Ottoman Empire," 161.
[143] Kurat, "How Turkey Drifted into World War I," 294–5; Bodger, "Russia and the End of the Ottoman Empire," 96.

powers supported Russian policy by turning down Ottoman requests for loans and diplomatic agreements, thereby contributing further to the Ottomans' sense of isolation. This Anglo-French attitude, moreover, served only to solidify Ottoman apprehension of these powers' intentions towards them.

The German declaration of war on Russia, on August 1, 1914, unleashed the events that would become the First World War. During the period of Ottoman neutrality, declared on August 3 and effective until the Ottoman entry in the final days of October 1914, relations between the Ottomans and the Entente deteriorated steadily as the German presence in the Ottoman capital grew. That the Sublime Porte signed an alliance with Germany on August 2 without ever even sounding out the British on a possible Anglo-Ottoman alliance reflected Ottoman calculations and sensibilities. The Ottoman leaders had lost hope of achieving Ottoman sovereignty and independence through cooperation with Britain. Examination of the British archival records, moreover, has shown that the Foreign Office hardly fought to pull the Ottomans to the side of the Entente. Although London did not learn of the secret German–Ottoman alliance until the Ottomans entered the war, the arrival of the German warships, the SMS *Goeben* and the SMS *Breslau*, in Istanbul on August 10, must have signaled to the British that the Ottomans would definitely side with the Central Powers. This impression, moreover, must have deepened further when the members of the British naval mission, headed by Rear-Admiral Limpus, were taken off the ships and reassigned to desk jobs in the Ottoman navy ministry as early as August 15.[144]

Nevertheless, despite the clear position taken by both sides, contact between London and Istanbul continued. In response to a note by Winston Churchill, the first sea lord, advising neutrality, Enver Pasha promised that the Ottomans would cooperate with Britain under the following condition. He demanded that the British government pay generous compensation to the Ottoman navy, which had been deprived of two British-manufactured warships, the *Sultan Osman* and the *Reşadiye*, promised by the end of July 1914. Churchill replied that such payments would be made only if the *Goeben* and the *Breslau*, the two German men-of-war that had escaped the Mediterranean navies of the Entente and entered the Straits, left Ottoman waters permanently. Similar exchanges followed. Meeting with the British ambassador, Cemal Pasha claimed that the Porte would join the Entente powers if the latter consented to the abolition of the capitulations and agreed not to interfere in the empire's

---

[144] Joseph Heller, "Sir Louis Mallet and the Ottoman Empire: The Road to War," *Middle Eastern Studies* 12 (January 1976): 5 and 8.

internal affairs. Again, little came of the proposal, and the British inaction illustrates "that by the end of August the Foreign Office was pretty sure that the Porte's entry into the war [on the side of the Central Powers] was inevitable."[145]

It was quite likely that the Ottoman leaders were none too surprised about the aloof attitude of the Entente. Their suspicion of the Entente's ultimate designs on Ottoman territory was confirmed, if confirmation were needed, by an intercepted telegram written by the Russian ambassador. On August 6, four days prior to the arrival of the two German battleships, Giers wrote to St. Petersburg:

I believe that Turkey, and maybe also Bulgaria, will go with us. [Turkey] fears German defeat but wishes to get some real gain out of the current war. Although I somewhat mistrust [Turkey], I do not think we can push her away, since that would mean pushing her into the arms of our enemies. The formation of a Balkan league, which includes Turkey, can be to our advantage only to that point in time when circumstances permit our own firm entrance into the Straits. I therefore dare to express the viewpoint that it would be desirable to continue negotiations with the [Sublime] Porte concerning a possible understanding between us.[146]

As they read this document, the Ottoman leaders knew that they faced once again the threat that Russia posed to the empire's very existence. Neutrality, now that Europe was in flames, was no longer a viable option in the Ottomans' relations with the European powers. Rather, the Ottoman leaders believed that the empire's long-term security and economic development could be achieved only through an alliance with Berlin.

---

[145] Ibid., 9–10, 13.
[146] BA-MA, RM 40 – 457, sheet 254, Giers to St. Petersburg, August 6, 1914, no. 631. Also in *IBZI*, Series I, vol. 2, no. 9, Giers to Sazonov, August 5, 1914, 6–7.

4   The Great War as great opportunity: the Ottoman July Crisis

As European armies took to the battlefields in early August 1914, Ottoman statesmen achieved a major diplomatic victory by forming a defensive alliance with the Great Power of their choice. The German Empire was widely considered to possess the best and strongest of the European land armies and the only one that might defend the empire against Russian designs on the Straits and eastern Anatolia. Ottoman statesmen, moreover, hoped that the war would be a short one and that the alliance, good until 1918 and renewable beyond that, would usher in a new period of relative Ottoman security during which the empire could be consolidated and its institutions modernized without fear of external threats. Once the Ottomans secured the alliance with Berlin, however, they found themselves engaged in a delicate balancing act. Hoping for a swift conclusion of the war, the Ottomans intended to enjoy the benefits of their Great Power alliance in peacetime without active military intervention.

German–Ottoman alliance negotiations during the July Crisis

In the weeks following the assassination of Franz Ferdinand and his wife Sophie in Sarajevo on June 28, 1914, the Habsburg government enlisted international support for sharp action against Serbia. Vienna saw in Istanbul's cooperation an invaluable instrument for influencing the policies of its Balkan neighbors, Bulgaria and Romania. Bulgarian support could prove crucial to Austria-Hungary because Bulgaria was in a position to open a second front against the Serbian army.[1] If the Ottomans joined the Entente, however, Bulgaria would be left facing enemies on all sides and could not be expected to carry out offensive operations. Thus Foreign Minister Berchtold instructed his ambassador in Berlin to prod the

---

[1] Friedrich, *Bulgarien und die Mächte*, 115–17.

Auswärtiges Amt towards a formal alignment with the Ottoman Empire. On July 14, 1914, Ladislaus Count von Szögyény, Vienna's ambassador in Berlin, proposed to Foreign Secretary Jagow that the Ottomans be linked to the Central Powers. Jagow rejected Szögyény's proposal on the spot. The question of an Ottoman alliance was by no means a new one. Jagow summarized the German position on this question in two points. First, the Ottomans did not possess the military or political capacity "to take an aggressive stance against Russia" and thus had to be considered "a passive factor": an Ottoman alliance was destined to remain fruitless in any effort to counter Russian influence in the Balkans. Second, Jagow continued, the Triple Alliance was in no position to defend the empire's borders in eastern Anatolia against the Russian army, a provision Ottoman diplomats were certain to include in the terms of an alliance. These two reasons alone, according to Jagow, rendered pointless the pursuit of such an alliance.[2]

The position Jagow laid out was consistent with long-standing German policy towards the Near East, and reports from Istanbul gave him little reason to change course. The two individuals positioned best to appraise the Porte's potential as a German ally were General Otto Liman von Sanders, head of the military mission, and Ambassador Baron Hans von Wangenheim. Both Liman and Wangenheim felt the empire had little to contribute as an ally in either diplomatic or military terms. On the contrary, they stated, the empire would undoubtedly prove a dangerous liability for any of its partners.[3] It was on the basis of these reports from Istanbul that Jagow turned down Vienna's proposal for an Ottoman alliance of mid-July 1914.[4]

Vienna engaged in these efforts to bring the Ottomans into the fold of the Central Powers because, as we have seen, it hoped to gain the support, or at least the neutrality, of the Balkan states, especially Bulgaria, during the July Crisis. Bulgarian–Ottoman cooperation, moreover, seemed increasingly plausible. Both states considered Russia their enemy and hence sought the support of Russia's rivals, the Central Powers. Despite the recent war between them, Bulgarian and Ottoman forces had been fighting alongside one another since the Second Balkan War in an undeclared war against Serbian troops in the disputed region of Macedonia. Since the Treaty of Bucharest of August 1913, Bulgarian–Ottoman trade

[2] PA/AA, R 1913, Jagow to Wangenheim, July 14, 1914, no. 533, and Jagow to Szögyény, July 14, 1914, no. 910.
[3] PA/AA, R 14524, Wangenheim to Bethmann, May 9, 1914.
[4] PA/AA, R 1913, Jagow to Wangenheim, July 14, 1914, no. 533, and Jagow to Tschirschky, July 14, 1914, no. 910.

relations had been growing steadily.[5] Yet if the Ottomans remained internationally isolated, Berchtold feared, they might drift into the Russian camp after all and pull Bucharest and Sofia along with them, thereby substantially weakening Vienna's strategic position in the Balkans. Hence Berchtold had not only instructed Szögyény to push the Ottoman alliance in Berlin but also assigned Pallavicini, the ambassador in Istanbul, to sound out the Sublime Porte for its willingness. Pallavicini's subsequent activity rekindled the Ottoman hopes of joining the Triple Alliance and putting an end to the international vulnerability that so preoccupied the Ottoman statesmen.

It is difficult to say to what extent Pallavicini disclosed to Grand Vezir Said Halim Vienna's attempts to promote an Ottoman alliance in Berlin. Pallavicini must have provided sufficient clues, however, for immediately after the grand vezir reopened the subject of an alliance with the German ambassador. Meeting with Wangenheim on July 15 or 16, Said Halim restated the Porte's strong desire to break out of diplomatic isolation. He expressed his hope for an alliance between Bulgaria, Romania, and the Ottoman Empire under the protection of the Triple Alliance. Thus the grand vezir employed the crisis between Austria-Hungary and Serbia as a lever, seeking to nudge the Triple Alliance into accepting the Ottomans under its umbrella of security.[6]

A rejection, Said Halim suggested, could force the Ottomans into an alliance with Greece, a combination of grave concern to Austria-Hungary's position in the Balkans, as it would free Athens from the dangers of an Ottoman attack and allow it to support Serbia's stance against the Habsburgs. Pointing to an upcoming meeting in Brussels with the Greek prime minister, Eleutherios Venizelos, Said Halim exploited this fear further and claimed that Greece now appeared conciliatory on the issue of the Aegean islands. But, if forced to choose between the alliance with Bulgaria and Romania, on the one hand, and the islands, on the other, the Porte would opt for the alliance. The islands could be ceded to Greece, the grand vezir alleged, if the "complete removal of the Greek population from the Anatolian coast could be carried out first." Wangenheim was unimpressed: a Greek–Ottoman conciliation seemed highly unlikely to him. He sent on the grand vezir's remarks to Berlin without further comment, as his negative views on the subject of an Ottoman alliance were well known there.[7]

[5] Friedrich, *Bulgarien und die Mächte*, 129; Sinan Kuneralp, "Turco-Bulgarian Trade Relations on the Eve of World War One," *Turkish Review of Balkan Studies* 1 (1993): 92–3.
[6] PA/AA, R 1913, Wangenheim to Auswärtiges Amt, July 16, 1914, no. 346.
[7] Ibid.; "Türkiye-Romanya-Bulgaristan: Yeni Bir Balkan İttihadı İhtimali [Turkey-Romania-Bulgaria: The Possibility of a New Balkan Union]," *Tanin*, May 17, 1914.

On July 18, when Pallavicini set out to win Wangenheim towards an Ottoman alliance, the baron reported to Berlin that during the current crisis Pallavicini "hopes for the rescue of Austria less as the result of any energetic action on the part of his government [against Serbia] than through the arrangement of new alliances, and [Pallavicini] would like therefore to attach [the Sublime Porte] to Austria through Bulgaria. I oppose this idea most emphatically. [Turkey] is today without any question still worthless as an ally. She would only be a burden to her associates, without being able to offer them the slightest advantage ... [Turkey] can only be advised to keep away from every political adventure and to maintain friendly relations with all nations."[8] Wangenheim was thus repeating the German position that Jagow had conveyed to the Austro-Hungarian ambassador at Berlin, Szögyény, just four days earlier. Yet although Said Halim's advances received little favor in Berlin, Ottoman statesmen continued to press for an alliance with the Triple Alliance. If the Ottomans also perceived potential dangers in an alliance with Germany, the sources remain silent on this point. It is certain, however, that they harbored long-standing fears of a Russian attack, both on Istanbul and eastern Anatolia, and that they saw in the July Crisis an opportunity to address this threat head on. Thus, when Vienna was searching for international support during the July Crisis, Ottoman leaders were eager to provide it. Said Halim, Enver, and Talat expressed their hopes to Pallavicini that Vienna would take swift action against Serbia and they pledged their steadfast support for that event. They also claimed that Bulgaria and Romania would follow suit and likewise rally behind Vienna.[9]

On July 22, Enver Pasha continued the Ottoman pursuit for alliance.[10] He disputed Wangenheim's argument that the empire should steer clear of all alliances and concentrate solely on "military and administrative reorganization," as the ambassador had put it. Enver tried to persuade Wangenheim that no satisfactory reorganization of the empire could ever be accomplished without adequate international security. This view was

---

[8] PA/AA, R 19866, Wangenheim to Auswärtiges Amt, July 18, 1914, no. 349. The telegram is reproduced in English in Karl Kautsky, *Outbreak of the World War* (New York: Oxford University Press, 1924), no. 71.

[9] PA/AA, R 19866, Wangenheim to Auswärtiges Amt, July 21, 1914, no. 354. Also in Kautsky, *Outbreak*, no. 99.

[10] It is misleading, therefore, to regard this meeting as marking the beginning of the German–Ottoman negotiations leading to the signing of the alliance treaty of August 2, 1914, as is the case in Trumpener, *Germany and the Ottoman Empire*, 15 and 19, Howard, *Partition of Turkey*, 84, Mühlmann, *Deutschland und die Türkei*, 39, Weber, *Eagles on the Crescent*, 62–3 – though Mühlmann, Howard, and Weber acknowledge the role played by Vienna.

not simply his personal opinion, he explained, but represented the firm position of the CUP. According to Enver, the Ottoman leaders were committed to aligning with one or the other of the two Great Power blocs during the current crisis. A minority in the CUP hoped for closer ties to France and Russia, while the majority looked to the Triple Alliance. The speaker of the chamber of deputies, Halil Bey, Said Halim, Talat, and Enver himself controlled the majority, he claimed. Yet only decisive action on the part of Germany and its partners could save the Ottomans from becoming the "vassals of Russia,"[11] an image he hoped would set off alarm bells in Berlin.

Lest he appear to be threatening, however, Enver promised to meet Berlin halfway. Like Said Halim, he told Wangenheim that the cabinet was aware of the empire's current inability to take its place as a full member in a Great Power formation such as the Triple Alliance. He explained that the cabinet, therefore, wished only to form a "secondary alliance" with a smaller power under the protection of one of the two Great Power blocs. The alternatives were, on the one hand, an alliance with Bulgaria linked to the Triple Alliance, and, on the other hand, an alliance with Greece linked to the Triple Entente. An arrangement of this kind would put the armies and resources of not one but two smaller powers at the chosen alliance's disposal. Enver went on to say that the cabinet preferred an alliance with Bulgaria backed by the Central Powers. But if the Central Powers turned down their request, the Ottoman leaders would have no choice but to turn to the Entente.[12] Such talk certainly did not appear as a mere bluff to Berlin. Wangenheim had already reported that Britain and France actively sought a Greek–Ottoman alliance and that the probable outcome of such an alliance would be Greek support for Serbia in the event of war.[13]

Enver reminded the ambassador that recent attempts to conclude a Bulgarian–Ottoman alliance had faltered only for lack of the Central Powers' support. The Sarajevo assassination and the subsequent crisis, however, now had altered the international landscape entirely. At this point, his government could not simply await the outbreak of a third Balkan war without taking measures to defend itself. Alluding to military imperatives, Enver explained that Ottoman military preparations would begin immediately; with neighboring armies mobilized, his country could

---

[11] PA/AA, R 1913, Wangenheim to Auswärtiges Amt, July 22, 1914, no. 362, also in PA/AA, R 22402 and Kautsky, *Outbreak*, no. 117.

[12] Ibid.

[13] PA/AA, R 1913, Wangenheim to Auswärtiges Amt, July 22, 1914, no. 362. Also in PA/AA, R 22402, Wangenheim to Auswärtiges Amt, July 22, 1914, no. 362.

not trust that its neutrality would be respected. If the Central Powers disregarded these concerns once again, he reiterated, the empire would find itself forced to pursue Entente protection through the alliance with Greece. Wangenheim tried to change Enver's mind. He warned that the Ottomans would not benefit from joining the Triple Alliance, because it would bring them into open conflict with Russia. It would also cut off the empire from its main financial creditor, France, and dash any hopes for the empire's economic recovery. Moreover, a treaty with Germany would render eastern Anatolia the weakest strategic point of the entire Triple Alliance formation. Enver persisted, however, intimating that, if turned away, his government would have no choice but to approach the powers of the Entente.[14] Evidently, Enver was confident enough in Ottoman military capacity to play its part in a German alliance, and he held firm against Wangenheim's warning about the danger of Russia. A key aspiration, after all, was to use the German alliance to deal with long-standing Russian designs on Ottoman territory. This calculation was not entirely off the mark; future events proved that the Ottomans did indeed have the military strength to fight for four long years.

Wangenheim's report about his conversation with Enver on July 22, which reached Berlin the following day, made a deep impression on Kaiser Wilhelm II. The German emperor agreed with Enver's proposition that the ongoing crisis called for careful reconsideration of all standing policy. The Ottoman cabinet appeared resolved to side with the Entente if Berlin turned down its alliance proposal. Such a scenario would abruptly end two and a half decades of German investments and efforts to gain a sphere of dominance in the Near East, a horrifying picture the kaiser could not accept. Wilhelm II brushed aside Wangenheim's misgivings and his argument that the Ottoman Empire should stay out of any possible war and focus solely on its internal affairs. Wilhelm II noted: "Theoretically correct, but at the present moment wrong! The thing to do now is to get hold of every gun in readiness in the Balkans to shoot *for* Austria, and so a Turkish–Bulgarian alliance connected with Austria may well be accepted! ... That is better in any case than driving Turkey into the arms of the Triple Entente by theoretical scruples."[15] By the time the kaiser's instructions reached Istanbul,[16] Grand Vezir Said Halim Pasha, in a meeting with Wangenheim, had raised the stakes and now pressed urgently for Berlin's immediate decision. Said Halim revealed that Vienna's ambassador had implored him not to conclude an alliance with

[14] Ibid.   [15] Ibid. (Emphasis in original.)
[16] PA/AA, R 1913, Wedel to Auswärtiges Amt [Kaiser Wilhelm to Wangenheim], July 24, 1914, no. 128. Also found in Kautsky, *Outbreak*, no. 141.

Greece. He explained to Wangenheim that the Porte would gladly follow this plea but that it required a formal defensive alliance against Russia with Berlin or Vienna. Although Wangenheim continued to caution the Auswärtiges Amt against an alliance, he also conceded that the Ottoman Empire could side with the Entente if its proposal were rejected.[17]

Thus Said Halim and Enver had seized on the July Crisis as an opportunity to break out of the prolonged diplomatic isolation that had seemed like the mournful prelude to the empire's dismemberment. On July 24, when the kaiser received Wangenheim's telegram reporting his discussion with Enver, he wired an urgent reply to Istanbul the same night. The emperor was unequivocal: "Wangenheim must express himself to the Turks in regard to a connection with the Triple Alliance with unmistakably plain compliance, and receive their [requests] and report them! Under no circumstances can we afford to turn them away. A refusal or a snub would amount to her going over to Russo-Gallia, and our influence would be gone once and for all!"[18]

Wangenheim conveyed the kaiser's reaction to the grand vezir, and shortly thereafter, on July 27, Said Halim summoned Wangenheim and presented the terms of a "secret short-term German–Ottoman alliance directed against Russia." Said Halim would later claim that by "short-term" he had meant a duration of seven years, underscoring the Ottoman concern for long-term security. The *casus foederis* would become operative if Russia attacked either of the two signatory powers, or Germany's ally Austria-Hungary. The treaty would also be activated if Germany or a member of the Triple Alliance attacked Russia, a clause that was removed from the final version of the treaty, signed on August 2, by which point most of the treaty's terms had been overtaken by events. Instead, the German negotiators called for, and their Ottoman counterparts promised, immediate Ottoman action. Furthermore, Said Halim assured Wangenheim that the Porte did not expect protection against any power other than Russia. The treaty stipulated that in the event of war the German military mission would remain in the Ottoman Empire; the officers would take over the empire's general command as well as the direct command of one quarter of its troops. Berlin, therefore, could hope realistically to exercise military control over the entire Near East, save Egypt. Said Halim asked that all further negotiations be conducted in

---

[17] PA/AA, R 22402, Wangenheim to Auswärtiges Amt, July 23, 1914, no. 364. Also in Kautsky, *Outbreak*, no. 149.

[18] PA/AA, R 22402, Wedel to Auswärtiges Amt, July 24, 1914, no. 130. For the kaiser's marginalia, see PA/AA, R 1913, Jagow to Wilhelm, July 24, 1914, no. 122, and Kautsky, *Outbreak*, no. 149, whose translation is used here.

the strictest secrecy, insisting that even his colleagues in the cabinet as well as his ambassador at Berlin, Mahmud Muhtar Pasha, be excluded from the negotiations.[19] Throughout these talks of July 23–27, 1914, Wangenheim evidently became even less anxious about the possibility that the Ottomans, if rebuffed, would join the other side. Still opposing the alliance, he suggested to the Auswärtiges Amt that the Ottomans, if turned down, would probably seek an alliance with Bulgaria without Triple Alliance protection rather than go over to the Entente.[20]

Kaiser Wilhelm II was not about to take that risk. On July 28 Chancellor Bethmann Hollweg conveyed the kaiser's strong support for the grand vezir's proposal, and he instructed the baron to begin final negotiations based on a draft Bethmann had included. The secret agreement was to include the following five provisions. Point 1 called for both parties to maintain strict neutrality during the current crisis between Austria-Hungary and Serbia. Point 2 required the Ottoman Empire to take up arms against Russia if Russia attacked Austria-Hungary and thereby required Germany to enter the conflict on Austria-Hungary's side. Point 3 provided for the Liman mission to remain in the empire in the event of war and stipulated that the actual Ottoman high command be placed at the disposal of the military mission if the Porte entered the war. Point 4 stated that Germany committed itself to defend all current Ottoman territorial possessions against encroachments by Russia. Point 5, the only point the grand vezir would reject, limited the duration of the treaty to the duration of the current crisis between Austria-Hungary and Serbia.[21] This final point, to Said Halim, defeated the very purpose of the alliance, and it illustrated the difference between German and Ottoman strategy behind the treaty. Berlin thought of the alliance as a way to gain the upper hand during the July Crisis, while Istanbul perceived it as the road to long-term security by deterring attacks on the Ottoman Empire.

The grand vezir, therefore, immediately rejected Point 5 with the explanation that the "end" of the current conflict was not something that could ever be positively fixed. He also argued that Point 5 was unacceptable in any case because after the current crisis the empire would be left to face the wrath of the Triple Entente for having supported the Central Powers. When he had spoken of a "short-term" agreement,

[19] PA/AA, R 22402, Wangenheim to Auswärtiges Amt, July 27, 1914, no. 370. Also in Kautsky, *Outbreak*, no. 285.
[20] PA/AA, R 1913, Wangenheim to Auswärtiges Amt, July 27, 1914, no. 371. Also in Kautsky, *Outbreak*, no. 256.
[21] PA/AA, R 22402, Bethmann to Wangenheim, July 28, 1914, no. 275. Also in Kautsky, *Outbreak*, no. 320.

Said Halim explained, he had meant a seven-year treaty that would serve as a first step towards a long-term treaty. Thus he was willing to consent to a treaty running for the same duration as General Liman's contract, that is, until late 1918.[22] The Auswärtiges Amt accepted the grand vezir's amendment and recommended to Bethmann the immediate conclusion of an alliance effective until the end of 1918. Bethmann minuted in the margin: "Please notify grand vezir immediately that we accept duration of the treaty until 1918 as wished by the Porte, and that we are ready for immediate conclusion of the treaty."[23] On July 31, the Ottoman leaders kept up the pressure by venting their anxiety about the imminence of a Russian attack to Wangenheim. If a German–Ottoman alliance was not concluded right away, they might have no choice but to pre-empt the Russian attack by siding with the Entente. Wangenheim wrote that "[i]f we want to conclude with the Ottomans, it is high time to do so now. Otherwise we might have 300,000 Ottoman [troops] against rather than with us. General Liman has begun to doubt that the Ottoman Empire will declare itself for Germany."[24]

Said Halim and Enver had persuaded Berlin to sign an alliance treaty with the Ottoman Empire by suggesting they would otherwise be forced to side with the Entente. Their success was no doubt aided by Kaiser Wilhelm II's own vision of a worldwide Muslim revolution that would be inspired by the Ottoman sultan-caliph, orchestrated by Enver Pasha, and staged by the millions of colonized Muslim subjects in the empires of the Entente, from Morocco to India to Central Asia. Crucial to the Ottoman diplomatic achievement, however, was not the promise of an Islamic revolution but the promise of immediate, and substantial, military operations.

Throughout the German–Ottoman negotiations, Said Halim sought to put at ease the Entente's representatives in the capital. Meeting with Giers, he assured the Russian ambassador that the Porte would do everything in its power to stay out of the conflict embroiling Austria-Hungary and Serbia. Giers was not holding his breath; he surmised that the Ottomans would enter the war at the first opportunity for making gains, be it on the side of the Triple Alliance or on the side of the Triple

---

[22] PA/AA, R 22402, Wangenheim to Auswärtiges Amt, July 30, 1914, no. 385. Bethmann's marginalia are dated July 31, 1914. The text of the telegram, without Bethmann's marginalia, is reproduced in Kautsky, *Outbreak*, no. 411.

[23] PA/AA, R 22402, Wangenheim to Auswärtiges Amt, July 30, 1914, no. 385. Also in Kautsky, *Outbreak*, no. 411; PA/AA, R 1913, Bethmann to Wangenheim, July 31, 1914, no. 290.

[24] PA/AA, R 22402, Wangenheim to Auswärtiges Amt, July 31, 1914, no. 392. Also in Kautsky, *Outbreak*, no. 517.

Entente.[25] Giers was an experienced and insightful diplomat, and he immediately saw Austria-Hungary's harsh ultimatum for what it was: an effort to reverse Serbia's triumphs of the Balkan Wars. Giers supported strong Russian backing for Serbia. If Austria-Hungary emerged from the crisis victorious over Serbia, the entire Balkan peninsula would henceforth be dominated by the Central Powers. Such a shift would also pull in the Ottomans. To prevent such an outcome, Giers went so far as to suggest pre-emptive Russian action against its Ottoman neighbor. Germany and Austria-Hungary's success in the Balkans "will create such an unacceptable situation for us that the time is perhaps no longer distant when we ourselves, in order to find a way out, must take the initiative of war upon ourselves." Thus Giers saw an "urgent and absolute necessity to strengthen our Black Sea Fleet as rapidly as possible and to put our land forces into full combat readiness, so that the moment of our action, which could appear any time, does not surprise us and find us unprepared."[26] Had the *Goeben* and the *Breslau* not arrived in the Straits on August 10, providing for the defense of Istanbul, might the Russian Black Sea Fleet have made a grab for the Ottoman capital and the Straits region?

The signing of the German–Ottoman alliance, August 2, 1914

On August 1, 1914, Chancellor Bethmann Hollweg sent final authorization to his ambassador for the signing of a treaty of alliance with the Ottoman Empire. Bethmann included a single new condition. He instructed Wangenheim to sign the treaty only if the Ottoman forces would undertake significant military operations immediately, as Germany was declaring war on Russia the same day. To ascertain the extent of Ottoman military strength, Wangenheim was to consult Liman von Sanders and act according to the general's recommendation. "If General Liman is convinced," Bethmann wrote, "that in the event of war with Russia Turkey will take direct and significant action for us, Your Excellency is authorized to conclude the alliance treaty effective until 1918 with clause regarding extension."[27]

Wangenheim went to work immediately, meeting with both Liman and Enver. The two military leaders determined that the empire was able and

[25] *IBZI*, Series I, vol. 5, no. 78, Giers to Sazonov, July 25, 1914, 66; ibid., Series I, vol. 5, no. 439, Giers to Sazonov, August 1, 1914, 269.
[26] *IBZI*, Series I, vol. 5, no. 154, Giers to Sazonov, Highly Confidential, July 27, 1914, 125–6.
[27] PA/AA, R 22402, Bethmann to Wangenheim, August 1, 1914, no. 296. Also in Kautsky, *Outbreak*, no. 547. Compare with PA/AA, R 22402, Wangenheim to Auswärtiges Amt, July 30, 1914, no. 385, which is an earlier and slightly different version of the treaty.

willing to field an army against Russia, and Wangenheim acceded to their assessment.[28] In his report, the ambassador summarized the discussion in some detail. At the meeting, Liman had acknowledged that the precise form of Ottoman intervention turned on the course of action chosen by Bulgaria and Romania. If Bulgaria did not join the Central Powers, then the role of the Ottoman army would be to keep Bulgaria neutral. This caveat became crucial in the following weeks, as Bulgaria remained undecided and Berlin insisted on Ottoman entry nonetheless. According to Wangenheim, Liman and Enver agreed that the further concentration of troops along the Anatolian border with Russia would amount to little. Russia would not be sufficiently threatened by such forces, and thus would not draw away additional troops from the European theater. For Liman, Ottoman action needed to exert a direct impact on the eastern front of the war in Europe, where Russia was fighting Germany and Austria-Hungary. "Everything depends on the Ottoman forces attacking at the vital point," Wangenheim wrote about the military deliberations.[29] Such an attack on Russia could be launched only by way of Bulgaria and Romania, or an attack by sea.

The meeting between Liman and Enver on August 1 also opens a fascinating window on the famous story of the two German ships, the SMS *Goeben* and SMS *Breslau*, which escaped the hot pursuit of an Anglo-French fleet across the eastern Mediterranean. Wangenheim's report reveals that it was Enver Pasha who requested that the two warships join the Ottoman fleet in Istanbul, a request the German ambassador supported.[30] On August 3, Cemil Bey, the Ottoman military attaché in Berlin, had already informed Enver that he had learned from the Auswärtiges Amt "very confidentially" that Kaiser Wilhelm II might agree to send the *Goeben* to Istanbul and, subsequently, to send it "alongside the Ottoman navy into the Black Sea."[31] Wangenheim underscored the importance of Enver's request: "With the *Goeben*, even a landing on Russian territory would be possible. Romania and Bulgaria would at the same time be protected against a Russian invasion." Asked once again to evaluate Ottoman willingness to enter the war, Wangenheim replied that the Porte was ready to commit troops against Russia. The ambassador based his opinion on "the views of the Comité [the Committee of Union and Progress, the effective force behind the government] and the

---

[28] PA/AA, R 22402, Wangenheim to Auswärtiges Amt, August 2, 1914, no. 407.
[29] Ibid. (Emphasis in original.)
[30] PA/AA, R 22402, Wangenheim to Auswärtiges Amt, August 2, 1914, no. 407.
[31] ATASE, BDH, Klasör 243, Yeni Dosya 1009, Fihrist 7–2, Cemil to Enver, August 3, 1914.

important ministers." He qualified his assessment only slightly: "I cannot, of course, accept any responsibility for what the Ottoman Empire would do if the Triple Alliance was decisively defeated," but, he concluded, "I am in agreement with Liman, and I find that the requirements for signing the treaty are fulfilled. I will therefore probably sign today."[32] He added that Liman had informed him about an understanding with Enver according to which "actual Ottoman military command" would be transferred to the officers of the German military mission.[33] Despite some personal misgivings about the alliance and Ottoman military capacity, the ambassador signed the alliance on August 2, 1914: "Alliance treaty signed this afternoon at four o'clock. Text to follow. Wangenheim."[34] Shortly thereafter, Liman issued orders for mobilization to the seventy-one members of the German military mission in Istanbul.[35]

Berlin had signed the alliance treaty in exchange for an Ottoman pledge to stage significant military operations against either Russia or British-held Egypt more or less immediately. The individual making the pledge was War Minister Enver Pasha, and throughout the following three months he would repeat the promise on several occasions. Over the same period, however, he would also provide explanations to his German allies as to why such immediate entry could not yet be realized.

Alliance and mobilization

With the Habsburg declaration of war on Serbia on July 28, 1914, Enver had taken a number of military measures even before the signing of the German alliance. He had ordered detachments from the First Army Corps to the northern end of the Bosporus, at Midhat Çiftliği and Zekeriya Köyü. Additional units were to be armed and replenished with reserves to meet wartime requirements, and torpedo boats were to ready for action at the northern end of the Bosporus.[36] Enver issued mobilization orders on August 1, with August 3 as the first day of mobilization.[37] The cabinet endorsed Enver's mobilization orders the next day, on

[32] PA/AA, R 22402, Wangenheim to Auswärtiges Amt, August 2, 1914, no. 407.
[33] PA/AA, R 22402, Wangenheim to Auswärtiges Amt, August 2, 1914, no. 409. Also in Kautsky, *Outbreak*, no. 733.
[34] PA/AA, R 1913, Wangenheim to Auswärtiges Amt, August 2, 1914, no. 408. Reproduced in Kautsky, *Outbreak*, no. 726.
[35] ATASE, BDH, Klasör 63, Yeni Dosya 316, Fihrist 4 to 4–2, Liman to All Members of the Military Mission, August 2, 1914.
[36] BOA, A.VRK 791–87, War Minister Enver to Grand Vezir, 5 Ramazan 1332 and 15 Temmuz 1330 (July 28, 1914).
[37] BOA, A.VRK 791–97, War Minister Enver to the Grand Vezir, 9 Ramazan 1332 and 19 Temmuz 1330 (August 1, 1914). In fact, the Bolayır battalion by Gallipoli received

August 2,[38] and Sultan Mehmed Reşad V issued an imperial decree authorizing the cabinet's decision.[39] In the Black Sea, the Russian navy stopped and searched Ottoman ships on August 3, but during the following weeks it stayed clear of Ottoman vessels and was sighted only occasionally, at points off the coast at Ereğli and Sinop.[40] The cabinet declared martial law,[41] and it prorogued the Ottoman legislative body, the chamber of deputies.[42]

With the alliance in place, Enver expanded his powers as commander-in-chief.[43] He informed the grand vezir of the establishment of a General Headquarters on August 2, the day the alliance was signed. The new office, headed by Enver, would henceforth carry out several of the responsibilities formerly discharged by various ministries of the government. Among the most far-reaching of these duties was the handling of correspondence with foreign states, which became subject to approval by General Headquarters when not conducted by it directly.[44]

From Berlin, Military Attaché Cemil Bey reported meetings with Chief of the General Staff Moltke and War Minister Erich von Falkenhayn. For now, Cemil Bey had good news. According to his German colleagues, Greece would not actively support Serbia, and Romania would "definitely" join the Central Powers, eventually. Russia had withdrawn an army corps

mobilization orders as early as July 31, 1914, see ATASE, BDH, Klasör 4611, Yeni Dosya 9, Fihrist 6–1, 18 Temmuz 1330 (July 31, 1914); see also ATASE, BDH, Klasör 4611, Yeni Dosya 9, Fihrist 11, 13, 13–1, and 13–2 for additional orders.

[38] BOA, MV 236–17, 10 Ramazan 332 and 20 Temmuz 1330 (August 2, 1914). This document is a draft copy of the cabinet's decision and bears no signatures. Also *IBZI*, Series I, vol. 5, no. 441, Leontiev to Danilov, August 1, 1914, 270; ibid., Series I, vol. 5, no. 478, Giers to Sazonov, August 2, 1914, 291, and ibid., Series I, vol. 5, no. 508, Giers to Sazonov, August 3, 1914, 303–4, where Giers reports on his meeting with Said Halim, who explains Ottoman mobilization plans.

[39] BOA, BEO.NGG 236, Harbiye Gelen, 322677, Grand Vezir to War Ministry, Navy Ministry, and Interior Ministry, 20 Temmuz 1330 (August 2, 1914).

[40] ATASE, BDH, Klasör 508, Yeni Dosya 1986, Fihrist 1–12 (22 Temmuz 1330, August 4, 1914), 1–14 (25 Temmuz 1330, August 7, 1914), 2–11 (24 Temmuz 1330, August 6, 1914), 2–25 (18 Ağustos 1330, September 1, 1914), 2–26 (19 Ağustos 1330, September 2, 1914), 2–27 (19 Ağustos 1330, September 2, 1914), 2–33 (24 Ağustos 1330, September 5, 1914).

[41] BOA, MV 236–16, 10 Ramazan 1332 and 20 Temmuz 1330 (August 2, 1914). This document is a draft copy of the cabinet's decision and bears no signatures. See also the grand vezir's communication of this decision in BOA, BEO.NGG 236, Harbiye Gelen, 322677, Grand Vezir to War Ministry and to Interior Ministry, 20 Temmuz 1330 (August 2, 1914).

[42] The chamber of deputies convened for the last time on August 2, 1914, see *MMZC*, 20 Temmuz 1330. It reconvened on December 14, 1914.

[43] Enver Pasha's new title was Deputy Commander-in-Chief (*Başkumandan Vekili*), in deference to the supreme, but nominal, Commander-in-Chief, the Ottoman sultan.

[44] BOA, A.VRK 791–101, Deputy Commander-in-Chief Enver to the Grand Vezir, 10 Ramazan 1332 and 20 Temmuz 1330 (August 2, 1914).

from the Caucasus to the European theater. In addition, Berlin was sending munitions for the Ottoman army.[45]

Ottoman military planners also hoped to reinforce the navy with Austro-Hungarian and German ships. On August 3, Enver asked the grand vezir to place such a request through the German and Habsburg embassies: "In order to prepare for war, the Ottoman army is in definite need of a great number of vessels in addition to Ottoman vessels. Therefore, the Austro-Hungarian and German embassies shall be contacted for the use of their vessels currently in Ottoman waters and the Sea of Marmara for the purpose of transporting Ottoman troops."[46] In a "very confidential and urgent note," Enver instructed the commander of the southern Dardanelles to permit entry into the Straits to any "German and Austro-Hungarian warship."[47] Any such ships admitted into the Straits were authorized to proceed northward towards the capital.[48]

On August 8 Ahmed Reşid Bey, the foreign ministry's political affairs director, informed the grand vezir that the German embassy had authorized all but three of the German vessels currently in Ottoman waters to be handed over to military authorities.[49] Vienna was less obliging, stating simply that no Austro-Hungarian vessels were available for Ottoman mobilization efforts at the time.[50]

Aided by the provisions of martial law, Enver sought to concentrate the government's executive powers in the office of General Headquarters. Said Halim nevertheless attempted to counter Enver's grip on power by demanding that all important decisions taken by General Headquarters still be submitted to deliberation by the full cabinet. The ensuing tension

[45] ATASE, BDH, Klasör 243, Yeni Dosya 1009, Fihrist 4, Cemil Bey to War Ministry, Very Confidential, 21 Temmuz 1330 (August 3, 1914).

[46] BOA, BEO.NGG 171, Hariciye Gelen, 322697, War Ministry to the Grand Vezir, 11 Ramazan 1332 and 21 Temmuz 1330 (August 3, 1914).

[47] ATASE, BDH, Klasör 4611, Yeni Dosya 10, Fihrist 4, 1–4, Enver to the Commander of the Southern Dardanelles, Very Confidential and Urgent, 22 Temmuz 1330 (August 4, 1914); and ATASE, BDH, Klasör 4611, Yeni Dosya 10, Fihrist 1–61, Very Confidential, 22 Temmuz 1330 (August 4, 1914).

[48] ATASE, BDH, Klasör 4611, Yeni Dosya 10, Fihrist 1–5, Commander of the Southern Straits to the Office of the Commander-in-Chief, 22 Temmuz 1330 (August 4, 1914), and Enver to Commander of the Southern Straits, 22 Temmuz 1330 (August 4, 1914).

[49] BOA, BEO.NGG 171, Hariciye Gelen, 322697, Grand Vezir to the Foreign Ministry, 11 Ramazan 1332 and 21 Temmuz 1330 (August 3, 1914); BOA, BEO.NGG 236, Harbiye Gelen, 322746, Foreign Ministry to the Grand Vezir, 15 [sic] Ramazan 1332 and 26 Temmuz 1330 (August 8, 1914), and Grand Vezir to War Ministry, 16 Ramazan 1332 and 26 Temmuz 1330 (August 8, 1914).

[50] BOA, BEO.NGG 236, Harbiye Gelen, 322761, Foreign Ministry to the Grand Vezir, 17 Ramazan 1332 and 27 Temmuz 1330 (August 9, 1914); BOA, BEO.NGG 236, Harbiye Gelen, 322794, Grand Vezir to the Deputy Commander-in-Chief, 19 Ramazan 1332 and 29 Temmuz 1330 (August 11, 1914).

is reflected in the correspondence between the commander-in-chief and the grand vezir. On August 3, without consulting the cabinet or the grand vezir, Enver ordered the immediate closure and mining of the southern end of the Dardanelles (*Bahr-i Sefid*), and the northern end of the Bosporus (*Bahr-i Siyah*),[51] leaving only secret passages for friendly vessels.[52]

Since the Berlin Congress of 1878, international law had effectively closed the Straits to all non-Ottoman military vessels. The Straits consist of two narrow waterways, separated by the Sea of Marmara. The northern one, the Bosporus, connects the Sea of Marmara to the Black Sea. The southern one, the Dardanelles, connects the Sea of Marmara with the Aegean and the Mediterranean seas. Merchant vessels of any flag, however, were guaranteed free passage through the Straits.[53] As we have seen, Russian industrialization and modernization depended on the hard currency that agricultural exports brought to the country, as 90 percent of Russia's grain trade and a full 50 percent of all its exports made their way to market via the Black Sea and the Straits.[54] The closure of the Straits thus posed a profound threat to the Russian economy. By August 5, the Straits had been mined.[55] When Said Halim questioned Enver's orders, the war minister retorted that, as commander-in-chief, he was authorized to close the Straits at any time upon his personal judgement.[56] Said Halim objected, insisting that something as significant as the closure of the Straits, other than in the event of war, remained a question to be determined only by a comprehensive cabinet decision.[57] After all, the decision to close the Straits entirely was bound to have a profound impact on Ottoman relations with Russia, which would consider it a provocation on the part of an ostensibly neutral power.

---

[51] ATASE, BDH, Klasör 87, Yeni Dosya 448D, Fihrist 2–1, 21 Temmuz 1330 (August 3, 1914) for Enver's order; BOA, BEO.NGG 40, Bahriye Gelen, 322698, Deputy Commander-in-Chief Enver to the Grand Vezir, 11 Ramazan 1332 and 21 Temmuz 1330 (August 3, 1914). Also see the navy minister's communication that the Straits have successfully been mined and the light buoys extinguished, Ibid., Navy Minister Ahmed Cemal to the Grand Vezir, 22 Temmuz 1330 (August 4, 1914), and ATASE, BDH, Klasör 87, Yeni Dosya 450, Fihrist 2–2, 21 Temmuz 1330 (August 3, 1914).

[52] ATASE, BDH, Klasör 87, Yeni Dosya 450, Fihrist 18–2, Şevki to Deputy Commander-in-Chief, 21 Temmuz 1330 (August 3, 1914); ibid., BDH, Klasör 87, Yeni Dosya 450, Fihrist 18–7, Cevad to Deputy Commander-in-Chief, 2 Ağustos 1330 (August 15, 1914).

[53] The Sublime Porte, The Ministry of Foreign Affairs, *Boğazlar Meselesi* [The Straits Question] (Istanbul: Matbaa-i Amire, 1334 [1918]), 32–4.

[54] Rich, *Great Power Diplomacy, 1814–1914*, 425.

[55] ATASE, BDH, Klasör 87, Yeni Dosya 450, Fihrist 2–3 to 2–6, 2–9.

[56] BOA, BEO.NGG 237, Harbiye Giden, 322947, Deputy Commander-in-Chief Enver to the Grand Vezir, 27 Ramazan 1332 and 6 Ağustos 1330 (August 19, 1914).

[57] BOA, BEO.NGG 237, Harbiye Giden, 322947, Grand Vezir to War Ministry, 7 Ağustos 1330 (August 20, 1914).

Nevertheless, Said Halim put a good face on a bad situation, explaining to the Russian ambassador that it was indeed the cabinet that had decided both on the declaration of strict neutrality and on the mining of the Bosporus and the Dardanelles with passage-ways open to friendly merchant ships. For his part, Giers ascribed the mining of the Straits to the scheming of the German military mission, and he regarded it as evidence of a German plan to drag the Ottomans into war. Giers warned St. Petersburg that the Russian Black Sea Fleet must not engage in any activity that might be interpreted as hostile. Otherwise, according to Giers, the Ottomans might panic and close the Straits completely, or worse, take action against Russian forces.[58]

Once the war was afoot, Enver ordered the requisitioning of foreign, mainly Russian, merchandise docked in Ottoman ports, including Russian oil and foodstuffs. Not only the Russian embassy,[59] but initially even the Ottoman foreign ministry objected.[60] The navy ministry, too, disclaimed any responsibility for these seizures, stating that it had not requisitioned any freight belonging to foreign companies.[61] Nor was the war ministry technically responsible. It was Enver's commissions for war tax (*teklif-i harb komisyonları*), a special wartime agency, that had carried out the seizures.[62] Enver claimed such measures were prescribed by Ottoman law and were thus perfectly legitimate under the present state of mobilization and extraordinary circumstances.[63] Talat, at the interior ministry, took a similar position.[64] Enver argued that foreigners living in the empire were subject to "war taxes in order to secure our homeland's

---

[58] *IBZI*, Series I, vol. 5, no. 557, Giers to Sazonov, August 4, 1914, 322; *BDOW*, vol. 11, no. 586, Beaumont to Grey, August 3, 1914, 311–12.

[59] BOA, BEO.NGG 236, Harbiye Gelen, 322765, Foreign Ministry to the Grand Vezir, 17 Ramazan 1332 and 27 Temmuz 1330 (August 9, 1914); BOA, BEO.NGG 236, Harbiye Gelen, 322883, Political Director of the Foreign Ministry Ahmed Reşid to the Grand Vezir, 22 Ramazan 1332 and 2 August 1332 (August 15, 1914); BOA, BEO.NGG 172, Hariciye Gelen, 322945, Political Director of the Foreign Ministry Ahmed Reşid to the Grand Vezir, 27 [sic] Ramazan 1332 and 7 August 1330 (August 20, 1914); BOA, BEO. NGG 236, Harbiye Gelen, 322977, Political Director of the Foreign Ministry Ahmed Reşid to the Grand Vezir, 5 Şevval 1332 and 14 August 1330 (August 27, 1914).

[60] BOA, BEO.NGG 236, Harbiye Gelen, 322765, Foreign Ministry to the Grand Vezir, 13 Ramazan 1332 and 23 Temmuz 1330 (August 5, 1914).

[61] BOA, BEO.NGG 50, Bahriye Giden, 322825, Navy Minister to the Grand Vezir, 27 Temmuz 1330 (August 9, 1914); ibid., Navy Minister to the Grand Vezir, 30 Temmuz 1332 (August 12, 1914).

[62] BOA, BEO.NGG 50, Bahriye Giden, 322825, War Minister to the Grand Vezir, 30 Temmuz 1330 (August 12, 1914).

[63] BOA, BEO 322999, War Minister to the Grand Vezir, 5 Şevval 1332 and 13 August 1330 (August 26, 1914).

[64] BOA, BEO 322956, Interior Ministry to the Grand Vezir, 28 Ramazan 1332 and 7 August 1330 (August 20, 1914).

defense [*müdafaa-i vatanın selâmetini temin için*]" – never mind that the Ottomans had not yet declared war. Enver added that "the duties and sacrifices required [by war] do not apply only to Ottoman citizens," but to the entire population, citizens and non-citizens alike.[65] Soon thereafter, the cabinet concurred with Enver's argument and ruled legitimate the collection war taxes from non-Ottoman citizens for the sake of the nation's security. In its deliberation of the question, the cabinet pointed to similar policies implemented by the Entente governments in recent days.[66]

These Ottoman requisitions had been most heavily influenced by the British decision on August 1 to confiscate the warships *Sultan Osman* and *Reşadiye*, ships that the Porte had ordered and paid for. In fact, in late July a crew had arrived in London with the intention of taking charge of the ships and piloting them back to Istanbul. Whereas Enver responded with confiscations of his own, as we have seen, Navy Minister Cemal Pasha initially, on August 4, favored responding with a diplomatic protest, demanding return of the full amount paid, 5 million Ottoman pounds, plus 1 million Ottoman pounds in damages.[67] (Later, as we shall see, Berlin granted the Porte a loan of over 5 million Ottoman pounds as the final incentive for intervention.) The cabinet had endorsed Cemal's proposal and passed a formal decision to that effect,[68] but Enver's unilateral action effectively overrode the cabinet's decision. The Russian government responded to the requisitions by detaining Ottoman citizens in Russian ports and preventing them from returning to the empire; in Batum over a thousand Ottomans awaited permission to leave the country.[69] The Ottoman government also worried about its ships in Mediterranean ports, exposed to attack by British naval forces. As early as August 9, the Porte issued warnings to the commanders to take precautions for the safety of their vessels since "the possibility of war with England is not unlikely."[70]

---

[65] BOA, BEO.NGG 50, Bahriye Giden, 322825, Deputy Commander-in-Chief Enver to the Grand Vezir, 13 Ramazan 1332 and 23 Temmuz 1330 (August 5, 1914).

[66] BOA, MV 191–27, 20 Ramazan 1332 and 30 Temmuz 1330 (August 12, 1914), carrying the signatures of nine cabinet members, including those of Enver and Said Halim. An official Ottoman protest was submitted only after the Ottoman entry into the war, see BOA, BEO.NGG, 172, Hariciye Gelen, 324407, 1 Kanun-i Evvel 1330/25 Muharrem 1333 (December 14, 1914). For a discussion of Russian measures, see Eric Lohr, *Nationalizing the Russian Empire: The Campaign against Enemy Aliens during World War I* (Cambridge, MA: Harvard University Press, 2003), 1–30.

[67] BOA, BEO.NGG 40, Bahriye Gelen, 322782, Navy Ministry to the Grand Vezir, 22 Temmuz 1330 (August 4, 1914).

[68] BOA, MV 191–22, 17 Ramazan 1332 and 27 Temmuz 1330 (August 9, 1914).

[69] BOA, BEO.NGG 236, Harbiye Gelen, 322841, Foreign Ministry to the Grand Vezir, 21 Ramazan 1332 and 31 Temmuz 1330 (August 13, 1914).

[70] ATASE, BDH, Klasör 87, Yeni Dosya 450, Fihrist 13, 27 Temmuz 1330 (August 9, 1914), Levazımat-ı Müdüriyeti Riyaset-i Aliyesi'ne.

Like Wangenheim, General Liman von Sanders also reported on the signing of the alliance and its prospects. Writing General Helmuth von Moltke, the chief of the general staff, about his meeting with Enver on August 1, he outlined exactly what the war minister had promised in military terms. One hundred and twenty thousand troops would be massed at Edirne for joint action with Bulgarian forces against Russia. These troops would be ready for action on the thirtieth day of mobilization, that is, on September 1. Romania's support for such an operation would be essential, however, as a joint Bulgarian–Ottoman campaign against Russia would have to cross Romanian territory. A second Ottoman army of 90,000 troops would be massed south of Edirne for action against either Greece or Russia. This second army required sixty days of mobilization to get ready. Five further Ottoman divisions would be headquartered along the Ottoman–Russian border in eastern Anatolia.[71]

The arrival of the SMS *Goeben* and the SMS *Breslau*

The events on the western front were yet to unfold when Enver made the request that became one of the war's most notorious episodes: the dispatch of the German battleship SMS *Goeben* to Istanbul. Like Wangenheim, Liman supported Enver's request and on August 2 wrote to Berlin that the "transfer of the *Goeben* is highly desired here to bring the very passive Ottoman fleet to action and to paralyze the Russian Black Sea Fleet. A free hand in the Black Sea is of the greatest importance for all operations [on land]."[72] The German navy ministry granted Liman's request immediately, informing the *Goeben*'s captain, Admiral Wilhelm Souchon, of the new alliance by radio and instructing him to go to Istanbul right away.[73] Meanwhile, the news of an ostensibly secret German–Ottoman alliance reached St. Petersburg with remarkable speed. Already on August 2, at 9.08 a.m., Commander of the Russian Naval Forces in the Black Sea Eberhardt informed his navy ministry: "From an intercepted telegram. Turkey has declared full mobilization and has joined our enemies."[74]

On the eve of the war, the Russian Black Sea Fleet was still considered superior to the Ottoman navy, but Istanbul had been rebuilding its naval forces and catching up rapidly. It had added two German warships of an older model to its fleet in 1910 and ordered two dreadnoughts from British companies in August 1911, with a delivery time of three years.

[71] PA/AA, R 1913, Wangenheim to Auswärtiges Amt, August 2, 1914, no. 406.
[72] Ibid.   [73] BA-MA, RM 40 – 455, Tirpitz to Souchon, August 3, 1914.
[74] *IBZI*, Series I, vol. 5, no. 516, Grigorovich to Sazonov, August 3, 1914, 306–7, relaying Eberhardt's telegram of August 2, 1914.

Russian military leaders were alarmed, and they warned of the grave dangers that resulted from losing mastery over the Black Sea. Persuaded, the Duma authorized the launching of a naval program in June 1912 that provided for a major expansion of the naval forces in the Black Sea. The expansion was premised on the formula to afford the Russian fleet superiority one and a half times that of the Ottoman fleet.[75]

The signing of the German–Ottoman alliance on August 2 followed the Austro-Hungarian declaration of war on Serbia on July 28 and the German declaration of war on Russia on August 1. Liman pressed Enver for immediate and active contribution to the Central Powers' war efforts. Fully aware that no Ottoman forces were ready for battle and that both the German and the Austro-Hungarian ambassadors actually opposed entry at this point, Enver claimed to support Liman's call for immediate intervention nonetheless. This was a mere gesture; Enver did not yet issue any orders for an attack. Unable to see through Enver's intentions, Wangenheim wrote to Berlin that "Enver and Liman want to declare war on Russia immediately in order to confiscate three valuable Russian steamers with wireless equipment here [in Istanbul]. The grand vezir and I are opposed to it." Continuing to advise against intervention himself, the German ambassador pointed to the incomplete state of mobilization. He also reminded the Auswärtiges Amt that Sofia had not yet committed itself to action, and he speculated that if the Ottomans declared war, Britain would confiscate the warship *Sultan Osman*, already behind its scheduled delivery date of August 1, and a second warship, the *Reşadiye*, to be delivered shortly thereafter. The baron concluded that, in any event, German headquarters should instruct Liman right away whether to take military action. That same day, on August 3, the Porte declared its armed neutrality during the current war.[76] Almost immediately after the Ottomans learned that the two British ships were being confiscated, news reached the capital that the Greek government had succeeded in purchasing two battleships from the United States, the USS *Idaho* and the USS *Mississippi*, which were transferred to the Greek navy and renamed *Kilkis* and *Limnos*,[77] pouring salt on the wound created by the British action.

---

[75] Republic of Turkey, Chief of the General Staff, *Deniz Harekâtı*, vol. VIII, by Saim Besbelli, *Birinci Dünya Harbi'nde Türk Harbi* (Ankara: Genelkurmay Basım Evi, 1976), 36–42; Halpern, *Mediterranean Naval Situation*, 298–9, 304, 316–17, and *A Naval History of World War I* (Annapolis: Naval Institute Press, 1994), 223–5.

[76] PA/AA, R 22402, Wangenheim to Auswärtiges Amt, August 3, 1914, no. 416. Also in Kautsky, *Outbreak*, no. 795.

[77] Halpern, *Mediterranean Naval Situation*, 351–2.

Despite their eager embrace of the German alliance, the Ottoman leaders were intent on postponing intervention for as long as possible. Initially they succeeded in doing so mainly by exploiting Berlin's fears of their defection to the Entente side. In playing this game, they also received support from Ambassador Wangenheim. Unlike Liman and the Auswärtiges Amt, Wangenheim believed that intervention would not benefit Germany. He did not have much faith in the Ottoman military – not an unreasonable view given its performance in the Balkan Wars – and thus he thought it would not be able to hold its own in battle against the forces of a Great Power. Berlin read the situation differently. Foreign Secretary Jagow warned Wangenheim on August 4 that Britain was on the verge of declaring war on Germany and that an immediate Ottoman declaration of war on Russia seemed necessary for that reason alone. Jagow feared that the British entry into the war could propel Istanbul into the camp of the Entente.[78]

The Ottomans, and Said Halim in particular, fueled these fears in the attempt to strengthen their bargaining power *vis-à-vis* Germany. Meeting with Wangenheim on August 4, Said Halim alluded to friendly assurances held out to his government by Maurice Bompard, the French ambassador, and Giers, his Russian counterpart. The grand vezir assured Wangenheim that his government was not considering seriously such approaches, especially since they stipulated the dismissal of the German military mission. Said Halim also mentioned that Giers appeared to believe in the authenticity of the Ottoman statement of neutrality, announced the previous day, August 3. Having sufficiently rattled the German ambassador – by speaking of Entente-courting and evoking the dismissal of the Liman mission – Said Halim made an urgent case for maintaining the appearance of armed neutrality. Without it, according to the grand vezir, both the use of the Black Sea fleet and mobilization efforts more generally would be severely undermined.[79] These remarks, intended for an audience in Berlin, were the result of astute calculation; they mollified the German objections to the Porte's declaration of neutrality. At the same time, Said Halim assured his allies that he put the alliance with Germany ahead of all other diplomatic considerations.

Thus Said Halim made it clear to Berlin that at the heart of the Entente's demands stood the removal of the German military mission. This point was intended to restrain General Liman von Sanders, whose

---

[78] PA/AA, R 22402, Jagow to [Embassy at] Pera, August 4, 1914, no. 313. Also in Kautsky, *Outbreak*, no. 836. England declared war on Germany on August 4, 1914.

[79] PA/AA, R 22402, Wangenheim to Auswärtiges Amt, August 4, 1914, no. 423. Also in Kautsky, *Outbreak*, no. 854.

continued, and increasingly angry, insistence on immediate intervention had become difficult to manage. In fact, the general would eventually go so far as to request the military mission's recall over the issue of continued Ottoman neutrality.[80] The grand vezir hoped his comments would lead Berlin to urge patience on Liman. The general's rash conduct in dealing with the Ottoman authorities, Berlin had reason to assume, might convince Said Halim to grant Liman his wish and dismiss the mission after all. With the mission out of Istanbul, the empire would be free to take up Bompard and Giers on their promises of Entente protection. Instead, Said Halim implied, Berlin ought to consider, and appreciate, the benefits of Ottoman neutrality.[81] The grand vezir's tactics worked, and Berlin instructed Liman to exercise patience and to respect Ottoman neutrality for the time being.

For Said Halim and his colleagues the gravity of the situation intensified after the arrival of a cable from Tevfik Pasha, the Ottoman ambassador at London, on 4 August. Jagow's alarm as to the potential effect of a British entry into the war had not been amiss. Tevfik now reported that London had ordered general mobilization and that it was joining its allies in the fight against the Central Powers.[82] With the *Goeben* steaming for the Dardanelles it would be difficult to preserve neutrality once the German ships joined the Ottoman navy. Said Halim informed Wangenheim that the squadron led by the *Goeben*, whose dispatch had been requested by Enver and Said Halim on August 1, would not be permitted to enter the Straits until an alliance treaty had been signed with Bulgaria. Whether Said Halim was acting on his own accord, and undercutting Enver, remains unknown. With the Entente in hot pursuit of the *Goeben*, the grand vezir used that critical moment to bring about a decision in Sofia. He explained to Wangenheim that the prolonged uncertainty about Bulgaria's course of action made it impossible for the Sublime Porte to admit the squadron into the Straits. Hostile powers might regard the entry of the ships as the end of Ottoman neutrality. It could offer the pretext, for example, for a Bulgarian attack from Thrace backed by Russia. Sofia had evaded alliance negotiations, Said Halim fumed, despite Pallavicini's full assurances that it would join the Central Powers, and thus it could not be fully trusted. The grand vezir now demanded that Berlin force Sofia's

---

[80] PA/AA, R 22402, [German Deputy Foreign Secretary] Zimmermann to Jagow, August 20, 1914, no. 23.

[81] PA/AA, R 22402, Wangenheim to Auswärtiges Amt, August 4, 1914, no. 423. Also in Kautsky, *Outbreak*, no. 854.

[82] BOA, A.VRK 792–2, Navy Minister to the Grand Vezir, 22 Temmuz 1330 (August 4, 1914), reports Tevfik Pasha's telegram of August 2, 1914. Britain declared war on Germany the same day.

hand. Otherwise, his government would have no choice but to suspect foul play and to prepare for a Bulgarian attack as soon as the German ships arrived. The grand vezir also admonished Wangenheim for Romanian fence-sitting; the Bucharest government, too, had not been open to alliance negotiations as the grand vezir had been led to expect by Berlin. Short of a Bulgarian–Ottoman alliance, Said Halim told Wangenheim, he could not support all the articles of the alliance with Germany, and he would have to resign as a consequence. Finally, he promised to authorize the ships' entry into the Straits as soon as a Bulgarian–Ottoman alliance was signed.[83] Quite clearly, then, Said Halim, sought to exploit the July Crisis for maximum effect. He not only pursued the alliance with Germany, through which the Ottomans hoped to gain international security after the war, but also a Balkan alliance to secure the empire's western borders that had been the site of such devastating wars so recently.

The Ottoman excuse for not allowing the German ships' entry was a plausible one. Both Wangenheim and Pallavicini endorsed Said Halim's insistence on the Bulgarian guarantee. The German ambassador wired the Auswärtiges Amt that the ships' entry into the Straits would be seen as an Ottoman declaration of war on the Entente, and that therefore it was more than reasonable for Istanbul to insist on the Bulgarian alliance prior to allowing entry to the ships. If Sofia could not be won over, Wangenheim suggested in cold calculation, Berlin should promise the Ottomans territorial gains in Bulgarian Thrace.[84]

Yet the Ottoman excuse was no more than that. As we shall see, there is evidence that the Sublime Porte itself sought to prevent the conclusion of a Bulgarian–Ottoman alliance, as both powers preferred to stay out of the war while preserving their association with the Central Powers.

On August 10, the German squadron did enter the Straits – without, however, a Bulgarian–Ottoman alliance or the grand vezir's resignation.[85] Said Halim had asked Wangenheim for a midnight meeting, around 1 a.m. on August 6, in order to discuss the situation of the portless ships outside the Straits. The grand vezir explained that the cabinet had held an extensive meeting – although no records of this meeting on the evening of August 5 have turned up in the papers of the cabinet, the Meclis-i Vükelâ, and it is unlikely that all cabinet members were privy to it – and had "unanimously" decided to allow the ships into the Straits under the following six conditions:

---

[83] PA/AA, R 1913, Wangenheim to Auswärtiges Amt, August 4, 1914, no. 429.
[84] PA/AA, R 1913, Wangenheim to Auswärtiges Amt, August 6, 1914, no. 437.
[85] ATASE, BDH, Klasör 244, Yeni Dosya 1012, Fihrist 17, Commander of the Southern Dardanelles to War Ministry, 29 Temmuz 1330 (August 11, 1914).

(1) Germany must support the abrogation of the capitulations.

(2) Germany must support Ottoman negotiations with Bulgaria and Romania and must see to it that the Ottoman Empire receive its fair share when dividing war spoils with Bulgaria.

(3) Germany must not conclude any peace until all Ottoman territory had been liberated from enemy occupation resulting from the current war.[86]

(4) In the case of Greek intervention and Greek defeat, Germany must support the return of the Aegean islands to the Ottoman Empire.

(5) Germany must secure a small border change in eastern Anatolia that would allow for direct contact with the Russian Muslims there.

(6) Germany must procure appropriate reparations to be paid to the Ottoman Empire.

Wangenheim accepted the new demands, reasoning that doing so would be binding only in the event that Germany gained "absolute control over European affairs" at the end of the war.[87] Shortly after his meeting with Said Halim, Wangenheim saw Enver, who took personal and full credit for the cabinet's decision; whether Wangenheim felt gratitude is doubtful, however. Enver requested that the squadron enter the Dardanelles early in the morning, remain in the Sea of Marmara, and then proceed through the Bosporus at dusk.[88]

---

[86] There is nothing here that indicates that "Ottoman territory" meant anything beyond the current boundaries of the Ottoman Empire, i.e. it did not refer to any lost territories in the Balkans (1912/13), North Africa (1911), or elsewhere. Point 5, however, seems to refer directly to territory lost to Russia in 1877–8: Ardahan, Batum, and Kars.

[87] PA/AA, R 22402, Wangenheim to Auswärtiges Amt, August 6, 1914, no. 438. Perhaps Wangenheim did not realize that the Ottomans were serious about implementing their first condition, the abrogation of the capitulations, in the near future. When the Ottomans did in fact declare the capitulations abrogated on September 9, 1914, Wangenheim decried it as a ploy of the Entente. He claimed that the Entente had supported Said Halim in this declaration, based on the calculation that the Ottomans would join the Entente in the current war in exchange. The Entente could afford to support the abrogation, according to Wangenheim, since the Entente powers would partition the Ottoman Empire in case of an Entente victory, and, conversely, enjoy no rights or privileges in the event of an Entente defeat in any case. Wangenheim did not so much object to the financial implications of abolishing the capitulations, as to the legal ones. He could not imagine how the Europeans could continue their political and commercial activities under Ottoman law and without special legal protection. The Auswärtiges Amt instructed Wangenheim *not* to protest the Ottoman declaration or take any other measure that would antagonize the Ottomans. See BA-B, R 901/25150, Wangenheim to Auswärtiges Amt, September 9, 1914, no. 765; BA-B, R 901/25150, Wangenheim to Auswärtiges Amt, September 10, 1914, no. 768; BA-B, R 901/25150, Zimmermann to Wangenheim, September 11, 1914, no. 663; *IBZI*, Series II, vol. 6/1, no. 244, Giers to Sazonov, Urgent, Copies to Bordeaux and London, September 10, 1914, 183–4.

[88] PA/AA, R 22402, Wangenheim to Auswärtiges Amt, August 6, 1914, no. 438; ATASE, BDH, Klasör 4611, Yeni Dosya 10, Fihrist 1–22, Enver to the Commander of the Southern Dardanelles, Urgent, 24/25 Temmuz 1330 (August 6/7, 1914).

During the first few days following the signing of the German–Ottoman alliance, Ottoman statesmen had managed to stay out of the war without jeopardizing the alliance. At the same time, the German government, through the chief of the military mission, General Liman von Sanders, had pressed the Ottoman leaders for an immediate declaration of war on Russia. Liman was told that intervention, despite Enver's stated commitment to it, was impossible for the moment because of the military's unreadiness and the uncertainty surrounding Bulgaria's course of action. Said Halim pledged his good faith, and he proposed a four-power defensive alliance consisting of Bulgaria, Greece, the Ottoman Empire, and Romania. He suggested that Germany's mediation would be necessary for its conclusion, and that the outcome would be a neutral bloc in the Balkans completely isolating Serbia.[89] From Istanbul's view, this scenario offered the Ottomans security within the international system without intervention, a strategic objective that would remain elusive over the next few months.

From Berlin's view, the defensive nature of such an alliance would be of little help, and it would also ignore the terms of the alliance signed on August 2. The Auswärtiges Amt considered the Balkan proposal to be largely unachievable and, if achievable at all, an extremely time-consuming and complicated undertaking since it required satisfying the competing territorial demands of each state.[90] Perplexed by these suggestions, Chancellor Bethmann Hollweg urged: "The Ottoman Empire and Bulgaria must be made to take immediate action against Russia or Serbia. Therefore, the four-way alliance [between Bulgaria, Greece, the Ottoman Empire, and Romania] based on *neutrality* is unacceptable."[91]

Said Halim summoned Wangenheim once again to discuss the future status of the *Goeben* and the *Breslau*. According to the grand vezir, his government had accepted the great likelihood of an Entente declaration of war following the ships' arrival. Said Halim and his colleagues had taken this risk in the expectation of a Bulgarian alliance. Now that Bulgaria might strike not with but *against* the empire, however, the German ships would have to be either disarmed or sold to the Ottomans, he argued. He would therefore announce the purchase of the two ships the next day, on August 11. Finally, the ships would not be permitted to go into the Black Sea until Bulgaria had declared itself openly for the Central Powers.[92]

[89] PA/AA, R 22402, Wangenheim to Auswärtiges Amt, August 9, 1914, no. 463.
[90] PA/AA, R 22402, Bethmann to Constantinople, August 10, 1914, no. 350.
[91] PA/AA, R 22402, Bethmann to Constantinople, August 10, 1914, no. 350. (Emphasis in original.)
[92] BA-MA, RM 40 – 671, sheet 4 and reverse, [signed] Wangenheim, August 10, 1914; ATASE, Klasör 245, Yeni Dosya 1018, Fihrist 12, Ahmed Reşid to War Ministry, communicating reports from the Ottoman ambassador at Belgrade, Cevad Bey, August 3, 1914.

Only with great difficulty and immense cost would Berlin eventually be able to overcome Ottoman procrastination. For the next several weeks, the Porte continued to point to incomplete mobilization and Bulgarian uncertainty as justifications for its non-intervention. As we have seen, both of these issues had been discussed at length during the meeting between Enver, Liman, and Wangenheim on August 1, 1914. Its fierce efforts notwithstanding, the German government proved unable to bring about a Bulgarian–Ottoman alliance.[93] It had, however, granted Enver's request for naval support in hopes that the two warships would dislodge the Ottomans out of their neutrality. Bethmann wrote to Wangenheim:

The *Goeben* must enter the Dardanelles right away and must <u>not</u> be in danger of being disarmed there. [Arrival and continued armed condition of the *Goeben*] will render Ottoman neutrality untenable. The Ottoman government should not worry about English threats. The English fleet in the Mediterranean is not sufficient to force the Dardanelles. The *Goeben* was called for by the Ottoman government and [the *Goeben*] has put itself in grave danger to answer this call.[94]

The chancellor was certainly correct in pointing out that the Ottomans themselves had called for the *Goeben*. For the Porte, the danger now lay in the possibility that their newly won ally might pack up and abandon the alliance altogether. This fear was not unfounded. In fact, Berlin sent instructions to Admiral Souchon, the commander of the *Goeben* and the *Breslau*, to act unilaterally and break out into the Black Sea or into the Aegean should Ottoman support for action not be forthcoming. It was a sign of Berlin's desperation that it considered such an enterprise, even as a much less preferred fallback position.[95]

It must be asked whether the German warships altered the military balance of powers. Did the dispatch of the *Goeben* and the *Breslau* to Istanbul give the German–Ottoman forces naval superiority in the Black Sea? Although the battlecruiser *Goeben* enjoyed the status of most powerful single battleship in both the eastern Mediterranean and the Black Sea, no German–Ottoman combination possessed the strength to engage Entente forces in a major sea battle in either body of water. While the two German ships were speedier than any enemy formation, the threat

[93] German diplomats did manage to secure an early verbal Romanian pledge of benevolent neutrality. PA/AA, R 22402, Jagow to Sofia, August 5, 1914, no. 54.
[94] PA/AA, R 22402, Bethmann to Constantinople, August 10, 1914, no. 350. (Emphasis in original.)
[95] BA-MA, RM 40 – 455, sheet 198, Admiralty Staff to Souchon, August 10, 1914.

they posed consisted primarily of hit-and-run operations and their ability
to disengage from unpromising naval encounters.[96]

The Porte's efforts to resist the German pressure to enter the war, as we
have seen, were aided by none other than Ambassador Wangenheim himself. On August 14, he warned his colleagues in Berlin that the *Goeben*'s
excursion into the Black Sea would precipitate an Entente attack on the
Straits, a campaign that, according to Admiral Souchon, the squadron's
commander – and contrary to Bethmann's wire – stood a reasonable chance
of success. Evidently the Ottomans had requested the ships to fortify their
naval capacity and to strengthen defensive positions at the Straits, but they
were not eager to use the *Goeben* and the *Breslau* to open hostilities against
Russia at this point. Wangenheim also reminded Berlin that the Ottoman
public had celebrated the "purchase" of the German ships as a major
victory, and therefore he advocated playing along with the Ottoman conceit
that the ships had been properly bought. He advised that the ships should
not enter the Black Sea until the Dardanelles were completely secured.[97]

[96] Halpern, *Naval History of World War I*, 223–5; Miller, *Superior Force*, 12–13. Unlike
Halpern, Miller claims that German–Ottoman naval forces commanded superiority of
the Black Sea in August 1914, *Superior Force*, 251.
[97] PA/AA, R 22402, Wangenheim to Auswärtiges Amt, August 14, 1914, no. 499.

5 Tug of war: Penelope's game

> So by day she [Penelope] would weave at her great and growing web – by night, by the light of torches set beside her, she would unravel all she'd done. Three whole years she deceived us blind, seduced us with this scheme.
>
> Homer, *The Odyssey*, Book II

In mid-August, Military Attaché Cemil Bey reported that Berlin had begun to consider extreme measures for bringing Bulgaria and Romania into the war. He had been assured by foreign ministry officials that once the Ottomans took the field, Bulgaria and Romania were certain to follow. Berlin held King Ferdinand personally responsible for Bulgaria's inaction, and Cemil even learned of discussions within the Auswärtiges Amt about assassinating the Bulgarian monarch.[1] Enver instructed Cemil to convey once again the reasons why the Ottomans could not yet take up active intervention. First, mobilization remained incomplete, and on those grounds alone a forward move now would only backfire and impair the Central Powers' overall war efforts. Second, the departure of the *Goeben* and the *Breslau* from the Straits for action in the Black Sea would thrust not only the Straits but also the capital into grave danger, and it would also prematurely subject eastern Anatolia to a Russian attack from the Caucasus. Enver concluded that Bulgaria should take up arms first and at least march against Serbia; to this end Enver would send a special envoy that same day to Sofia to get the ball rolling.[2] Enver's message must have had a confusing effect in Berlin, for the argument itself was muddled. If indeed Ottoman mobilization remained incomplete and the Straits were insufficiently protected against an Entente naval

---

[1] ATASE, Klasör 243, Yeni Dosya 1009, Fihrist 5, Cemil to War Ministry, 31 Temmuz 1330 and August 13, 1914.

[2] ATASE, Klasör 243, Yeni Dosya 1009, Fihrist 7–5, Cemil to War Ministry, August 13, 1914.

attack, how would these serious problems be resolved by a Bulgarian attack on Serbia?

While Berlin called for a favorable decision in Sofia, Bulgarian–Ottoman negotiations were underway in Istanbul as well. Interior Minister Talat Bey and Navy Minister Cemal Pasha led these negotiations, and Enver and Said Halim also met with the Bulgarian representative, Andrei Toshev. To shore up Bulgarian confidence, both German and Ottoman negotiators revealed the existence of the secret German–Ottoman alliance to their Bulgarian counterparts. These attempts to persuade Sofia to join the Central Powers failed, however. After a week of Bulgarian–Ottoman negotiations the two sides agreed, on August 15, on the basic terms for a defensive alliance, one that also provided for Romanian participation. These terms of the treaty, which failed to call for joint offensive operations by the signatories, could only have been a major disappointment for Berlin.[3]

The defensive nature of the alliance was by no means accidental: Cemal and Talat had suggested to Toshev that the two sides should prolong the negotiation process and thereby preserve their mutual neutrality until the outcome of the war became more predictable. And Grand Vezir Said Halim communicated this policy of joint neutrality directly to Prime Minister Radoslavov, who agreed fully.[4] The Ottoman representative in Sofia, moreover, was not instructed to work towards a Bulgarian–Ottoman agreement, though he might have been briefed about the negotiations with Toshev subsequently. Instead, he denied the existence of a German–Ottoman alliance and told his Bulgarian colleagues that his government intended to maintain its policy of neutrality.[5]

As a result of the alliance, Bulgarian leaders could put aside fears of an Ottoman attack for the time being and feel somewhat secure in their declared neutrality. The option of joining the Entente presented considerable obstacles for the Bulgarians, who sought the annexation of Serbian territory in Macedonia and Romanian territory along the western Black Sea coast, and who hoped to secure their disputed possession of the Mediterranean coast. The Entente could have won Bulgarian support only in exchange for substantial territorial promises, promises that

---

[3] PA/AA, R 22402, Wangenheim to Auswärtiges Amt, August 15, 1914, no. 505.

[4] Hall, *Bulgaria's Road to the First World War*, 290; Friedrich, *Bulgarien und die Mächte*, 123 and 132–3; F. A. K. Yasamee, "Ottoman Empire," in *Decisions for War, 1914*, ed. Keith Wilson (New York: St. Martin's Press, 1995), 242; see also the published diary of Cavid Bey, "Birinci Cihan Harbine Türkiye'nin Girmesi," *Tanin*, 19 Birinciteşrin 1944 (October 19, 1944).

[5] PA/AA, R 1913, Tschirschky to [Auswärtiges Amt], August 6, 1914.

would have necessarily been made at the expense of Greece, Romania, and Serbia.[6]

That such Entente promises were never entirely out of the question was certainly appreciated in Istanbul, and thus the possibility of a Bulgarian attack on eastern Thrace was never fully ruled out. Ahmed Reşid, the foreign ministry's political director, kept military leaders informed regarding a possible Bulgarian attack on Ottoman Thrace. Even after the signing of the defensive treaty with Bulgaria on August 19, Ahmed Reşid cautioned about the possibility of Bulgarian–Serbian collaboration against Ottoman positions. According to recent intelligence, he reported, Serbia was promising the Bulgarian government territorial gains in eastern Macedonia in exchange for neutrality. For this reason, he explained, Bulgaria was keeping only a limited number of troops on the border with Serbia. Ahmed Reşid grimly concluded that all military measures must be in place to confront a potential Bulgarian attack.[7] Such warnings were certainly justified, not only because of recent experience in the First Balkan War but also because Sofia found itself under considerable pressure for armed intervention from both the Central Powers and the Entente, and, in particular, from Russia.[8]

Ali Fethi Bey, the Ottoman ambassador in Sofia, reported a similarly pessimistic appraisal directly to Enver Pasha. In unequivocal language, more than six weeks prior to the German–Ottoman attack on Russian positions in the Black Sea, the ambassador stressed his "complete agreement" with Enver's view that "everything must be done to destroy and annihilate the Triple Entente."[9] But bringing Sofia into the war on the side of the Ottoman Empire and its allies, Ali Fethi believed, would prove difficult and perhaps even impossible. For Bulgaria to march with the Ottomans against the Serbs, the French Army first must be defeated entirely, and even the Russian Army partially: without these military successes on the part of the Central Powers, Bulgarian action remained "outside the realm of possibilities."[10]

[6]   Friedrich, *Bulgarien und die Mächte*, 130–1; *IBZI*, Series I, vol. 4, no. 251, Savinski to Sazonov, July 29, 1914, 177–8; ibid., Series I, vol. 4, no. 254, Savinski to Sazonov, July 29, 1914, 179–80; ibid., Series I, vol. 4, no. 555, Strandtmann to Sazonov, August 4, 1914, 321–2; ibid., Series II, vol. 6/1, no. 9, Giers to Sazonov, August 5, 1914, 6–7.
[7]   ATASE, BDH, Klasör 509, Yeni Dosya 1989, Fihrist 9, Ahmed Reşid to War Ministry, 20 Ağustos 1330 (August 31, 1914); ibid, Klasör 568, Yeni Dosya 2189, Fihrist 3, Ahmed Reşid to War Ministry, 7 Ağustos 1330 (August 20, 1914).
[8]   Hall, *Bulgaria's Road to the First World War*, 288–95.
[9]   TTK, Enver Paşa Arşivi, no. 1338, Ali Fethi to Enver, 27 Ağustos 1330 (September 9, 1914).
[10] Ibid.

And even though Mustafa Kemal, the military attaché in Sofia (and the future president of the Turkish Republic), reported on August 19 that according to the Bulgarian war minister his country would declare mobilization within the next three days and attack Serbia, Bulgarian and Ottoman diplomats had effectively already decided against such action.[11] And so, less than a week later, Mustafa Kemal reported from Sofia that "since the signing [of the defensive treaty between us] there has not been a single indication that the war minister's statement regarding the probable attack on Serbia will be implemented." While he continued to urge for Bulgarian action against Serbia, according to his instructions, he expressed doubts that Sofia would go to arms before waiting out the confrontation between the French and German armies on the western front.[12]

Even after the Bulgarian–Ottoman alliance of August 19, the Radoslavov government continued to walk a tightrope between the Entente and the Central Powers. Sofia's foreign policy objectives, in the main, remained what they had been since 1878: the unification of ethnic Bulgarians through the creation of a Greater Bulgaria that encompassed all of Macedonia, Dobruja on the western Black Sea, and eastern Thrace including Edirne/Adrianople. These aims could not easily be satisfied by joining either of the blocs, since possession of Macedonia and Dobruja conflicted with the interests of Greece and Serbia and designs on eastern Thrace meant designs on the Ottoman Empire. For that reason, the Radoslavov government secretly promised both alliance blocs benevolent neutrality in exchange for territorial concessions. By mid-1915, this tactic would begin to falter, and Bulgarian neutrality proved insufficient to achieve territorial expansion. Despite advanced negotiations with the Entente, Sofia was ultimately moved to action by the Central Powers' victories at Gallipoli and on the eastern front. Its aims, it now decided, could be satisfied only through joining the Central Powers. On September 6, 1915, Bulgaria signed a five-year alliance treaty with the Central Powers, and Bulgarian troops engaged Serbian armies on October 11, 1915, almost a full year after Ottoman intervention.[13]

Said Halim, acting in conjunction with Enver and Talat, was directly involved in the negotiations with Sofia. During the week of meetings with Toshev in Istanbul, he sent word to Prime Minister Radoslavov

[11] ATASE, BDH, Klasör 243, Yeni Dosya 1009, Fihrist 10, Mustafa Kemal to War Ministry, 6 Ağustos 1330 and August 19, 1914.
[12] ATASE, BDH, Klasör 243, Yeni Dosya 1009, Fihrist 10–1, Mustafa Kemal to War Ministry, 8 Ağustos 1330 (August 21, 1914).
[13] Hall, *Bulgaria's Road to the First World War*, 285–328.

suggesting that the alliance be postponed until Sofia had concluded a satisfactory agreement with Romania.[14] The grand vezir also sent a copy of the draft agreement to Wangenheim on August 15, and Enver and Talat visited the German ambassador that same afternoon to mollify the expected reaction. They knew full well that the Germans had hoped for a joint Bulgarian–Ottoman military offensive. Enver and Talat, in a piece of theater, complained about the document, claiming that the terms of the draft were the most they could squeeze out of Toshev. They also claimed that they had sought an agreement for joint offensive action. Enver and Talat pretended to mistrust Toshev and explained that they were so outraged about the defensive nature of the agreement that they themselves would travel to Sofia immediately. Thus, in their meeting with the ambassador, they formally registered their commitment to the German–Ottoman alliance and their strong support for intervention. Wangenheim sent word to that effect to Berlin:

[Enver and Talat will travel to Sofia] and negotiate with the Bulgarian government directly. They said they would use threats in order to get the Bulgarians to strike immediately against the Serbs. [They would use threats] because the Ottoman Empire does not want to be told that it did not do everything in its power to fulfill its obligations towards Germany. They said the [Ottoman] government was earnestly contemplating a strike against Russia as soon as possible.[15]

In other words, Enver and Talat claimed that they, as well as the entire cabinet, were ready for military intervention and that they were working eagerly towards removing the final obstacle, the uncertainty of Bulgaria's course of action. This claim, however, as we have seen, was insincere and served to hide the Ottoman preference for continued armed neutrality. The same day, Enver attempted to capitalize on these assurances and requested armaments from the German manufacturer Krupp through General Liman von Sanders, to be delivered without cash payment.[16]

As for Wangenheim, the ambassador had opposed the alliance with the Ottoman Empire from the beginning on the grounds that the empire was militarily too weak to be of any value to the Central Powers. It was ironic, therefore, that he was instructed to sign the alliance treaty on condition that the empire be capable of launching operations and making a

---

[14] Friedrich, *Bulgarien und die Mächte*, 132.
[15] PA/AA, R 22402, Wangenheim to Auswärtiges Amt, August 15, 1914, no. 505. In fact, Talat and Halil, not Enver, left for Sofia August 15, 1914. A "treaty of friendship" was signed on August 19, 1914, without military consequence.
[16] PA/AA, R 22402, Wangenheim to Auswärtiges Amt, August 15, 1914, no. 516; Enver was repeating an earlier request for equipment and *matériel*, see ATASE, BDH, Klasör 244, Yeni Dosya 1012, Fihrist 12 and 12–1, Enver to Cemil, 23 Temmuz 1330 (August 5, 1914).

significant military contribution. Against his own better judgement, he had signed on the basis of Liman's revised assessment, as he had been instructed. And yet, even after the signing, Wangenheim's outlook continued to be based on his own, independent negative assessment of Ottoman military capabilities. During the late summer and fall of 1914, the ambassador wrote several times to Berlin that he thought any Ottoman campaign would be premature and advised Berlin against forcing an offensive on the Porte.[17]

Because the Auswärtiges Amt was working intensely for intervention, however, Wangenheim's reports to Berlin were crafted to convey the impression that he, too, supported intervention. Nonetheless, he consistently backed the Ottomans' arguments against intervention, and asserted repeatedly that Berlin would not profit from premature Ottoman action. Following the failure – in German eyes – of the Bulgarian–Ottoman negotiations, for example, he rationalized the Porte's hesitation to his superiors: "No Ottoman statesman will assume the responsibility of waging war against three Great Powers without the guarantee of Constantinople's security."[18]

Wangenheim also argued that the international situation had changed drastically since August 2. At the time of signing, he explained, Italy was still a committed member of the Triple Alliance, and the Ottoman Empire was therefore justified in counting on Italian naval forces in the Mediterranean to play a role in the defense of the Straits. Since Italy's change of direction – away from the Central Powers – operations across the Black Sea had been rendered a much more dangerous undertaking. As soon as a German–Ottoman naval expedition left the Bosporus, Wangenheim posited, the Entente would declare war. He added that both the fortifications specialist Schack and Admiral Souchon judged that the Dardanelles could not be held without the *Goeben*. If Britain took Istanbul, the fate not just of the two ships but of the whole empire would be sealed. The arrival of a foreign power in the capital would spell partition – and without German participation. For these reasons, Wangenheim declared, he and Pallavicini, his Habsburg counterpart, could not advise their governments to push for the attack on Russia by sending the *Goeben* and the *Breslau* into the Black Sea, with or without Ottoman troops.[19]

Then the ambassador shifted to the balance of powers in the Balkans. Even if Bulgaria could not be won over and persuaded to take action, the formation of a "small triple alliance" consisting of Bulgaria, the Ottoman

[17] PA/AA, R 22402, Wangenheim to Auswärtiges Amt, August 15, 1914, no. 505.
[18] Ibid.   [19] Ibid.

Empire, and Romania, should be embraced despite its defensive nature. In that way, Bulgaria would still become part of the Triple Alliance system, and the "small triple alliance" would represent 700,000 troops, formidable enough to face Russia. Thus a Russian attack on the Straits would be an attack on the "small triple alliance" as well as on the Triple Alliance proper, by virtue of the German–Ottoman alliance.[20] Here, the ambassador was allowing his imagination to get the better of him: it must have seemed implausible even then that Bulgaria and Romania would take up arms against the Russian giant because it had attacked the Ottoman Empire.

Wangenheim continued to argue steadfastly against intervention. Germany would remain master of the Straits thanks to its two ships stationed there, and the ships would be an important bargaining chip at the eventual peace conference. Russia was holding back troops initially designated for its western front because of the Ottoman threat, and thus the alliance was paying off already, even without intervention.[21] As a member of the "small triple alliance," the empire would pose an even greater threat to Russia than it did now. Continued armed neutrality, Wangenheim pointed out, allowed the navy to finish the fortification installations at the Straits, to complete ongoing repairs on its ships, and to continue its training exercises. In making these arguments, Wangenheim was not only conveying what he had been told by his Ottoman colleagues but was also defending their position because he considered it to be the best available policy for the Ottoman Empire and thus for Germany.[22]

It was not only Bulgaria's ambiguous attitude about which the Ottoman leaders expressed concerns to their German allies. When Enver and Said Halim had requested the dispatch of naval reinforcement to Istanbul, they asked not only for the *Goeben* but for Austro-Hungarian vessels as well. Vienna had denied the request. The loss of Italy as a Triple Alliance partner further disturbed the naval balance in the eastern Mediterranean, as Wangenheim had been quick to remind the Auswärtiges Amt in his report of August 15. When Berlin and Liman stepped up their demands for a naval attack on the Russian Black Sea coast during the first weeks of August, therefore, Ottoman statesmen argued that the departure of the *Goeben* and the *Breslau* from the capital would render the Dardanelles indefensible against the British and French navies in the eastern Mediterranean, a situation worsened by the lack of Italian and Austro-Hungarian naval

---

[20] Ibid.
[21] Ibid.; confirmed in *IBZI*, Series II, vol. 6/1, no.147, Sazonov to Basili, August 22, 1914, 109–10.
[22] PA/AA, R 22402, Wangenheim to Auswärtiges Amt, August 15, 1914, no. 505.

support. The status of the Straits, and the question as to whether they could be forced open by the Entente navies, became a bone of contention and continued to be debated back and forth between Berlin and Istanbul.[23]

How did the Entente powers respond to the news of Ottoman mobilization, the declaration of neutrality, reports of an alliance with Germany, and the arrival of the two German ships a week later? In London, Winston Churchill, the first sea lord, called for an aggressive policy to launch an attack on the Straits and to sink the two ships if necessary. Was this mere posturing or a realistic assessment? The Entente's failure to take the Straits in 1915 would suggest that success in mid-1914 would have been difficult to achieve. In any case, Churchill's position met with overwhelming opposition. The prime minister, Herbert Henry Asquith, the foreign secretary, Grey, and the war secretary, General Herbert Kitchener, all opposed the idea. Their argument was driven by political concerns. Britain could not initiate an attack on the empire of the Muslim caliph, which had declared its neutrality, no matter how flimsy that neutrality might have been. Attacking first might inspire revolts among the Muslims living in the Entente's colonial possessions, most notably in British India.[24] And throughout the following months, the British government was concerned not to break off relations with the Sublime Porte but to delay her entry as long as possible, and to be sure that, when the break did happen, it was widely acknowledged that it was brought about by the Ottomans themselves and not by the Entente.

From St. Petersburg, Sazonov called on the British foreign office to prevent the shipmaker Armstrong Whitworth from delivering the *Sultan Osman* to the Ottoman crew that had arrived on the Tyne to take charge of the new dreadnought. Sazonov instructed his ambassador to London, Count Benckendorff, to impress on Grey "the enormous significance" of this issue for the Russian government.[25] By August 3, the British government had declared that the two ships could not be delivered, because of the outbreak of war in Europe.[26] Once the *Sultan Osman* and the *Reşadiye* had been confiscated, Russian anxiety over the possibility of an Ottoman attack calmed, only to be stirred up again by the arrival of the *Goeben* and the *Breslau*. The Russian military attaché in Istanbul, General

---

[23] BA-MA, RM 40–55, sheets 3–10, Souchon to Chief of the Admiralty Staff and additional correspondence, August 15–19, 1914; PA/AA, R 22402, Wahnschaffe to Bethmann, August 21, 1914.

[24] Miller, *Superior Force*, 215–16 and 218.

[25] *IBZI*, Series I, vol. 5, no. 281, Sazonov to Benckendorff, July 30, 1914, 195.

[26] *IBZI*, Series I, vol. 5, no. 399, Benckendorff to Sazonov, 254; ibid., Series I, vol. 5, no. 507, Giers to Sazonov, August 3, 1914, 303.

Leontiev, suggested that the Porte would eventually tip one way or the other between the two blocs, but he was quick to add that Russia could await its neighbor's decision with a cool head: the Ottomans' weak armed forces posed no military threat.[27]

Slightly more concerned, Ambassador Giers warned that the Ottomans might wage a pre-emptive war against Russia. The Ottoman leaders, he thought, were convinced that St. Petersburg would use the European war as the pretext for seizing the Straits.[28] On August 5, Leontiev visited Enver Pasha to inquire about the war ministry's latest views. Enver welcomed his colleague with a stunning proposal. He explained that the ongoing mobilization was not directed against any particular power and that, once mobilized, Ottoman forces could march alongside those of Russia if St. Petersburg so desired: Enver was proposing an alliance! In return for military support, the war minister asked for the Russian government's promise to foster peaceful relations between the Ottomans and their Balkan neighbors. Such improved relations, Enver posited, could be achieved by returning the Greek-held Aegean islands or Bulgarian-held western Thrace. In return for these territorial changes, Enver continued, Greece could receive the Epirus region on the Adriatic, Bulgaria could receive Macedonia, and Serbia could receive Bosnia.[29] Here, Enver, famous for his reputation as a pro-German war hawk and vision of a pan-Islamic empire, proposed an alliance against Germany and suggested the cession of (Muslim) Albanian Epirus to Greece.

Over the next two weeks, Enver, together with Said Halim and Talat, continued to pitch an Ottoman–Russian alliance to Giers and Leontiev. The very day before the arrival of the German warships in the Straits, Enver told his Russian colleagues that he expected to face a great deal of opposition in the cabinet, but that he was confident in his ability to push through the alliance with St. Petersburg, if only the Russian leaders accepted. If they did, Enver claimed, he would put all of his forces at Russia's disposal, and he would immediately dismiss all German officers and specialists now in Ottoman service. More specifically, Enver proposed a five- to ten-year defensive alliance, so that the empire might enjoy a measure of security against its Balkan neighbors. The Russian government would also have to mediate the return of the Aegean islands and western Thrace to Ottoman sovereignty (Enver had spoken of one or the other, not both, in his meeting with Leontiev). Evidently, the Ottoman leaders had succeeded in winning over Giers and Leontiev, both of whom

---

[27] *IBZI*, Series I, vol. 5, no. 561, Leontiev to Danilov, August 4, 1914, 323–4.
[28] *IBZI*, Series I, vol. 5, no. 479, Giers to Sazonov, August 2, 1914, 291–2.
[29] *IBZI*, Series II, vol. 6/1, no. 8, Giers to Sazonov, Urgent, August 5, 1914, 5.

strongly recommended accepting the alliance immediately.[30] Giers reasoned that in the case of an Entente victory, Bulgaria and Greece could be easily compensated at the expense of Austria-Hungary. He also warned that turning down Enver's offer would cement the Ottomans' relations with the Central Powers for good.[31]

Back in St. Petersburg, Foreign Minister Sazonov read the situation differently. Not yet informed of the German ships' arrival in Ottoman waters, he reminded Giers that the Ottomans posed no military threat to Russia whatsoever and instructed him simply to stall negotiations with Enver until Bulgaria's stance became clear. Then, Sazonov raised the stakes: Giers should intimate that if the Porte took any action not sanctioned by Russia it risked the loss of all of Anatolia.[32]

Giers, on the other hand, saw great potential in the Ottomans' alliance proposal. He felt that it offered what Russia so strongly desired, and on highly favorable terms. The conclusion of an Ottoman–Russian alliance would mean the dismissal of the Liman mission and hence the end of German influence. As a result, the Sublime Porte would become militarily, if not politically, dependent on the Russian Empire. According to Giers, "the historic moment has finally arrived in which we have the opportunity to make the Ottoman Empire submit to us."[33]

If such an alliance had materialized, it would certainly have marked a diplomatic revolution; not only would it have altered the course of the First World War, as Russia could have been supplied through the Straits by its Entente partners, but it undoubtedly would also have charted a different path for the history of the modern Middle East.

Remarkably, Giers and Leontiev continued to support the Ottoman alliance proposal even after the arrival of the two German ships. The alliance, Leontiev argued, would guarantee the neutrality of two key Balkan powers, Bulgaria and Romania, and would be worth concluding for that consideration alone. Germany, in turn, would suffer an irreparable blow in the Balkans, a blow that might prove decisive for the outcome of the entire war.[34] Despite Giers's sustained advocacy of the alliance, Sazonov hoped to pull Bulgaria into the Entente camp without such as step.[35] Once the German warships arrived in the Straits, St. Petersburg

[30] *IBZI*, Series II, vol. 6/1, no. 48, Giers to Sazonov, August 9, 1914, 32–3.
[31] *IBZI*, Series II, vol. 6/1, no. 49, Giers to Sazonov, August 9, 1914, Urgent, 33.
[32] *IBZI*, Series II, vol. 6/1, no. 50, Sazonov to Giers, August 10, 1914, 33–4.
[33] *IBZI*, Series II, vol. 6/1, no. 60, Giers to Sazonov, Urgent, August 10, 1914, 40–1.
[34] *IBZI*, Series II, vol. 6/1, no. 69, Giers to Sazonov, August 11, 1914, 47.
[35] *IBZI*, Series II, vol. 6/1, no. 84, Giers to Sazonov, August 12, 1914, 59; ibid., Series II, vol. 6/1, no. 41, Sazonov to Savinski, Urgent, August 9, 1914, 27–8; ibid., no. 81, Savinski to Sazonov, August 12, 1914, 56.

had a strong argument for delaying its reply, and Sazonov considered the dismissal of the German crew a prerequisite to any further deliberations on the question.[36] Yet Giers and Leontiev continued to support the proposal. On August 13, Giers surmised that a German–Ottoman alliance probably had been signed, but that the Ottoman offer should be pursued nonetheless. He wrote that Greece must give up the disputed Aegean islands and Bulgaria should cede western Thrace, "which is inhabited predominantly by Muslims."[37] (Never mind that Giers, at other times, could advocate Russian seizure of the Straits region.) Leontiev added that the Ottomans' territorial demands should be granted, and that the restoration of the Aegean islands and western Thrace was necessary to appease the sense of violation that prevailed among the Ottoman populace. The frankness with which Enver Pasha described the Ottoman outlook to Leontiev is astonishing. The war minister explained that German equipment and personnel strengthened Ottoman forces and that therefore it was not in the Porte's interest to remove the German presence. He understood full well, Enver continued, that the German military advisors now in the empire wished nothing more than to bring the Ottomans into the war against Russia. But if St. Petersburg accepted the alliance proposal, Enver Pasha would tell the German officers "without a minute's hesitation: now you are our enemies, and I ask you to leave," because, he told Leontiev, "[I have] only Ottoman interests" in mind.[38]

Were the Ottomans sincere throughout these talks with St. Petersburg, even after they had signed an alliance with Germany, had taken in two German warships, and were in the midst of negotiating an alliance with Bulgaria against Russia? Might the Ottomans have terminated their alliance with Germany and dismissed the military mission in exchange for the return of lost territories and a Russian defensive guarantee of the empire's future territorial integrity? Giers and Leontiev considered the Ottoman offer to be genuine. They believed that the Ottoman leaders were intent on profiting from the European war, if necessary through a Russian alliance. The Porte's representative at St. Petersburg, Fahreddin Bey, also sought to impress upon the Russian government directly the idea of an Ottoman–Russian alliance. In his meetings, Fahreddin listed as the empire's objectives the preservation of its territorial integrity, the transfer of German businesses to Ottoman possession, and a Russian promise not

[36] *IBZI*, Series II, vol. 6/1, Note 2 to no. 55, Sazonov to Giers, August 12, 1914, 37.
[37] *IBZI*, Series II, vol. 6/1, no. 93, Giers to Sazonov, Urgent, August 13, 1914, 63–4.
[38] *IBZI*, Series II, vol. 6/1, no. 94, Leontiev to Danilov, August 13, 1914, Enver Pasha's Proposal for the Conclusion of a Military Alliance, 64–9; ibid., Series II, vol. 6/1, no. 107, Giers [Leontiev] to Sazonov, August 15, 1914, 80–1.

to support Armenian nationalist aspirations in eastern Anatolia. Sazonov accepted the first two but rejected the third of these demands. The Armenian reform project must proceed, the foreign minister insisted.[39]

For Sazonov, the objective lay in keeping the Ottomans outside the war for as long as possible, and he disagreed with Giers and Leontiev that an alliance presented the best way of achieving that objective. With the arrival of the *Goeben* and the *Breslau*, Ottoman naval power in the Black Sea had been strengthened considerably, and the Entente governments correspondingly increased their efforts to keep the Ottomans neutral – and the by now two-week-old war as confined as possible. Sazonov had a different plan for keeping the Porte outside the war. He suggested to his allies that the Entente issue a guarantee of territorial integrity in exchange for Ottoman neutrality and demobilization. The island of Limnos could also be conceded, as it was critical for the security of the southern Straits; Greece could be compensated with Epirus. German businesses and commercial concessions in the empire could go to the Ottomans as well. While the Entente partners agreed on keeping the Porte neutral, by August 19, 1914, their ambassadors in Istanbul had presented only a verbal proposal, offering to guarantee the empire's territorial integrity in exchange for neutrality, leaving alone for now the questions of demobilization, the return of Limnos or any other territory, and the fate of German commercial possessions. Giers found that handing back Limnos by itself, without the larger islands of Chios and Mytilene, would be insufficient to end the Ottoman sense of vulnerability in western Anatolia. The demand for demobilization, moreover, seems to have been eliminated on the initiative of the London and Paris governments, who warned that such a demand could be interpreted in Istanbul as a threat and should therefore not be included.[40]

Giers and Leontiev did not hide their disappointment in the eventual Entente proposal. In a long telegram to Sazonov on August 19, Leontiev reiterated that only territorial concessions were capable of bringing the Ottoman Empire into the fold of the Entente. Leontiev warned that the Ottoman armed forces were improving daily in quality and number, and that it now looked as if they could field an army of 400,000 men rather than the previous lower estimate of 200,000. Evidently, Enver Pasha had succeeded in convincing Leontiev of his commitment to neutrality. If the

---

[39] *IBZI*, Series II, vol. 6/1, no. 72, Sazonov to Giers, August 12, 1914, 49–50.

[40] *IBZI*, Series II, vol. 6/1, no. 99, Giers to Sazonov, Urgent, August 14, 1914, 73; ibid., Series II, vol. 6/1, no. 100, Sazonov to Benckendorff, August 15, 1914, 73–4; ibid. Series II, vol. 6/1, no. 110, Sazonov to Benckendorff, August 16, 1914, 82–3; ibid., Series II, vol. 6/1, no. 138, Giers to Sazonov, Urgent, August 19, 1914, 102–3; see the notes to these telegrams for subsequent correspondence.

Central Powers achieved clear successes on the battlefield, Leontiev cautioned, the Ottomans might jump into the mix after all in order to reap territorial gains. The Porte's understanding with Bulgaria would greatly endanger Russia's southern flank. Russia's interest would not be served with Ottoman demobilization, but rather with the dismissal of the German military from Istanbul, precisely the measure Enver offered to implement "happily," Leontiev argued.[41]

Like Sazonov, Sir Edward Grey, the British foreign secretary, opposed the idea of granting territorial concessions to the Ottomans. The Russian ambassador at London, Benckendorff, doubted whether Grey would ever participate in any "promise to the Ottoman Empire that restored to her the Christian provinces." Any Ottoman declaration of neutrality would never be a true one and would inevitably last only until the arrival of the first news of German military successes.[42] Grey considered Greece a far preferable ally, and for that reason, too, he opposed the idea of returning Limnos to Ottoman control. While he supported the general idea of promising the security of Ottoman borders, Grey had no patience with the Porte's demands. Echoing Sazonov's earlier warning, he sent a stern message to Istanbul: if the Ottomans took action hostile to the interests of the Entente, and if Germany were subsequently defeated, then "the consequences for Turkey will be totally unpredictable."[43]

Although the Entente governments reached agreement on a written, collective note, they did not submit such a statement until August 28. Eventually, the written declaration "guarantee[d] the integrity of the Ottoman territory" in exchange for the empire's neutrality. The note reminded the Porte that it would be obligated, as a neutral power, to grant free passage through the Straits to all merchant ships and to dismiss the crews of the *Goeben* and the *Breslau*.[44] But by the time the Entente ambassadors presented the note, their governments had already become convinced that the Ottomans were only waiting for the right moment to join the Central Powers. The question of what course of action Bulgaria would take was increasingly considered pivotal by both alliance blocs. On August 24, four days before the guarantee of territory, Sazonov

[41] *IBZI*, Series II, vol. 6/1, no. 136, Giers (forwarding Leontiev's report) to Sazonov, Urgent, August 19, 1914, 99–101.

[42] *IBZI*, Series II, vol. 6/1, no. 98, Benckendorff to Sazonov, Private, August 14, 1914, 72, and Note 3 to this document.

[43] *IBZI*, Series II, vol. 6/1, no. 118, Benckendorff to Sazonov, Urgent, August 17, 1914, 88–9; also ibid., Series II, vol. 6/1, no. 119, Grey to Buchanan, August 17, 1914, 89, for a British telegram intercepted and decoded by Russian intelligence.

[44] *IBZI*, Series II, vol. 6/1, no. 148, Aide-mémoire of the British Embassy in St. Petersburg to the Russian Foreign Minister, August 23, 1914, 110–11; ibid., Series II, vol. 6/1, no. 173, Sazonov to Izvolskii, Benckendorff, Giers, Urgent, August 28, 1914, 129.

instructed his diplomats in the European capitals that Bulgaria must be won over before the Ottomans entered the war: "According to our intelligence reports the Ottoman Empire may take action in the next few days, and therefore negotiations with Bulgaria may not be delayed," for the Ottoman decision to go with the Central Powers would pull Bulgaria into that camp as well.[45] The Entente proved unsuccessful, however, in its attempt to secure the territorial concessions from Greece and Serbia that were necessary to tempt Sofia.[46]

Throughout the month of August, one of the central German objectives for the Ottoman theater was being met; Russian headquarters had decided not to withdraw any of its forces from the Caucasus to the eastern front. In late August, Russian headquarters even decided to move additional troops from Turkestan into the Caucasus, troops that might otherwise have been deployed on the eastern front.[47] These additional troops, however, were not intended to play a defensive role.

Russian military planners sought to "maintain the closest of relations with the Armenians and the Kurds" in order to prepare for the outbreak of war with the Ottoman Empire. For this reason, the army should undertake the necessary preparations for "the rapid transportation of weapons and provisions across the [Ottoman–Russian] border and for the distribution of these among the population on the other side of the border."[48] In the following weeks the Russian government decided "to prepare a rebellion of the Armenians, Assyrians, and Kurds for the event of war" with the Ottoman Empire. The instructions issued by the Russian foreign ministry prescribed that the groups that were to lead this rebellion would be "formed under the supervision of our consuls in Azerbaijan and the

[45] *IBZI*, Series II, vol. 6/1, no. 151, Sazonov to Izvolskii and Benckendorff, August 24, 1914, 113–14; ibid., Series II, vol. 6/1, no. 172, Sazonov to Izvolskii, Urgent, August 28, 1914, 128–9.

[46] *IBZI*, Series II, vol. 6/1, no. 2, Sazonov to Strandtmann, August 5, 1914, 2; ibid., Series II, vol. 6/1, no. 106, Strandtmann to Sazonov, August 15, 1914, 79–80; ibid., Series II, vol. 6/1, no. 144, Sazonov to Benckendorff, August 21, 1914, 106–7; ibid., Series II, vol. 6/1, no. 146, Aide-mémoire of the British Embassy in St. Petersburg to the Russian Foreign Minister, August 22, 1914, 108–9; ibid., Series II, vol. 6/1, no. 149, Izvolskii to Sazonov, August 23, 1914, 111–12; ibid., Series II, vol. 6/1, no. 153, Sazonov to Izvolskii, to Benckendorff, to Giers, to Demidov, to Poklevskii, and to Strandtmann, August 24, 1914, 115–16; ibid., Series II, vol. 6/1, no. 160, Basili to Sazonov, August 25, 1914, 120; ibid., Series II, vol. 6/1, no. 174, Sazonov to Izvolskii and to Benckendorff, August 28, 1914, 130–1; ibid., Series II, vol. 6/1, no. 185, Izvolskii to Sazonov, August 29, 1914, 140; ibid., Series II, vol. 6/1, no. 229, Sazonov to Demidov, September 7, 1914, 173–4; ibid., Series II, vol. 6/1, no. 264, Sazonov to Savinski, September 16, 1914, 201–2.

[47] *IBZI*, Series II, vol. 6/1, no. 147, Sazonov to Basili, Director of the Diplomatic Office at Russian Headquarters, August 22, 1914, 109–10, bearing Tsar Nicholas II's note of approval, August 23, 1914.

[48] *IBZI*, Series II, vol. 6/1, no. 191, Sazonov to Goremykin, August 30, 1914, 144–5.

commanders of our units there, under complete secrecy from the Persian administration. Rifles have been prepared, but these will be distributed only at the necessary moment."[49]

Throughout September 1914, the Entente ambassadors continued to pursue an agreement on Ottoman neutrality, despite clear signs that the Sublime Porte had moved deeper still into the Central Powers' camp. Russian intelligence intercepted and deciphered some of the diplomatic correspondence coming in and out of Istanbul. Thus St. Petersburg followed German and Austro-Hungarian assessments of Ottoman military strength and strategic utility. Those in the Russian foreign ministry knew, therefore, that in early September the majority of German military advisors in the capital viewed the Dardanelles as vulnerable and requiring fortification work before military operations could be risked. But they also knew that high officials in Berlin and some officers in Istanbul, such as Liman, urged immediate action in the hope that intervention would win over Bulgaria and Romania.[50]

Istanbul's response to the offer of security-for-neutrality by the Entente was also ambiguous. For some, the Ottoman negotiators had "left no doubt of Turkey's intention to move against Greece."[51] Why, then, did the Entente continue negotiations? Evidently, during the hard-fought months of August to October, the months that saw the highest casualty rates of the war, the Entente placed great importance on keeping the Porte out of the war.

Grey argued that the Entente must hold back from opening the war against the Ottoman Empire. At this point, war in the Ottoman Empire would be a needless distraction, as the decisive theaters were on the eastern front and in Belgium. The military focus must be on defeating Germany.[52] Grey also believed that the only danger the empire posed was through the two German ships, and therefore Entente diplomats pursued several attempts to get the German crews dismissed from Istanbul – and just the crews, since the ships alone would be useless in Ottoman hands, British experts believed.[53] Grey was convinced that as long as Germany failed to achieve success on the battlefield, the Ottomans would remain

[49] *IBZI*, Series II, vol. 6/1, no. 295, Klemm to Giers, September 23, 1914, 227–8.
[50] *IBZI*, Series II, vol. 6/1, no. 210, Pallavicini to Berchtold, Decoded in the Russian Foreign Ministry, September 2, 1914, 160. For other examples, see *IBZI*, Series II, vol. 6/1, no. 297, The Russian Foreign Minister's Report for the English Ambassador at St. Petersburg, September 23, 1914, 227, and ibid., Series II, vol. 6/2, no. 411, Giers to Sazonov, Please Decipher Personally, October 25, 1914, 327.
[51] *IBZI*, Series II, vol. 6/1, no. 203, Izvolskii to Sazonov, September 1, 1914, 153.
[52] *IBZI*, Series II, vol. 6/1, no. 97, Benckendorff to Sazonov, August 14, 1914, 71–2.
[53] *IBZI*, Series II, vol. 6/1, no. 76, Benckendorff to Sazonov, August 12, 1914, 52–3.

neutral: they "must be aware that if Turkey brings about a war and if Germany suffers setbacks, their [fears that Russia will bring about the partition of the Ottoman Empire] will probably be realized."[54]

This fate the Ottomans deserved; Grey maintained that "if Turkey makes a decision for war, she will bear the war's most severe consequences." Therefore, "it is imperative for the British government that the break with the Ottomans be obvious, but the result of Turkey's own action." In Grey's view, reasons to justify war with the Ottoman Empire could already be found, but he argued that it would be much more expedient to leave "the responsibility for [bringing the empire into war] squarely with Turkey and Germany." Tsar Nicholas II agreed fully with Grey's assessment. Hence the Russian government decided against mining the northern Straits, because such an operation could not have been kept secret, and it would have provided Ottoman leaders with the argument that Russia had attacked the empire, an argument the Entente evidently was unwilling to concede.[55]

Why, then, were the Entente governments so eager to place the responsibility for the end of relations with the Ottomans on Istanbul itself? Perhaps we may see in the Entente position the laying of the groundwork and the preparing of postwar legitimacy for partitioning the Ottoman Empire, i.e. for the British annexation of Egypt, for the formalization of French control in Syria, and, of course, for the incorporation of the Straits region into Russia. This partition could be carried out much more effectively, and with greater legitimacy, if the Ottomans could be shown clearly to have been the aggressors.

In line with Grey, Sazonov instructed both his ambassador at Istanbul and the commander of the Russian Black Sea Fleet, Admiral Eberhardt, to delay open confrontation. The Ottomans were unlikely to take action so long as Germany and Austria-Hungary failed to deliver the military successes they had promised. Thus they should not be provoked into war at this point. Reversing his earlier instructions, Sazonov now directed Eberhardt not to engage the *Goeben* in the Black Sea should the German battlecruiser steam northward, except "in the case that success was assured." Sazonov stressed that "from the political point of view, which is shared by France and England, it is very important that a war against Turkey, if it proves unavoidable, is caused by Turkey itself." For Britain, and to a lesser degree for Russia and France, it remained a key consideration not to alienate and even antagonize the large number of Muslim

---

[54] *IBZI*, Series II, vol. 6/1, no. 101, Benckendorff to Sazonov, August 15, 1914, 75; ibid., Series II, vol. 6/1, no. 103, Izvolskii to Sazonov, August 15, 1914, 76–7.
[55] *IBZI*, Series II, vol. 6/1, no. 176, Benckendorff to Sazonov, August 28, 1914, 132–3.

subjects. If Bulgaria could be brought to the Entente side, Sazonov added, the Ottoman factor would be neutralized.[56]

As the empire's mobilization efforts proceeded, aided by German officers and *matériel*, the Russian government reassessed the Ottoman military threat. Registering the naval advantage the *Goeben* and the *Breslau* gave them, Sazonov warned Eberhardt once more against a possible encounter with the Ottoman fleet in the Black Sea, this time cautioning the naval commander that "we must do whatever is necessary in order to avoid a clash" with the Ottoman forces. A clash now, Sazonov explained, "would preoccupy a portion of our forces, and it could engulf the entire Balkan peninsula and prevent our joined action with Serbia against Austria." Eberhardt should engage the German–Ottoman naval forces only after very careful calculation, because of the "disastrous results a failure in such a confrontation would have for us." Not only would the Ottomans gain "unrivaled control over the Black Sea," but a Russian defeat would also have a deep psychological impact on the neutral Balkan powers.[57]

In Istanbul, Ambassador Giers shared Sazonov's nervousness, which only intensified throughout the subsequent weeks. By the first days of October, Giers believed that if the cabinet did not declare war against the Entente, then the "Germans will create an incident that will thrust Turkey into the war," and perhaps "even against her wishes." Giers reiterated "the heavy blow even a partial defeat of our fleet" in the Black Sea would mean to the Russian war effort. The confiscation of the two Ottoman ships by the British government had greatly exacerbated the anti-Entente and, in particular, anti-British feelings in both government circles and in the realm of "public opinion."[58]

The endangered alliance

On August 16, 1914, Enver requested through Admiral Souchon that Germany send a team of naval technicians and specialists to Istanbul. The mission was charged with reorganizing and overhauling the fortifications at the Straits against an attack from the sea. For this task Souchon requested two admirals, ten officers, and a hundred additional personnel. Another team of officers, engineers, and technicians should be sent to replace the British naval mission, which had been relegated to office

[56] *IBZI*, Series II, vol. 6/1, no. 182, Sazonov to Basili, August 29, 1914, 137–8.
[57] *IBZI*, Series II, vol. 6/1, no. 245, Sazonov to Eberhardt, September 11, 1914, 184–5.
[58] *IBZI*, Series II, vol. 6/1, no. 354, Giers to Sazonov, Private, October 3, 1914, 278–80, and Series II, vol. 6/1, no. 363, Giers to Sazonov, Confidential, October 5, 1914, 285–7.

assignments in mid-August. Berlin granted this request with great speed, and a Special Commando Unit (*Sonderkommando*), consisting of 26 officers and 520 men headed by Admiral Guido von Usedom, arrived disguised as factory workers in late August.[59]

In order to place Enver's request for the naval mission, the Ottoman military attaché in Berlin, Cemil Bey, had met with officials at the German navy office. In that meeting, Admiral von Capelle, the deputy navy secretary, promised that all requests for officers, troops, engineers, scientists, and *matériel* would be granted in full. But he also emphasized that the Straits were already secure from any Entente assault and that the Ottomans therefore were free to launch their own operation across the Black Sea. He pointed to the great potential for Ottoman gains: "Turkey has a future in the Caucasus and its surroundings. If we are successful, these [regions] will be yours." Cemil Bey concluded that the German leadership was convinced that "if the *Goeben* and the *Breslau* go into the Black Sea and sink the Russian Fleet and burn down [the Russian ports] then Bulgaria and Romania's hesitation will disappear and the two governments will finally also take action."[60]

Shortly thereafter, Cemil met personally with the navy secretary, Admiral Alfred von Tirpitz, who had been away on the inspection of troops with Kaiser Wilhelm II. Tirpitz felt strongly about immediate intervention: if the Porte refused to decide for war now, then the two German ships should be turned loose into the Black Sea, where they would be free to attack Russian targets. He suggested that the Ottomans could pretend to protest such an attack, even by firing rounds into the air when the ships departed! And Tirpitz insisted once again that Bulgaria and Romania would be won over to the Central Powers when the Ottomans finally decided for war. In this way, the admiral remarked, the "world of Islam" would win, adding that for this reason an Ottoman army corps should also "march on Egypt and threaten the Canal."[61] In a second meeting with Cemil, Tirpitz averred "in definite terms" that the Straits were secure from attack already, this time making the point that the British would have "long ago" forced the Straits in pursuit of the German ships were they capable of doing so.[62]

[59] BA-MA, RM 40–55, sheets 3–10, Souchon to Chief of the Admiralty Staff and additional correspondence, August 15–19, 1914; PA/AA, R 22402, Wahnschaffe to Bethmann, August 21, 1914; TTK, Kâzım Orbay Arşivi, no. VI/82, Humann, August 25, 1914. The figures vary slightly throughout the documentation.
[60] ATASE, BDH, Klasör 243, Yeni Dosya 1009, Fihrist 7, Cemil to Enver, 3 Ağustos 1330 (August 16, 1914).
[61] ATASE, BDH, Klasör 243, Yeni Dosya, 1009, Fihrist 7–4, Cemil to Enver, Extremely Urgent, August 16, 1914.
[62] ATASE, BDH, Klasör 243, Yeni Dosya, 1009, Fihrist 7–1, Cemil to Enver, Extremely Urgent, 4 Ağustos 1330 (August 17, 1914).

From the Ottoman perspective, however, the German naval mission's arrival in late August 1914 served to guarantee the further delay of intervention until fortification projects at the Straits were completed. The Ottoman leaders seem to have persuaded even Souchon of this necessity, as the admiral consented to the postponement of action until fortifications were overhauled, the fleet trained, and mobilization completed. How the Ottomans succeeded in winning over the German admiral remains an open question, especially since Berlin had given the admiral the go-ahead if he wanted to break out into the Black Sea, even without the Porte's authorization.[63]

In contrast to Wangenheim's long dispatch to Berlin of August 15, in which the ambassador had counseled patience and recounted the benefits of Ottoman armed neutrality, General Liman von Sanders provided his own, alternative assessment. He had discussed with Enver the possibility of an operation against British-occupied Egypt and decided that it was out of the question in the near future because of the logistical problems such a campaign posed. Liman explained that instead he and Enver planned to transport five army corps by sea and to disembark these troops near Odessa on the Russian Black Sea coast, with the intention of attacking the flank of the Russian army operating against Austria-Hungary.[64] Berlin embraced this apparent opportunity, and Kaiser Wilhelm II immediately wired a "very urgent" telegram, reiterating that he did not care about the precise shape of Ottoman military action. And in any case, he remarked, the particular conditions could not be judged from so far away as Germany. The kaiser exhorted that "any [form of] Ottoman action is welcome"[65] – although Berlin continued to favor the expedition against Egypt. These unequivocal demands by the kaiser brought the German–Ottoman tensions to a head.

The first German–Ottoman crisis over Ottoman intervention, August 19–22

Kaiser Wilhelm II's renewed demands for military action reached Enver Pasha on August 19. Wiring directly from the German embassy, Enver expressed his regret for the delay. Playing on Wilhelm II's well-known faith in the idea of revolutionizing Muslim populations under British and French colonial rule, Enver claimed that the necessary preparations for a

[63] BA-MA, RM 40 – 455, Sheet 251, Souchon to Admiralty Staff, August 17, 1914.
[64] PA/AA, R 22402, Zimmermann to Jagow, August 18, 1914, no. 11.
[65] PA/AA, R 22402, Imperial Suite to Auswärtiges Amt [Kaiser Wilhelm II to Wangenheim], August 18, 1914, no. 5.

massive uprising were proceeding quietly but successfully. He described for the kaiser in some detail the various special revolutionary commissions allegedly active in the Caucasus, India, Persia, and northern Africa. Wangenheim endorsed the war minister's reply: "Enver's good intentions in sparking a pan-Islamic revolution cannot be questioned. For its success, it will be important that we defeat our enemies." The ambassador thus seconded Enver, but at the same time he reminded Berlin that any Ottoman success depended foremost on military victory achieved by the Central Powers.[66] This was a classic deadlock: while the Germans demanded intervention to achieve military victory, the Ottomans demanded German military victory before they were willing to commit to intervention.

The same day, Enver requested 4,000 rifles from Germany through Wangenheim, to be delivered in expedited fashion. The request was a sobering follow-up to Enver's message to the kaiser. He explained that the rifles were needed in the Caucasus in order to arm the Muslim populations, particularly in Georgia, and to advance the revolutionary causes there. Reaffirming his commitment to the pan-Islamic idea and German interests, Enver threw in some good, though vague, news for Wilhelm II, claiming that significant forces in Afghanistan and Persia would declare themselves against Russia.[67] Once again, the war minister was holding out the prospect of Ottoman action in the near future while in the meantime requesting supplies. This would become the familiar pattern in which Enver and his colleagues managed to delay intervention while drawing on German military and financial support.

German pressure for intervention emanated not only from Wilhelm II and the Auswärtiges Amt. Frustrated with the Ottoman tactic of delaying intervention, Liman submitted a request to Berlin that, in the face of continued neutrality, he and the entire military mission be recalled. Liman had met with Enver regarding the new fortification structures at the Straits. The war minister had claimed that there was no need for fortification work any longer because of the new Balkan alliance that Halil and Talat were currently setting up in Sofia, and because hostilities were thus highly unlikely to ensue. Why Enver would make such an assertion is unclear, since the overall Ottoman strategy aimed at improving the empire's military posture. Perhaps Enver was attempting to set

---

[66] PA/AA, R 22402, Zimmermann to Jagow, August 19, 1914, no. 15, which was based on BA-MA, RM 40 – 456, sheets 356–58, Humann to Wangenheim [here, copy for Souchon], Bericht an den Herrn Botschafter [Report to the Ambassador], August 17, 1914.

[67] PA/AA, R 22402, Zimmermann to Jagow [Enver Pasha to German Headquarters], August 20, 1914, no. 30; Bihl, *Die Kaukasus-Politik der Mittelmächte*, 230.

limits on the German officers' freedom of action. In any case, Enver's nonchalance about the fortifications question outraged the German general, who in the face of this doubletalk now argued that there was no point in the military mission remaining in the empire any longer. Remarkably, in this tense atmosphere, Wangenheim took Enver's side and described Liman as utterly unreasonable. He reported that Enver indeed favored military action but needed to take certain factors into consideration, most importantly the attitudes of Bucharest and Sofia. To undermine Liman's complaint, Wangenheim portrayed Enver as an uncompromising pro-German war hawk, even though Enver at this point explicitly opposed intervention. Wangenheim suggested that Liman receive the kaiser's praise for his service but that he should be sternly advised to exercise restraint. Berlin should reason with Liman that once the Ottoman defensive alliance was signed with Bulgaria and Romania, it would take only a Russian advance against Romania or the Bosporus to bring the empire into war.[68] Although Wangenheim's arguments found some traction in Berlin, the ambassador's position would grow increasingly untenable in the weeks to come, as the Sublime Porte persisted in its inaction while continuing to draw on German military aid.

To support his position, Wangenheim instructed the embassy's military attaché, Major Karl von Laffert, to wire Berlin explaining the slow progress of mobilization. In the report that followed, Laffert backed Wangenheim and the Ottoman leaders and called for more time to complete military preparations. Aware of General Liman von Sanders's assessments to the contrary, Laffert explained that he had met with the ranking members of Liman's mission, all of whom agreed with Laffert that the time was not yet ripe for intervention. In line with the Ottoman position, Laffert emphasized that no action could be hoped for before the conclusion of an alliance with Bulgaria and Romania.[69]

Wangenheim also dispatched Lieutenant Commander Hans Humann (*Korvettenkapitän*), a liaison at the embassy and a childhood companion of Enver's, to probe the war minister for details about his conversations with Liman. Enver complained that the general had been pressuring him incessantly for military action. He had told Liman that he agreed with him "as a soldier, but that as a minister he could not allow himself to be

---

[68] PA/AA, R 22402, Zimmermann to Jagow, August 20, 1914, no. 23.
[69] PA/AA, R 22402, Zimmermann to Jagow, August 20, 1914, no. 25. Indeed, a few days later, Lieutenant Colonel Kress von Kressenstein, a member of the military mission, reported that Ottoman action would prove premature at this time, see BA-MA, RM 40 – 456, sheets 352–3 and reverse, Kress to German Headquarters, August 25, 1914, and also BA-MA, RM 40 – 456, sheets 354–5, Laffert to [German Headquarters], August 26, 1914.

guided by emotions and that he had the duty to think first and foremost politically and act within his country's overall political framework." Here Enver, the alleged war hawk, was showing a different face. He argued that Germany benefited from the Sublime Porte's policy of armed neutrality, as Russia had been compelled to leave behind troops in the Caucasus otherwise deployed in European theaters. The same was true for Britain in Egypt, Enver claimed. He insisted that these factors were tangible contributions to the Central Powers' war effort, and if Berlin did not appreciate them, the military mission could be recalled and the Ottoman army demobilized. Then, Enver quickly expressed his hope that the mission would not be recalled, as it would leave the empire defenseless. Enver added that demobilization would signal a "fiasco" not only of Ottoman but also of German policy and a "triumph for the powers of the Entente."[70]

Wangenheim's advice on managing Liman – to praise him and counsel patience – was followed in Berlin. Kaiser Wilhelm II sent Liman instructions ordering him to stay put and to work in concert with Enver: "I expect cooperation with Enver, to whom you are to convey my full trust and to pass on my greetings."[71] Nevertheless, the ambassador's elaborations on the question of Ottoman neutrality produced consternation. Foreign Secretary Jagow laid down Berlin's view. "We counted on definite, active intervention following the alliance with the Ottoman Empire. It was this expectation that caused us to grant the Ottoman request for the dispatching of the Goeben and the Breslau." He was alarmed to learn from Enver's statement that it would take a Russian attack on the Bosporus or an invasion of Romania to bring the empire into the war. Perplexed, Jagow objected that both events seemed highly unlikely, and he suspected that Enver's statement was a pretext for delay. Jagow urged the Ottomans to finally carry out their part of the alliance, referring to all of the technical and material support that Germany was providing. He pointed to the Usedom mission, the team of about 550 naval personnel, including fortification and artillery specialists, which Enver had requested. Berlin was adamant: "We expect now that the Ottoman government will decide on immediate action."[72]

[70] PA/AA, R 22402, Zimmermann to Jagow, August 20, 1914, no. 32.
[71] PA/AA, R 22402, Wilhelm to Auswärtiges Amt, August 20, 1914, not numbered. And PA/AA, R 1913, Bethmann to Auswärtiges Amt, August 20, 1914, no. 17.
[72] PA/AA, R 22402, Jagow to Wangenheim, August 20, 1914, no telegram number. For a summary of German *matériel*, personnel, and financial support provided as of August 20, 1914, see BA-MA R 40 – 4, sheet 158 and reverse, Meldung über den Fortgang der Aktion zur Unterstützung der Türkei [Information on the progress of support to Turkey], Boedicker to Jagow, August 20, 1914.

Wangenheim conveyed Berlin's message once again to Enver, but the war minister refused to budge. Instead, Enver replied on August 22 that Ottoman hands were tied as long as the Bulgarian and Romanian positions remained undefined, stating that the wavering attitudes of the two Balkan powers "placed reasonable limits on an active Ottoman policy." Enver also claimed that Halil and Talat's absence from the capital temporarily weakened his position in the cabinet. Thus he once again fended off strong German pressure, making his case for Ottoman neutrality.[73] Although Enver frequently declared his support for immediate action, it is clear that he repeatedly, and openly, opposed it. Wangenheim also reported a telephone conversation with Enver in which the war minister had claimed that Sofia would launch a major offensive on Serbia within two or three days. Enver suggested that German diplomats thus focus their attention on the Bulgarian prime minister, and in the days that followed, Berlin's pressure shifted away from Istanbul and towards Sofia. Enver, for the moment, had defused the crisis.[74] Aided by Wangenheim, August came and went and the Ottoman leaders still managed to preserve their alliance with Germany without entering the war.

Between neutrality and alliance

On August 19, the Bulgarian and Ottoman governments finally signed a "treaty of friendship and alliance." Yet for all the Ottoman insistence on an alliance with Bulgaria before entering the war, military action was still not forthcoming.[75] Enver now reversed himself yet again, and began to focus on the vulnerability of the Dardanelles to an Entente naval attack. Attaché Laffert repeated the fear that, in all likelihood, the Straits could not be held against an assault, particularly if the *Goeben* and the *Breslau* were not in the southern Dardanelles but were instead operating against the Russians in the Black Sea. He pointed out that currently the two ships were guarding the northern Bosporus, and that as a result they were a six-hour journey away from the Aegean Sea, the point of any Entente attack. If the *Goeben* and the *Breslau* moved now against Odessa, the Straits would become particularly vulnerable to the British. According to Laffert, the German naval officers in Istanbul all agreed that a British attack launched from the Aegean could not be withstood. He recommended that the

---

[73] PA/AA, R 1913, Wangenheim to Auswärtiges Amt, August 22, 1914, no. 575; PA/AA, R 22402, Zimmermann to Bethmann, August 22, 1914, no. 66.
[74] PA/AA, R 22402, Zimmermann to Jagow, August 20, 1914, no. 26.
[75] For the treaty, see Sinan Kuneralp, ed., *Recueil des Traités, Conventions, Protocoles, Arrangements et Déclarations signés entre l'Empire Ottoman et les Puissances Étrangères, 1903–1922*, vol. I, *1903–1916* (Istanbul: Éditions Isis, 2000), 297–8.

German warships should not leave the Straits until these were sufficiently fortified. The most promising option for military action, Laffert concluded, was a joint Bulgarian–Ottoman overland campaign against Serbia. Such a campaign would free up Austro-Hungarian forces, which in turn could be used on the Russian front.[76]

Wangenheim agreed with all of these arguments. The Straits had to be given priority, he said, and the Porte should not be faulted for its hesitation. Given Italy's continued neutrality, he added, the strategic assumptions on which the Ottomans had accepted the alliance with Germany had changed radically. He also shifted the responsibility for Ottoman passivity on to Austria: "Had the Austrians sent a naval division [to Constantinople], as they had previously indicated they would, the Ottoman Empire would now be ready for action."[77]

Romania, too, was to be blamed for the lack of Ottoman battlefield action, Wangenheim continued. The Romanian government had refused to make a promise not to attack Bulgaria should its southern neighbor get involved in the war. He concluded that not only Austria-Hungary but also "Italy and Romania should be blamed if an Ottoman action is currently not possible." Addressing what was perhaps his government's greatest concern, Wangenheim reassured the Auswärtiges Amt that there was no danger of losing the empire to the Entente now: even though Istanbul was not ready for war at this point, it remained fully committed to its German ally.[78]

For Berlin, all this was a bitter pill to swallow. Navy Secretary Tirpitz, writing in Chancellor Bethmann Hollweg's name, hit back. He overruled the evaluations coming out of Istanbul and declared the Dardanelles secure, even without the constant presence of the *Goeben* and the *Breslau*. Once the members of the Usedom mission had taken up their posts, so Tirpitz argued, the ships would be entirely free for action in the Black Sea. The Tirpitz/Bethmann note shows Berlin pressing for intervention of any type: "an attack by our ships in the Black Sea or an attack by the torpedo boats against the British blockade [in the Aegean] would draw

---

[76] PA/AA, R 1913, Wangenheim to Auswärtiges Amt, August 24, 1914, no. 595, reaching Jagow the following day, see PA/AA, R 22402, Zimmermann to Jagow, August 25, 1914, no. 113.

[77] PA/AA, Wangenheim to Auswärtiges Amt, August 26, 1914, no. 609, forwarded to the German Foreign Secretary as PA/AA, R 22402, Zimmermann to Jagow, August 26, 1914, no. 131.

[78] Ibid.; Romanian leaders worried not only about raising Russian ire, they also rightly suspected Bulgarian designs on the Southern Dobruja region, which had changed from Bulgarian to Romanian hands during the Second Balkan War in 1913, see Friedrich, *Bulgarien und die Mächte*, 124.

the Ottoman Empire into the war, which is our most urgent interest."[79] Wangenheim understood the message, and sought to moderate it. Enver was ready for war, he noted, but work on the fortifications at the Dardanelles required at least another eight to fourteen days, according to Admiral Usedom. Mobilization, too, the ambassador pointed out, demanded about the same time. The baron reassured Berlin once again that there was now no danger of Istanbul switching sides, nor, he claimed, did Enver fear a British forcing of the Straits, not even a successful one. Enver made the remarkable claim that British forces, once inside the Straits or in the Sea of Marmara, would not be able to land anywhere.[80] Whether Enver really held this view is questionable, and it is probable that the war minister made this statement in order to allay German fears of an Ottoman last-minute switch to the enemy side.

As late as September 1914, key German officials in Istanbul were disinclined to force the empire into the war. Souchon reported to Ottoman headquarters that British ships outside the southern Dardanelles were jamming the navy's radio signals and actively incapacitating communication lines. He argued that such tactics should be considered a "military act" equivalent to harassing Ottoman ships in open waters. But when the argument did not elicit a strong reaction, Souchon did not push the issue further.[81] Lieutenant Colonel Friedrich Kress von Kressenstein joined Enver and Wangenheim in helping to make the Ottomans' case. In a report of August 27, Kress argued that the armed forces had not yet recovered from the Balkan Wars and that intervention could bring only failure. Kress believed that a "sufficiently long period of peace" was necessary to successfully implement military reforms.[82] A little later, the German officer again shared the "view of the Turkish statesmen" and pointed to their legitimate concern over a Bulgarian attack in Thrace as

---

[79] For Tirpitz's draft see PA/AA, R 22402, Tirpitz to Bethmann Hollweg, August 28, 1914. For the eventual document sent to Wangenheim, see PA/AA, R 1913, Bethmann Hollweg to Auswärtiges Amt, August 28, 1914, no. 26; BA-MA, RM 40 – 457, sheet 241, for Souchon's copy.

[80] PA/AA, R 22402, Zimmermann to Jagow, August 30, 1914, no. 198. For Wangenheim's explicit statement that the Ottoman Empire would definitely not change sides, see PA/AA, R 1913, Wangenheim to Auswärtiges Amt, August 26, 1914, no. 609. The Usedom mission's work on the Dardanelles fortification did not commence, for logistical reasons, until September 7, 1914. See BA-MA RM 40 – 1, sheet 5, Usedom to Mueller, September 9, 1914.

[81] TTK, Kâzım Orbay Arşivi, no. VI/134, Souchon to Ottoman General Headquarters, August 28, 1914.

[82] ATASE, BDH, Klasör 46, Yeni Dosya 215A, Fihrist 1–4 and 1–5, Kress to Ottoman General Headquarters, August 27, 1914; see also ATASE, BDH, Klasör 46, Yeni Dosya 215A, Fihrist 3–5 to 3–7, Kress to Ottoman General Headquarters, September 4, 1914.

soon as the Ottoman forces engaged Russia in the Black Sea or the Caucasus, or Britain in Egypt.[83]

Nonetheless, during the first days of September, with several Balkan powers still neutral, German and Austro-Hungarian diplomats set their hopes on forming a broad Balkan alliance linked to the Central Powers. Greek–Ottoman negotiations proceeded in Bucharest, with Halil and Talat as the Sublime Porte's representatives. For a brief period it appeared as if the two parties could set aside their dispute regarding the Aegean islands by agreeing on a twenty-five-year lease of Chios and Mitylene to Greece under Ottoman sovereignty. As part of such a settlement, the two powers would conclude a defensive alliance. But the negotiations broke down over the question of what Greece would do if Bulgaria attacked Serbia. While the Ottomans (and Berlin) demanded that Greece remain neutral in the case of a Bulgarian attack on Serbia, the Greek prime minister held fast to his government's commitment to Serbia.[84] That commitment stemmed from the alliance between Greece-Serbia that was signed in July 1913, which promised mutual aid in the case that either partner suffered an attack. This treaty should have become operative, of course, when Serbia was attacked by Austria-Hungary in July 1914, but Athens claimed that it was applicable only if the aggressor was one of the small Balkan states. Now the Greek government affirmed its military support to Serbia if an attack were to come from Bulgaria.[85] In fact, neither Greece nor Romania had been genuinely engaged in these negotiations with the Central Powers, and both secretly favored an alliance with the Entente.[86] Hence, no Balkan league under the aegis of the Central Powers lay within the reach of Berlin or Vienna in August/September 1914.

The German war plans used in 1914 were developed by the late chief of the general staff, Alfred von Schlieffen, and expanded upon considerably after 1905 by the general staff of his successor, Helmuth von Moltke (the

---

[83] ATASE, BDH, Klasör 46, Yeni Dosya 215, Fihrist 3–26 to 3–28, Beurteilung der Lage am 6.9.1914 [General Assessment of September 6, 1914].

[84] PA/AA, R 22402, Zimmermann to Jagow, August 31, 1914, no. 213; PA/AA, R 22402, Zimmermann to Jagow, September 2, 1914, 234; PA/AA, R 22402, Zimmermann to Jagow, September 3, 1914, no. 258; PA/AA, R 22402, Zimmermann to Jagow, September 3, 1914, no. 260; PA/AA, R 22402, Zimmermann to Jagow, September 4, 1914, no. 277; see also the memoirs of the Ottoman ambassador at Athens, Galip Kemali Söylemezoğlu, *Hatıralarι: Atina Sefareti (1913–1916)*, Canlı Tarihler, no. 5 (Istanbul: Türkiye Yayınevi, 1946), 213 and 219.

[85] Lynn H. Curtright, *Muddle, Indecision and Setback: British Policy and the Balkan States, August 1914 to the Inception of the Dardanelles Campaign* (Thessaloniki: Institute for Balkan Studies, 1986), 26.

[86] Both Romania and Greece eventually joined the Entente, in August 1916 and June 1917, respectively. Bulgaria entered the war on the side of the Central Powers in October 1915.

younger). These plans provided for a two-front war against France in the west and Russia in the east, and they sought to mitigate the principal problem Germany faced on the battlefield: shortage of manpower. Thus the general staff planned a primary campaign against France in the west, where the density of German railways provided the advantages of speed and flexibility. Victory over France would then allow the deployment of German divisions to the east in support of the armies of Austria-Hungary and now, if it could be made to move, the Ottoman Empire.[87] Once war broke out, however, German forces found themselves bogged down at the Marne, fighting not only French but British forces as well. For the Ottomans, who were counting on German military success as the basis for their participation in the war, bad news from the western front fostered hesitation and delay throughout the following months.

Having sent military and naval missions under Liman, Souchon, and Usedom, the German high command itself stepped up the pressure for Ottoman intervention. The chief of the general staff, General Helmuth von Moltke, cabled Liman directly on September 4:

It is wished that the Ottoman Empire lead an attack soon, at the very latest after the completion of the Dardanelles defenses, [now being] expedited. [Shape of] operations based [on your] judgement. [Operations] across Black Sea against Odessa and those against Egypt [appear] particularly promising.[88]

Moltke's message signaled the beginning of a tightened policy towards the empire at German headquarters. All requests for personal, material, and financial aid now were to be placed on hold until the empire took an active military role. The Ottomans got the message. They responded by reaffirming their commitment to the German alliance and to the war efforts of the Central Powers. To make this point as explicitly as possible, Enver inquired from Admiral Souchon when the German–Ottoman "fleet will be

---

[87] For the recent debate as to what extent, if any, Schlieffen's 1905 memorandum provided the basis for German war planning in 1914, see Terence Zuber, "The Schlieffen Plan Reconsidered," *War in History* 6 (1999): 262–305, and the responses by Terence Holmes, Robert T. Foley, and Annika Mombauer. See also the reviews of Zuber's *Inventing the Schlieffen Plan: German War Planning, 1871–1914* (New York: Oxford University Press, 2002).

[88] PA/AA, R 22402, Moltke to Wangenheim [for Liman], September 4, 1914, and BA-MA, RM 40 – 454, sheet 338, Moltke to Liman, September 4, 1914. Liman shared the message with Souchon, see BA-MA, RM 40 – 456, sheet 346, Liman to Souchon, September 13, 1914. Souchon's reply reflects Liman's preference for the Odessa campaign, while Berlin favored the expedition against Egypt, BA-MA, RM 40 – 456, sheet 347–48, Souchon to Liman, September 14, 1914.

in a position to seek out and fight successfully the Russian fleet" – as if it had been the fleet's lack of preparation that had held him back.[89]

Interior Minister Talat Bey also reiterated his commitment to Germany and the joint war effort. Newly returned from alliance negotiations in Bucharest and Sofia, he visited Wangenheim and expressed his frustration at the Balkan obstacles to Ottoman intervention. Romania continued to refuse a written promise not to attack Bulgaria if the latter entered the war, Talat lamented. As for the Bulgarians, they refused to take action without precisely such a guarantee from Bucharest. Negotiations with Bulgaria would forge ahead, and Talat repeated the now-familiar line that the Ottoman army would march immediately once Sofia entered the war. Should the grand vezir oppose intervention after Bulgaria's decision, Talat claimed that he and his colleagues would enter the war anyway and force Said Halim's resignation. Given that Talat, as we have seen, was not actually interested in a Bulgarian–Ottoman offensive alliance, it follows that he too was working to gain additional time in the hope that the war would be decided before the Ottomans were forced to intervene. Reporting his conversation to Berlin on September 6, Wangenheim contended that an operation against Odessa would not be possible for at least another ten to fourteen days for logistical reasons. He also challenged the plan itself, noting that the officers of the Usedom mission considered the landing on the open Russian coast to be highly problematic because only a small number of troops could be set ashore in such an operation. The troops would be so limited in number that they would not be able to push their way to Galicia, where they would be needed to reinforce the Austro-Hungarian army. For these reasons, Wangenheim recommended focusing on a campaign against the British in Egypt rather than the naval operation against Russia,[90] a major shift in the war plans under deliberation, although one Berlin too favored.

In a subsequent telegram the same day, Wangenheim indicated that the Porte's finances were dwindling rapidly and that the authorities were certain to turn to Berlin for financial support sooner rather than later. In response to Moltke's strong words of September 4, and in an attempt to salvage the continuation of German aid, Wangenheim suggested that Berlin provide financial support initially only for those military undertakings

[89] BA-MA, RM 40 – 454, Enver to Souchon, September 6, 1914, sheet 335. Souchon's reply stated that the fleet could be ready for a naval attack against Russia within a few days, by September 13. That readiness, however, was not acted upon, see BA-MA, RM 40 – 454, sheet 336–7, Souchon to Enver, September 10, 1914.
[90] PA/AA, R 1914, Wangenheim to Auswärtiges Amt, September 6, 1914, no. 725, forwarded to Jagow as PA/AA, R 22402, Zimmermann to Jagow, September 6, 1914, no. 302.

designed to support primarily German interests. Although it is unclear whether Wangenheim was expressing his personal opinion, or whether he was conveying Ottoman requests without explicitly saying so, he recommended that Berlin finance Ottoman operations "such as the push against Egypt, [an operation] from which the Ottoman Empire can expect no real advantage. Later on, however, we will also have to consider subsidies for the [Ottoman] army in Europe."[91]

It is striking that Wangenheim persistently requested further aid for the Ottomans while defending their neutrality, despite the demand from his superiors for immediate action. It also becomes clear from Wangenheim's correspondence that the purpose behind Ottoman military action was to serve German objectives. This rationale is evident, especially in the eventual German–Ottoman campaign against the Suez Canal in February 1915. After the war, one of the key planners behind the campaign, Kress, wrote in a private letter to the German Near East scholar Karl Süssheim that the empire had nothing to gain from the Egyptian expedition launched in 1915. On the contrary, no one expected the successful crossing of the canal, let alone the capture of Egypt or Cairo. The sole purpose of the campaign, according to Kress, was to compel a British troop build-up there. In this way, the operation would draw troops away from the western front and provide relief there to the Central Powers.[92]

The German "no" to Ottoman requests for military aid, September 10, 1914

Thus German authorities did not care much about the specific shape Ottoman intervention would take. In response to Wangenheim's report, Bethmann retorted that the Sublime Porte should open hostilities against Russia even if troops could not be landed and no real military objective would be achieved. The chancellor also offered the Egyptian option as an alternative:

Only an attack against the Suez Canal could prove truly decisive. A large-scale Turkish undertaking against English rule in Egypt seems currently out of the question, however. But it seems possible to obtain Enver's approval now for an expedition against the Suez Canal of twenty to thirty thousand men, marching from Damascus via Jerusalem or Maan ... I ask that you discuss this plan first with the German experts and with the military and naval leaders, [Liman and Souchon] and that you then get Enver's opinion [regarding this plan] and report

---

[91] PA/AA, R 22402, Zimmermann to Jagow, September 6, 1914, no. 308.
[92] Library of Congress, Karl Süssheim Papers, Friedrich Kress von Kressenstein to Karl Süssheim, August 20, 1919.

back, including what Enver would demand in terms of weapons and ammunition. I emphasize once again the urgency of this matter and place its solution in your energetic hands.[93]

Wangenheim's discussion of Suez with Enver and Liman, however, simply provided both men with the opportunity to fill out their wish lists. The latter requested the dispatch of ten additional officers from Germany for the attack on the canal. Enver said he needed a minimum of six quick-firing field artilleries (*Schnellfeuerbatterien*) along with ammunition. The war minister also seized the opportunity to renew previous requests for ammunition and to place new ones: "Completely lacking is ammunition for the four 10.5 cm howitzers. [For] these he [Enver] asks provisionally for a minimum of eight thousand rounds."[94]

Enver made known his preference for an offensive in the Caucasus rather than the Egyptian campaign, claiming that collaboration with the Georgian population would be more fruitful. Indispensable for such an invasion, however, were rifles and ammunition for the Georgians. He had requested these weapons before, Enver reminded the ambassador, and he now pushed for their prompt delivery. Passing on Enver's request, Wangenheim seemed to apologize for this counter-demand by pointing to the bad news arriving from the battlefront. The Austro-Hungarian defeat by Russian forces at Lemberg in mid-September had upset the Ottoman leadership. Enver's commitment to the alliance and intervention remained unshaken, Wangenheim insisted, but these reassurances had begun to ring hollow in Berlin. Enver regularly overstated his enthusiasm for intervention in order to make up for the delay, and, by extension, to keep German financial support and *matériel* flowing. Even though Istanbul's tactics must by now have been glaringly transparent, Wangenheim dutifully proclaimed once more that "Enver is still prepared to strike at any cost and at any time," and he relayed the war minister's statement that he did not "fear the Anglo-French fleet, even if it should enter the Dardanelles, because, in any case, it could not land." And Enver did offer something tangible: a naval demonstration in the Black Sea that would pass by the Bulgarian and Romanian port cities Varna and Constanta, thereby putting pressure, through intimidation, on the two Balkan states. He even suggested that the fleet could also engage Russian naval forces. These disparate promises for intervention deeply dismayed those

[93] PA/AA, R 22402, Bethmann to Wangenheim, September 7, 1914 [draft], no. 35. A copy of Bethmann's telegram reached Admiral Souchon on September 8, 1914. See BA-MA, RM 40 – 457, sheet 235, and BA-MA, RM 40 – 4, sheet 153.
[94] PA/AA, R 1914, Wangenheim to Auswärtiges Amt, September 8, 1914, no. 745, forwarded to Jagow as PA/AA, R 22402, Zimmermann to Jagow, September 9, 1914, no. 336.

in Berlin. Presenting yet another vague plan for action, Wangenheim's closing remark clouded the picture only further:

I will try everything in my power to succeed in carrying through the naval demonstration. Should I not succeed, it will only remain for the *Goeben* and the *Breslau* to break through the Bosporus and begin the operation themselves. This [event] would probably drag the Ottomans along. Speedy Austrian victories in Galicia are hoped for.[95]

Jagow sent a brief reply indicating that Enver's request had been forwarded to the German war minister, and declared that "quick Ottoman action against Russia" had now become urgent. He acknowledged that the expedition against Egypt required additional time, and endorsed the idea of a naval demonstration in the Black Sea.[96] Jagow feared that insistence on the Egyptian campaign would only delay the Ottoman decision: "If we press for an expedition against Egypt, which requires several more weeks of preparation, *prior* to a declaration of war, we give the Ottoman Empire a certain right to consider a declaration of war premature and to postpone it further." Then Jagow put forth his own view on how to bring about intervention. Once the fleet entered the Black Sea, "[e]verything else will follow."[97]

If the Ottoman leaders, and Wangenheim, had assumed that additional military aid would be forthcoming in order to bring Istanbul closer to intervention, the reply of September 10 by General Falkenhayn, the war minister, must have come as a surprise. In agreement with the general staff, Falkenhayn explained, he had decided to stop all further "requests for officers, artillery, and ammunition." No such requests "should be honored until the Ottoman Empire was at war with Germany's enemies." Thus, "from the moment hostilities begin, [Ottoman] wishes will be followed to the greatest extent possible."[98]

Enver set out immediately to test his ally's new policy, inquiring through his military attaché in Berlin, Cemil Bey, about four 28 cm guns, which had been built by Krupp for the Belgian army but confiscated along with their ammunition. Enver asked for the cannons to be installed at the Dardanelles against an Entente naval attack. Berlin stuck to its hard line. From a war ministry official Cemil learned that the guns and further aid would be forthcoming immediately upon intervention. Demanding

---

[95] PA/AA, R 1914, Wangenheim to Auswärtiges Amt, September 8, 1914, no. 752.
[96] PA/AA, R 1914, Jagow to Auswärtiges Amt, September 9, 1914, no. 117, and its draft in PA/AA, R 22402, Jagow to Wangenheim, September 9, 1914, no. 117.
[97] PA/AA, R 22402, Jagow to Zimmermann, draft dated September 10, 1914. (Emphasis in original.)
[98] PA/AA, R 22402, Jagow to Wangenheim, September 10, 1914, no. 121.

that the Ottomans finally throw in their lot with Germany, he sweetened the pill by touching on Berlin's larger vision for the Ottoman Empire: "Germany is now so involved in the Ottoman Empire that our prestige and principal war aim incontrovertibly demand that we should support the Ottoman Empire in the future also." But intervention was necessary first. Cemil assured his colleague that the delay resulted neither from any lack of commitment among the members of the cabinet nor from any other political consideration, but stemmed only from the slow pace of mobilization.[99]

The Ottomans continued their attempts at restoring the flow of German aid. A "representative of the naval office," probably Enver's confidant Hans Humann, inquired on the Porte's behalf whether Berlin would provide 25 million German Marks, or about 1.35 million Ottoman pounds,[100] for the expedition against Egypt. Jagow's deputy, Arthur Zimmermann, suggested that a larger amount of 100 million German Marks, or about 5.4 million Ottoman pounds, should be offered as a general war subsidy, to be paid out in installments once Ottoman military action got underway.[101] Responding to Bethmann's instructions of September 7 regarding the Egypt expedition, Liman claimed that the campaign required much smaller funds, that is, about 100,000 Ottoman pounds, or less than 2 million German Marks.[102] Consulting with Jagow, Zimmermann stressed that Liman's proposal should be understood as a first installment and that a general schedule for subsidies should be implemented along the lines of his own recent proposal.[103] Eventually Jagow approved the disposition of 100,000 Ottoman pounds for the expedition against Egypt but maintained that any further subsidies could come only after Ottoman intervention. This was it! The German government would categorically reject any further requests for aid from now on.[104] Chancellor Bethmann Hollweg concurred with the decision

---

[99] PA/AA, R 22402, General Headquarters to Auswärtiges Amt, September 11, 1914.

[100] One Ottoman pound exchanged for about 18.5 German Marks and 1.1 British pounds; see Şevket Pamuk, "Evolution in the Ottoman Monetary System," in Suraiya Faroqhi, Bruce McGowan, Donald Quataert, and Şevket Pamuk, *An Economic and Social History of the Ottoman Empire*, vol. II, *1600–1914* (Cambridge: Cambridge University Press, 1994; paperback edn., 1997), 972.

[101] PA/AA, R 22402, Zimmermann to Jagow, September 10, 1914, Report No. 11.

[102] PA/AA, R 1914, Wangenheim to Auswärtiges Amt, September 11, 1914, no. 785.

[103] PA/AA, R 22402, Zimmermann to Jagow, September 12, 1914, no. 393.

[104] PA/AA, R 1914, Jagow to Auswärtiges Amt, September 13, 1914, no. 140. Bethmann approved the transfer of 100,000 Ottoman pounds in gold (1.85 million German Marks) three days later; see PA/AA, R 22402, Zimmermann to Jagow, September 16, 1914, which bears Chancellor Bethmann's handwritten approval.

demanding a declaration of war against Russia before further subsidies were granted.[105] The Ottomans had exhausted German patience.

Meanwhile, the Bulgarian prime minister, Radoslavov, intimated that his country would remain neutral for the time being because of a possible Romanian attack.[106] Wangenheim reported that Sofia's declaration had visibly rattled Ottoman circles: "The Ottomans will not send their troops into the Black Sea as they said earlier. [They will not do so] until Bulgaria has entered the war." An expedition against the Russians in Batum, Wangenheim explained, was still possible, but it would require the arming of the Georgian population with rifles, still due to arrive in Istanbul.[107] Yet, with an Ottoman campaign in the Balkans out of the question in the face of Bulgarian neutrality and the Egyptian expedition in need of additional preparation, Kaiser Wilhelm II, evidently brushing aside Wangenheim's objections, pressed for the naval attack on Russia. Through his chief of the admiralty staff, Admiral Hugo von Pohl, the kaiser instructed Souchon to take the fleet into the Black Sea and to attack the Russian fleet. Souchon was notified that:

His Majesty the Kaiser wants energetic action in the Black Sea, as soon as you feel strong enough and the Dardanelles have been rendered defensible against an attack. Objective of the operation is to neutralize the Russian Black Sea Fleet and to gain naval supremacy in the Black Sea.[108]

But the specific form of Ottoman intervention still mattered little to Berlin, as long as it did in fact occur, and as soon as possible. War could even be brought about by attacking the Entente ships patrolling the southern mouth of the Dardanelles, lying in wait for the *Goeben* and the *Breslau* in case they attempted to re-enter the Aegean. Wilhelm II suggested: "Continue to pursue [plans for the] impairment of enemy forces outside the Dardanelles through attacks with torpedo boats."[109]

---

[105] PA/AA, R 22402, Jagow to Zimmermann, September 12, 1914, Reply to Report No. 11.
[106] PA/AA, R 22402, Michahelles to Auswärtiges Amt, September 9, 1914 (telegram number illegible).
[107] PA/AA, R 1914, Wangenheim to Auswärtiges Amt, September 11, 1914, no. 779, and submitted to Jagow as PA/AA, R 22402, Zimmermann to Jagow, September 13, 1914, no. 394.
[108] PA/AA, R 22402, Pohl to Jagow, September 12, 1914, Report no. 93. These instructions reached Ambassador Wangenheim and Admiral Souchon in Istanbul on September 14, 1914. See PA/AA, R 1914, Bethmann to Auswärtiges Amt, September 14, 1914, no. 43. Copy for Navy Ministry in BA-MA, RM 5 – 2320, Bethmann to Auswärtiges Amt, September 14, 1914, no. 43. Bethmann's telegram conveying Wilhelm's instructions was drafted by Jagow on September 14, 1914, see PA/AA, R 22402, Jagow to Wangenheim, [draft] September 14, 1914, no. 7.
[109] Ibid.

Grand Vezir Said Halim Pasha took advantage of the new international dynamic generated by the July Crisis. As a result of the conflict between Austria-Hungary and Serbia, the Central Powers could no longer reject Ottoman appeals for alliance, and the grand vezir succeeded in concluding an alliance with Germany on August 2, 1914. In his efforts to form the alliance, Said Halim was aided by Enver, without whose promise of immediate military action Berlin would not have been won. During the weeks to follow, the Ottoman leaders found themselves under intense German pressure to deliver the military support as promised. They had hoped either to stay outside the war entirely or to enter it only in its final stages, but their paramount foreign policy concern was to preserve the alliance they had formed with Germany and to preserve it into the postwar period. As a result, Enver vociferously declared his commitment to war even while stalling on any concrete action. From the Ottoman perspective, what would come to be known as the Great War was, for the moment, a Great Opportunity. Those at the helm of state hoped that through the German alliance the empire could regain its international security and, eventually, its international status.

6   Salvation through war?

Their negotiations with German representatives in Istanbul from August through October 1914 reveal an Ottoman leadership that viewed participation in the war as an acceptable but perhaps avoidable policy, and sought to delay entry for as long as possible. The goal was to preserve the German–Ottoman alliance and the ability to draw on German assistance during the war and, even more importantly, after the war, with no great expenditure of Ottoman resources or blood.

At least theoretically, Ottoman decision-makers still enjoyed two alternatives. The first – alignment with the Entente – would have entailed the dismissal of the three German military missions from the empire, headed respectively by General Liman von Sanders, Admiral Souchon, and Admiral Usedom, and consisting of over a thousand German officers and personnel. The loss of this military aid effectively would have meant Ottoman demobilization and future reliance on Britain, France, and/or Russia. The second entailed commitment to and financial reliance on Germany, and consequently the willingness to participate in the war on the side of the Central Powers. This second option held the promise of long-term international security and economic development in the framework of a Great Power alliance. Said Halim Pasha, in particular, viewed the alliance chiefly as a means to long-term Ottoman recovery.

Joining either bloc, however, brought with it a host of dangers. On the one hand, given the well-known Russian territorial and extensive British and French economic interests in the empire, joining the Entente would place the empire's future at the discretion of its alliance partners. Alignment with the Central Powers, on the other hand, would bring the empire into open hostility with Britain, France, and Russia. Since the most important determinant of Ottoman policy in 1914 was the concern for long-term international security and economic development, the German–Ottoman negotiation process throughout the summer of 1914 must be seen in this context. And even after the empire entered the war, these concerns continued to shape decision-making in Istanbul. Once

they launched the naval attack on Russia across the Black Sea in late
October 1914, therefore, the Ottoman leaders went to work immediately
to expand the terms of the August treaty, which was revised and then
signed on January 11, 1915.[1]

Once Berlin declared on September 10, 1914, its refusal to provide any
further material or financial assistance until the Ottomans took up arms,
key cabinet members abandoned the policy of delay. As the ultimatum
was followed by urgent demands for intervention from the highest ranks in
Berlin, including Kaiser Wilhelm II, War Minister Falkenhayn, and
Chancellor Bethmann Hollweg, the alliance became strained to the
point of rupture. Given the Ottoman leaders' hope for long-term
German–Ottoman cooperation, it became necessary to shed the image
of the hesitant and self-serving coquette, playing off one suitor against the
other, and instead to accept the role of committed and loyal spouse.
Enver, in particular, fulfilled this role by acting as the uncompromising
war hawk.

During the days following Falkenhayn's notification that Germany
would not provide additional assistance until the Ottomans entered the
war, Enver initially sought to soften Berlin's attitude by going back to the
prospect of a joint Bulgarian–Ottoman campaign in the Balkans.[2] At a
meeting on September 13, Enver assured Wangenheim, Liman,
Souchon, and Usedom that he had once again offered Sofia immediate
military cooperation. A joint operation, Enver explained, would be two-
pronged, with one front moving against Serbia, and a second front, if
Romanian cooperation could be secured, against Russia. Should the
Romanians decide not to join the Bulgarian–Ottoman forces, Ottoman
troops would march through Bulgaria and guard the Bulgarian northern
border against a Romanian attack. As a result, the Bulgarian army would
have a free hand against Serbia. Such an operation could take place within
three weeks' time, provided Bulgaria mobilized immediately. The decision, therefore, according to the Porte, once again rested with the
Bulgarian government.[3]

---

[1] ATASE, BDH, Klasör 1649, Yeni Dosya 41, Fihrist 8–8/2.

[2] PA/AA, R 1914, Wangenheim to Auswärtiges Amt, September 12, 1914, no. 791, reaching
Jagow the next day, see PA/AA, R 22402, Zimmermann to Jagow, September 13, 1914,
no. 401.

[3] PA/AA, R 1914, Wangenheim to Auswärtiges Amt, September 13, 1914, no. 795, reaching
Jagow on September 13, see PA/AA, R 22402, Zimmermann to Jagow, September 13,
1914, no. 401; BA-MA, RM 40 – 282, sheet 61, Humann to Souchon, Besprechung mit
Oberstleutnant v. Kress am 12. September 1914 [Conversation with Lieutenant Colonel
Kress on September 12, 1914].

Enver understood his role and continued to appear fully committed to intervention. He was aided by divisions in Germany's own military establishment. When at the same meeting Souchon, Usedom, and Wangenheim opposed the operation proposed by Liman, an attempt to land troops near Odessa on Russia's Black Sea coast, with Souchon pointing to the dangerous nature of the mission, Enver expressed his support for Liman's plan despite the high risk that it entailed. Reporting back to Berlin, Wangenheim wrote that Liman's operation "has only about a 10 percent chance [of success] according to the admirals," but "Liman seems to have won over Enver to it." A few days later, however, Enver joined the rest of the Ottoman cabinet in refusing to authorize the fleet to go into the Black Sea, suggesting that he was in less of a hurry than he had led his German colleagues to believe.[4]

Given the German officers' verdict against the Odessa operation, Berlin did not back Liman's plan, despite Enver's apparent support for it. Instead, it suggested a naval encounter in the Black Sea, sufficient to bring the Ottomans into war, though without any hope of landing troops and threatening Russian operations on the eastern front. Berlin's strategists hoped that Ottoman intervention would fire up a global rebellion among the millions of Muslim subjects living under Entente colonial rule in North Africa, India, and Central Asia. Once the clash in the Black Sea brought the caliphate into the war, the Ottoman forces could stage campaigns into territories controlled by the enemy but with majority Muslim populations:

The expedition against Egypt and anti-British Islamic movements continue to be our central war aim. Please inform Liman that this is His Majesty's wish ... Our military authorities consider a landing of troops in Odessa prior to gaining naval superiority in the Black Sea to be impossible because of the danger posed to the transports [by the Russian fleet]. His Majesty orders that General Liman be informed of this decision.[5]

---

[4] PA/AA, R 1914, Wangenheim to Auswärtiges Amt, September 13, 1914, no. 795. Wangenheim requested appropriate instructions for Liman to be sent immediately in order to resolve the dispute (*Streitfrage*) among the German leaders.

[5] PA/AA, R 1914, Bethmann Hollweg to Auswärtiges Amt, September 14, 1914, no. 43. Copy for Navy Ministry in BA-MA, RM 5 – 2320, sheets 3–4. Bethmann's telegram conveying Wilhelm's orders was drafted by German Foreign Secretary Jagow, see PA/AA, R 22402, Türkei Nr. 18, Jagow to Wangenheim, draft dated September 14, 1914, no. 7. Wilhelm's orders had reached the Auswärtiges Amt in a memorandum by the German Chief of the Admiralty Staff Pohl, see PA/AA, R 22402, Türkei Nr.18, Pohl to Jagow, September 12, 1914, Report no. 93.

This telegram, signed by Chancellor Bethmann Hollweg and arriving in Istanbul on September 14, 1914, also included a message for Admiral Souchon from Kaiser Wilhelm II: stage "energetic action in the Black Sea as soon as you feel strong enough."[6]

During the subsequent days, German military leaders reinforced the kaiser's orders. Falkenhayn, by now also the chief of the general staff, wrote Liman during the critical days of mid-September: "As I explained in my letter of August 10 … an expedition against Egypt is of great importance." Given the circumstances, however, Falkenhayn instructed Liman to take whatever the Ottomans offered: "in the meantime, it is central to our objectives that Turkey take some action. Your Excellency is therefore instructed to accept any plans for action suggested by Turkey, and you are to subordinate to this objective unconditionally any reservations about such operations you might have."[7]

The Germans hoped for a number of new developments from an Ottoman entry into the war: anti-colonial, Islamic revolutions in Entente territories; Russian assignment of additional troops to the Caucasus and the Black Sea regions; a shift in Bulgarian and Romanian opinion as the Central Powers demonstrated naval superiority in the Black Sea; and even the acceleration of Ottoman preparations for the expedition against Egypt.

The second German–Ottoman crisis over Ottoman intervention, September 14–22

In the Balkans, the Austro-Hungarian offensive against Serbia was turning into a debacle. This unexpected setback caused grave concern among the prospective allies of the Central Powers. The Ottoman delegation in charge of concluding a military convention with Bulgaria returned empty-handed from Sofia for a second time.[8] With the weak showing of the Habsburg army, Bulgaria's King Ferdinand and Prime Minister

[6] PA/AA, R 1914, Bethmann Hollweg to Auswärtiges Amt, September 14, 1914, no. 43, and BA-MA, RM 40 – 454, sheet 332, Bethmann Hollweg to Souchon, September 14, 1914.
[7] PA/AA, R 22402, Falkenhayn to Liman, September 16, 1914.
[8] For the initially promising news out of Sofia turning into bad news, see PA/AA, R 1914, Michahelles to Auswärtiges Amt, September 14, 1914, no. 137; PA/AA, R 22402, Zimmermann to Jagow, September 15, 1914, no. 422; PA/AA, R 1914, Michahelles to Auswärtiges Amt, September 15, 1914, no. 140; PA/AA, R 22402, Zimmermann to Jagow, September 16, 1914, no. 437; and BA-MA, RM 40 – 457, sheet 232, Corcovado to Goeben, September 16, 1914.

Radoslavov were increasingly unwilling to give in to the demands of their own nationalists at home for what they regarded a costly war against Romania and Serbia, the kingdom's recent enemies of the Balkan Wars. In the end, Bulgarian leaders maintained their policy of neutrality until October 1915, when financial aid from Berlin and the hope of regaining lost territories in Macedonia finally enticed them to join the Central Powers.[9] In autumn 1914, however, since no Bulgarian relief for the Austro-Hungarian forces could be expected, Berlin and Vienna called for Ottoman action more urgently than ever.

Charged with the kaiser's orders of September 14, Admiral Souchon immediately went to work towards taking the entire Ottoman fleet, led by its new flagship, the *Goeben*, into the Black Sea. He notified Cemal and Enver that the fleet would go into the Black Sea for naval exercises the following day.[10] Enver evidently authorized the maneuver initially, but in characteristic fashion the authorization was withdrawn soon afterwards. Souchon, who had been appointed commander-in-chief of the Ottoman navy, was furious. He fully intended to carry out the kaiser's orders. As a result, an intense confrontation ensued between German and Ottoman leaders about whether Souchon was subordinate to German or Ottoman orders.

Austria-Hungary's failure to defeat its small Serbian neighbor exacerbated this heated situation, as did, even more, the spectacular defeats Russia inflicted on Habsburg forces in Galicia – totaling losses of 350,000 men – on the eastern front during September.[11] Admiral Usedom, head of the team of German fortification and artillery specialists that had arrived in Istanbul in late August, described the atmosphere in a letter of September 18 to Admiral Georg von Müller, chief of the kaiser's naval cabinet in Berlin. Usedom reported that "the general situation here has not changed. Bulgaria has not taken a stand [for us]. The mood in Turkey against war is stronger than ever, a result of the negative news from Galicia and the fact that news has not yet arrived here from the western front."[12] As a result of these early Austrian defeats, the Ottomans refused to go ahead with Souchon's plans. They ordered the "cancellation of the fleet's maneuver in the Black Sea, by which we hoped to force a decision through an encounter with Russian ships, or, if these did not show themselves, by sending a strong message to Bulgaria and Romania."[13] Usedom then tried

[9] Friedrich, *Bulgarien und die Mächte*, 133–279.
[10] BA-MA, RM 40 – 454, sheet 333, Souchon to Enver and Cemal, September 14, 1914.
[11] Strachan, *The First World War*, vol. I, *To Arms*, 356.
[12] BA-MA, RM 40 – 1, sheet 9, Usedom to Müller, September 18, 1914. [13] Ibid.

to force the Ottomans' hand, potentially risking the German–Ottoman alliance altogether:

> The situation cannot be tolerated in this manner any longer. We have offered the Turks our ships, officers, crew as well as innumerable weapons and equipment without anything in return. Souchon will therefore take the fleet out to the Black Sea the day after tomorrow, with four or five ships and a few torpedo boats. If the Turkish ships are kept back, he will take out only his own two ships, [the *Goeben* and the *Breslau*] flying the Turkish flag. And, I think, in that way the die will be cast.[14]

Relations between the two allies had reached boiling-point. It had become abundantly clear that the alliance could survive only if the Ottomans at last took action.

The mystery of Enver's "authorization" and its subsequent withdrawal was soon solved. On September 19, Wangenheim reported to his superior in Berlin, Deputy Foreign Secretary Arthur Zimmermann, that an embassy informant, perhaps Humann, had learned about a heated cabinet meeting on September 16; that is, two days after the kaiser's exigent demand for immediate Ottoman action. During the course of the meeting, Grand Vezir Said Halim had declared once again his strict opposition to the fleet's proposed excursion into the Black Sea, correctly surmising that Souchon would use the opportunity to cause an incident with the Russian fleet. Said Halim had already articulated his thoughts about naval maneuvers in the Black Sea to the German embassy on several occasions since the warships' arrival on August 10, 1914. He viewed such maneuvers as dangerous activity that would involve the empire in a war with Russia at an untimely moment – which of course was precisely what Berlin desired. According to the informant, Enver had refused to withdraw instructions to take the fleet into the Black Sea now that they had been issued to the German admiral. The grand vezir then threatened to resign, upon which Talat, the interior minister, intervened and pressured Enver to withdraw the order. According to Wangenheim, Talat made his case by promising Enver that no minister would oppose Black Sea maneuvers once Bulgaria had decided on action. Eventually Enver withdrew the order, but he emphasized that this would be the first and last time he reversed an order already issued.[15]

---

[14] Ibid.

[15] PA/AA, R 1914, Wangenheim to Auswärtiges Amt, September 19, 1914, no. 836; BA-MA, RM 40 – 4, sheets, 113–15, Besprechung mit Enver Pascha am 26.9.1914 [Conversation with Enver Pasha on September 26, 1914]. Smaller parts of the fleet were still permitted to exercise in the Black Sea, however. See BA-MA, RM 40 – 457, sheet 347, Enver to Souchon, September 19, 1914.

In fact, the cancellation of Souchon's authorization can be traced back to Cemal Pasha, the navy minister, who had written the admiral immediately upon learning of the planned naval excursion. In vituperative language (*zinhar*, "beware!"), Cemal admonished Souchon not to undertake any actions without prior instructions: "The fleet's entry into the Black Sea represents a political act [*bir siyasî teşebbüs olub*] on the part of the Ottoman government." Such a naval maneuver, he continued, was "inappropriate [*münasib değildir*]" and could be authorized only by cabinet decision (*buna ancak kabine heyeti canibinden karar verilmek ve ona müsteniden icra edilmek lazımdır*). Instead of pursuing such activities, Cemal rather condescendingly concluded, Souchon should turn his attention to the upcoming ceremonial naval parade, scheduled for September 17. Souchon then immediately instructed Humann to lodge a protest with Enver.[16]

Cemal notified his colleagues in the cabinet that the question of naval maneuvers would be discussed at their next meeting,[17] and Enver sent a telegram to Souchon ordering him to postpone the excursion until further notice (*donanmanın Karadeniz'e çıkması emr-i ahire kadar te'hir edilmişdir*).[18] In the meantime, Admiral Souchon submitted personally his protest to Said Halim to no avail. Humann, in a meeting with Enver on the morning of September 20, demanded a comprehensive statement on just what was the admiral's capacity as the commander-in-chief of the Ottoman navy.[19] The same day, Enver took Humann's question to yet another cabinet meeting. This meeting produced a detailed reply to Humann and Souchon's protests, describing the Porte's position regarding Souchon and the question of taking the fleet into the Black Sea. In what amounted to a significant change in policy, the cabinet acknowledged Souchon's right to accept and carry out orders from Berlin, even if these orders contradicted Ottoman wishes and interests. Remarkably, Enver emphasized that "the current political situation did not allow the Ottoman government to authorize" naval maneuvers in the Black Sea, regardless of whether the admiral promised "not to provoke any incidents that would result in war." The cabinet thus acknowledged that the German admiral could not be expected to "put aside his love for his fatherland and sense of duty" once out at sea. The reply also stated that

[16] ATASE, BDH, Klasör 87, Yeni Dosya 449, Fihrist 1, Souchon to Cemal, 1 Eylül 1330 (September 14, 1914), and Cemal to Souchon, 1 Eylül 1330 (September 14, 1914); BA-MA, RM 40 – 457, Cemal to Souchon, sheet 354 and reverse, September 14, 1914.
[17] BA-MA, RM 40 – 457, sheet 350, Humann to Souchon, September 19, 1914.
[18] BA-MA, RM 40 – 457, sheet 349, Enver to Souchon, September 16, 1914.
[19] BA-MA, RM 40 – 456, sheets 447–9, Humann to Souchon, September 20, 1914.

the cabinet could not prevent Souchon from taking out the *Goeben* and the *Breslau* into the Black Sea, nor from attacking the Russian fleet or coast. In that event, however, the Sublime Porte would make a statement disavowing the admiral's action and stating that it occurred against Ottoman orders. Ottoman ships, moreover, could not be sent into the Black Sea, because such action would most probably be understood by the Entente as the end of neutrality, an outcome deemed undesirable at the moment.[20] Enver added that his government would request Berlin to change Admiral Souchon's status to that of an *Ottoman* admiral, a change that would permit Souchon to take Ottoman ships into the Black Sea as well, without violating the government's declaration of neutrality. Asked about this change, Souchon noted on October 5: "If I can continue to do as I please with the German ships, I have no objections to becoming a Turkish admiral and getting a firmer grip on the Turkish ships."[21]

More importantly, Humann also learned that the speaker of the Ottoman chamber of deputies, Halil Bey, would embark on a trip to Berlin to present the reasons preventing the empire's entry into the war and to seek the German government's support for continued neutrality.[22] As always, and as Ottoman decision-makers themselves knew, these efforts simultaneously to preserve the German alliance and to maintain a policy of neutrality were in direct conflict. Now, perhaps, their string had run out.

Wangenheim then met with Grand Vezir Said Halim Pasha on the question of Souchon's authority. The ambassador declared that the *Goeben* and the *Breslau* were still German ships and would refuse to take Ottoman orders. Said Halim retorted that the cabinet feared Admiral Souchon would attack the Russian fleet against their wishes; he and the

---

[20] BA-MA, RM 40 – 456, sheets 452–4, Humann to Souchon, September 20, 1914. Based on the information provided by Enver to Humann in this meeting, Wangenheim reported to Berlin regarding the current impasse, see PA/AA, R 1914, Wangenheim to Auswärtiges Amt, September 21, 1914, no. 847.

[21] The Ottoman ambassador at Berlin, Mahmud Muhtar Pasha, submitted a request for Souchon's entry into the Ottoman navy as admiral to the German government on September 23, 1914. Souchon, a rear admiral (*Konteradmiral*) in the German navy, carried the rank of vice-admiral in the Ottoman navy, see PA/AA, R 22402, Zimmermann to Jagow, September 23, 1914, no. 533. The offer was accepted immediately in Berlin, see PA/AA, R 1914, Jagow to Auswärtiges Amt, September 24, 1914, no. 193. Souchon seems not to have been contacted about the issue until October 5, 1914, see BA-MA, RM 40 –456, sheets 302–3, Vertrauliche Mitteilungen vom 5. Oktober 1914 [Confidential Report of October 5, 1914], Humann to Souchon.

[22] BA-MA, RM 40 – 456, sheets 452–4, Humann to Souchon, September 20, 1914; PA/AA, R 1914, Wangenheim to Auswärtiges Amt, September 21, 1914, no. 847.

cabinet felt the appropriate moment for such action had not yet arrived. Wangenheim, in turn, warned that by continuing to stall intervention, the Ottoman Empire was increasingly losing any future claims to the spoils of the war. If the empire waited for victory to be assured before it intervened, the German government would hardly reward the Ottomans for their participation. This argument represented Berlin's principal leverage over its Ottoman ally. Wangenheim urged that the empire fulfill its part of the alliance and make up for its earlier foot-dragging by taking the following steps forthwith. First, the Sublime Porte should demonstrate naval superiority in the Black Sea through decisive action against the Russian navy, thereby winning over Bulgaria and Romania to the side of the Central Powers and elevating its own standing in the Islamic world. Second, the Porte should advance Muslim agitation against the Entente, towards which end Germany would provide financial and material aid. And, finally, the Ottoman government should keep troops mobilized against Romania in order to keep that Balkan country neutral if it could not be won over to the Central Powers.[23]

While Wangenheim was obligated to follow Berlin's orders to force intervention, he was at the same time, as we have seen, personally opposed to it. Hence, while he claimed to be doing everything in his powers to bring the Ottomans to action, the ambassador continued to justify Ottoman passivity in his correspondence with Berlin. He pointed out that "Liman, the admirals, and I [work] constantly and with greatest efforts" towards Ottoman entry.[24] Ottoman non-intervention stemmed from continued uncertainty in the Balkans and the other active theaters of war. The Central Powers' setbacks in Galicia and the stalemate on the western front were feeding Ottoman doubts and hesitation.[25] Wangenheim also reminded his superiors of the turmoil the German demands were creating within the Ottoman government itself. Enver had withdrawn Souchon's authorization for all fleet maneuvers in the Black Sea only in the face of a major cabinet crisis, in which the grand vezir, Said Halim Pasha, had threatened to resign.[26]

[23] PA/AA, R 1914, Wangenheim to Auswärtiges Amt, September 20, 1914, no. 848; PA/AA, R 22402, Zimmermann to Jagow, September 21, 1914, no. 505. See also Ahmad, "Ottoman Armed Neutrality and Intervention," 68–9, and Trumpener, *Germany and the Ottoman Empire*, 40–1.
[24] PA/AA, R 1914, Wangenheim to Auswärtiges Amt, September 19, 1914, no. 834.
[25] Ibid.
[26] PA/AA, R 1914, Wangenheim to Auswärtiges Amt, September 19, 1914, no. 836. Wangenheim's telegram to Berlin was based on information provided by Naval Captain Humann, see BA-MA, RM 40 – 457, sheet 350, Humann to Souchon, September 19, 1914.

It is quite possible, however, that the meeting of September 16 proceeded much less dramatically than Enver's account to Humann suggests. We can never be entirely sure, because although theoretically all cabinet meetings were recorded and cabinet decisions transmitted to the appropriate government agencies for implementation, the meeting of September 16 was not. And, in fact, not putting down in writing cabinet decisions of a political character appears to have been the usual practice.[27]

Based on positions taken by Enver during the previous and following weeks, it is likely that Enver consented to the view of his colleagues and that he favored postponement of military intervention as well. The specter of a cabinet crisis and the possibility of the grand vezir's resignation in fact served as yet another excuse to Berlin for the delay in military action. The news of the grand vezir's resignation would itself signal a loss of prestige for Germany in a world that was acutely aware of an existing "arrangement" between the current Ottoman cabinet and the Central Powers. In the propaganda war waged between the two camps attempting to woo the neutral Balkan states and to retain or acquire Italy, Said Halim's resignation would have been interpreted as a blow to Germany and a sign that its paramount presence in Istanbul could no longer be taken for granted. Once again Enver could portray himself as being turned away from an interventionist course only at the final moment and under the heaviest of political pressure in the cabinet.[28]

In mid-September 1914, therefore, the cabinet asserted itself successfully in staying out of the war in the face of Berlin's strong demands for intervention. At the same time, however, the alliance was becoming increasingly fragile. The Germans let the Ottomans know that they were in real danger of squandering any claims to a serious role in peace negotiations at war's end. That prospect dashed Ottoman hopes for future international security with German protection. The heated confrontation over naval maneuvers was eventually eased by the efforts of Ambassador Wangenheim, who instructed Souchon to be patient and filed a lengthy report detailing the ways in which neutrality actually benefited the German war effort. The Sublime Porte for its part promised to authorize Black Sea maneuvers under Souchon after the latter had officially been made an Ottoman admiral. Increasingly, the Ottoman leaders were forced

---

[27] See the records of the Ottoman cabinet, Meclis-i Vükelâ, at the Ottoman Archives of the Turkish Prime Ministry, BOA, MV 190–MV 194 and MV 235–MV 237, covering the period July–November 1914.

[28] Evaluating the same telegram of September 19, 1914, Ulrich Trumpener expressed similar concerns: *Germany and the Ottoman Empire*, 42.

to choose between the alliance with Germany and their policy of non-belligerence. According to a colleague, Talat for one was aware of the danger: "We are caught vacillating in the middle. Each passing day we lose the confidence of our allies while compounding the enmity of the others. That's called eating up your capital; therefore, we must make up our minds."[29]

Alliance or neutrality?

Indeed, in Berlin the Auswärtiges Amt was considering drastic measures. Jagow asked General Liman von Sanders to report on possible ways by which the Ottoman Empire could be coerced into war. Although Liman's actual reply has not turned up in the archives and may have been destroyed, we can deduce his recommendations from Wangenheim's assessment of them, solicited by Jagow on September 23.

Liman had advised that the Germans threaten to withdraw all support and officers, a tactic Wangenheim warned could result in a major diplomatic debacle for Germany. The Entente's proposals for an Ottoman alliance had foundered precisely on this point: the dismissal of the German officers. If Germany were to recall its officers on its own, it would be virtually throwing the Ottomans into the arms of the Entente; the Sublime Porte would surely present the departure of the Germans as meeting Entente conditions for an alliance: "Herr von Liman would appreciate Turkish benevolent neutrality more, if he knew about the incredible efforts the Triple Entente is making in order to remove us from our position here."[30] Wangenheim thus contradicted Liman's assertion that the empire's neutrality only drained German resources. "I rather believe that benevolent Turkish neutrality is currently much more valuable to us than a premature Turkish declaration of war."[31] He explained:

Turkey currently controls the Straits and the Black Sea. It has mobilized an army of over half a million and is thus an important factor in all questions regarding the

[29] Ahmad, "Ottoman Armed Neutrality and Intervention," 65–6, citing Halil Bey (Menteşe), *Cumhuriyet*, November 15, 1946, Ali İhsan Sâbis, *Harp Hatıralarım: Birinci Dünya Harbi* (Istanbul: Nehir, 1990), vol. II, 33–5, Y. T. Kurat, "How Turkey Drifted into World War I," and Bayur, *Türk İnkılâbı Tarihi*, vol. III/i, *1914–1918 Genel Savaşı*, 229–30.
[30] PA/AA, R 22402, Wangenheim to Jagow, September 24, 1914, no. 3, arriving in Berlin on the morning of September 26, 1914. A second copy [*Abschrift*] is found in PA/AA, R 1914. Wangenheim's telegram bypassed Zimmermann, who instructed Wangenheim to resend it, see PA/AA, R 1914, Zimmermann to Wangenheim, October 7, 1914 [draft], no. 895. For Zimmermann's inquiry regarding Wangenheim's missing telegram, see PA/AA, R 22403, Zimmermann to Jagow, October 10, 1914, no. 689.
[31] PA/AA, R 22402, Wangenheim to Jagow, September 24, 1914, no. 3.

Near East, particularly the Balkans. Since Turkey knows that its strength depends almost entirely on our officers, it will have to suit its policies to Germany's wishes for as long as [it] needs our officers. Germany is hence currently in charge of Turkish affairs and is therefore able to control, through Turkey, the Straits, the Black Sea, and, to a certain extent, also the Balkans.[32]

Ottoman action, Wangenheim wrote, "depends on our successes" in the war, "and particularly on Austria, as well as on the attitude of Bulgaria."[33] To Jagow's question of whether forcing the empire into war "prior to a decision in Galicia would compromise the expedition against Egypt,"[34] the baron left no doubt. "A sudden declaration of war on Russia would probably preclude the much more significant expedition against Egypt."[35] Premature intervention might also lead to a political shake-up in the capital and remove the leading pro-German figures from their current positions. And "in any case," he added, "it is better that Turkey strike at a moment when it is ready to carry out the tasks it has been given, when the Caucasus and Egypt [expeditions] have been sufficiently prepared."[36] Thus Wangenheim continued to support the Porte's policy of non-intervention then in place, one he saw as working to Germany's own advantage, and recommended that Berlin accept it as well.

Wangenheim's reasoning, however, was not shared by Berlin. Alarmed by recent news about a substantial British offer of political and financial support in exchange for Ottoman neutrality,[37] Berlin exhorted immediate action. From a tactical perspective, too, military specialists were pointing to the need to act rapidly. In a detailed operational report of September 3, 1914, Lieutenant Colonel Kress von Kressenstein warned that a naval strike against Odessa and the landing of troops there would have to be launched by the end of September at the latest because of weather conditions.[38] Thus despite its plausible argument, Wangenheim's report

[32] Ibid.   [33] Ibid.
[34] PA/AA, R 1914, Jagow to Constantinople [Ambassador Wangenheim], September 23, 1914, no. 13.
[35] Ibid.   [36] PA/AA, R 22402, Wangenheim to Jagow, September 24, 1914, no. 3.
[37] BA-MA, RM 40 – 4, sheets 125–6, Vertrauliche Mitteilungen vom 22.9.14 [Confidential Report of September 22, 1914].
[38] BA-MA, RM 40 – 130, sheets 343–5, Kress to Headquarters, Gesichtspunkte für die Durchführung einer Uebersee-Expedition [Considerations for the Execution of a Naval Expedition], September 3, 1914. Kress suggested landing four army corps at Odessa under the command of General Liman; received by the Ottomans as ATASE, BDH, Klasör 46, Yeni Dosya 215A, Fihrist 3 and 3–1, Kress to Ottoman General Headquarters, September 3, 1914; see also BA-MA, RM 40 – 281, sheets 306–8, Kress to Headquarters, Beurteilung der Lage am 4. September 1914 [General Assessment of September 4, 1914].

failed to convince his superiors, who continued to push for a quick strike against Russia.

At the same time, the Ottoman leadership was bracing itself, in growing recognition that the war was unfolding in unexpected ways. From Cemil Bey in Berlin arrived extensive analyses of recent military developments and their implications for Ottoman policy. The German plan on the western front had "partially failed," and the German army there now faced "a very difficult assignment." Thus, "it will not be possible to occupy France in a few weeks' time as had been thought," and he added that instead "it will most likely be necessary to advance piece by piece and this task will take much longer than previously thought." Cemil explained that "because of this situation Berlin wishes very much that we enter the war against Russia right away." From recent conversations "with high-ranking individuals at the [German] foreign, war, and navy offices," Cemil had learned even worse intelligence. Austria-Hungary's forces ran the risk of suffering substantial defeats against the Russian armies. One immediate consequence might be the loss of Romania to the Entente, and thus perhaps Bulgaria as well. For that reason, Cemil concluded, Berlin was urging the Ottomans to take control of the Black Sea and to attack Russian ports there. The German foreign office had also repeatedly urged that the Ottoman Third Army advance into the Caucasus.[39]

These calls for intervention intensified as the Central Powers' military machine began to sputter. In Cemil's words, "originally their calls for our participation stemmed from the wish to gain an ally. Now they feel the need for our support in the light of ever-increasing difficulties. They put more hope in us than Romania or Bulgaria." Despite these military set-backs, and even some instances of panic among German ranks, Cemil felt that their alliance partner would emerge victorious in the end. He added a crucial qualification, however: if the French armies were not decisively defeated soon, an eventual German success could amount to no more than a "weak victory."[40]

Wilhelm II's instructions of September 24 to Souchon reflect the mounting urgency Cemil Bey had described: "In coordination with the ambassador [Wangenheim] continue insisting on taking the entire Turkish fleet [into the Black Sea]."[41] When Berlin inquired a few days

[39] ATASE, BDH, Klasör 243, Yeni Dosya 1009, Fihrist 24–1 to 21–5, Cemil to Enver, 11 Eylül 1330 (September 24, 1914).
[40] Ibid.
[41] PA/AA, R 22402, Pohl to Auswärtiges Amt [forwarding the kaiser's instructions for Souchon], September 24, 1914, no. 135; PA/AA, R 1914, Jagow to Auswärtiges Amt, September 24, 1914, no. 191; BA-MA, RM 40 – 454, sheet 319, Wilhelm to Souchon, September 24, 1914.

later about the admiral's immediate plans, Souchon replied that he intended "soon to engage the Russian fleet and commercial vessels with the *Goeben*, the *Breslau*, and the Turkish fleet. As long as this is not possible for political reasons, I will continue training the Turkish ships and plan to stage a naval demonstration in the Black Sea," thereby making a show of Ottoman naval power, directed towards Romania in particular.[42] Souchon's response caused jaws to drop in Berlin. Evidently Wangenheim had persuaded the admiral to remain patient and await further developments. "Please cable as soon as possible," the Auswärtiges Amt demanded, "which political reasons currently prevent our ships and the Turkish fleet from striking against Russian naval forces and commerce."[43] Since the Ottoman cabinet had offered to make Souchon an admiral in the Ottoman navy, with the authority to maneuver with the entire fleet, Berlin insisted, "a naval strike seems ready even without the explicit approval of the Porte, particularly now that the Dardanelles have been mined shut. The Porte apparently *wants* to be forced into a decision [*Die Pforte* will *offenbar zur Entscheidung gezwungen werden*]."[44]

Thus for Berlin Ottoman intervention was only partially about military power, that is, about diverting Russian and British troops; it was also about prestige and effect. Intervention could be employed to woo the Balkan states and, as we have seen, to spark anti-colonial rebellions among the Entente's Muslim subjects.

On October 1, 1914, Mahmud Muhtar, the Porte's ambassador in Berlin, met with Deputy Foreign Secretary Zimmermann, who was well aware of the Ottomans' growing financial constraints and who had already proposed a loan-for-entry deal on September 10. Mahmud Muhtar requested a loan of over 5 million Ottoman pounds. He explained that the loan was "needed urgently in order to maintain mobilization." Zimmermann replied that "the money was available immediately upon the Porte's" entry into the war. Now Mahmud Muhtar sought to negotiate, inquiring whether a smaller loan of half a million pounds could be

---

[42] BA-MA, RM 40 – 457, sheet 338 reverse, Souchon to Wangenheim [for Zimmermann], September 30, 1914; PA/AA, R 1914, Wangenheim to Auswärtiges Amt, September 30, 1914, no. 940, and forwarded to Jagow next day, see PA/AA, R 22403, Zimmermann to Jagow, October 1, 1914, no. 618.

[43] PA/AA, R 1914, Auswärtiges Amt to Wangenheim, October 4, 1914, no. 862.

[44] Ibid. (Emphasis in original.) This is a draft prepared by the Deputy Foreign Secretary, Arthur Zimmermann. The Straits had been closed after an Ottoman ship exiting the Straits into the Aegean had been turned around by the British on September 27, 1914. See BA-MA, RM 40 – 1, sheets 12–13, Usedom to Wilhelm II, October 15, 1914.

granted without intervention. "Such a demonstration of friendship," the ambassador pleaded, "would have an enormous impact on the morale in the entire Muslim world." The loan would also expose those in Istanbul who argued that "Germany would not be able to provide the necessary financial assistance to the Porte" throughout the war. Mahmud Muhtar added special force to his request by stressing his supposed personal commitment to intervention: Souchon should simply attack the Russian fleet in the Black Sea and "thereby pull along the elements that are hesitating."[45] In Mahmud Muhtar's request we see once again the Ottoman tactic of playing on the German hope for a Muslim anti-colonial and anti-Entente uprising. It was also characteristic of Ottoman–German relations during this period that although the Sublime Porte had no intentions of publicizing the German loan the ambassador did not hesitate to speak of the loan's "enormous impact" among Muslims the world over.

Once Zimmermann obtained the nod from Arthur Gwinner, the speaker of the Deutsche Bank, and Karl Helfferich, the German financial advisor at the Sublime Porte, Zimmermann recommended a loan of 5 million Ottoman pounds. The loan would carry a 5 to 6 percent rate of interest, and would be paid directly to the Ottoman grand vezirate without going through the Finance Minister Cavid Bey, whose opposition to intervention was well known – a back-room deal that opened wide the door for corruption. While 250,000 Ottoman pounds would be paid out right away, an amount of 750,000 pounds would follow after intervention. Furthermore, half a million Ottoman pounds would be paid out each month until the payments had reached the total of 5 million. The initial loan, therefore, was designed to cover a maximum period of eight months. Did the Ottomans assume the war would last no longer than that, or did they count on a subsequent loan? In his memorandum recommending the loan, Zimmermann pointed out that in the event the Ottomans took the money without striking against Russia, the loss would be kept to the relatively small amount of a quarter of a million Ottoman pounds. "At the same time," he concluded, "the danger of a partial demobilization for lack of money would be eliminated."[46] That very night, October 1, the Auswärtiges Amt agreed to meet the Ottoman request and approved Zimmermann's method for handling the loan.[47]

[45] PA/AA, R 22403, Zimmermann to Jagow, October 1, 1914, no. 613.   [46] Ibid.
[47] PA/AA, R 22403, Jagow to Zimmermann, October 1, 1914 [draft], no. 65.

The Germans took several more days to work out the exact terms,[48] without, however, informing the Sublime Porte of its approval,[49] possibly with the intention of straining Ottoman nerves. In the attempt to encourage a favorable decision, Grand Vezir Said Halim approached Wangenheim with a proposition that once again demonstrated the Ottoman leaders' long-term vision of their cooperation with Germany. He suggested the creation of a German naval base in the Sea of Marmara, with German naval forces responsible for the protection and defense of the Ottoman Empire against any naval threat. Souchon found the creation of such a "protection fleet" to be "very practical" and pointed out that it would afford not only German control over the Sea of Marmara, but "over the Bosporus as well."[50] Like the grand vezir, Talat and Enver also offered assurances.[51] In a meeting with Humann on October 2, Enver stated that the Dardanelles would remain closed despite Entente efforts to reopen them, and he emphasized that the closure would have an adverse effect on the economies of both Romania and Russia. As for Ottoman mobilization, the war minister explained, an army of over 300,000 men had been mobilized, plus labor battalions (*amele taburları*), into which he had "put all the unreliables: Greeks, Armenians, etc."[52] A German loan in return for these efforts, the Ottomans argued, was therefore well deserved. Humann reported that Enver had also made an ideological point:

In this great mobilization, he [Enver] always believed that the great sacrifices that the people have to make must primarily advance the people's national identity

---

[48] The loan agreement was concluded on October 5, 1914, see BA-MA, RM 5 – 2308, Capelle to Tirpitz, October 6, 1914, which also makes clear that Zimmermann, in particular, pressed for a naval attack on Russia by the Ottoman fleet under Souchon. See also BA-MA, RM 40 – 457, sheet 223, October 5, 1914, for Souchon's notification of the loan agreement. The Ottoman cabinet apparently took a decision endorsing the loan agreement, see BOA, MV 237–102 and 102A [draft], [29 Teşrin-i Evvel 1330 (November 11, 1914)]. The draft approves a loan from the German government of over 5 million Ottoman lira at 6 percent interest. The draft bears no signatures.

[49] The Sublime Porte was notified of the loan's approval by Ambassador Wangenheim on the afternoon of October 5, 1914, see PA/AA, R 2123, Vertrauliche Mitteilungen vom 5. Oktober 1914 [Confidential Report of October 5, 1914], compiled by Naval Captain Humann and submitted to the Auswärtiges Amt by Ernst Jäckh; cf. Ernst Jäckh Papers, Yale University Library.

[50] BA-MA, RM 40 – 456, sheets 310–12, Vertrauliche Mitteilungen vom 1. Oktober 1914 [Confidential Report of October 1, 1914] and Souchon's marginalia in green pencil. A copy of the report, compiled by Naval Captain Hans Humann and distributed to the various German agencies in the Ottoman capital, was forwarded to the Auswärtiges Amt by Ernst Jäckh and is found in PA/AA, R 1914.

[51] For Talat: PA/AA, R 1914, Vertrauliche Mitteilung vom 2.X.14 [Confidential Report of October 2, 1914].

[52] PA/AA, R 1914, Besprechung mit Enver Pascha am 2. Oktober 1914 [Conversation with Enver Pasha on October 2, 1914], reported by Humann, and also found in BA-MA, RM 40 – 4, sheets 94–7.

[*vornehmlich seiner völkischen Erziehung zugute kommen sollen*]. He looks at the current example set by Germany: the tireless willingness of all to sacrifice, commitment of the whole person to the fatherland. A people [which lacks such commitment] has no right to exist. It is a most difficult task to teach this highest and most important virtue to the people of Abdülhamid [II], but it is indispensable. The Balkan war was lost at the time mainly because everyone thought of himself, no one of the fatherland [*Vaterland*], he [Enver] believes. The people must embrace the idea that it is shameful to do nothing when the fatherland is in danger.[53]

Still unaware that the loan had already been approved, the next day Enver discussed with Humann the severe financial difficulties facing the empire and the absolute necessity of a German loan. The entire army had been placed on half-pay and Finance Minister Cavid was urging the cabinet to adopt a decision for partial demobilization for financial reasons. Playing on the great importance Berlin attached to the Suez expedition, Enver warned that financial problems "slowed down especially the preparations [for the expedition] against Egypt," and he added that the Ottoman army urgently needed howitzer cannons for the expedition as well.[54]

With the approval of the loan, Germany's military and political leaders expected immediate and tangible results. Zimmermann impressed on the German representatives in Istanbul and Tehran that "the sooner Russia enters into conflict with Turkey and Persia the better. Please work towards this aim by any possible means."[55] Wangenheim tried one last time to persuade his superiors that they were harming Germany's own interests. On October 6, he resubmitted to Zimmermann his report of September 24.[56] "I am today still of the opinion," the ambassador insisted, "that Turkey's neutrality, benevolent towards us, is" of greater value than "Turkey's premature involvement in the war, which would be a very risky undertaking [*aleatorisches Unternehmen*]." Saying he lacked confidence in the strength of the Ottoman armed forces, Wangenheim feared a swift defeat of the empire that would put an end to German influence in the region. "If Turkey declares war," he commented, "[Turkey] will be of value to us only for as long as it remains undefeated … one lucky torpedo by the Russian fleet incapacitating the *Goeben* would mean the destruction of the entire Turkish fleet and render impossible any further military

---

[53] Ibid.
[54] PA/AA, R 1914, Besprechung mit Enver Pascha am 3. Oktober 1914 [Conversation with Enver Pasha on October 3, 1914]. Same report in BA-MA, RM 40 – 4, sheets 91–2.
[55] PA/AA, R 1914, Zimmermann to Wangenheim, October 4, 1914 [draft], no. 872.
[56] PA/AA, R 22402, Wangenheim to Jagow, September 24, 1914, no. 3. As indicated above, Wangenheim's telegram had bypassed Zimmermann, who instructed Wangenheim to resend it on October 7, see PA/AA, R 1914, Zimmermann to Wangenheim, October 7, 1914 [draft], no. 895.

efforts in the Black Sea." Wangenheim once again recounted the tangible benefits of Ottoman neutrality: political influence on Romania, cutting off Russian commerce and supplies, and preparation of the prospective expeditions against the Caucasus, Egypt, and Afghanistan. An Ottoman declaration of war, he warned, would most likely lead to a "Russian invasion of Armenia" and the British annexation of Egypt. The line of German supplies to the Ottoman Empire, crossing Romania, would also be severed. But Wangenheim also reported that the Ottoman government had ceased to insist on Bulgarian action before entering the war: "As soon as we achieve a decisive victory in France or Galicia, the entire [Ottoman] land and sea forces will be at the disposal of German interests … If we are victorious in Russia or France, Souchon can commence military action in the Black Sea immediately."[57] Souchon also received a copy of the ambassador's report.[58]

Then Wangenheim attempted to ease the German pressure. The Istanbul government was now firmly under the control of Enver and any fears about the Ottomans switching sides were unwarranted. The possibility that Said Halim could orchestrate such a shift, as suggested by the Auswärtiges Amt, was completely unfounded. As a result of several conversations he had had about this question with Enver, "the grand vezir's sympathy belongs to Germany, although he does not want to break with England entirely." Said Halim's conduct, he argued, was quite understandable, since as long as the Ottomans had not entered the war, a pre-emptive attack by the Entente had to be avoided by maintaining a working relationship. The ambassador assured Berlin that contrary to "allegedly reliable information," the empire would not abandon Germany's side under any circumstances except in the event Germany suffered decisive defeat on the battlefield.[59] But Berlin remained wary; only recently Wangenheim himself had correctly reported learning "from two reliable, independent sources" that the Triple Entente had offered the Sublime Porte abrogation of all capitulations and a loan in exchange for demobilization and dismissal of the German officers.[60]

Wangenheim was fighting a losing battle. Three influential leaders of the cabinet and the CUP, apprehensive about the fate of their loan application, finally decided that further delay would dangerously jeopardize the alliance.

---

[57] PA/AA, R 1914, Wangenheim to Auswärtiges Amt, October 6, 1914, no. 985.
[58] BA-MA, RM 40 – 4, sheets 79–80, reaching Souchon on the evening of October 6, 1914.
[59] PA/AA, R 1914, Wangenheim to Auswärtiges Amt, October 8, 1914, no. 995.
[60] PA/AA, R 1914, Wangenheim to Auswärtiges Amt, September 20, 1914, no. 849; for Entente willingness to revise the commercial, though not legal, aspects of the capitulations regime, see *IBZI*, Series II, vol. 6/1, no. 286, Sazonov aide-mémoire to British and French ambassadors at St. Petersburg, Buchanan and Paléologue, September 21, 1914.

At a meeting on the evening of October 8, Enver, Halil, and Talat decided to present to Berlin a plan for intervention. At that date they had still not received a final word about the German loan, and evidence suggests that they had become seriously concerned about the possibility of Germany's abandoning the alliance. Wangenheim explained to Berlin that Enver, Halil, and Talat were poised to press Cemal and Said Halim either to join them or to leave their offices. A precondition for entry, however, remained German financial support. Once that was granted, Souchon would be issued secret orders to attack Russian naval forces, possibly as early as Monday, October 12, 1914. The attack would proceed without a prior declaration of war, ostensibly in order to gain an element of surprise; in fact, however, in order to be able to maintain later that Russian forces had opened fire first. Wangenheim made it clear to Berlin that he did not endorse the attack, and that his "reservations about a premature Turkish entry" persisted. He also questioned the results Berlin expected from such an Ottoman naval attack: "I also do not believe that Turkish belligerence in the Black Sea will be sufficient in triggering revolutions in India, Persia, Egypt, etc." Yet the ambassador at the same time conceded that if Germany did not seize the current opportunity and strongly support the Ottoman plan, future bad news from the European military theaters could render the Porte immobile at a later point.[61]

Berlin ignored Wangenheim's misgivings and embraced the proposal on the spot. Chancellor Bethmann Hollweg replied to Wangenheim: "Please work towards immediate action [*Bitte auf sofortiges Losschlagen hinwirken*]. Financial support has already been granted through negotiations with Turkish ambassador."[62] In part, Berlin's impatience can be ascribed to the fear that the Ottomans might settle with the Entente after all, despite Wangenheim's claims to the contrary. Every day the Germans received new reports of ongoing negotiations between Entente representatives and prominent Ottomans. Cavid, in particular, was believed to have the potential to redirect Ottoman policy. Some members of the cabinet, according to German sources, were already meeting behind Enver and Cemal's backs.[63]

In Istanbul, Cemal had joined Enver, Halil, and Talat in supporting the naval attack on Russia. They met with Wangenheim on the morning of October 11 and told him of their decision to instruct Souchon to strike

---

[61] PA/AA, R 1914, Wangenheim to Auswärtiges Amt, October 9, 1914, no. 1010.

[62] PA/AA, R 22403, Zimmermann to Jagow, October 10, 1914, no. 702; PA/AA, R 1914, Jagow to Auswärtiges Amt, October 11, 1914, no. 254, reporting Bethmann's instructions for Wangenheim.

[63] PA/AA, R 2123, Vertrauliche Mitteilungen vom 6. Oktober 1914 [Confidential Report of October 6, 1914].

against the Russian fleet as soon as the embassy put aside 2 million Ottoman pounds for them. Although the money need not be paid out until after the strike, it was essential to have the funds on hand. "Because of Romania's [wavering] attitude," Wangenheim reported, Cemal, Enver, Halil, and Talat insisted that "the necessary funds for the conduct of a longer war" be physically present in the capital prior to the outbreak of hostilities.[64] This new precondition delayed Ottoman entry for an additional two and a half weeks.

In a conversation with the Austro-Hungarian ambassador, Count Johann von Pallavicini, on October 12, Said Halim divulged that he did not object to the naval attack on Russia. He was only concerned that Russian submarines could damage the *Goeben* and the *Breslau* and thereby eliminate "one of the most effective instruments at any [future] peace negotiations."[65]

Enver submitted the Ottoman war plan for General Helmuth von Moltke's endorsement, although by that point Moltke had already been replaced as the chief of the general staff by Erich von Falkenhayn. The plan, drawn up by Major Colonel Friedrich Bronsart von Schellendorf, Enver Pasha's chief of staff,[66] consisted of six points. It was a tall order.

1. The fleet shall gain naval superiority in the Black Sea by attacking the Russian fleet without prior declaration of war. Timing at Souchon's choosing. Following the Russian declaration of war, His Majesty the Sultan will declare holy war against the enemies of Germany, Austria-Hungary, and the Ottoman Empire.
2. The Turkish army positioned in Armenia [i.e. northeastern Anatolia] will hold back the Russian forces in Transcaucasia.
3. The VIII Army Corps will move towards Egypt and may be supported by the XII Army Corps if necessary. But crossing into Egypt will not be possible for another six weeks.
4. In the event an agreement can be reached with Bulgaria, Turkish troops will partially move [through Bulgarian territory] against Serbia and partially cover against Greece and Romania if necessary.

---

[64] PA/AA, R 1914, Wangenheim to Auswärtiges Amt, 11 October 1914, no. 1022. A carbon copy of the document with Zimmermann's marginalia is found in PA/AA, R 22403; BA-MA, RM 40 – 4, sheets 61–3, Bericht über die Beratung beim Botschafter am 11.10.1914 [Report on the Conference with the Ambassador on October 11, 1914]. The final version of the loan agreement was signed on November 11, 1914 by Wangenheim and Talat, see BA-MA, RM 40 – 4, sheets 3–4, Vertrauliche Mitteilungen vom 12. November 1914 [Confidential Report of November 12, 1914].
[65] PA/AA, R 2123, Vertrauliche Mitteilungen vom 13.10.1914 [Confidential Report of October 13, 1914].
[66] At least according to General Ali İhsan Sâbis, *Harp Hatıralarım: Birinci Dünya Harbi* (Istanbul: Nehir, 1990), vol. II, 76–7.

5. If Romania also joins our side, Turkish troops will [cross through Bulgarian territory and] fight alongside the Romanian army against Russia.

6. A naval operation against Odessa with 3–4 army corps is currently under preparation. Execution [depends on] gaining naval superiority in the Black Sea and benevolent neutrality of Romania and Bulgaria. Timing also dependent on progress of German–Austrian offensive in Russia.[67]

"Please indicate," Enver concluded, "whether our intentions correspond with yours."[68] In requesting German authorization in such a formal manner, the war minister documented full Ottoman commitment to the German war effort. Such a demonstration, the Ottoman leaders hoped, would oblige the Germans to back the empire in the future and entitle the Porte to equal participation in the eventual postwar settlement.

Deputy Foreign Secretary Zimmermann urged headquarters to approve Enver's general plan without delay, regardless of any modifications that might be desired by the generals. Any such changes, he noted, must be left for a later time, and what mattered most of all was intervention: "The second gold shipment has also arrived in Constantinople, so now Enver's condition for a Turkish action has been met."[69] General Falkenhayn agreed. "The German High Command approves Enver Pasha's operational plan in all points," and Falkenhayn reiterated the continued importance of the expedition against Egypt.[70]

Unknown to either Germans or Ottomans, the Russian government was following these negotiations closely. Thanks to intercepts, Foreign Minister Sazonov was able to inform Admiral Eberhardt on October 20 that "Turkey has received gold from Germany, a Turkish operation in the next few days is possible." Russian intelligence had also succeeded in intercepting Pallavicini's note to Vienna of October 17, in which the ambassador reported that the Ottoman leaders had signed an agreement with Wangenheim "committing themselves to immediate military action as soon as two million of the promised one hundred million pounds has arrived in Constantinople." On October 25, Giers warned Sazonov that

[67] PA/AA, R 1914, Wangenheim to Auswärtiges Amt, October 22, 1914, no. 1087, based on Humann's report about his conference with Enver, see BA-MA, RM – 4, sheets 34–5, Humann to Wangenheim, October 22, 1914 and BA-MA, RM – 4, sheets 39–40, Enver to Moltke, October 22, 1914.

[68] Ibid.; the Italian government made this point throughout the summer of 1914, for an example see PA/AA, R 1914, Wangenheim to Auswärtiges Amt, September 8, 1914, no. 752.

[69] PA/AA, R 22403, Zimmermann to Jagow, October 23, 1914, no. 800.

[70] PA/AA, R 22403, Falkenhayn to Auswärtiges Amt, October 23, 1914, no. 2073P, and PA/AA, R 1914, Jagow to Auswärtiges Amt, October 24, 1914, no. 305.

the Ottoman "fleet will take action as soon as Thursday [October, 29, 1914]."[71] The Russians knew what was coming.

Even at the final moment, however, the Porte, still backed by Wangenheim, made a last-ditch effort to win over Berlin for a postponement, this time by pointing to Italy as the obstacle. Citing a conversation with Pallavicini, Wangenheim warned his superiors that intervention could provoke Rome to join the Entente and to launch an attack on Austria-Hungary. Italy, in control of the former Ottoman provinces in Libya, feared that Ottoman intervention would set loose anti-colonial agitation there. Prime Minister Antonio Salandra's government thus shared the concerns of the other colonial powers of the Entente. Pallavicini's own fears had recently been rekindled by conversations with Halil and Talat, who exploited Vienna's anxieties by conjuring the specter of an Italian attack. Thus even at this point when preparations for Ottoman action were well advanced, Wangenheim was still detailing at great length the reasons why intervention should be considered premature, with the potential of backfiring.[72]

In making the case against intervention once again, the ambassador noted that the representatives of Austria-Hungary, Bulgaria, and Italy were agreed that Ottoman entry at this point would be mistaken: "The Austrian military attaché [Pomiankowski] ... has filed a sharp protest with the Austrian general staff against the untimely intervention of Turkey, stating that it was irresponsible to expose Austria to an Italian attack because of the Turkish action." The Bulgarian representative, too, had voiced his reservations. If the Ottoman war effort were successful, Bulgaria would support it. If not, Toshev had claimed, pro-Russian policy would carry the day and probably lead to a joint Bulgarian–Romanian campaign against the Ottoman Empire.[73] And the Italian government, as we have seen, feared the potential effects on Italian interests in North Africa. To allay the anxieties of the Italian government, Berlin and Vienna repeatedly requested of Enver to offer reassuring statements in regard to Tripoli, which Enver did.[74] Halil and Talat, moreover, pointed to the woeful conditions winter weather would pose for a campaign in the Caucasus, even as they insisted that the expedition against British-held

---

[71]   *IBZI*, Series II, vol. 6/1, no. 401, Sazonov to Eberhardt, October 20, 1914, Urgent, 320, and Note 1 for subsequent correspondence, 320.

[72]   PA/AA, R 1914, Wangenheim to Auswärtiges Amt, October 24, 1914, no. 1094. Wangenheim's telegram was, in part, based on the confidential report provided by Naval Captain Humann, see PA/AA, R 2123, Besprechung mit Enver Pascha am 23. Oktober 1914 [Conversation with Enver Pasha on October 23, 1914].

[73]   Ibid.

[74]   PA/AA, R 1914, Wangenheim to Auswärtiges Amt, October 26, 1914, no. 1113.

Egypt could take place, at the earliest, in six weeks' time. The Egyptian expedition would be jeopardized entirely, however, if supply lines through Romania were disrupted, a very likely occurrence in the event of Ottoman intervention,[75] since Bucharest would not permit transit of *matériel* to a belligerent power. Pallavicini, and evidently Wangenheim too, shared many of the Ottoman leaders' doubts.[76]

Even the Ottoman statesmen most committed to the alliance with Germany were voicing serious concerns about action at that time. Both Enver and Talat believed that a naval attack on Russia would not suffice for mobilizing the colonized Islamic populations against their British, French, and Russian overlords, as the Germans hoped. Such large-scale popular resistance, they claimed, required simultaneous campaigns against the Russians in the Caucasus and the British in Egypt, which were not yet possible. According to Wangenheim, the Ottoman leaders believed that adequate preparations for the successful pursuit of their war aims were still not complete. Even Enver had made known his reservations, although this time he did not openly object to intervention. Indeed, "Enver sends word," Wangenheim wrote, "that he is still resolved to bring about the immediate opening of war against Russia." To back this claim, Enver had informed Wangenheim that the document containing the secret orders for Souchon had already been drawn up and signed and would be handed over to Souchon the same day.[77]

Enver's conduct laid bare the conviction that the alliance with Germany had to be preserved at all cost. If the German government could not be swayed to value the Ottoman Empire as a non-combatant ally, the Ottomans must be willing to enter the war in exchange for support in the new international order following the war. But even now Enver, like Wangenheim, was not enthusiastic about the final step to intervention, as the ambassador made clear:

I have the impression that Enver Pasha personally doubts that Souchon's attack with the Turkish fleet on the Russians will have any kind of effect on the Islamic world if there are no simultaneous campaigns against the Caucasus and Egypt, which are currently out of the question. But he is intent on fulfilling, under any circumstances, the treaty concluded with us and on keeping his promise.[78]

---

[75] PA/AA, R 1914, Wangenheim to Auswärtiges Amt, October 24, 1914, no. 1094.
[76] Vienna claimed, however, that Pallavicini had pressed Enver, Halil and Talat for Ottoman entry, see PA/AA, R 22403, Zimmermann to Jagow, October 25, 1914, no. 818.
[77] PA/AA, R 1914, Wangenheim to Auswärtiges Amt, October 24, 1914, no. 1094; PA/AA, R 22403, Zimmermann to Jagow, October 25, 1914, no. 820.
[78] Ibid.

On October 18, Admiral Souchon instructed Humann to obtain written orders from Enver addressed to the Ottoman naval officers that were to participate in the attack on Russia. The orders were to be drawn up both in German and Ottoman Turkish, and they were to instruct the Ottoman officers to follow any order issued by the German commanders of the ships.[79] These secret orders, sixteen copies in sealed envelopes, were issued and signed by Navy Minister Cemal Pasha and handed over to Humann on October 24. The orders were intended to prevent any possibility of Ottoman disobedience to their German superiors during the operation.[80] On October 27, those Ottoman officers designated to participate in the operation received these orders,[81] along with instructions to destroy the documents after the attack.[82] Enver then authorized Souchon to conduct maneuvers in the Black Sea. Once at sea, Souchon would be instructed by radio to open another sealed order, issued by Enver, ordering the fleet to attack Russian naval forces.[83] Should Enver be unable to secure cabinet backing prior to the operation, he would radio Souchon "do not open the [sealed] order," the signal that the admiral should go ahead with the attack on his own authority while preserving deniability to Enver.[84]

Even now the Ottoman leadership had not given up hope for a postponement. Enver informed the German general staff that he intended to dispatch a small delegation of officers to Berlin to discuss military questions.[85] Falkenhayn replied that the delegation's visit would be welcome,

[79] BA-MA, RM 40 – 454, sheet 309, Souchon to Humann, October 18, 1914.
[80] BA-MA 40 – 454, sheet 306, Humann to B[usse], October 25, 1914; BA-MA, RM 5 – 2308, Wangenheim to Auswärtiges Amt, October 24, 1914, no. 1101, and PA/AA, R 22403, Zimmermann to Jagow, October 25, 1914, no. 820. This is also related by Sâbis, *Harp Hatıralarım*, vol. II, 97 and 102.
[81] BA-MA, RM 40 – 457, sheet 313, [Humann] to Souchon, no date, which includes a German translation of Cemal's order.
[82] BA-MA, RM 40 – 454, sheet 196, Souchon to ships, [November] 4, 1914.
[83] BA-MA, RM 40 – 457, sheet 323, Enver to Chief of the Ottoman Fleet Ottoman Admiral Souchon (An den Chef der Ottomanischen Flotte Ottomanischen Admiral Souchon), October 24, 1914; Wangenheim received a copy of Enver's written order on October 24, 1914, see PA/AA, R 2123; BA-MA, RM 5 – 2308, Wangenheim to Auswärtiges Amt, October 24, 1914, no. 1101; PA/AA, R 22403, Zimmermann to Jagow, October 25, 1914, no. 820; BA-MA, RM 40 – 456, sheet 247 and reverse, Enver to Humann [copy in Humann's handwriting], October 24, 1914; PA/AA, R 1914, Wangenheim to Auswärtiges Amt, October 25, 1914, no. 1107, where Wangenheim emphasized that he had insisted on a written order by Enver, precluding later claims that Germany had fooled the Ottomans into entering the war; PA/AA, R 22403, Zimmermann to Jagow, October 25, 1914, no. 826.
[84] PA/AA, R 1914, Wangenheim to Auswärtiges Amt, October 24, 1914, no. 1094.
[85] PA/ AA, R 22403, Zimmermann to Jagow, October 24, 1914, no. 816. The delegation was to be led by General Bronsart von Schellendorf and Lieutenant Colonel Hakkı Bey.

but warned that the Black Sea operation must still proceed as planned.[86] Next day, Halil Bey, speaker of the chamber of deputies, was assigned to lead the delegation, which traveled to Berlin to lay out the empire's great difficulties in fighting a major war at this point. Enver explained this last attempt at delay to Humann:

Halil will be traveling to Berlin for political discussions. He believes that our intervention will hurt German interests more than advance them. I, Talat Bey, and Cemal, however, are prepared for action, but we did not want to reject Halil's wish. He will discuss in Berlin the general situation, and if ... [Berlin] insists on our immediate intervention anyway, he [Halil] will be on our side.[87]

Thus despite Enver's dismissive tone towards Halil's mission, the Ottoman leaders still hoped, by having Halil personally present the case against intervention, to buy a few more days' time.

In fact, even Enver's authorization to Souchon on October 24 did not amount to an order for the naval attack. Souchon still awaited Wangenheim's green light, noting that he would "act only in accordance with the ambassador, since I cannot evaluate the political situation independently."[88] But it did mark the end of the Porte's active resistance to Berlin's calls for intervention. And in any case, it was evident that Souchon, once in the Black Sea, would be inclined to provoke an incident. In Souchon's own words, he "would not, so to speak, prevent the cannons from discharging by themselves," if he encountered "the Russian fleet or parts of it in favorable conditions."[89]

The Auswärtiges Amt was disturbed by all the recent bad political news from Istanbul. Berlin was unsettled in particular by the possibility that the Ottoman strike against Russia might not result in the intensely hoped for confrontation of Muslims everywhere against the Entente, especially if, as was quite possible, Russia treated the attack as a purely German operation. As a result, the Auswärtiges Amt pressed for the Ottoman expedition against the British in Egypt in order to achieve a greater effect on Muslim populations around the world. But Wangenheim reiterated that a quick expedition against Egypt seemed highly unlikely, as a result of incomplete preparations. But he agreed with his superiors that a naval attack against Russia, "carried out almost entirely by the *Goeben*," should indeed be followed by a land campaign. "Otherwise we risk Russia's

---

[86] PA/AA, R 22403, Falkenhayn to Auswärtiges Amt, October 25, 1914, no. 7658.
[87] BA-MA, RM 40 – 456, sheet 247 and reverse, October 24, 1914; PA/AA, R 1914, Wangenheim to Auswärtiges Amt, October 25, 1914, no. 1107; PA/AA, R 22403, Zimmermann to Jagow, October 25, 1914, no. 826.
[88] BA-MA, N 156–2, sheet 2, Note by Souchon, October 25, 1914.   [89] Ibid.

interpreting the advance of the fleet ... as merely a German operation and Russia might not even declare war on Turkey."[90]

By October 1914, Berlin's increasing impatience with the Ottoman leadership had extended to Ambassador Wangenheim as well. In order to control Wangenheim directly and to force him to take a harder line on intervention, the Auswärtiges Amt dispatched a special envoy, Richard von Kühlmann, to Istanbul.[91] The move proved to be effective, and Wangenheim's steady resistance began to crumble. Humann, who had worked so diligently in facilitating communication between the two sides generally and between Enver and Wangenheim in particular, lamented during the last week of October the imminence of Ottoman action in the Black Sea:

Now events have developed faster than we imagined yesterday morning, and we now suddenly face the end of our first "phase."

Here at the embassy, Kühlmann pushes very strongly for striking out [Losschlagen] against Russia. His argument is: Berlin has given orders, and now the ambassador must see to it that the action happens ... He [Kühlmann] believes that the admiral [Souchon] no longer has a choice, because the action is something quite political and is militarily only of secondary importance; the government [Reichleitung] has ordered so![92]

Humann, like Wangenheim, had a much deeper understanding of the Ottoman situation than either Kühlmann or Berlin. He believed that the Ottoman leaders were sufficiently committed to Germany not to turn towards the Entente and that, for the reasons so often elaborated by Wangenheim, the policy of armed neutrality benefited Germany's war effort. According to Humann, Wangenheim even believed "that action at this time was foolish. But, Berlin wants it! And there is nothing he can do to change that." As far as Humann was concerned, only the complete annihilation of the Russian Black Sea Fleet, a very unlikely outcome, could justify a naval encounter.[93]

The naval attack on Russia, October 27–31, 1914

On October 27, 1914, Admiral Souchon took the Ottoman fleet into the Black Sea with the express intention of causing war between the Ottoman Empire and Russia. Souchon informed Wangenheim from sea that the maneuver was being conducted "under the pretense of naval exercises

[90] PA/AA, R 1914, Wangenheim to Auswärtiges Amt, October 26, 1914, no. 1113.
[91] BA-MA, RM 5 – 2308, Capelle to Tirpitz, Telephondepesche, October 6, 1914.
[92] BA-MA, RM 40 – 457, sheets, 308–12, Humann to Busse, October 25, 1914.
[93] Ibid.

[*unter Vorwand Flottenmanöver*]" and that he intended to "attack the Russian fleet upon Enver's telegram per agreement or at a suitable opportunity."[94]

Once out at sea, Souchon awaited Enver's wireless instructions either to open the sealed orders for the attack on the Russian coast or, depending on the political situation in the capital, not to open them. This was the agreed-upon signal for Souchon to launch the attack without written authorization. Then Enver added yet another twist. He sent no radio instructions at all and thereby forced the final decision on the German admiral.[95]

Two days later, in the early morning hours of October 29, Souchon informed Wangenheim that "yesterday the Russian fleet disturbed exercises of the Turkish fleet constantly" and that "today hostilities were opened."[96] The German–Ottoman fleet had sunk two Russian warships, the minelayer *Prut* and the gunboat *Kubanetz*, which, the admiral claimed (falsely, as we shall see), were "engaged in hostile activity in front of the Bosporus." The *Goeben*, he added, successfully shelled the Black Sea port Sevastopol.[97] According to Souchon, the *Prut* was carrying 700 mines intended for the northern mouth of the Bosporus, more than "justifying the Turkish attack."[98] A report claiming Russia had attacked the Ottoman fleet was delivered to the authorities in the capital.[99]

---

[94] BA-MA, RM 5 – 2308, sheets 1–3, Souchon to Chief of the Naval Staff, October 27, 1914; PA/AA, R 22403, Zimmermann to Jagow, October 27, 1914, no. 842.

[95] BA-MA, RM 40 – 184, sheet 109, Akten des Sonderkommandos der Marine in der Türkei, Kritische Stellungnahme des Admirals Souchon zum türkischen Operationsplan Herbst 1914, June 5, 1924.

[96] PA/AA, R 1914, Wangenheim to Auswärtiges Amt, October 29, 1914, no. 1146; PA/AA, R 22403, Zimmermann to Jagow, October 29, 1914, no. 858.

[97] BA-MA, RM 5 – 2308, Wangenheim to Auswärtiges Amt, October 29, 1914, no. 1159; BA-MA, RM 5 – 2308, Wangenheim to the Staff of the Admiralty, arrived October 30, 1914; BA-MA, RM 40 – 54, sheet 28, Souchon to Etappe, October 29, 1914; BA-MA, RM 40 – 54, sheet 29, Souchon to Etappe, October 30, 1914; PA/AA, R 22403, Zimmermann to Jagow, October 30, 1914, no. 870. The gunboat *Kubanetz* was sunk off Odessa, the *Prut* was sunk off the port of Sevastopol. Several additional vessels were also sunk or substantially damaged, including the Russian gunboat *Donetz*, see BA-MA, RM 5 –2308, Souchon to Wilhelm, Sheet 104, November 3, 1914. Also see Halpern, *Naval History of World War I*, 63.

[98] PA/AA, R 1914, Wangenheim to Auswärtiges Amt, October 30, 1914, no. 1163; PA/AA, R 22403, Zimmermann to Jagow, October 31, 1914, no. 878. PA/AA, R 1914, Wangenheim to Auswärtiges Amt, October 31, 1914, no. 1174, also in BA-MA, RM 5 – 2308; PA/AA, R 22403, Zimmermann to Jagow, November 1, 1914, no. 889.

[99] The report is paraphrased in Republic of Turkey, *Birinci Dünya Harbi'nde Türk Harbi*, vol. I, *Osmanlı İmparatorluğu'nun Siyasi ve Askeri Hazırlıkları ve Harbe Girişi*, rev. Akbay, 218, citing documentation found in the Historical Division of the Turkish General Staff, Ankara, Turkey.

The same day, Said Halim received a short memorandum from War Minister Enver Pasha alleging that the Russian navy had attacked the Ottoman squadron conducting training maneuvers in the Black Sea. The news was not entirely bad, however. Ottoman forces had not suffered any damage or losses from the attack, the ships had succeeded in sinking one enemy gunboat and one torpedo boat, and they had taken three Russian officers and eighty-three crew members prisoner. The Russian "attack," in other words, had been successfully thwarted.[100]

Two days later, Enver reported through official channels to the grand vezirate the latest information regarding the naval encounter. He provided a doctored description of the events that had occurred in the Black Sea. The account was allegedly based on statements made by Russian officers and crew taken prisoner-of-war during the engagement. Enver claimed that the Russian naval commanders leading the attack had previously served on the Russian ambassadorial yacht in Istanbul, implying that the attack stemmed from long-term Russian planning. This was an important consideration, as it evoked the century-old threat of Russian occupation of Istanbul and the Straits. Enver elaborated:

The commission sent to interrogate the Russian prisoners has found that on October 27, 1914, a Russian fleet accompanied by three submarines left Sevastopol and headed south. After laying 200 mines, the [minelayer] *Prut* continued its southward course on the following day, on October 28, 1914. We have learned that the *Prut* had been in preparation [for this mission] since October 18, 1914. In keeping with their plan, the Russians left behind only a minimum number of warships required for the defense of the region around Sevastopol. In light of the statements made by the [captured] officers and men, and in light of the fact that at the time [of the encounter] a part of our navy was out in the Black Sea while the main part of our navy was inside the Bosporus, the Russian plan has become clear. The Russians were planning to mine [the northern end of] the Bosporus and to cut off thereby our squadron in the Black Sea from any support. The Russian fleet was going to attack our squadron in the Black Sea, and expected that our fleet inside the Bosporus would rush out to the Black Sea, run into the mines, and perish. The commanders of the [Russian] ships had spent one to two years in Istanbul on the [Russian] ambassadorial yacht two or three years ago and possessed excellent knowledge of the Bosporus region. The total number of crew members was around 250. Four officers, one of whom was wounded, one physician and seventy-two men have been taken to Izmit.[101]

[100] BOA, A.VRK 793/29, Office of the Deputy Commander-in-Chief to the Grand Vezir, 16 Teşrin-i Evvel 1330/9 Zilhicce 1332 (October 29, 1914).
[101] BOA, A.VRK 794/32, Deputy Commander-in-Chief Enver to the Grand Vezir, 18 Teşrin-i Evvel 1330 (October 31, 1914).

An Ottoman–Russian naval engagement in the Black Sea that would precipitate the empire's entry into the war was precisely the incident Said Halim had been so eager to avoid. Aware of Berlin and Vienna's urgent desire to see the Ottoman Empire actively involved in the war, the grand vezir had opposed Ottoman naval maneuvers in the Black Sea since the second half of August. When an incident did occur on October 29, Said Halim certainly suspected, if he did not firmly believe, that the reports he was receiving were meant only to disguise the actual event, a German–Ottoman naval attack on Russia.

At the German embassy, Wangenheim learned that Grand Vezir Said Halim Pasha and Finance Minister Cavid Bey had protested the outbreak of war in the cabinet and portrayed it as the doing of a few cabinet members.[102] Said Halim, moreover, refused to accept "responsibility for the hostile action."[103] In contrast, Cemal and Enver sent notes of congratulation to the admiral.[104] On October 30, 1914, the Sublime Porte issued a public communiqué describing the incident as a Russian attack on the Ottoman fleet, stating that "the Imperial Government will no doubt protest with its utmost vigor against this hostile act that the Russian fleet conducted against a minor section of our fleet."[105] To the public, such a statement confirmed the widely held view of Russia's hostile designs. To the Entente, it eliminated any doubt that the Porte was committed to war against them. The Entente ambassadors in Istanbul, Maurice Bompard, Michael Nikolaevich Giers, and Louis Mallet, promptly declared their intention to depart and requested their passports.[106]

Cemal Pasha saw to it that the Russian prisoners-of-war were kept strictly isolated so as to preserve the lie of a Russian attack. It had also been his idea to publish an "official statement" concerning the Black Sea attack in order to "depict the Russians as the aggressors as soon as

---

[102] PA/AA, R 1914, Wangenheim to Auswärtiges Amt, October 30, 1914, no. 1160, also in BA-MA, RM 5 – 2308, sheet 23; PA/AA, R 22403, Zimmermann to Jagow, October 30, 1914, no. 875.

[103] BA-MA, RM 40 – 454, sheet 296 and reverse, Wangenheim to Souchon, October 30, 1914.

[104] Both messages, sent by wireless radio, in BA-MA, RM 40 – 454, sheet 297, Okmeydanı to Souchon, October 30, 1914, and ibid., Enver to Souchon October 30, 1914.

[105] "Le Gouvernement Impérial protestera sans doute avec la dernière vigueur contre cet acte hostile dirigé par la flotte russe contre une minime partie de notre flotte." See PA/AA, R 1914, Wangenheim to Auswärtiges Amt, October 31, 1914, no. 1175, also in PA/AA, R 22403, Wangenheim to Auswärtiges Amt, October 31, 1914, no. 1175.

[106] PA/AA, R 22403, Zimmermann to Jagow, October 31, 1914, no. 890; PA/AA, R 22403, Zimmermann to Jagow, November 2, 1914, no. 907.

possible." And an official protest denouncing the Russian action was to be lodged with the Great Powers as well.[107]

Intervention and its impact on German–Ottoman relations

On the evening of October 31, Enver invited his old friend Hans Humann to discuss the most recent developments. Here Humann learned that earlier that day twenty-seven members of the CUP had gathered to reach a consensus on the next course of action. Seventeen members voted for war against Russia, while ten members opposed it. During this meeting, according to Enver, evidence was presented demonstrating that the Russian fleet had intended to mine the Bosporus in preparation for hostile action against the Ottoman capital and the Straits.[108] It remains unclear exactly what this documentation consisted of, but it was certainly manipulated if not fabricated entirely.[109] What can be said, however, is that this meeting was pivotal, for the CUP might have decided that it was not yet time for war and taken steps to reverse these events. It is unlikely, moreover, that anyone was fooled by the documentation presented at the gathering that evening; the October 31 decision for war grew out of the conviction that the time for the inevitable military encounter with Russia had arrived.

Humann also learned that the cabinet had convened twice that day. During the first of these meetings, the grand vezir, along with four other ministers, submitted his resignation. In the afternoon, a CUP delegation met the grand vezir and showed him the "evidence" for a Russian attack, asking him to retract his resignation and remain in office. Meeting in the late afternoon, the cabinet, too, was presented with the so-called proof of Russian culpability. Enver explained further that he, Cemal, Halil, and Talat stood by the decision for war as they had promised at the time of the

---

[107] ATASE, BDH, Klasör 87, Yeni Dosya 449, Fihrist 1–1, Ahmed Cemal [to Enver?], 16 Teşrin-i Evvel (October 29, 1914).

[108] PA/AA, R 2123, Vertrauliche Mitteilungen vom 31. Oktober 1914 [Confidential Report of October 31, 1914], also in BA-MA, RM 40–456, sheets 238–45. Drawing on this report, often verbatim, Wangenheim related the information to Berlin, see PA/AA R 22403, Zimmermann to Jagow, November 2, 1914, no. 907, which includes Wangenheim's telegram, no. 1205.

[109] See BA-MA, RM 5 – 2308, Souchon to Wilhelm II, November 3, 1914, which shows that the German–Ottoman fleet sailed without any encounters to the Russian coast and opened fire in the early morning of 29 October. The months-long discussions of a naval attack against Russia, too, expose the claim that the Russian fleet was agitating in Ottoman waters. Trumpener reached the same conclusion; see "Turkey's Entry into World War I: An Assessment of Responsibilities," 379.

loan agreement. As a concession to Said Halim, a conciliatory note would be sent to the Russian government. Humann, despite his earlier misgivings, opposed the idea of such a note vehemently. It "discredited" Admiral Souchon, he said, and could turn Ottoman public opinion against Germany. Humann warned Enver that if Germany, "tired of waiting and promises, turned away from Turkey, the demise of the empire is certain." Humann asked Enver to reconsider the note to Russia and did not fail to point out that a German–Russian understanding at the expense of the Ottoman Empire could end the German–Russian conflict. Despite this threat, Enver held firm, replying that he had been alone in the cabinet in opposing the note.[110] Humann's threat, though only once documented to this level of clarity, had hung over each phase of the negotiation process between the two allies since the signing of the treaty on August 2.

In the cabinet's note, Said Halim maintained that the Ottoman authorities "deeply regret the fact that a hostile act, provoked by the Russian fleet, has disturbed the two countries' friendly relations." The grand vezir pledged to put in place precautionary measures to avoid any such incidents in the future. The Ottoman fleet, he continued, would no longer be authorized to maneuver in the Black Sea, and he expressed the hope that the Russian fleet would likewise refrain from conducting naval operations there.[111]

Humann need not have worried. The Russian government left the grand vezir's conciliatory note unanswered. Instead, it recalled its diplomatic corps and retaliated on the Russian–Ottoman border at Erzurum, while British and French warships opened fire on Çanakkale at the southern Dardanelles and on Aqaba from the Red Sea.[112] On November 10, the Ottoman cabinet officially declared war on Russia and its allies, Britain and France. A few days later, it also declared war on Belgium, Montenegro, and Serbia. The cabinet's declaration insisted that the Russian fleet had been sailing towards the Bosporus "with the intention of laying mines" when it opened fire on the "part of the Ottoman fleet that was exercising in the Black Sea." Ottoman forces had only then returned fire. According to the cabinet, the government had sought to resolve the

---

[110] PA/AA, R 2123, Vertrauliche Mitteilungen vom 31. Oktober 1914 [Confidential Report of October 31, 1914], also in BA-MA, RM 40 – 456, sheets 238–45; PA/AA R 22403, Zimmermann to Jagow, November 2, 1914, no. 907, which includes Wangenheim's telegram no. 1205.

[111] *IBZI*, Series II, vol. 6/1, no. 445, Sazonov to Izvolskii and to Benckendorff, November 1, 1914, 355.

[112] ATASE, BDH, Klasör 87, Yeni Dosya 450, Fihrist 5–2, Emin (for Said Halim) to War Ministry, 30 Teşrin-i Evvel 1330 (November 12, 1914); *IBZI*, Series II, vol. 6/1, no. 446, Sazonov to Izvolskii and to Benckendorff, Urgent, November 1, 1914, 355–6.

incident through an investigation, but the Russian government had shown no interest and had instead chosen to attack the empire.[113] But, as we have seen, whether anyone in the cabinet actually believed this description of the "Black Sea Incident," is doubtful. Cemal, Enver, Halil, Said Halim, and Talat, at least, knew the real story.

To their considerable relief, the Ottoman leaders learned that the Radoslavov government was resisting staunchly Russian pressures to take up arms against Istanbul. Their ambassador at Sofia, Ali Fethi, reported that St. Petersburg's official approaches had been turned down in no uncertain terms, and that Radoslavov had been applauded in a special meeting of the Bulgarian legislature when he depicted the Ottomans as friends and Serbs as foes. Later on, Radoslavov had declared Serbia the greatest Bulgarian enemy and claimed that Bulgarians, too, would soon reach for the gun.[114]

Having declared war on Great Britain, France, and Russia, the Ottomans now called for an expansion of the current terms of the alliance in exchange. Already at the time of its signing, they had demanded that the treaty cover a period of at least five years, while the Germans had suggested a treaty lasting for the duration of the war.[115] Following the naval attack, the Ottomans now pressed for a change in the length of the treaty from five to ten years. Halil had delivered the cabinet's request through Wangenheim, who supported the proposal and advised its acceptance. The Ottomans also requested amending the treaty so that it would guarantee German protection not only against an attack from Russia but also Britain, France, and any combination of smaller states. Wangenheim remarked that such a revision of the treaty was necessary to keep the current Ottoman cabinet intact. He also pointed out that, in any case, the Central Powers could honor the treaty only in the event of decisive military victory.[116]

While Berlin hesitated in approving the proposal, Vienna strongly supported it. Ambassador Pallavicini urged its rapid adoption. Should the Central Powers win the war, Pallavicini argued, close collaboration with the Ottoman Empire would be one of its most significant and

---

[113] BOA, MV 237–90, 28 Teşrin-i Evvel 1330/21 Zilhicce 1332 (November 10, 1914); BOA, BEO.NGG 171, Hariciye Gelen, 323983, 30 Teşrin-i Evvel 330/23 Zilhicce 1332 (November 12, 1914), which includes Enver to Said Halim, 3 Teşrin-i Sani 330/28 Zilhicce 1332 (November 16, 1914), no. 3987.

[114] ATASE, BDH, Klasör 566, Yeni Dosya 2186, Fihrist 4, Ali Fethi, 12 Teşrin-i Sani 914 (November 12, 1914).

[115] See chapter 4.

[116] PA/AA, R 22403, Zimmermann to Jagow, November 4, 1914, no. 927. For Trumpener's treatment of the Ottoman initiative, see his *Germany and the Ottoman Empire*, 108–13.

tangible results. The Habsburg foreign minister, Count Berchtold, felt the same way.[117] Back in Berlin, Deputy Foreign Secretary Zimmermann also recommended approval. But Jagow and Bethmann considered the new terms unnecessary and even dangerous. "The current world war," the reply stated, "has been caused in no small part by the exaggeration of the alliance systems ... Expansion of the alliance against *all* states would give rise to the formation of a new system of coalitions, which we wish to avoid entirely." The chancellor also pointed to the fact that the current treaty, with a term of five years, already had a renewal clause for an additional five years to be decided on when the first five-year period concluded. The treaty, therefore, needed no amendment.[118]

Berlin's rejection of the proposal caused a sharp reaction in Istanbul. The revision of the treaty, Wangenheim fired back, was an absolute necessity for the empire's political stability:

> In order to appease the grand vezir, Cavid, and their backers, Enver and his friends had expressed the wish to expand the alliance and improve the credit agreement. They had counted on a favorable response from Berlin. The fact that we have not given them a [positive] decision as of yet has increased the tensions here by the day. I am unable to meet with the grand vezir personally.[119]

The Ottomans' posturing as reported by Wangenheim had its intended effect, and Berlin reversed its decision. Bethmann instructed the ambassador to inform Said Halim of his consent to the treaty's extension until 1920 and its automatic renewal until 1926 unless one of the Powers wished to terminate it.[120] After a period of negotiation, Said Halim and Wangenheim signed the final version of the revised treaty on January 11, 1915.[121] In addition, Said Halim insisted on "a letter that included the promise" that Germany would support the empire financially "for the *entire* duration of the war." The Auswärtiges Amt promptly issued the letter.[122]

---

[117] PA/AA, R 22403, Zimmermann to Jagow, November 5, 1914, no. 960.

[118] PA/AA, R 1915, Bethmann Hollweg to Auswärtiges Amt, November 5, 1914, no. 97, based on Jagow's handwritten draft in PA/AA, R 22403, Jagow to Bethmann Hollweg, November 4, 1914, no. 97; PA/AA, R 1915, Jagow to Auswärtiges Amt, November 6, 1914, no. 343.

[119] PA/AA, R 22403, Zimmermann to Bethmann Hollweg, November 8, 1914, no. 80, which forwards Wangenheim's telegram no. 1262 and also bears Zimmermann's comments of approval.

[120] PA/AA, R 22403, Bethmann Hollweg to Wangenheim, November 9, 1914 [draft], no. 100.

[121] The text of the treaty is published in Kuneralp, *Recueil des Traités, Conventions, Protocoles*, vol. I, *1903–1916*, 313–14.

[122] PA/AA, R 22403, Zimmermann to Bethmann Hollweg, November 17, 1914, Report no. 12, conveying Wangenheim's request, and Zimmermann's and Jagow's support for it. (Emphasis in original.)

Following the attack on the Russian fleet and the shelling of Russian port cities on October 29–31, Russian troops crossed the border into Erzurum Province on the morning of November 1, 1914.[123] The outbreak of war also marked the beginning of the arrest of citizens of the Entente and the wholesale seizure of enemy property in the empire. Enver issued instructions for the search of Entente embassies and consulates and the seizure of businesses, goods, and ships belonging to the governments or citizens of Russia, Britain, France, and Belgium. From Said Halim, Enver requested that civil officials assist army commanders in following these orders.[124] And even prior to any of the Sublime Porte's official declarations of war, the Fourth Army centered at Hama (in today's Syria) began arresting Belgian, British, French, and Russian citizens on November 2, including diplomatic consuls and their staff.[125]

Talat, the interior minister, agreed with Enver's orders for seizing British and French ships along with those belonging to Russian nationals. He thought, however, that foreign businesses, except for those of Russia, should for the time being be left alone until the cabinet had taken a comprehensive decision regarding such enterprises.[126] Talat's position was approved by the cabinet, and a detailed procedure for the treatment of enemy officials, citizens, and property was drawn up shortly thereafter, on November 15, 1914.[127]

Throughout August-October 1914, as Austro-Hungarian and German attempts failed to bring Bulgaria, Romania, and the Ottoman Empire into the war on their side, Berlin's pressure for immediate Ottoman intervention mounted. Germany not only declared its intention of withholding any further assistance until its ally had joined it on the battlefield, but also threatened to recall its personnel instrumental to the Ottoman mobilization effort. The departure of German personnel and *matériel*, including the departure of the *Goeben* and the *Breslau*, would have returned the country to its former state of isolation during a time when the empire's neighbors were armed to the teeth and fully mobilized.

More importantly, however, allowing the rupture of the German–Ottoman alliance would have meant putting an end to the crucial

---

[123] BOA, A.VRK 794/33, Talat to Said Halim, 19 Teşrin-i Evvel 1330 (November 1, 1914), presenting three telegrams from Erzurum Province.
[124] BOA, A.VRK 794/35, Enver to Said Halim, 19 Teşrin-i Evvel 1330 (November 1, 1914).
[125] ATASE, BDH, Klasör 243, Yeni Dosya 1009, Fihrist 40 and 40–1, Fourth Army Commander Zeki Pasha to Office of the Deputy Commander-in-Chief, 20 Teşrin-i Evvel 1330 (November 2, 1914).
[126] BOA, A.VRK 794/49, Talat to Said Halim, 22 Teşrin-i Evvel 1330/15 Zilhicce 1332 (November 4, 1914).
[127] BOA, MV 194–36, 2 Teşrin-i Sani 330/26 Zilhicce 1332 (November 15, 1914), carrying the signatures of eight ministers.

long-term goals associated with it. That the Ottoman leaders were unwilling to do so can be seen explicitly in Said Halim Pasha's proposal of October 1, 1914, for the creation of a long-term German naval base in the Sea of Marmara, which would have given the Germans a considerable role in the empire's security. The same impulse for a long-term arrangement is also evident in the Ottomans' demand for extending the terms of the alliance to 1920, renewable until 1926.

Enver Pasha, too, directly engaged in the attempt to preserve the alliance without fulfilling its military obligations. In meetings with his German counterparts as late as October 1914, he enumerated the advantages the Central Powers were reaping from the closure of the Straits. In time, however, through threats to terminate the alliance and abandon Ottoman interests entirely, perhaps even settling the war through agreements with the Great Powers by partitioning the Ottoman Empire altogether, Berlin had prevailed.

Conclusion: the decision for war remembered

In the war's final month of fighting, Enver Pasha issued the following letter to his general staff on October 18, 1918:

The situation that has been created by the attack of the Entente on the Macedonian front and the riots in Bulgaria have forced the Bulgarian government to propose a separate peace with our enemies. Bulgaria is therefore no longer our ally. In consultation with our allies we have jointly proposed peace negotiations to our enemies on the basis of the Wilsonian principles. The purpose of our entry into the war on the side of Germany, Austria-Hungary, and Bulgaria was to engage as many enemy troops as possible and to keep these away from the European theater, where the outcome of the war would be decided. The Ottoman army and navy fully pursued this objective without interruption. And they have until now completely fulfilled this task on all fronts despite many sacrifices. As a result of the new situation, the present government has decided to resign. As a member of this government, I have also asked our commander-in-chief [Sultan Mehmed Reşad V] to release me from the office of the chief of the general staff.[1]

For the Ottomans, the war was over.

Following the collapse of their armies in the second half of 1918, the Central Powers had no choice but to sue for peace. In Istanbul, a new cabinet headed by Ahmed İzzet Pasha replaced the wartime government. Talat, grand vezir (and pasha) since February 1917, continued to wield much of his previous authority, however, and controlled the formation of his successor's cabinet. The new cabinet faced the impossible task of negotiating the terms of the peace settlement with the victorious Entente powers and salvaging as much as possible of the empire and its sovereignty. Central to this task was the prosecution and punishment of the former Ottoman leaders who had directed the war against the Entente. And although the most prominent members of the former government fled the country immediately after the official signing of the armistice on October 30, 1918, the majority of cabinet members eventually faced trial. To a great extent, the sentencing of the wartime leaders served to placate

---

[1] ATASE, BDH, Klasör 1649, Yeni Dosya 42, Fihrist 1 and 1–1, Enver, October 18, 1918.

188

the Entente powers, and it has rightly been characterized as a "show trial."[2]

The interrogation of the wartime cabinets accused the cabinet members of the following ten transgressions:

1. Entering the war without reason and at an untimely moment.
2. Falsely stating to the chamber of deputies the real reasons and course of events behind the declaration of war.
3. Rejecting the honorable and salutary offers by the Entente governments following mobilization and prior to the declaration of war, and allowing the Empire to be drawn into war without obtaining any kind of guarantee from Germany and without securing an advantage.
4. Permitting, for purely personal reasons, the squandering of the vitality of the people [*millet*] by entrusting the war to incompetent and profligate hands, and [permitting] the undertaking at all battlefronts of foolish operations contrary to military science.
5. Turning the country into a scene of calamity by issuing temporary laws, ordinances, and regulations completely irreconcilable with the rule of law, human rights, and especially the spirit and letter of our Constitution.
6. Concealing, merely in order to protect the position [of certain individuals], events of the war that did not concern strategy and did not have to be kept confidential; and failing to inform the people in a timely manner of the disastrous consequences that would ensue from allowing the enemy to trample over portions of the exalted homeland.
7. Refusing the Entente governments' repeated peace offers during the war years, particularly following the Russian Revolution, and thus inviting today's inauspicious outcome.
8. Destroying the country's economy through profiteering and misappropriation, by guaranteeing that a few private individuals and corporations would accumulate wealth, rather than taking measures to alleviate the needs of the people in the face of the hardships of war.
9. Infringing upon the freedom of press and correspondence by putting in place political and military censorship without any necessity or basis in law, and barring the importation of European news reports.
10. Participating in the atrocities by supporting bands of brigands in violation of personal freedoms and property rights by bringing about administrative chaos within the country.[3]

[2] Sina Akşin, *İstanbul Hükümetleri ve Milli Mücadele* (Istanbul: Cem Yayınevi, 1976), 17–70.
[3] *Said Halim ve Mehmed Talat Paşalar Kabinelerinin Divan-ı Âliye Sevkleri Hakkında (Divaniye) Mebusu Fuad Bey Merhum Tarafından Verilen Takrir Üzerine Bera-ı Tahkikat*

The responses to these questions framed the subsequent narration of the Ottoman entry into the First World War. Those who testified depicted Enver as a loose cannon who forced the empire into the war through secret dealings with German agents. This image of Enver as a single-minded dictator prepared to join the German side in battle at any price has demonstrated an impressive historiographic resilience. But as the examination of Ottoman publications on the eve of the war has shown, the public, or, at least, the broader elite, supported an alliance with Germany and saw war as a desirable path to reclaiming the empire's independence and economic stability.

Although most authors of political memoirs writing in the era of the modern Turkish Republic denied their support for the ultimately ill-fated alliance with Germany, a few acknowledged their earlier convictions. These authors stated that, before the war, they indeed believed in the advantages that could be gained from the German–Ottoman Alliance of 1914. Galip Vardar, a former officer and committed CUP member, whose memoirs were published in 1960, noted that the "most difficult question" the CUP would ever have to answer was the question of why it decided for war in 1914. Vardar provided the following explanation:

Everybody is in agreement that the Ottoman Empire entered this war with the approval of the Unionist cabinet which was in power. And many even claim that in this [approval] the roles of Talat, Enver, and Cemal pashas were predominant. Moreover, those who examine this question carefully, hold first and foremost one person responsible. And that is War Minister Enver Pasha. They say: Enver Pasha was the personal friend of the German emperor Wilhelm II. During his time in Berlin as military attaché, [Enver] won [Wilhelm II's] trust and favor ... It was Enver who permitted the two German warships Goeben and Breslau, which were in great danger in the Mediterranean, to maneuver through the minefields at Çanakkale and take refuge in Istanbul. It was again Enver who took the admiral of those ships, [Wilhelm] Souchon, into Ottoman service, and who later allowed [Souchon] to go out into the Black Sea under the pretext of naval exercises. Therefore Enver personally led the empire into the war. Many have reached this [above] conclusion. This is not the truth. The truth is that the leaders of the CUP favored siding with Germany for emotional reasons [his itibariyle], that they remained under the impact of the tragic disasters of the Balkan Wars, that they feared Russia, that they had to find money, and that, finally, they went with the flow of events and entered the war with hesitation.[4]

Kura İsabet Eden Beşinci Şube Tarafından İcra Olunan Tahkikat Ve Zabt Edilen İfadatı Muhtevidir [Fifth Parliamentary Investigation Committee] (Istanbul: Meclis-i Mebusan Matbaası, 1334 [1918]), 5–6; cf. Osman Selim Kocahanoğlu, İttihat-Terakki'nin Sorgulanması ve Yargılanması: Meclis-i Mebusan Tahkikatı, Teşkilat-ı Mahsusa, Ermeni Tehcirinin İçyüzü, Divan-ı Harb-i Örfi Muhakemesi (Istanbul: Temel, 1998), 52–3.
[4] Galip Vardar, İttihad ve Teraki İçinde Dönenler, dictated to Samih Nafiz Tansu (Istanbul: İnkilâp Kitabevi, 1960), 253–5.

A mix of pride, sense of violation, and revenge imbued the Ottoman intellectual climate on the eve of the First World War. The human suffering and territorial losses experienced by the Ottomans in 1911–13 resulting from the Tripolitanian and Balkan wars had been harrowingly illustrated by the arrival of Muslim refugees. Contemporary publications sought to mobilize society and ready it against further calamity. These publications sent out an emotional rallying cry to a psychologically vulnerable public. These emotions were recast in social Darwinian terms, and journals like *Büyük Duygu* (The Great Yearning) argued that the road to the future led through war. Enver Pasha, perhaps the most influential Ottoman decision-maker, also subscribed to the ideas promoted in the literature of the time.[5] Since the late eighteenth century, the Ottomans had observed a gradual but unmistakable shift in the balance of international power towards the states of Western Europe. Despite repeated efforts at reform, the empire never successfully kept up with the technological and industrial developments in Europe. As a result, the Ottomans' vast empire increasingly fell subject to the political and financial interests of outsiders. In theory, only diplomacy offered an opportunity for the empire to maintain control over its own affairs. Finding an ally among the states of the Great Powers would have offered a measure of real security and greater autonomy in the empire's political economy, which was frequently at the mercy of European investors. This thinking explains the urgency of Ottoman efforts to put an end to diplomatic isolation and to seize the opportunity of a German alliance during the July Crisis of 1914.

Only rarely does the historian get a clear statement by the decision-makers themselves as to the rationale behind their decisions. On one such occasion Talat Pasha emphasized that the alliance with the Central Powers was part of a strategy to achieve long-term security, economic development, and, eventually, national recovery. He explained this strategy and rationale in a letter of October 23, 1917, to Ernst Jäckh, the self-proclaimed German expert on the Near East and government liaison in Istanbul:

It would be wrong to consider our alliance with Germany as a temporary political combination. The Turco-German alliance is the result of a concrete policy based on the community of interests. The quadruple alliance which has proved itself during three years of war will, with the help of God, be able to triumph over the

[5] See his conversation with Hans Humann in PA/AA, R 1914, Besprechung mit Enver Pascha am 2. Oktober 1914 [Conversation with Enver Pasha on October 2, 1914], reported by Humann, and also found in BA-MA, RM 40 – 4, sheets 94–7.

difficulties of the moment and ensure for our countries a glorious peace and a future of prosperity.[6]

Only an alliance with Germany offered any prospect of fulfilling this long-term strategy, since the Entente states all had concrete territorial ambitions in the Near East and had shown no interest in genuine diplomatic cooperation with the Ottoman Empire.

Said Halim Pasha, the grand vezir during the July Crisis, was in this sense not far from Talat in his thinking. Following Franz Ferdinand's assassination on June 28, 1914, Said Halim skillfully redoubled efforts to conclude the alliance with Berlin. He did so primarily by exploiting Vienna's sense of insecurity during the Sarajevo Crisis, and by invoking the possibility of a Greek–Ottoman alliance that would assure Greek support to Serbia, a frightening prospect for the Habsburgs. Enver and Talat followed up on Said Halim's efforts and met with the Austro-Hungarian and German ambassadors, Johann von Pallavicini and Hans von Wangenheim, reiterating the Ottoman desire to form an alliance with the Central Powers. In a meeting with Wangenheim on July 22, Enver emphasized that he was speaking on behalf of the entire Committee of Union and Progress, and the war minister held out once again the prospect of a Greek–Ottoman or even an Entente–Ottoman alliance. Thus, far from pursuing a policy that only he himself supported, Enver Pasha was the chief negotiator of an alliance strategy backed by the Ottoman decision-making elite.

The policy of feigning readiness to join the Entente, moreover, had the intended effect on Kaiser Wilhelm II. Sensing an opening, Said Halim had offered immediately a "secret short-term German–Ottoman alliance directed against Russia."[7] In a recently discovered manuscript penned by the former grand vezir himself just before his assassination in Rome in 1921, Said Halim described his meetings with Wangenheim. He wrote, "During our discussions about Russia's schemes I took the occasion to tell him [Wangenheim] that the only way to put an end to Russia's aggression would be an alliance with Germany."[8] And, by 1921, Said Halim

---

[6] Ernst Jäckh Papers, Yale University Library, Box 2, Folder 43, Talat to Ernst Jäckh, October 23, 1917: "Il serait erroné de considérer notre alliance avec l'Allemagne comme une combinaison politique passagère. L'Alliance Turco-Allemande est le résultat d'une politique concrète basée sur la communauté d'intérêts. La quadruple alliance qui a fait ses preuves durant les trois années de guerre saura, avec l'aide de Dieu, triompher des difficultés du moment et assurer à nos pays une paix glorieuse et un avenir de prosperité."

[7] PA/AA, R 22402, Wangenheim to Auswärtiges Amt, July 27, 1914, no. 370. Also in Kautsky, *Outbreak*, no. 285.

[8] "Au cours d'un de nos entretiens sur les agissements de la Russie, je saisis l'occasion pour lui dire que le seul moyen de mettre fin aux agressions de la Russie serait une alliance avec l'Allemagne." See Said Halim Paşa, *L'Empire Ottoman et la Guerre Mondiale* (Istanbul: Éditions Isis, 2000), 8.

evidently had not changed his mind, saying that "[in] effect the alliance with Germany was then the most desirable thing for Turkey."[9] In an interview with the *New York Times*, appearing on February 22, 1915, Said Halim declared that in making their decision for war Turkey's leaders had been "tired of the hypocrisy actuating the powers of the Triple Entente when dealing with Turkey." The grand vezir added that the Ottoman Empire "knew that to enter into relations with Great Britain, France, and Russia would have been a harmful factor in respect to the country's interest." Finally, the grand vezir stated, the Ottoman "people want a chance to work out their destiny."[10]

While Berlin initially perceived the treaty as a measure to steer through the tumultuous days of the July Crisis, the Ottomans harbored much grander hopes. To them, the alliance meant long-term military security and a chance to gain momentum for political stability and economic development. The irony, of course, is striking: rather than ushering in a period of stability, as they had hoped, the alliance committed the Ottomans to fighting a war that rang the empire's death knell.

The Ottomans won Berlin for an alliance not only by threatening to join the enemy camp, the Triple Entente, but also by promising substantial military support to the war effort of the Central Powers. They did so primarily through the efforts of Enver Pasha, who conducted the final alliance negotiations with the German ambassador, Hans von Wangenheim, and the head of the German military mission, Otto Liman von Sanders. This re-examination of the German–Ottoman negotiations during August–November 1914 strongly suggests that the image of Enver Pasha as war hawk dazzled by Germany's military power and by pan-Islamist dreams is untenable. By 1914, Enver Pasha, like the majority of the Ottoman elite, perceived the interests of the international system to oppose the continued existence of the Ottoman Empire. And, to the Ottomans, fighting back appeared possible only within the context of an alliance with the German Empire.

Nor was Enver eager to dive into the war: the Ottomans only entered after three months of foot-dragging, deception, and protracted negotiations with Berlin, and only after the German–Ottoman alliance came close to rupturing. Once the Ottoman leaders secured the alliance with Germany on August 2, 1914, they focused their energies on postponing any military engagement. When the Germans, and especially Liman, pressed Istanbul for action, the Ottomans repeatedly insisted on the

---

[9] "En effet, l'alliance avec l'Allemagne était la chose la plus désirable alors pour la Turquie." See Said Halim Paşa, *L'Empire Ottoman*, 8.

[10] "Turkey Distrusted Allies, Says Halim," *The New York Times*, February 22, 1915.

necessity of an alliance with Bulgaria and for more time to complete their mobilization efforts. It was Germany's refusal to provide further military aid, and its threat to abandon them and to conclude a separate peace with Russia, that finally drew the Ottomans into war.

In 1914 Ottoman public life was charged with feelings of despair and violation at the hands of the Great Power system. These strong emotions also imbued Ottoman diplomacy. The empire's statesmen sought revenge against a system that they believed had betrayed them, while at the same time imagining that war would set the stage for national renewal and reinvigoration. The assassination of Franz Ferdinand in Sarajevo unleashed a new international dynamic that afforded the Ottomans a historic opportunity for self-assertion. While the empire's demise after the war has been understood as a sign of a failure of leadership, the tenets under which they operated did not die with them. Militarism, nationalism, and modernization continued to define the political landscape of the Turkish nation-state that emerged after the First World War.

Finally, one might speculate that, given the incompleteness of the nationalizing process in the Ottoman territories in 1914, the diverse peoples of the region might have managed to continue their fare within the old Ottoman framework. The radical change in leadership after January 1913, however, suggests that the time in which "continuation" would have been an option had already passed.

Bibliography

I. UNPUBLISHED DOCUMENTS

OTTOMAN

Askeri Tarih ve Stratejik Etüt Başkanlığı (ATASE), Archives of the Turkish General Staff, Ankara, Turkey
BDH, Birinci Dünya Harbi, First World War

Başbakanlık Osmanlı Arşivi (BOA), Ottoman Archives of the Prime Ministry, Istanbul, Turkey
A.VRK, Sadaret Evrakı, papers of the Grand Vezirate
BEO.NGG, Bab-ı Âli Evrak Odası, Nezaretler Gelen-Giden, Document Office of the Sublime Porte, Incoming and Outgoing Correspondence
MV, Meclis-i Vükelâ Mazbataları, Decisions of the Ottoman Cabinet

Library of Congress, Washington, DC
Karl Süssheim Papers

Türk Tarih Kurumu Arşivi (TTK), Archives of the Turkish Historical Society, Ankara, Turkey
Enver Paşa Evrakı, Enver Pasha Papers
Kâzım Orbay Evrakı, Kâzım Orbay Papers

GERMAN

Politisches Archiv des Auswärtigen Amts (PA/AA), Political Archives of the Foreign Office, Berlin, Germany
R 1912, Deutschland 128 No. 5, Beitritt der Türkei zu dem Bündnisvertrage zwischen Deutschland, Österreich und Italien
R 1913, Deutschland 128 No. 5, Beitritt der Türkei zu dem Bündnisvertrage zwischen Deutschland, Österreich und Italien
R 1914, Deutschland 128 No. 5, Beitritt der Türkei zu dem Bündnisvertrage zwischen Deutschland, Österreich und Italien
R 1915, Deutschland 128 No. 5, Beitritt der Türkei zu dem Bündnisvertrage zwischen Deutschland, Oesterreich und Italien
R 2123, Deutschland 135 No. 1, Die deutsche Botschaft in Konstantinopel

R 2125, Deutschland 135 No. 1, Die deutschen Missionen im Auslande, Botschaft Konstantinopel

R 14501, Orientalia Generalia No.5, Politik der Mächte bezüglich der Balkanhalbinsel, der Türkei und der Meerengen

R 14503, Orientalia Generalia No. 5, Politik der Mächte bezüglich der Balkanhalbinsel, der Türkei und der Meerengen, December 1913–April 1914

R 14524, Orientalia Generalia No. 5 Geheim, Die Politik der Mächte bezüglich der Balkanhalbinsel und der Meerengen, November 1909–June 1914

R 19866, Der Weltkrieg, Krieg 1914

R 22402, Grosses Hauptquartier No.185, Türkei Nr.18, Haltung der Türkei, Vertrag mit Deutschland und Österreich

R 22403, Grosses Hauptquartier No. 186, Türkei Nr.18, Haltung der Türkei, Vertrag mit Deutschland und Österreich

Bundesarchiv-Militärarchiv (BA-MA), German Federal Military Archives, Freiburg i.Br., Germany

RM 5 Admiralstab der Marine, 1890–1919

2308, unnamed

2320, unnamed

RM 40, Dienst- und Kommandostellen der Kaiserlichen Regierung im Mittelmeer und im Osmanischen Reich, 1906–18

1, Abschriften der Berichte an S.M. und Admiralstab, September 1914–September 1917

4, Politische Nachrichten und allgemeine Nachrichten über den Kriegsverlauf

54, Geheim, Mittelmeerdivision und Flotte, Sonderkommando Türkei, August 1914–September 1915

55, Zusammenstellung des Sonderkommandos, August 1914–September 1915

106, Militärmission, October 1913–June 1914

130, O[perations]-Akten, September 1914–June 1918

184, Akten des Sonderkommandos der Marine in der Türkei, Kritische Stellungnahme des Admirals Souchon zum türkischen Operationsplan Herbst 1914, 1914–24

282, Andere Operationsvorarbeiten, September 1914–October 1915

454, Operations-Befehle, September 1914–July 1915

455, Kriegsausbruch, August 1914–October 1914

456, Politisches, August 1914–August 1916

457, Politisches, August 1914–August 1916

564, Militärpolitische Berichte (Reisepläne), November 1912–March 1913

575, Bildung einer ständigen Mittelmeer-Division (MMD), July 1913–July 1914

671, Politisches, 6 August 1914–October 1914

N 80, Papers of Bruno von Mudra, 1851–1931, General der Infanterie

1, Privatkorrespondenz mit Freiherr von der Goltz, Einlauf, 10 September 1899–6 August 1915

N 156, Papers of Wilhelm Souchon, 1864–1946, Admiral, Chef der Mittelmeerdivision, Oberbefehlshaber der türkischen und bulgarischen Seestreikräfte

2, Privatdienstliche Korrespondenz, Wilhelm Souchon mit Vorgesetzten und
    Kameraden, Ein- und Auslauf, August 14, 1914–November 23, 1923
N 737, Papers of Goltz, Colmar Freiherr von der, 1843–1916, preussischer
    Generalfeldmarschall
5, Berichte über Türkei Aufenthalte

**Bundesarchiv Berlin-Lichterfelde (BA-B), German Federal Archives
Berlin-Lichterfelde**
R 901, Auswärtiges Amt
25150, die Aufhebung der Kapitulationen in der Türkei und ihr Ersatz durch
    Rechtsverträge, November 1913–November 1915

Yale University Library, New Haven, CT
Ernst Jäckh Papers

II. PUBLISHED DOCUMENTS AND OFFICIAL HISTORIES

Austria-Hungary, Foreign Ministry. *Österreich-Ungarns Aussenpolitik: Von der bosni-
    schen Krise 1908 bis zum Kriegsausbruch 1914*, 8 vols., ed. Ludwig Bittner, Alfred
    Francis Pribram, Heinrich Srbik, and Hans Uebersberger. Vienna:
    Österreichischer Bundesverlag; 1930; reprinted, Nendeln: Kraus Reprint,
    1972.
Germany, Foreign Office. *Die Grosse Politik der Europäischen Kabinette, 1871–1914:
    Sammlung der Diplomatischen Akten des Auswärtigen Amtes (Im Auftrage des
    Auswärtigen Amtes)* [*GP*], 40 vols., ed. Johannes Lepsius, Albrecht
    Mendelssohn Bartholdy, and Friedrich Thimme. Berlin: Deutsche
    Verlagsgesellschaft für Politik und Geschichte, 1922–7.
Great Britain. *British Documents on the Origins of the War, 1898–1914* [*BDOW*],
    11 vols., ed. G. P. Gooch and Harold Temperley. London: His Majesty's
    Stationery Office, 1936.
Kautsky, Karl. *Outbreak of the World War*, trans. Carnegie Endowment for
    International Peace. New York: Oxford University Press, 1924.
Kuneralp, Sinan, ed. *Recueil des Traités, Conventions, Protocoles, Arrangements et
    Déclarations signés entre l'Empire Ottoman et les Puissances Étrangères,
    1903–1922*, vol. I, *1903–1916*. Istanbul: Éditions Isis, 2000.
Ottoman Empire. *Meclis-i Mebusan Zabıt Ceridesi* [MMZC, Proceedings of the
    Ottoman Chamber of Deputies]. Istanbul: Meclis-i Mebusan Matbaası, 1914.
*Said Halim ve Mehmed Talat Paşalar Kabinelerinin Divan-ı Âliye Sevkleri Hakkında
    (Divaniye) Mebusu Fuad Bey Merhum Tarafından Verilen Takrir Üzerine Bera-ı
    Tahkikat Kura İsabet Eden Beşinci Şube Tarafından İcra Olunan Tahkikat Ve Zabt
    Edilen İfadatı Muhtevidir* [Fifth Parliamentary Investigation Committee].
    Istanbul: Meclis-i Mebusan Matbaası, 1334 [1918].
The Sublime Porte, The Ministry of Foreign Affairs. *Boğazlar Meselesi* [The
    Straits Question]. Istanbul: Matbaa-i Amire, 1334 [1918]).
Republic of Turkey, Chief of the General Staff. *Birinci Dünya Harbi'nde Türk Harbi*,
    vol. I, *Osmanlı İmparatorluğu'nun Siyasî ve Askerî Hazırlıkları Ve Harbe Girişi*.

Genelkurmay Askeri Tarih ve Stratejik Etüt Başkanlığı Yayınları, 1970. Revised by Cemal Akbay. Ankara: Genelkurmay Basım Evi, 1991.

Birinci Dünya Harbi'nde Türk Harbi, vol. VIII, *Deniz Harekâtı*, by Saim Besbelli. Ankara: Genelkurmay Basım Evi, 1976.

Soviet Union. *Die Internationalen Beziehungen im Zeitalter des Imperialismus [IBZI]*: Dokumente aus den Archiven der Zarischen und der Provisorischen Regierung herausgegeben von der Kommission beim Zentralexekutivkomitee der Sowjetregierung unter dem Vorsitz von M. N. Pokrowski (Einzig berechtigte deutsche Ausgabe Namens der Deutschen Gesellschaft zum Studium Osteuropas herausgegeben von Otto Hoetzsch). Series I–III. Berlin: Reimar Hobbing, 1931–43.

III. CONTEMPORARY PUBLICATIONS AND MEMOIRS

A. *Balkan Harbi'nde Neden Münhezim Olduk* [Why We Were Routed in the Balkan War]. Part I. Kütübhane-i İntibah, Tüccarzade İbrahim Hilmi, no. 9. Istanbul: Kütübhane-i İslam ve Askeri, 1329 [March 1913–March 1914].

Balkan Harbi'nde Neden Münhezim Olduk: Askeri Mağlubiyetimizin Esbabı [Why We Were Routed in the Balkan War: The Causes of Our Military Defeat]. Part II. Kütübhane-i İntibah, Tüccarzade İbrahim Hilmi, no. 12. Istanbul: Kütübhane-i İslam ve Askeri, 1329 [March 1913–March 1914].

Ahmed Emin [Yalman]. "The Development of Modern Turkey as Measured by its Press." *Studies in History, Economics, and Public Law* 59 (1914): 1–142.

Ahmed Saib. *Tarih-i Meşrutiyet Ve Şark Mesele-i Hazırası* [The History of the Constitutional Period and the Current Eastern Crisis]. Istanbul: Necm-i İstikbal Matbaası, 1328 Hicrî. [1910].

Ahmed Salâhaddin. *Makedonya Meselesi Ve Balkan Harb-i Ahiri* [The Macedonian Question and the Latest Balkan War]. Dersaadet: Kanaat Matbaası, 1331 [March 1915–March 1916].

Berlin Kongresi'nin Diplomasi Tarihine Bir Nazar [The Diplomatic History of the Berlin Congress]. Külliyat-ı Hukuk Ve Siyasiyatdan Birinci Kitab. n.p., 1327 [March 1911–March 1912].

Akçuraoğlu Yusuf. "Türk, Cermen Ve Islavlar'ın Münasebat-ı Tarihiyeleri [Historical Relations among the Turks, Germans, and Slavs]." Address delivered November 19, 1914. [Istanbul]: Kader Matbaası, 1330.

Büyük Duygu: Onbeş Günde Bir Çıkar, Türkün Risalesidir [The Great Yearning: The Turk's Bimonthly Journal]. Bab-ı Âli Caddesinde Cemiyet Kütübhanesi. Yıl 1, Sayı 1, 2 Mart 1329–Yıl 1, Sayı 26, 18 Kanun-i Sani 1329 [Number 1, March 15, 1913–Number 26, January 31, 1914].

Cami [Abdurrahman Cami Baykut]. *Osmanlılığın Atisi: Düşmanları Ve Dostları* [The Ottoman Future: Its Enemies and Its Friends]. Istanbul: İfham Matbaası, 1331 [5 Kanunisani 1328/January 18, 1913].

Cavid. "Birinci Cihan Harbine Türkiye'nin Girmesi" [Turkey's Entry into the First World War]. *Tanin*, 15 Birinciteşrin 1944–2 Ağustos 1945 [October 15, 1944–August 2, 1945].

Foerster, Wolfgang, *Generalfeldmarschall Colmar Freiherr von der Goltz: Denkwürdigkeiten*. Berlin: E. S. Mittler und Sohn, 1929.

Hafız Hakkı, Binbaşı [Major]. *Bozgun* [Morale and Defeat]. Tüccarzade İbrahim Hilmi Series. Dersaadet: Matbaa-i Hayriye, 1330 [March 1914–March 1915].

Hüseyin Kâzım. *Rum Patriği'ne Açık Mektub: Boykot Müslümanların Hakkı Değil Midir?* [An Open Letter to the Greek Orthodox Patriarch: Do Muslims Not Have the Right to Boycott?]. Istanbul: Yeni Turan Matbaası, 1330 [March 1914–March 1915].

Karabekir, Kâzım. *Tarih Boyunca Türk-Alman İlişkileri* [Turkish-German Relations in History], ed. Orhan Hülagü and Ömer Hakan Özalp. Istanbul: Emre, 2001.

Türkiye'de Ve Türk Ordusunda Almanlar [Germans in Turkey and in the Turkish Military], ed. Orhan Hülagü and Ömer Hakan Özalp. Istanbul: Emre, 2001.

Cihan Harbine Neden Girdik, Nasıl Girdik, Nasıl İdare Ettik [Why We Entered the War, How We Entered It, and How We Administered It], vol. II, *Cihan Harbine Nasıl Girdik?* [How We Entered the World War]. Istanbul: Tecelli Basımevi, 1937.

Liman von Sanders, [Otto]. *Fünf Jahre Türkei, 2nd edn.* Berlin: August Scherl, 1920.

Mandelstam, André N. *Das armenische Problem im Lichte des Völker- und Menschenrechts.* Berlin: Georg Stilke, 1931.

Martı, Metin, ed. *Bahriye Nazırı ve 4. Ordu Kumandanı Cemal Paşa: Hatırat* [The Memoirs of Navy Minister and Fourth Army Commander Cemal Pasha], 5th edn. Istanbul: Arma, 1996.

Mehmed Emin. *Ey Türk Uyan* [O Turk, Awake!]. [Istanbul]: Babikyan Matbaası, 1330 [March 1914–March 1915].

Mehmed Şerif. *Edirne Vilayetinden Rumlar Niçin Gitmek İstiyorlar? İzmir Mebusu Emanuelidi Efendi'ye* [Why Do Greek Ottomans Want to Leave Edirne Province? (A Letter) To Emanuelidi Efendi, Member of the Chamber of Deputies from Izmir]. Edirne: Edirne Sanaii Mektebi Matbaası, 1330 [March 1914–March 1915].

Menteşe, Halil. *Osmanlı Mebusan Reisi Halil Menteşe'nin Anıları* [Memoirs of the Speaker of the Ottoman Chamber of Deputies Halil Menteşe], ed. İsmail Arar. Istanbul: Hürriyet Vakfı, 1986.

Mühlmann, Carl. *Deutschland und die Türkei, 1913–1914: Die Berufung der deut- schen Militärmission nach der Türkei 1913, das deutsch-türkische Bündnis 1914 und der Eintritt der Türkei in den Weltkrieg (Unter Benutzung und Mitteilung bisher unveröffentlichter politischer Dokumente dargestellt).* Politische Wissenschaft. Berlin-Grunewald: Rothschild, 1929.

Naci İsmail. *Londra Konferansı'ndaki Meselelerden: Anadolu'da Türkiye Yaşayacak Mı? Yaşamayacak Mı?* [One of the Matters at the London Conference: Will Turkey Survive in Anatolia?], attrib. Jones Moli, trans. Habil Adem [pseud.] Istanbul: İkbal Kütübhanesi, n.d.

Mağlub Milletler Nasıl İntikam Alırlar [How Do Defeated Nations Take Revenge?], attrib. Belak, trans. Habil Adem [pseud.]. Dersaadet: İkbal Kütübhanesi, 1332 h. [November 1913–November 1914].

Ömer Seyfeddin. *Yarınki Turan Devleti* [Tomorrow's State of Turan]. Türk Yurdu Kütübhanesi. Istanbul: Kader Matbaası, 1330 [March 1914–March 1915].

Özdemir [Şehbenderzade Filibeli Ahmed Hilmi]. *Türk Ruhu Nasıl Yapılıyor? Her Vatanperverden, Bu Eserciği Türklere Okumasını Ve Anlatmasını Niyaz Ederiz*

[How the Turkish Spirit is Formed: We Ask of Each Patriot to Read and Relate this Booklet to the Turks]. İkaz-ı Millet Kütübhanesi, no. 1. Darülhilâfe: Hikmet Matbaa-i İslamiyesi, 1329 [March 1913–March 1914].

Parvus. *İngiltere Galib Gelirse . . . : İtilaf-ı Müselles'in Zafer Ve Galibiyetinde Husule Gelecek Tebedüllat-ı Araziye* [If England is Victorious ... Territorial Changes in the Event of Triple Entente Victory]. Türk Yurdu Kütübhanesi. Umumi Harb Neticelerinden, no. 2. Istanbul: Kader Matbaası, 1330 [March 1914–March 1915].

Recai. Foreword to *Almanya Nasıl Dirildi? Harbe Nasıl Hazırlanıyor?* [How Germany Revived and How It is Preparing for War]. Translation of *La préparation de la lutte économique par l'Allemagne*, by Antoine de Tarlé. Dersaadet: Nefaset Matbaası, 1329 [March 1913–March 1914].

Said Halim Paşa, *L'Empire Ottoman et la Guerre Mondiale*. Studies on Ottoman Diplomatic History VIII. Istanbul: Éditions Isis, 2000.

Sâbis, Ali İhsan. *Harp Hatıralarım: Birinci Dünya Harbi* [My War Memoirs: The First World War], 4 vols. Nehir Edition. Istanbul: Nehir, 1990.

Söylemezoğlu, Galip Kemalî. *Hatıraları: Atina Sefareti (1913–1916)* [Memoirs: The Athens Embassy (1913–1916)]. Canlı Tarihler, no. 5. Istanbul: Türkiye Yayınevi, 1946.

Süleyman Nazif. *İki İttifakın Tarihçesi: İttifak-ı Müselles-İttifak-ı Müsenna* [The History of the Two Alliances: Triple Alliance–Dual Alliance]. n.p.: Muhtar Halid Kütübhanesi, 1330 [March 1914–March 1915].

Tanin [Echo], Istanbul.

Toshev, Andrei. *Balkanskite voini*. Plovdiv and Sofia: H. G. Danov, 1931.

Tüccarzade İbrahim Hilmi. *Türkiye Uyan* [Turkey Awake]. Kütübhane-i İntibah, no. 13. Dersaadet: Kütübhane-i İslam ve Askerî, 1329 [March 1913–March 1914].

"Turkey Distrusted Allies, Says Halim." *The New York Times*, February 22, 1914.

Vardar, Galip. *İttihad Ve Terraki İçinde Dönenler* [The Games inside (the Committee of) Union and Progress], dictated to Samih Nafiz Tansu. Istanbul: İnkılâp Kitabevi, 1960.

Yusuf Ziya. Afterword to *Anadolu'nun İstikbali ve Akdeniz Meselesi* [Anatolia's Future and the Mediterranean Question]. Translation of *Problème méditerranéen*, 1913], by Charles Vellay. Kütübhane-i İntibah, Tüccarzade İbrahim Hilmi, no. 10. Istanbul: Kütübhane-i İslam ve Askeri, 1329 [March 1913–March 1914].

IV. SECONDARY SOURCES

Adanır, Fikret. "Der jungtürkische Modernismus und die nationale Frage im Osmanischen Reich." *Zeitschrift für Türkeistudien* 2 (1989): 79–91.

Ahmad, Feroz. "Ottoman Armed Neutrality and Intervention, August–November 1914." *Studies on Ottoman Diplomatic History* 4 (1990): 41–69.

  The Young Turks: The Committee of Union and Progress in Turkish Politics, 1908–1914. Oxford: Oxford University Press, 1969.

  "Great Britain's Relations with the Young Turks, 1908–1914." *Middle Eastern Studies* 2 (July 1966): 302–29.

Akşin, Sina. *Jön Türkler ve İttihat ve Terakki*. Istanbul: Remzi, 1987.

İstanbul Hükümetleri ve Milli Mücadele. Istanbul: Cem Yayınevi, 1976.

Akmeşe, Handan Nezir. *The Birth of Modern Turkey: The Ottoman Military and the March to World War I*. New York: I. B. Tauris, 2005.

Alexandris, Alexis. "The Greek Census of Anatolia and Thrace (1910–1912): A Contribution to Ottoman Historical Demography." In *Ottoman Greeks in the Age of Nationalism*, ed. Dimitri Gondicas and Charles Issawi, 45–76. Princeton: Darwin Press, 1999.

Anderson, M. S. *The Eastern Question, 1774–1923: A Study in International Relations*. New York: St. Martin's Press, 1966.

Anscombe, Frederick F. *The Ottoman Gulf: The Creation of Kuwait, Saudi Arabia, and Qatar*. New York: Columbia University Press, 1997.

Arıkan, Zeki. "Balkan Savaşı ve Kamuoyu." In *Bildiriler: Dördüncü Askeri Tarih Semineri*, 168–88. Ankara: Genelkurmay Basımevi, 1989.

Audoin-Rouzeau, Stéphane and Annette Becker. *14–18: Understanding the Great War*, trans. Catherine Temerson. New York: Hill and Wang, 2002.

Aydemir, Şevket Süreyya. *Makedonya'dan Ortaasya'ya Enver Paşa*, 3 vols. Istanbul: Remzi Kitabevi, 1971.

Aydın, Cemil. *The Politics of Anti-Westernism in Asia: Visions of World Order in Pan-Islamic and Pan-Asian Thought*. New York: Columbia University Press, 2007.

Baberowski, Jörg. "Nationalismus aus dem Geist der Inferiorität: Autokratische Modernisierung und die Anfänge muslimischer Selbstvergewisserung im östlichen Transkaukasien, 1828–1914." *Geschichte und Gesellschaft* 26 (*Aspekte des Nationalismus*) (2000): 371–406.

Baykara, Tuncer. "Birinci Dünya Savaşı'na Girişin Psikolojik Sebepleri." In *Bildiriler: Dördüncü Askeri Tarih Semineri*, 360–6. Ankara: Genelkurmay Basımevi, 1989.

Bayur, Yusuf Hikmet. *Türk İnkılâbı Tarihi*, 3 vols. Ankara: Türk Tarih Kurumu Basımevi, 1940–67.

Berkes, Niyazi. *The Development of Secularism in Turkey*. Montreal: McGill University Press, 1964.

Beşirli, Mehmet. *Die europäische Finanzkontrolle im Osmanischen Reich in der Zeit von 1908 bis 1914: Die Rivalitäten der britischen, französischen und deutschen Hochfinanz und der Diplomatie vor dem Ersten Weltkrieg am Beispiel der türkischen Staatsanleihen und der Bagdadbahn*. Berlin: Buch und Mensch, 1999.

Bihl, Wolfdieter. *Die Kaukasus-Politik der Mittelmächte*, vol. I, *Ihre Basis in der Orient-Politik und ihre Aktionen, 1914–1917*. Veröffentlichungen der Kommission für Neuere Geschichte Österreichs. Vienna: Böhlau, 1975.

Birinci, Ali. *Hürriyet ve İtilâf Fırkası: II. Meşrutiyet devrinde İttihat ve Terakki'ye karşı çıkanlar*. Istanbul: Dergâh Yayınları, 1990.

Bobroff, Ronald P. *Roads to Glory: Late Imperial Russia and the Turkish Straits*. London: I. B. Tauris, 2006.

Bodger, Alan. "Russia and the End of the Ottoman Empire." In *The Great Powers and the End of the Ottoman Empire*, 2nd edn., ed. Marian Kent, 76–110. London: Frank Cass, 1995.

Bosworth, R. J. B. "Italy and the End of the Ottoman Empire." In *The Great Powers and the End of the Ottoman Empire*, 2nd edn., ed. Marian Kent, 52–75. London: Frank Cass, 1996.

Brummett, Palmira. *Image and Imperialism in the Ottoman Revolutionary Press, 1908–1911*. Albany: State University of New York Press, 2000.

Burak, Durdu Mehmed. *Birinci Dünya Savaşı'nda Türk–İngiliz İlişkileri*. Ankara: Babil, 2004.

Corrigan, H. W. S. "German–Turkish Relations and the Outbreak of War in 1914: A Re-Assessment." *Past and Present* (April 1967): 144–52.

Curtright, Lynn H. *Muddle, Indecision and Setback: British Policy and the Balkan States, August 1914 to the Inception of the Dardanelles Campaign*. Thessaloniki: Institute for Balkan Studies, 1986.

Davison, Roderic H. "The Armenian Crisis, 1912–1914." *American Historical Review* 53 (April 1948): 481–505.

Demirhan, Pertev. *Generalfeldmarschall Freiherr von der Goltz: das Lebensbild eines grossen Soldaten. Aus meinen persönlichen Erinnerungen*. Göttingen: Göttinger Verlagsanstalt, 1960.

Farah, Irmgard. *Die Deutsche Pressepolitik und Propagandatätigkeit im Osmanischen Reich von 1908–1918: Unter Besonderer Berücksichtigung des "Osmanischen Lloyd"*. Stuttgart: Steiner, 1993.

Fischer, Fritz. *Krieg der Illusionen: Die deutsche Politik von 1911 bis 1914*. Düsseldorf: Droste, 1969.

  Griff nach der Weltmacht: Die Kriegszielpolitik des kaiserlichen Deutschland, 1914/18. Special Edition. Düsseldorf: Droste, 1967.

  "Deutsche Kriegsziele, Revolutionierung und Separatfrieden im Osten 1914–1918." *Historische Zeitschrift* 188 (1959): 249–310.

Friedrich, Wolfgang-Uwe. *Bulgarien und die Mächte, 1913–1915*. Stuttgart: Franz Steiner Verlag, 1985.

Fuhrmann, Malte. *Der Traum vom deutschen Orient: Zwei deutsche Kolonien im Osmanischen Reich, 1851–1918*. Frankfurt: Campus Verlag, 2006.

Fulton, L. Bruce. "France and the End of the Ottoman Empire." In *The Great Powers and the End of the Ottoman Empire*, 2nd edn., ed. Marian Kent, 141–71. London: Frank Cass, 1996.

Geertz, Clifford. "The Integrative Revolution." In *Old Societies and New States: The Quest for Modernity in Asia and Africa*, ed. C. Geertz. New York: The Free Press: 1963.

Ginio, Eyal. "Presenting the Desert to the Ottomans during WWI: The Perspective of *Harb Mecmuası*." *New Perspectives on Turkey* 33 (2005): 43–62.

  "Mobilizing the Ottoman Nation during the Balkan Wars (1912–1913): Awakening from the Ottoman Dream." *War in History* 12 (April 2005): 156–77.

Gürsoy, Selçuk. "*Liva el-Islam*'da Enver Paşa'nın Yazıları." *Toplumsal Tarih* 50 (February 1998): 24–34.

Hacipoğlu, Doğan. *29 Ekim 1914: Osmanlı İmparatorluğu'nun 1. Dünya Harbine Girişi*. Istanbul: Deniz İkmal Grup Komutanlığı, 2000.

Hall, Richard C. *The Balkan Wars, 1912–1913: Prelude to the First World War*. New York: Routledge, 2000.

Bulgaria's Road to the First World War. Boulder: East European Monographs, 1996. Distributed by Columbia University Press.

Halpern, Paul G. *The Mediterranean Naval Situation, 1908–1914*. Harvard Historical Studies. Cambridge, MA: Harvard University Press, 1971.

A Naval History of World War I. Annapolis: Naval Institute Press, 1994.

Hanioğlu, M. Şükrü. *Preparation for a Revolution: The Young Turks, 1902–1908*. New York: Oxford University Press, 2001.

The Young Turks in Opposition. New York: Oxford University Press, 1995.

ed. *Kendi Mektuplarında Enver Paşa*. Istanbul: Der Yayınları, 1989.

"Jön Türk Basını." In *Tanzimat'tan Cumhuriyet'e Türkiye Ansiklopedisi*, vol. III, ed. Murat Belge, 844–50. Istanbul: İletişim Yayınları, 1985.

Hanna, Martha. *The Mobilization of the Intellect: French Scholars and Writers during the Great War*. Cambridge, MA: Harvard University Press, 1996.

Heller, Joseph. *British Policy towards the Ottoman Empire, 1908–1914*. London: Frank Cass, 1983.

"Sir Louis Mallet and the Ottoman Empire: The Road to War." *Middle Eastern Studies* 12 (January 1976): 3–44.

Helmreich, Ernst Christian. *The Diplomacy of the Balkan Wars, 1912–1913*. Harvard Historical Studies. Cambridge, MA: Harvard University Press, 1938.

Herrmann, David G. *The Arming of Europe and the Making of the First World War*. Princeton Studies in International History and Politics. Princeton: Princeton University Press, 1996.

Hiller, Marlene P. *Krisenregion Nahost: Russische Orientpolitik im Zeitalter des Imperialismus, 1900–1914*. Europäische Hochschulschriften. New York: Peter Lang, 1985.

Hobsbawm, Eric and Terence Ranger, eds. *The Invention of Tradition*. Cambridge: Cambridge University Press, 1983; Canto edn., 1996.

Howard, Harry N. *The Partition of Turkey: A Diplomatic History*. Norman: University of Oklahoma Press, 1931.

Jelavich, Charles and Barbara. *The Establishment of the Balkan National States, 1804–1920*. A History of East Central Europe, ed. Peter F. Sugar and Donald W. Treadgold, vol. VIII. Seattle: University of Washington Press, 1977.

Jensen, Geoffrey. "Military Nationalism and the State: The Case of *Fin-de-siècle* Spain." *Nations and Nationalism* 6 (2000): 257–74.

Joll, James. "1914: The Unspoken Assumptions." Inaugural lecture delivered 25 April 1968, The London School of Economics.

Kaiser, Hilmar. *Imperialism, Racism, and Development Theories: The Construction of a Dominant Paradigm on Ottoman Armenians*. Ann Arbor: Gomidas Institute, 1998.

Kampen, Wilhelm van. "Studien zur deutschen Türkeipolitik in der Zeit Wilhelms II." Unpublished Ph.D. diss., University of Kiel, Germany, 1968.

Karaömerlioğlu, M. Asim. "Helphand-Parvus and His Impact on Turkish Intellectual Life." *Middle Eastern Studies* 40 (November 2004): 145–65.

Karpat, Kemal H. *The Politicization of Islam: Reconstructing Identity, State, Faith, and Community in the Late Ottoman State*. New York: Oxford University Press, 2001.

Karsh, Efraim and Inari Karsh. *Empires of the Sand: The Struggle for Mastery in The Middle East, 1789–1923.* Cambridge, MA: Harvard University Press, 1999.

Kayalı, Hasan. *Arabs and Young Turks: Ottomanism, Arabism, and Islamism in the Ottoman Empire, 1908–1918.* Berkeley: University of California Press, 1997.

Kedourie, Elie. *England and the Middle East: The Destruction of the Ottoman Empire, 1914–1921,* new edn. Boulder: Westview Press, 1987.

Kennedy, Paul. *The Realities behind Diplomacy: Background Influences on British External Policy, 1865–1980.* London: Fontana Press, 1981.

Kerner, Robert J. "The Mission of Liman von Sanders." *Slavonic Review* 6 (1927–8): 12–27, 344–63, 543–60 and *Slavonic Review* 7 (1928–9): 90–112. "Russia, the Straits, and Constantinople, 1914–1915." *Journal of Modern History* 1 (September 1929): 400–15.

Khalidi, Rashid Ismail. *British Policy towards Syria and Palestine, 1906–1914: A Study of the Antecedents of the Hussein–McMahon Correspondence, the Sykes–Picot Agreement, and the Balfour Declaration.* St Antony's Middle East Monographs. London: Ithaca Press, 1980.

Kocahanoğlu, Osman Selim. *İttihat-Terakki'nin Sorgulanması ve Yargılanması: Meclis-i Mebusan Tahkikatı, Teşkilatı Mahsusa, Ermeni Tehcirinin İçyüzü, Divan-ı Harb-i Örfi Muhakemesi.* Istanbul: Temel, 1998.

Koch, H. W., ed. *The Origins of the First World War: Great Power Rivalry and German War Aims,* 2nd edn. London: Macmillan, 1984.

Kröger, Martin. "Letzter Konflikt vor der Katastrophe: Die Liman-von-Sanders-Krise, 1913/14." In *Vermiedene Kriege: Deeskalation von Konflikten der Großmächte zwischen Krimkrieg und Erstem Weltkrieg, 1856–1914,* ed. Jost Dülffer, Martin Kröger, and Ralf-Harald Wippich, 657–71. Munich: R. Oldenbourg, 1997.

Kuneralp, Sinan. "Turco-Bulgarian Trade Relations on the Eve of World War One." *Turkish Review of Balkan Studies* 1 (1993): 89–98.

Kurat, Y. T. "How Turkey Drifted into World War I." In *Studies in International History,* ed. K. Bourne and D. C. Watt, 291–315. London: Longmans, 1967.

Kürsat-Ahlers, Elçin. "Die Brutalisierung von Gesellschaft und Kriegsführung im Osmanischen Reich während der Balkankriege (1903–1914)." In *Gewalt im Krieg: Ausübung, Erfahrung und Verweigerung von Gewalt in Kriegen des 20. Jahrhunderts,* ed. Andreas Gestrich. Jahrbuch für Historische Friedensforschung V (Münster: Lit-Verlag, 1995): 51–74.

Kushner, David. *The Rise of Turkish Nationalism, 1876–1908.* Totowa: Frank Cass, 1977.

Laitinen, Kauko *Chinese Nationalism in the Late Qing Dynasty: Zhang Binglin as an Anti Manchu Propagandist.* Scandinavian Institute of Asia Studies. London: Curzon Press, 1990.

Landau, Jacob M. *Pan-Turkism: From Irredentism to Cooperation,* 2nd edn. Bloomington: Indiana University Press, 1995.
The Politics of Pan-Islam: Ideology and Organization. New York: Oxford University Press, 1994.

Lannon, Francis. "1898 and the Politics of Catholic Identity in Spain." In *The Politics of Religion in an Age of Revival,* ed. Austen Ivereigh, 56–73. London: Institute of Latin American Studies, 2000.

Lohr, Eric. *Nationalizing the Russian Empire: The Campaign against Enemy Aliens during World War I.* Cambridge, MA: Harvard University Press, 2003.

Makdisi, Ussama. "Ottoman Orientalism." *American Historical Review* 107 (June 2002): 768–96.

Masters, Bruce. *Christians and Jews in the Ottoman Arab World: The Roots of Sectarianism.* Cambridge Studies in Islamic Civilization. Cambridge: Cambridge University Press, 2001.

McCarthy, Justin. *Death and Exile: The Ethnic Cleansing of Ottoman Muslims, 1821–1922.* Princeton: Darwin Press, 1995.

McKale, Donald M. *War by Revolution: Germany and Great Britain in the Middle East in the Era of World War I.* Kent, OH: Kent State University Press, 1998.

Miller, Geoffrey. *Straits: British Policy towards the Ottoman Empire and the Origins of the Dardanelles Campaign.* Hull: University of Hull Press, 1997.

Superior Force: The Conspiracy behind the Escape of Goeben *and* Breslau. Hull: University of Hull Press, 1996.

Mommsen, Wolfgang J., ed., with Elisabeth Müller-Luckner. *Kultur und Krieg: Die Rolle der Intellektuellen, Künstler und Schriftsteller im Ersten Weltkrieg,* Schriften des Historischen Kollegs, no. 34. Munich: R. Oldenbourg, 1996.

Moran, Daniel and Arthur Waldron, eds. *The People in Arms: Military Myth and National Mobilization since the French Revolution.* Cambridge: Cambridge University Press, 2003.

Müller, Herbert Landolin. *Islam, ğihād ("Heiliger Krieg") und Deutsches Reich: Ein Nachspiel zur wilhelminischen Weltpolitik im Maghreb, 1912–1918.* Europäische Hochschulschriften, no. 506. New York: Peter Lang, 1991.

Ortaylı, İlber. *Osmanlı İmparatorluğu'nda Alman Nüfuzu.* Ankara: Ankara Üniversitesi Siyasal Bilgiler Fakültesi Yayınları, 1981; reprinted, Istanbul: İletişim Yayınları, 1998.

Osterhammel, Jürgen and Niels P. Petersson. *Globalization: A Short History,* trans. Dona Geyer. Princeton: Princeton University Press, 2003.

Özcan, Azmi. *Pan-Islamism: Indian Muslims, the Ottomans and Britain (1877–1924).* The Ottoman Empire and Its Heritage. New York: Brill, 1997.

Özyüksel, Murat. *Osmanlı-Alman İlişkilerinin Gelişim Sürecinde Anadolu ve Bağdat Demiryolları.* Istanbul: Arba, 1988.

Pamuk, Şevket. *A Monetary History of the Ottoman Empire.* Cambridge Studies in Islamic Civilization. Cambridge: Cambridge University Press, 2000.

"Evolution in the Ottoman Monetary System." In Suraiya Faroqhi, Bruce McGowan, Donald Quataert, and Şevket Pamuk, *An Economic and Social History of the Ottoman Empire,* vol. II, *1600–1914,* 947–80. Cambridge: Cambridge University Press, 1994; paperback edn., 1997.

Polat, Nazım H. *Müdafaa-i Milliye Cemiyeti.* Kaynak Eserler, no. 52. Ankara: Kültür Bakanlığı, 1991.

Polk, William R., and Richard L. Chambers. *Beginnings of Modernization in the Middle East: The Nineteenth Century.* Chicago: University of Chicago Press, 1968.

Quataert, Donald. *The Ottoman Empire, 1700–1922,* 2nd edn. New Approaches to European History. Cambridge: Cambridge University Press, 2005.

Ralston, David B. *Importing the European Armies: The Introduction of European Military Techniques and Institutions into the Extra-European World, 1600–1914.* Chicago: University of Chicago Press, 1990.

Reynolds, Michael A. "The Ottoman–Russian Struggle for Eastern Anatolia and the Caucasus, 1908–1918: Identity, Ideology and the Geopolitics of World Order." Unpublished Ph.D. diss., Princeton University, 2003.

Rich, Norman. *Great Power Diplomacy, 1814–1914.* New York: McGraw-Hill, 1992.

Roshwald, Aviel. *Ethnic Nationalism and the Fall of Empires: Central Europe, Russia and the Middle East, 1914–1923.* New York: Routledge, 2001.

Şahin, Mustafa and Yaşar Akyol. "Habil Adem ya da nam-ı diğer Naci İsmail (Pelister) hakkında ..." *Toplumsal Tarih* 11 (November 1994): 6–14.

Schöllgen, Gregor. *Imperialismus und Gleichgewicht: Deutschland, England und die orientalische Frage,* 3rd edn. Munich: R. Oldenbourg, 2000.

Das Zeitalter des Imperialismus, 3rd edn. Oldenbourg Grundriss der Geschichte. Munich: R. Oldenbourg, 1994.

ed. *Escape into War? The Foreign Policy of Imperial Germany.* Providence: Berg, 1990.

Schwertfeger, Bernhard. *Weltkrieg der Dokumente: zehn Jahre Kriegsschuldforschung und ihr Ergebnis.* Berlin: Deutsche Verlagsgesellschaft für Politik und Geschichte, 1929.

Şeker, Nesim. "Demographic Engineering in the late Ottoman Empire and the Armenians." *Middle Eastern Studies* 43 (May 2007): 461–74.

Shils, Edward. "Primordial, Personal, Sacred and Civil Ties." *British Journal of Sociology* 8 (June 1957): 130–45.

Silverstein, Brian. "Islam and Modernity in Turkey: Power, Tradition and Historicity in the European Provinces of the Muslim World." *Anthropological Quarterly* 76 (Summer 2003): 497–517.

Somakian, Joseph Manoug. *Empires in Conflict: Armenia and the Great Powers, 1895–1920.* International Library of Historical Studies. New York: I. B. Tauris, 1995.

Spence, Jonathan D. *The Search for Modern China.* New York: W. W. Norton, 1990.

Strachan, Hew. *The First World War,* vol. I, *To Arms.* New York: Oxford University Press, 2001.

Swanson, Glen W. "War, Technology and Society in the Ottoman Empire from the Reign of Abdülhamid II to 1913: Mahmud Şevket and the German Military Mission." In *War, Technology and Society in the Middle East,* ed. V. J. Parry and M. E. Yapp, 367–85. New York: Oxford University Press, 1975.

Thaden, Edward C. *Russia and the Balkan Alliance of 1912.* University Park: Pennsylvania State University Press, 1965.

Toprak, Zafer. "Proto-globalization and Economic Change in the Late Ottoman Empire: A Commentary." *New Perspectives on Turkey* 35 (2006): 129–34.

İttihad-Terakki ve Cihan Harbi: Savaş Ekonomisi ve Türkiye'de Devletçilik. Istanbul: Homer, 2003.

Milli İktisat-Milli Burjuvazi: Türkiye'de Ekonomi ve Toplum (1908–1950). Türkiye Araştırmaları, no. 14. Ankara: Tarih Vakfı Yurt Yayınları, 1995.

Trumpener, Ulrich. "Germany and the End of the Ottoman Empire." In *The Great Powers and the End of the Ottoman Empire*, 2nd edn., ed. Marian Kent, 111–40. London: Frank Cass, 1996.

Germany and the Ottoman Empire, 1914–1918. Princeton: Princeton University Press, 1968.

"Turkey's Entry into World War I: An Assessment of Responsibilities." *Journal of Modern History* 34 (December 1962): 369–80.

Tunaya, Tarık Zafer. *Türkiye'de Siyasal Partiler*, vol. III, *İttihat ve Terakki, Bir Çağın, Bir Kuşağın, Bir Partinin Tarihi*, rev. edn. Istanbul: İletişim, 2000.

Turfan, M. Naim. *The Rise of the Young Turks: Politics, the Military and Ottoman Collapse, 1912–1913*. New York: I. B. Tauris, 2000.

Türkgeldi, Ali Fuat. *Mesâil-i Mühimme-i Siyâsiyye* [Key Political Events], vol. III, ed. Bekir Sıtkı Baykal. Ankara: Türk Tarih Kurumu Basımevi, 1966.

Weber, Eugen. *Peasants into Frenchmen: The Modernization of Rural France, 1870–1914*. Stanford: Stanford University Press, 1976.

Weber, Frank G. *Eagles on the Crescent: Germany, Austria, and the Diplomacy of the Turkish Alliance, 1914–1918*. Ithaca: Cornell University Press, 1970.

Yapp, M. E. "The Modernization of Middle Eastern Armies in the Nineteenth Century: A Comparative View." In *War, Technology and Society in the Middle East*, ed. V. J. Parry and M. E. Yapp, 331–66. New York: Oxford University Press, 1975.

Yasamee, F. A. K. "Colmar Freiherr von der Goltz and the Rebirth of the Ottoman Empire." *Diplomacy and Statecraft* 9 (July 1998): 91–128.

Ottoman Diplomacy: Abdülhamid II and the Great Powers, 1878–1888. Studies on Ottoman Diplomatic History VII. Istanbul: The Isis Press, 1996.

"Ottoman Empire." In *Decisions for War, 1914*, ed. Keith Wilson, 229–68. New York: St. Martin's Press, 1995.

Yetiş, Kâzım. "İkinci Meşrutiyet Devrindeki Belli Başlı Fikir Akımlarının Askeri Hareketlere ve Cepheye Tesiri." In *Bildiriler: Dördüncü Askeri Tarih Semineri*, 50–69. Ankara: Genelkurmay Basımevi, 1989.

Yılmaz, Veli. *1nci Dünya Harbi'nde Türk-Alman İttifakı ve Askeri Yardımlar*. Istanbul: Cem, 1993.

Zuber, Terence. *Inventing the Schlieffen Plan: German War Planning, 1871–1914*. New York: Oxford University Press, 2002.

"The Schlieffen Plan Reconsidered." *War in History* 6 (1999): 262–305.

Zürcher, Erik-Jan. "The Ottoman Empire, 1850–1912: Unavoidable Failure?," 1–10. *Turkology Update Leiden Project (TULP)* (No date). http://tulp.leidenuniv.nl/content_docs/wap/ejz31.pdf.

Turkey: A Modern History, 3rd edn. New York: I. B. Tauris, 2004.

"Greek and Turkish Refugees and Deportees, 1912–1924," 2. *Turkology Update Leiden Project (TULP)* (January 2003). http://tulp.leidenuniv.nl/content_docs/wap/ejz18.pdf.

"The Young Turks – Children of the Borderlands?," 1–9. *Turkology Update Leiden Project (TULP)* (October 2002). http://tulp.leidenuniv.nl/content_docs/wap/ejz16.pdf

"The Vocabulary of Muslim Nationalism." *International Journal of the Sociology of Language* 137 (1999): 81–91.

Index

Abdulhamid II, Sultan, 9, 24–5, 58
Adana massacres (1909), 9
Adrianople (Edirne), impact on attitudes
  of recovery of, 23–4
Ahenk (newspaper), 21
Ahmad, Feroz, 14
Ahmed Hilmi, Şehbenderzade, 29–31
Ahmed İzzet Pasha, 188
Ahmed Reşid Bey, 106, 121
Ahmed Rıza Bey, 59, 62
Ahmed Saib, 25
Akçuraoğlu Yusuf (later Yusuf Akçura),
  55–6
Ali Fethi Bey, 121
Ali Fethi, Bulgarian reaction to Ottoman
  naval attack, 184
Anatolia
  as Turkish homeland, 30–1
  ethnic cleansing, 48–9
  see also *Will Turkey Survive in Anatolia?*
  (Naci İsmail)
Armstrong. see dreadnoughts, Ottoman
  order for
Asquith, H.H., 81, 126
Austria-Hungary
  and German–Ottoman alliance, 93–4
  annexation of Bosnia-Herzegovina, 58–9
  issue of Ottoman loan, 62
  refusal of alliance, 61, 84

bab-ı âli baskını (the Raid on the Sublime
  Porte), 79
Baghdad Railway
  and German investments in Syria, 57
  disagreements settled, 83
  London's hindrances to extension of, 60
  strategic importance, 69–70
  use to colonize Anatolia, 27
Balkan Wars
  psychological impact in Ottoman Empire,
  21–3
  see also First Balkan War (1912–13)

battleships. see *Breslau*, SMS; dreadnoughts,
  Ottoman order for; *Goeben*, SMS;
  Greece; purchase of American
  battleships
Baykara, Tuncer, 14–15
Bayur, Yusuf Hikmet, *History of the Turkish
  Revolution*, 11–13
Bedirhan, Abdürrezak, 88
Benckendorff, A. K.
  and Liman von Sanders affair, 81
  doubts regarding Ottoman neutrality, 131
  intervention over British–Ottoman
  dreadnought sale, 126–7
  proposed Russian–British alliance, 47
Berchtold, Leopold, count von
  attitude to Ottoman–Romanian
  alliance, 89
  promotion of German–Ottoman alliance,
  93–4, 95
  rejection of Habsburg–Ottoman
  alliance, 84
  support for German–Ottoman treaty
  extension, 184–5
Berlin Congress (July 13, 1878), 5, 72–3
Bernhard von Eggeling, Russia and
  Ottoman war, 82
Bethmann Hollweg, Theobald von
  attitude to Ottoman neutrality, 116
  German–Ottoman negotiations during
  July Crisis, 100–1
  initial rejection of German–Ottoman
  treaty extension, 185
  on Entente attack on Straits, 117
  report on implications of First Balkan
  War, 71
  report on German–Ottoman alliance,
  70–1
  requires declaration of war before further
  funding, 150–1
  suggestion of attack on Suez Canal, 147–8
  telegram ordering Ottoman naval attack
  in Black Sea, 155–6

Bompard, Maurice, 112, 181
Bratianu, Ion, 87
Breslau, SMS
  and balance of power, 117–18
  arrival at Istanbul, 91
  arrival at the Straits, 110–18
  Ottoman "purchase" of, 118
  requested by Enver, 103–4, 113
Britain
  and Arab nationalism, 66
  attitudes towards in contemporary
    literature, 34
  military mission in Istanbul. *see* Limpus
    naval mission
  refusal of Anglo–Ottoman alliance, 59, 77
  rejection of Ottoman reform proposals, 60
  response to Ottoman mobilization, 126
  responsibility for hostilities, 54–5
  seizure of Ottoman territories, 57
  withholding of loans, 60
Büyük Duygu (journal), 36–8
Bulgaria
  alliance with Central Powers, 122
  and attack on Thrace after alliance, 121
  declaration of independence, 58
  likelihood of Ottoman alliance, 94–5
  neutrality, 156–7
  position in Greek–Ottoman war, 52–3
  rumored Ottoman alliance, 43
  see also Radoslavov, Vasil
Bulgarian–Ottoman alliance, 120, 122–3

Cami (Abdurrahman Cami Baykut), 33–6
Capelle, Eduard von, 136
capitulations, 14
Carol I, king of Romania, 87
Caucasus Desk (*Teşkilat-ı Mahsusa*), 89
Cavid Bey
  agreement of loan from France, 85
  exclusion from German–Ottoman loan, 167
  mission to obtain loans, 60
  potential to redirect Ottoman policy, 171
  protest at outbreak of war, 180–1
  urges cabinet to demobilize, 169
Cemal Pasha
  alliance attempt with the Entente, 90
  and Black Sea operation decision, 159
  approval of naval attack on Russia,
    171–2
  Bulgarian–Ottoman alliance
    negotiations, 120
  congratulatory note over naval attack on
    Russia, 181
  negotiations after start of First World
    War, 91–2

official statement on Black Sea naval
    attack, 181–2
  on national position in 1914, 19
  rejection of funding for Suez Canal
    expedition, 17
  response to confiscation of
    dreadnoughts, 109
  written orders for naval attack on
    Russia, 176
Cemil Bey
  and *Goeben* going to Istanbul, 103
  meetings with Moltke and Falkenhayn,
    105–6
  negotiations regarding Bulgaria, 119–20
  news of German need for Ottoman
    help, 165
  request for Dardanelles cannons, 149–50
  request for German naval mission, 136
Charykov, M., 82–3
Chios, 5, 42
  see also Talat Pasha, (Mehmed), proposed
    Bulgarian–Ottoman–Romanian
    alliance
Churchill, Winston, 91–2, 126
Constantinople Agreement (1915), 55
covert operations
  by Ottomans, against Russia, 89
  by Russia, against Ottoman Empire, 88
Crete, announced unification with Greece, 58
CUP (Ottoman Committee of Union and
    Progress)
  coup against Grand Vezir Kâmil Pasha, 79
  rise to power, 9
  vote for war, 182

Demidov, E.P., 49
Doumergue, Gaston, views on Straits
    question, 3–4
dreadnoughts, Ottoman order for
  and balance of power in Eastern
    Mediterranean, 49, 110–11
  attempt to reassure Russia regarding, 86
  demands for compensation for, 91
  Greek plans for pre-emptive war before
    delivery, 87
  Greek plans for war to prevent delivery, 43
  non-delivery and seizure of Russian
    merchandise, 108–9
  provoking Russian–British alliance, 47
  Russia blocking collection of, 61, 126–7
  Russian opposition to, 45–6

Eberhardt, Admiral, 134–5, 173–4
Edirne (Adrianople), recovery of, 23–4
education, and military effectiveness, 32–3

Emanuelidi Efendi, 52
Enver Pasha
  Aegean islands dispute, 46
  against declaration of *jihad*, 16–17
  and Bulgarian entry against Entente, 121
  and German ships in the Straits, 115
  arguments justifying German loan, 168–9
  attempt to make Balkan action
      conditional on Bulgaria, 154
  attempts to postpone Ottoman
      intervention, 111, 112, 119–20
  Black Sea operation, 157, 162
  Bulgarian–Ottoman alliance negotiations,
      120, 122–3
  complaint about Liman von Sanders,
      17–18, 139–40
  congratulatory note over naval attack on
      Russia, 181
  congratulatory telegram from Goltz, 17
  CUP coup against Grand Vezir Kâmil
      Pasha, 79
  death, 15–16
  false claim of Romanian offer of alliance, 85
  German refusal of loan, September 10,
      147–50
  German–Ottoman alliance negotiations
      during July Crisis, 96–8, 99, 101,
      102–3
  grandiosity, 15
  historical view of, 1–17, 190
  holy war rhetoric, 35–6
  letter calling for revenge, 38
  naval attack on Russia
      attempt to delay, 176–7
      authorization for, 177
      concerns over, 174–5
      ordered by Enver, 63, 64
      proposal, 170–1
      report to Said Halim of Russian
          "attack", 180–1
      written orders, 176
  negotiations after start of First World
      War, 91–2
  note from Said Halim Pasha on likelihood
      of war, 10–11
  offer of Black Sea naval demonstration,
      148–9
  Ottoman mobilization, 104–10
  pledged support for Vienna, 96
  power conflict with Said Halim, 106–7
  preference for Caucasus campaign, 148
  proposal of alliance with Russia,
      127–8, 129
  rejection of funding for Suez Canal
      expedition, 17

  request for arms while promising future
      action, 123, 138
  request for German naval mission, 135–6
  resignation letter, 188
  response to Kaiser Wilhelm II's demand
      for action, 137–8
  seizure of Entente ships and citizens, 186
  submission of war plan, 172
  successful recovery of Edirne
      (Adrianople), 23
  support of Liman's proposed Odessa
      attack, 155
  war ministry budget, 22
ethnic cleansing, 43–4, 47–8, 51–2

Fahreddin Bey, and alliance with Russia,
    129–30
Falkenhayn, Erich von
  approval of Ottoman war plan, 172, 173
  instruction to Liman on Ottoman
      action, 156
  meeting Cemil Bey, 105–6
  "No aid without hostilities" statement, 149
Ferdinand, king of Bulgaria, 119
First Balkan War (1912–13), 22–3, 71
Fischer, Fritz, 64
France
  agreement of Ottoman loan, 84–5
  intentions for French rule in Syria, 55
  postponement of Ottoman loan, 80–1

Germanos V, 53
German–Ottoman alliance
  casus foederis, 99
  crisis over Ottoman inaction, August
      1914, 137–41
  crisis over Ottoman inaction, September
      1914, 156–63
  existence revealed to Bulgaria, 120
  main provisions, 100, 102
  mention of, 99, 100–1
  negotiations during July Crisis, 93–102
  reasons for, 191–3
  Russian knowledge of, 110
  September 10, 147–52
  signing of, 102–4
  treaty extension, 184–5
Germany
  attitudes towards in contemporary
      literature, 34–5
  consideration of alliance, 35
  hopes from Ottoman entry into war,
      156, 166
  initial rejection of alliance, 62
  investments in Syria, 57

military mission in Istanbul, *see* Liman
von Sanders mission
naval mission in Istanbul in August
1914, *see* Usedom mission
plans for interim administration in
Istanbul, 78
protectorate over Ottoman Empire, 90–1
role in Ottoman entry into
war, 62–72
supply of warships and funds, 62
use of German ships by Ottomans, 106
war plans, 144–5
Giers, M. N.
Aegean islands dispute, 43–4
and Russian occupation of eastern
Anatolia, 75
apparent belief in Ottoman neutrality, 112
ascribed Strait's closure to German
military mission, 108
at Livadia meeting, 86–7
attempts to contain Ottoman–Greek
crisis, 51–2
concern at Ottoman pre-emptive war
against Russia, 127
concern over pushing Ottomans into
war, 135
departure from Istanbul, 181
intercepted telegram, 92
knowledge of Ottoman war plan, 173–4
note on Straits' annexation, 4
proposed trade of Limnos for Ottoman
neutrality, 45
recommending forcing open the Straits,
49–50
suggestion of pre-emptive Russian action,
101–2
support for Enver's proposed Russian-
Ottoman alliance, 127–9, 130–1
Goeben, SMS
and balance of power, 117–18
arrival at Istanbul, 91
arrival at the Straits, 110–18
Ottoman "purchase" of, 118
requested by Enver, 103–4, 110, 113
requested by Said Halim, 113
rumors of sale to Ottoman navy, 35
shelling of Sevastopol, 179
Goltz, Colmar von der
annexationist thinking, 65
congratulatory telegram on declaration of
war, 17
on German–Ottoman alliance, 69–70
reform of the Ottoman army, 69
report on implications of First Balkan
War, 71

Greece
Aegean islands dispute, 43
attempt to play on Russian fears over
Straits, 49
Great Power recognition of sovereignty
over Aegean islands, 46–7
June 12 demands, 50–1
non-support from Serbia, 50
purchase of American battleships, 111
rejection of Romanian mediation, 43–4
Russian concern over Aegean islands
dispute, 44–6, 49–50, 51
Greek–Ottoman negotiations, 144
Grey, Sir Edward
and Istanbul as international city, 78–9
and Liman von Sanders mission, 80–1
defense of Limpus mission, 46
justifying war with Ottomans, 134
on Egypt, 68
refusal of British–Ottoman alliance, 59
warning to Istanbul, 131
Gulkevich, K. N., 44–5, 77
Gwinner, Arthur, 167

Hafız Hakkı, 32–3
Halil Bey
call for nationalist movement, 27
claims in memoirs, 10
delegation to Berlin, 176–7
Greek–Ottoman negotiations, 144
proposal for naval attack on Russia, 170–1
hareket-i intibahiye, 19
Helfferich, Karl, 167
Helphand, Alexander (pseud.), 54–5
Hilmi Pasha, 46–7, 89
History of the Turkish Revolution (Bayur), 11–13
*How Germany Revived and How It Is
Preparing for War* (Recai), 31–2
Hüseyin Hilmi Pasha, 84
Hüseyin Kâzım Bey, 53–4
Humann, Hans
and Halil Bey's visit to Berlin, 160–3
and Ottoman Egypt expedition, 150
cabinet reversal of Black Sea operation
decision, 158
concerns over naval attack on Russia, 178
Enver's arguments on German loan, 168–9
on conciliatory note after naval attack on
Russia, 182–3
requested clarification of Souchon's
position, 159
sent to ask Enver about Liman
conversations, 139–40
written orders for naval attack on
Russia, 176

Hussein–McMahon Correspondence
(1915–16), 55

İbrahim Hakkı Pasha, and Baghdad Railway
extension, 60
Idaho, USS, 111
imposed historical amnesia, 13
intellectual/emotional climate within
Ottoman Empire, 29–36
attitudes to position of Ottoman Empire
and the International Order, 21–9
overview, 19–21, 39–41
international law, Ottoman loss of faith in,
21–2
Italy, challenges to Ottoman
territories, 57
Izmir, 43–4
Izvolskii, A. P., 3–4, 82–3, 84–5
İzzet Pasha, 85

Jagow, Gottlieb von
and Black Sea naval demonstration, 149
and coercion of Ottomans into
war, 163
approval of funding for Egypt
expedition, 150
attitude to British declaration of
war, 112
demand for action from Ottomans, 140
fear of formal partition, 68
German interest in Turkey, 67
German–Ottoman treaty extension,
185
reaction to Russian proposal for eastern
Anatolia, 73–4
rejection of German–Ottoman
alliance, 94
Joll, James, 18

Kâmil Pasha, Grand Vezir, 11,
59, 79
Kampen, Wilhelm van, 66
Kavalla, 52
Kâzım Karabekir, 20–1
Kılkis (battleship), 111
Kitchener, Horatio Herbert, 1st Earl
Kitchener of Khartoum, 68, 126
Kokovtsov, V. N., 81
Kress von Kressenstein, Friedrich, 143–4,
147, 164–5
Kubanetz (gunboat), sinking, 179
Kühlmann, Richard von, 178

Laffert, Karl von, 139, 141–2
Leontiev, General, 126–9, 130–1

Lichnowsky, Karl Max, Fürst von,
comparison of Liman mission with
Limpus mission, 80
Liman von Sanders mission
crisis surrounding, 3, 80–3
German-Ottoman alliance treaty
stipulations, 99, 100, 104
negotiations for, 79
resulting in increased German
influence, 63
Liman von Sanders, Otto
anger at delay in Ottoman intervention,
112–13, 138–9
on German–Ottoman alliance, 94
proposal to attack Odessa, 155
report of plans for Ottoman attack on
Russian army, 137
report on signing of German–Ottoman
alliance, 110
request for officers to attack Suez
Canal, 148
support of Enver's request for SMS
Goeben, 110
view sought for German–Ottoman
alliance, 102–3
Wangenheim evaluation of proposals to
coerce Ottomans into war, 163
Limnos
proposed trade for Ottoman neutrality, 45
strategic importance, 42
Limnos (battleship), 111
Limpus naval mission
assignment to desk jobs, 91
comparison with Liman von Sanders
mission, 80, 81
Limpus, Arthur Henry, 46
Livadia meeting, 85–7

Mahmud Muhtar Pasha, 79, 99–100, 166–7
Mahmud Şevket Pasha, 11, 79
Mallet, Sir Louis, 77, 181
Mediterranean Squadron
(*Mittelmeerdivision*, MMD), 71–2
Mehmed V Reşad, Sultan, 16–17, 104–5
Menteşe, Halil, *see* Halil Bey
Midhat Çiftliği, 104
Mississippi, USS, 111
Moltke, Helmuth von, the younger
cable demanding Ottoman action, 145
creation of German war plans, 144–5
meeting Cemil Bey, 105–6
submission of Ottoman war plan, 172
view of the war, 64
Müdafaa-i Milliye Cemiyeti (Society for
National Defense), 38

Mühlmann, Carl, 64–5
Mustafa Kemal, 15, 122
Mutius, Gerhard von, 70–1
Mytilene, xiii, 5, 42, 44–5, 46, 85–7, 144

Naci İsmail (pseud.), 25, 28–9
National Aid Society (*Osmanlı Donanma ve Muavenet-i Milliye Cemiyeti*), 53
naval attack on Russia by Ottoman Empire
    acceptance by Berlin, 171, 173
    approval of Said Halim, 172
    attempts to delay, 171–2, 174, 176–7
    concerns over, 174–5, 177–8
    conciliatory note, 183
    events, 178–82
    final authorization for, 177
    plan detail, 173
    proposal, 170–1
    Russian knowledge of, 173–4
    written orders, 176
Nazım Bey, Dr., 1908 London mission, 59
Nazım Pasha, death during CUP coup, 79
Nicholas II, tsar of Russia, 134
Noradonkyan Efendi, 62, 79

Ottoman Committee of Union and Progress (CUP), *see* CUP (Ottoman Committee of Union and Progress)
Ottoman Empire
    alliance attempts with the Entente, 90, 127–35
    alliance with Germany, 91–2
    cabinet meeting procedures, 162
    covert operations against Russia, 89
    CUP vote for war, 182
    declarations of war, 183–4
    Entente guarantee of territorial integrity, 3–4
    entry into 1914 war
        Bayur's view, 11–13
        historians' view, 1, 13
        psychological climate, 13–18, 191
        this book's view, 1–11, 193
    expulsion from Europe, 1
    financial situation, 59–60
    Great Power directive on military activities, 78–9
    international position after Balkan Wars, 77–9
    military weakness, 57–9
    mobilization, 104–10
    multi-national fleet off Istanbul, 78
    policy alternatives, September 1914, 153–4
    search for allies, 59, 61–2, 84, 85–7

    seizure of Entente ships and citizens, 186
    trial of wartime cabinet members, 188–90
    war plan, 172–3
    see also Bulgarian–Ottoman alliance; German–Ottoman alliance; Greek-Ottoman negotiations; naval attack on Russia by Ottoman Empire
Ottoman Future, The
    Its Enemies and Its Friends (Cami), 33
Ottoman Public Debt Administration, 59

Pallavicini, Johann von
    advised of Ottoman–Russian friendship, 84
    advising against sending *Goeben* and *Breslau* into Black Sea, 124
    Central Powers protectorate over Ottoman Empire, 68
    endorsement of Said Halim's insistence on Bulgarian guarantee, 114
    on Ottoman intervention and Italy, 174
    promotion of German–Ottoman alliance, 95, 96
    Said Halim's concerns over naval attack on Russia, 171–2
    support for German–Ottoman treaty extension, 184–5
Pan-Islamism
    as fabrication of the Triple Entente, 35
    German ideas of, 16
Parvus (pseud. of Alexander Helphand), 54–5
Pohl, Hugo von, 151
Poklevskii, S. A., 82
"post-war amnesia", 13
Prut (minelayer), sinking of, 179, 180

Radoslavov, Vasil, 52–3, 151, 184
Raid on the Sublime Porte, 79
Recai, 31–2
Reşadiye, *see* dreadnoughts, Ottoman order for
Romania
    Enver Pasha's proposal for Romanian mediation, 46
    on intervention in Greek–Ottoman war, 87
    refusal of alliance, 62
Rum
    expulsion from Ottoman Empire, 47–8, 51–2
    impossibility of coexistence with Muslims, 53
Rumeli, 5

Russia
  approval of warship to cruise Anatolian
    coast, 50
  Balkan league as holding measure, 92
  Black Sea fleet superiority, 110–11
  blocking collection of dreadnoughts, 61
  concern over Aegean islands dispute,
    44–6, 49–50, 51
  concerns over Ottoman naval strength, 61
  covert operations against Ottoman
    Empire, 88
  deal with Austria–Hungary over Bosnia-
    Herzegovina, 58
  dependence on Straits, 42
  knowledge of Ottoman war plan, 173–4
  Livadia meeting, 85–7
  obstacles to Ottoman reform, 60–1
  preparations for war with Ottomans,
    132–3
  promotion of Kurdish rebellion, 88
  reform proposal for eastern Anatolia,
    72–7
  response to Ottoman seizure of Russian
    merchandise, 109
  retaliation for Ottoman naval attack,
    183–4, 186
  seizure of Ottoman territories, 57
  see also Giers, M. N.; Sazonov, S. D.

Said Halim Pasha, (Mehmed)
  acquisition of Goeben and Breslau, 116
  Aegean islands dispute, 44–5
  attempt to enlist British support, 59
  attempts to force Bulgarian–Ottoman
    alliance, 113–14
  attempts to postpone Ottoman
    intervention, 112–13
  Bayur's view of, 11
  Bulgarian–Ottoman alliance negotiations,
    120, 122–3
  concerns over naval attack on Russia,
    171–2
  efforts for Habsburg–Ottoman alliance, 84
  ethnic cleansing, 48–9
  exploitation of July Crisis, 114
  German–Ottoman negotiations during
    July Crisis, 95, 99–100, 101–2
  meeting with Giers during July Crisis,
    101–2
  meeting with Wangenheim over Black Sea
    operation, 160–1
  negotiation of German–Ottoman treaty
    extension, 185
  note to Enver Pasha on likelihood of war,
    10–11

on German squadron's entry to Straits,
    114–15
  pledged support for Vienna, 96
  power conflict with Enver, 106–7
  reasons for German–Ottoman alliance,
    192–3
  refusal of responsibility for hostile action,
    180–1
  resignation threat, 158, 162
  suggestion for German naval base in Sea
    of Marmara, 168
  suspicion of Enver's memorandum on
    Russian "attack", 180–1
  view of German–Ottoman alliance and
    Ottoman recovery, 153
Sazonov, S. D.
  Aegean islands dispute, 44–5
  conditions for reforms in eastern
    Anatolia, 60–1
  intervention over dreadnought sale, 45–6,
    126–7
  keeping Ottomans outside the war, 130
  knowledge of Ottoman war plan,
    173–4
  on intervention upon closure of the
    Straits, 87
  on military intervention in eastern
    Anatolia, 74, 76
  opposition to Istanbul as international
    city, 78–9
  Ottoman territorial acquisition, 78
  policy on Straits' annexation, 4
  reaction to Liman von Sanders mission, 80
  rejection of Russian–Ottoman alliance,
    128–9
  war with Turkey, cause of, 134–5
  warnings of Balkan war escalation, 88
Schlieffen, Alfred von, 144–5
Sebiha, N., 38
Serbia, would not support Greece in war, 50
social Darwinism, 30
  see also Büyük Duygu (journal)
Society for National Defense (Müdafaa-i
    Milliye Cemiyeti), 38
Souchon, Wilhelm
  clarification of Porte's position regarding,
    159–60
  complaint to Enver about Cemal
    Pasha, 159
  complaint to Said Halim over Black Sea
    operation, 159
  Entente attack on Straits, 117
  instruction to break out of Straits, 117
  instruction to take action in Black Sea,
    151, 157, 165–6

instruction to take *Goeben* to
Istanbul, 110
on necessity of *Goeben* to hold the
Straits, 124
report of British jamming radio
signals, 143
sabotage by British naval mission, 46
Wangenheim's report on Ottoman
neutrality, 169–70
written orders for naval attack on
Russia, 176
see also naval attack on Russia by Ottoman
Empire
sources, 10
Straits
closure of, 107–8
conditions for German squadron's entry,
114–15
defensibility of, 117, 124, 125–6, 141–2
definition of, 107
Russian ambassador's note on
annexation, 4
Russia's dependence on, 42
Sublime Porte
1914 foreign policy challenges, 3
Raid on, 79
Sublime Porte's intelligence service,
Russian ambassador's note on
Straits' annexation, 4
Suez Canal
German–Ottoman campaign against, 147
see also Wangenheim, Baron Hans von,
suggestion to attack Egypt
Sukhomlinov, V. A., proposal to mass
Russian troops in Ottoman
territory, 76
Sultan Osman, see dreadnoughts, Ottoman
order for
surnames, xiii
Sykes–Picot Agreement (1916), 55
Syria, British challenge to Ottoman
authority, 57
Szögyény, Ladislaus, count von, and
German–Ottoman alliance, 94

Talat Pasha, (Mehmed)
and Black Sea operation
decision, 158
Bayur's view of, 11
Bulgarian–Ottoman alliance negotiations,
120, 122–3
claiming Balkan obstacles to Ottoman
intervention, 146
CUP coup against Grand Vezir Kâmil
Pasha, 79

ethnic cleansing, 43–4, 48
formal hearing on Greek Orthodox
Ottomans, 52
Greek–Ottoman negotiations, 144
Livadia meeting, 85–7, 90
on alliance or neutrality, 163
pledged support for Vienna, 96
postwar power, 188
proposal for naval attack on Russia, 170–1
proposed Bulgarian–Ottoman–Romanian
alliance, 87
reasons for German–Ottoman alliance,
191–2
seizure of Entente ships and citizens, 186
support of collection of war-taxes from
non-Ottomans, 108
Tanin (newspaper), 20
terminology, x–xi
Teşkilat-ı Mahsusa (Caucasus Desk), 89
Tevfik Pasha, 60, 77, 113
Thrace, 43–4
Tirpitz, Alfred von, 136, 142–3
Toshev, Andrei, 45, 120, 174–5
Treaty of Bucharest, 52
Treaty of San Stefano (March 3, 1878),
72–3
Triple Entente, attitudes towards in
contemporary literature, 34
Trumpener, Ulrich, 63–4

Ubeydullah Efendi, 23–4
Usedom mission, 135–7
Usedom, Guido von, 143, 153, 158

Vardar, Galip, 190
Venizelos, Eleftherios, 46–7
Vickers, *see* dreadnoughts, Ottoman
order for
Vorontsov-Dashkov, Prince I. I., 88

Wangenheim, Baron Hans von
and German squadron's entry to Straits,
114–15
color-coded maps, 67
endorsement of Enver pan-Islamic,
137–8
endorsement of Said Halim's insistence
on Bulgarian guarantee, 114
Enver's false claim of Romanian offer of
alliance, 85
fear of formal partition, 68
German–Ottoman alliance negotiations
during July Crisis, 95, 96–101, 102–4
misgivings over naval attack on Russia,
170–1, 175

Wangenheim, Baron Hans von (cont.)
  on balance of powers in the Balkans,
    124–5
  on German–Ottoman alliance, 94
  promotion of Ottoman action in Black
    Sea, 160–1
  proposed Bulgarian–Ottoman–Romanian
    alliance, 89
  reaction to Bulgarian–Ottoman alliance,
    122–3
  relationship with Enver Pasha, 17–18
  report of Enver's reversal on Black Sea
    operation, 158
  suggestion to attack Egypt, 146
  support for Enver regarding Liman, 139
  support for German–Ottoman treaty
    extension, 184, 185
  support of delayed Ottoman intervention,
    111, 112, 123–5, 142, 143, 146–7,
    148–9, 151, 161, 163–4, 169–70,
    174–5
  support of Enver's request for SMS
    Goeben, 110
  warning of Russian provocateurs in
    eastern Anatolia, 74–5
war ministry, budget approved without
    debate, 22
Wilhelm II, Kaiser
  and First Balkan War, 71
  annexationist thinking, 65
  demands for Ottoman action, 137–8

German–Ottoman alliance negotiations
    during July Crisis, 98–9, 100
  instructions to Liman on Enver, 140
  on Ottoman alliance, 62, 68–9, 70
  Ottoman naval attack in Black Sea, 151,
    155–6
  promotion of pan-Islamist ideology, 16, 66
  reform of Ottoman army, 69
  Russian troops on Ottoman border and
    partition, 75
  selected Liman as head of German
    military mission to Istanbul, 79·
  view of the war, 64
Will Turkey Survive in Anatolia? (Naci
    İsmail), 25–7, 28–9
women, attitudes toward, 32, 37

Young Turk Revolution (1908), 24

Zekeriya Köyü, 104
Zimmermann, Arthur
  agreement for German–Ottoman loan,
    166–8
  funding of Egypt expedition, 150
  report of Enver's reversal on Black Sea
    operation, 158
  support for German–Ottoman treaty
    extension, 185
  urged approval of Ottoman war plan, 173
  Wangenheim's report on benefits of
    Ottoman neutrality, 169–70